GW00392530

On Life-Writing

On Life-Writing

EDITED BY

Zachary Leader

OXFORD
UNIVERSITY PRESS

OXFORD
UNIVERSITY PRESS

Great Clarendon Street, Oxford, OX2 6DP,
United Kingdom

Oxford University Press is a department of the University of Oxford.
It furthers the University's objective of excellence in research, scholarship,
and education by publishing worldwide. Oxford is a registered trade mark of
Oxford University Press in the UK and in certain other countries

© the various contributors 2015

Some parts of this publication are available online as open access.
Chapter 12 is distributed under the terms of a Creative Commons
Attribution-NonCommercial-NoDerivatives 4.0 International
licence (CC BY-NC-ND), a copy of which is available at
http://creativecommons.org/licenses/by-nc-nd/4.0/.
Enquiries concerning use outside the scope of the licence terms
should be sent to the Rights Department, Oxford University Press,
at the above address.

Published in the United States of America by Oxford University Press
198 Madison Avenue, New York, NY 10016, United States of America

British Library Cataloguing in Publication Data
Data available

Library of Congress Control Number: 2015938206

ISBN 978–0–19–870406–5

Printed and bound by
CPI Group (UK) Ltd, Croydon, CR0 4YY

ACKNOWLEDGEMENTS

I am grateful to Jacqueline Baker, Lucy McClune, Rachel Platt, Rachael Nixon, Lydia Shinoj, Hayley Buckley, and Elizabeth Stone, of Oxford University Press and SPi Global for their support throughout. Thanks also to Douglas Matthews who compiled the index, and to Robert C. Ritchie, Steve Hindle, Carolyn Powell, and Juan Gomez of the Huntington Library, San Marino, California, for hosting the conference out of which the book grew. In addition, I am indebted to Catherine Wells-Cole, Jane McVeigh, and Lindsay Duguid, for advice and assistance.

Although every effort has been made to trace and contact copyright holders prior to publication this has not been possible in every case. If notified, the publisher will be pleased to rectify any omissions at the earliest opportunity.

CONTENTS

LIST OF FIGURES

Introduction

Zachary Leader

'Life-writing' is a generic term used to describe a range of writings about lives or parts of lives, or which provide materials out of which lives or parts of lives are composed. These writings include not only memoir, autobiography, biography, diaries, autobiographical fiction, and biographical fiction, but also letters, writs, wills, written anecdotes, depositions, court proceedings (*narratio* first existed not as a literary but as a legal term), marginalia, nonce writings, lyric poems, scientific and historical writings, and digital forms (including blogs, tweets, Facebook entries). The term itself is often traced to Virginia Woolf, who first used it in 'A Sketch of the Past' (1939), in connection with the difficulties and inadequacies of conventional biography, a word which itself 'literally means "life-writing". The two halves of the word derive from medieval Greek: *bios*, "life", and *graphia*, "writing" '.[1]

Some writers on life-writing distinguish between shorter forms, conceived of as source material, and 'life-writing proper' or 'extended life narratives' or 'formal biography and autobiography'; others distinguish between life-writing that is exemplary or formulaic, often associated with older periods, and the sort that seems or seeks to express more modern qualities: authenticity, sincerity, interiority, individuality. At least since the 1970s, theoreticians and historians of life-writing commonly fuse or meld sub-genres, as in the neologisms 'auto/biography', 'biofiction', 'biografiction', 'autonarration', and 'autobiografiction' (this last, surprisingly, the most venerable as well as the most ungainly of coinages, having first appeared in print in 1906).[2] The blurring of distinctions may help to

---

[1] Hermione Lee, *Biography: A Very Short Introduction* (Oxford: Oxford University Press, 2009), p. 5.

[2] For a history of life-writing neologisms see Max Saunders, *Self Impression: Life-Writing, Autobiografiction, and the Forms of Modern Literature* (Oxford: Oxford University Press, 2010), pp. 1–25.

account for life-writing's growing acceptance as a field of academic study, reflecting a wider distrust of fixed forms, simple or single truths or meanings, narrative transparency, objectivity, 'literature' as opposed to writing.

This volume offers a sampling of approaches to the study of life-writing, introducing readers to the range of forms the term encompasses, their changing fortunes and features, the notions of 'life', 'self', and 'story' which help to explain these changing fortunes and features, recent attempts to group forms, the permeability of the boundaries between forms, the moral problems raised by life-writing in all forms, but particularly in fictional forms, and the relations between life-writing and history, psychoanalysis, and philosophy. The chapters mostly select individual instances rather than survey historical, theoretical, or generic fields; generalizations are grounded in particulars. For example, the role of the 'life-changing encounter', a frequent trope in literary life-writing, is considered by Hermione Lee through a handful of examples, notably a much-storied meeting between the philosopher Isaiah Berlin and the Russian poet Anna Akhmatova; James Shapiro examines the history of the 'cradle to grave' life-narrative, as well as the potential distortions it breeds, by using the example of Shakespeare biography, in particular its attempts to explain the playwright's so-called 'lost years' (roughly, between the ages of nineteen and twenty-nine), about which we 'know nothing'; J. David Velleman, a philosopher, draws on the memoir, *After Long Silence* (1999), by Helen Fremont, as a means of examining the moral grounds for revealing repressed material as well as the respect repression at times deserves; Adam Foulds, the author of *The Quickening Maze* (2009), a novel that brings Tennyson and John Clare together, disarmingly defends the fictional depiction of historical figures by invoking the good faith of the writer, the good sense of the reader, and the great pleasure afforded by the physical 'embodiment' of 'people we know to have actually lived' (Chapter 5, page 290). Fleshly details bring alive Tolstoy's Napoleon and Saul Bellow's Ravelstein, a fictional portrait of the political philosopher Allan Bloom, and illustrate aspects of their characters.

The first half of the volume concerns itself with writing about the lives of others; the second half gives priority to writing about the self. That the distinction between self and other is not always clear is suggested throughout the volume, nowhere more so than in the chapters by Janis Freedman Bellow, Hermione Lee, and Karen A. Winstead, which could be thought of as forming a pivot or hinge between the two halves. Janis Freedman Bellow writes as the living model of a fictional character, Rosamund, in *Ravelstein* (2000). But she also writes as Saul Bellow's wife and as *Ravelstein*'s first reader (her initial reaction to the novel was to ask Bellow to remove the character of Rosamund completely). She was the devoted pupil and friend of Allan Bloom, and was much involved in Bellow's decision to reveal details of Bloom's private life and sexual history (a decision of which she disapproved). Her chapter is a memoir, a confession, and a study of the representation of real people in fiction. Lee's chapter on 'encounter narratives' draws equally on biographical, autobiographical, and poetical accounts of the meeting between Berlin and Akhmatova. Karen A. Winstead's chapter on the mysterious 'Margerie kempe of lynn', a flamboyantly eccentric fifteenth-century Englishwoman, leaves open, as do most scholarly accounts, the question of whether her 'boke' is biography or autobiography.

The chapters in the volume's second half raise questions about forms of self-description or self-presentation. Alan Stewart looks at the diaries of a single individual, Richard Stonley, from the early modern period (*c*.1500–1700), considering what Stonley chose to record and where and how he recorded it as factors which help us to understand how he thought of and attempted to make sense of his life. Joyce E. Chaplin stresses the unfixed nature of Benjamin Franklin's 'Autobiography', 'the world's most widely read unfinished work', partial and pirated versions of which began appearing shortly after Franklin's death in 1790. The decision by some editors to excise the scientific material Franklin clearly wanted included leads to interesting speculation about autobiographical convention. The genre of the confession, often associated with St Augustine, later with Rousseau and the Romantic period, is investigated by Blake Morrison, principally in relation to present-day examples. In addition to surveying a range of motives for confessional writing (he lists seven, excluding 'vanity and revenge'), Morrison offers a confessional account of his own efforts in the field. The moral questions raised by confessional writing are taken up in the chapter that follows, J. David Velleman's 'The Rights to a Life', and in Patrick Hayes's discussion of electronic forms of life-writing. Hayes weighs alarmist accounts of the online environment before making a qualified case for the expressive potential of digital forms, including blogging, tweeting, and Facebook entries. The two final chapters in the volume, those of Laura Marcus, 'Autobiography and Psychoanalysis', and Galen Strawson, 'The Unstoried Life', share a radical scepticism about the notions of self or individuality that underlie much autobiographical writing. Marcus draws on a variety of psychoanalytic theorists to call into question the assumption that the autobiographer and the subject are the same person. She also questions the assumption that individuals are single rather than multiple. Strawson, a philosopher, writes about 'narrative theory', a growing field of study in philosophy. There is now, he argues, 'a robust consensus' in both the humanities and psychoanalysis that 'life is life-writing, a narrative—autobiographical—activity', a consensus he challenges.

If the chapters in the second half of the volume complicate and call into question the truth claims of various forms of self-presentation or self-definition, those in the first half do the same for accounts of real-life others, whether biographical or fictional. Michael Dobson joins James Shapiro in linking approaches to Shakespeare's life to historical trends and factors, taking as his starting point the 'surprisingly rich and various history of depicting Shakespeare's childhood—of writing, in other words, about the bits of Shakespeare's life that came before he had done anything that would make him worth writing about.' William St Clair, in the chapter that follows, looks at the 'many other agents' apart from the biographer and the biographee who play a part in presenting lives in the Romantic period, including 'publishers, printers, designers, engravers, and manufacturers'. The attention St Clair pays to the material aspects of Romantic life-writing is one of several ways in which he suggests that its true character has been obscured by Romantic assumptions. At the same time, these aspects help to forward Romantic notions of immediacy and authenticity. Alison Booth writes about collective biography in the Victorian period, a very different species of life-writing. 'Prosopography' is the name given to these collections of lesser lives (lesser in several senses, first by being short, second by emphasizing common rather than individual features, third by often being about women as opposed to great men, as in such collections as *Gallant Ladies, Colonial Dames, Maids of Honour*). Booth draws comparisons between prosopography and the aggregating propensities of new media such as Facebook, LinkedIn, and other social networks. The conventions of such networks—the information they invite users to disclose, the topics or categories they identify as life-defining or life-explaining (friends, education, relationships, 'likes')—help to shape as much as to reveal a sense of what constitutes a self or a life. Finally, there are two chapters on the fictional representation of real-life figures: Adam Foulds's chapter focuses principally on historical figures, Janis Freedman Bellow's on contemporary or near-contemporary ones.

The book makes no attempt to cover all aspects of life-writing and its study. Other topics it might have discussed include human rights narratives or the testimonies of truth and reconciliation commissions; the journalistic profile or interview; the Theophrastan character; the keepsake book; the commonplace book; works of autobiographical fiction or poetry (*Sons and Lovers, The Prelude*); autobiografiction (*Tristram Shandy, Moll Flanders*); the representation of real-life figures on stage (*Julius Caesar, Galileo*); the use of anecdotes in life-writing; reading the life into the work, as opposed to the work into the life (which is deplored in several chapters here); the curated archive as a species of life-writing; the fashion for designating histories as biographies, as in *Chicago: A Biography* (2009) or *Biographies of Scientific Objects* (2000), behind which lie theoretical considerations ('object biography' is now a branch of cultural and social history, with supporting theory), as well as commercial ones (biographies sell better than histories).[3]

All the chapters in the book were commissioned for it and appear here for the first time. They are written by historians, philosophers, novelist/ poets, literary scholars, biographers, and autobiographers. The ordering of chapters within the book's two roughly designated sections is variously determined. One chapter leads to another, sometimes by way of shared theme, sometimes by period, sometimes by sub-genre, sometimes by a combination of factors. Four of the contributors to the book are volume authors for the forthcoming 'Oxford History of Life Writing', a seven-volume series. All the contributors were encouraged to consider the needs of a general as well as an academic audience, in keeping with the comparatively broad-based readership of the genres or sub-genres they mostly discuss. They were also encouraged to avoid abstruse terminology. I sought out contributors who were practitioners as well as academics, including those who if not exactly opposed to theory are not much given to

---

[3] For theories of 'object biography' see, for example, Bill Brown, 'Thing Theory' and W. J. T. Mitchell, 'Romanticism and the Life of Things: Fossils, Totems, and Images', *Critical Inquiry* 28:1 (Autumn 2001), pp. 1–22, 167–84; Janet Hoskins, 'Agency, Biography and Objects', in *Handbook of Material Culture*, ed. Christopher Tilley et al. (London: Sage, 2009), pp. 74–84; Arjun Appadurai, ed., *The Social Life of Things: Commodities in Cultural Perspective* (Cambridge: Cambridge University Press, 1986); Chris Gosden and Yvonne Marshall, 'The Cultural Biography of Objects', *World Archaeology* 31:2 (October 1999), pp. 169–78.

it. One potential contributor, the biographer Claire Tomalin, who is not an academic, explained in an email of 5 September 2013 her reasons for declining to write for the volume. I print the email below as an eloquent counterweight to the chapters that follow, in particular those, equally eloquent, which question the authority and supposed objectivity of traditional biography.

I have no theory of biography. Out of an interest in history and literature I found myself writing initially about women who seemed somewhat neglected or misrepresented by the official record. I moved on to other figures who caught my interest. I enjoy research hugely and spent many happy years at it. I wrote about Pepys because the standard biographies presented him as the great naval administrator whereas to me he seems much greater than that. I wrote about Hardy because I believed him when he said he was a poet who turned to fiction to earn his living, and it seemed worth taking this seriously. I went back to Dickens because I felt there was unfinished business for me after writing *The Invisible Woman* in which he has a minor role—and he is a colossus, as novelist and as man. I think a life story can be as interesting as fiction (sometimes more). The same building blocks are used, human behaviour and interaction, moral struggle, facing death and so on. I myself feel I have learned from the women and men I have written about and they stay in my mind as constant companions. I am often asked about them, offered more information, and so on. I know some writers have a theoretical objection to biography, but that seems to me a bit like having a theoretical objection to fiction: there is good and bad fiction, good and bad biography, crude biography and subtle biography. It can't be argued about in general. This is not the sort of thing that can be made into an academic essay. So sorrowfully I must say no.

1

Unravelling Shakespeare's Life

James Shapiro

As the eighteenth century came to a close, Edmond Malone, surely the most industrious and influential of Shakespeare's many biographers, voiced his deep frustration.[1] So much might have been learned about Shakespeare if only Malone's predecessors—who began gathering information about Shakespeare over a century earlier—had managed to speak with some of those who had known the playwright. Francis Meres, who praised Shakespeare's plays and poems so highly in *Palladis Tamia* in 1598, lived until 1646. William Cavendish, a poet and disciple of Ben Jonson, was born in 1593 and was still living in 1676. Why hadn't Thomas Fuller or John Aubrey contacted them or sought out others (such as Richard Brathwaite, who was eighteen years old when *King Lear* was first staged, had considered writing a history of the English poets, and didn't die until 1673)? Malone's litany of missed opportunities, which makes for painful reading, goes on and on.[2] And it wasn't just literary figures who might have been sought out: why didn't

---

[1] Malone completed the first section of his unfinished biography by late 1794 (Peter Martin, *Edmond Malone, Shakespeare Scholar: A Literary Biography* (Cambridge: Cambridge University Press, 1995), 186; a decade later, a third, he claimed, remained unwritten (for a discussion of this and the posthumous edition, see 257–76). See also S. Schoenbaum, *Shakespeare's Lives* (Oxford: Clarendon Press, 1991), 169–78.

[2] Edmond Malone, 'The Life of William Shakespeare', in *The Plays and Poem of William Shakspeare*, ed. James Boswell, 21 vols. (London, 1821), vol. 2, 1–11.

those who began visiting Stratford-upon-Avon in search of stories about Shakespeare speak to Shakespeare's younger daughter, Judith, who outlived her father by nearly a half-century, not dying until February 1662?[3]

Malone was painfully aware that the 1660s and 1670s marked a cut-off point: after that, it was no longer possible to learn from those with a personal connection to Shakespeare what he was like, what kind of father or friend or husband he was, what his religious or political beliefs were— things about his personality and private life we wish we knew.

Malone had another complaint, this one directed at Shakespeare's first biographer, Nicholas Rowe, who had appended a brief *Life* to his edition of the *Works* in 1709. Malone attacked Rowe for having mistaken anecdote, gossip, and surmise for evidence: 'it is somewhat remarkable', he writes, 'that in Rowe's *Life* of our author, there are not more than *eleven* facts mentioned; and of these, on a critical examination, eight will be found to be false'.[4] Malone was no less impatient with those, including Samuel Johnson, who had followed Rowe down this path, imagining that Shakespeare got his start holding horses at the playhouse in London, or those who proposed that, as a young man, Shakespeare apprenticed as a butcher or fled Stratford because he had been caught poaching deer. Such claims, in a phrase Malone repeats, were 'mere fiction',[5] that is, not grounded in documentary evidence. Despite the efforts of many researchers over the past three centuries or so, including Malone (who scoured the archives as no one before or since has done and even discovered the only surviving letter written to Shakespeare), we still know little about Shakespeare's childhood, and know barely more, aside from the fact that he married young and had three children, about his life before he left Stratford some time in the 1580s. Even more disappointingly, we don't know how Shakespeare spent the next decade, until the historical record picks up again in the early 1590s. These are called the 'lost years' or 'lost decade' for a reason: lost not to Shakespeare, who lived them, but permanently and almost entirely lost to us.

---

[3] Scott McCrea has done a major service to Shakespeare biography by showing that the tradition that John Ward, Vicar of Stratford, had made a note to speak with Judith but failed to act on time—a story accepted by most modern biographers (including me)—is mistaken and based on a misreading of Ward's notebooks. See his 'Mrs Queeny, RIP: A New Examination of Rev. John Ward's Notebooks', *Notes and Queries*, [n.s., 59], 257: 2 (June 2012), 182–5.

[4] Malone, *Plays and Poems of William Shakspeare*, vol. 2, 69–70.

[5] Malone, *Plays and Poems of William Shakspeare*, vol. 2, 118, 166.

Fast forward to the early twentieth-first century, and to the publication of influential cradle-to-grave biographies of Shakespeare written by some of our most prominent scholars and writers—including Peter Ackroyd's *Shakespeare: The Biography* in 2005, Stephen Greenblatt's *Will in the World: How Shakespeare Became Shakespeare* that same year, and René Weis's *Shakespeare Revealed: A Biography* in 2007—and you can see that some things haven't changed. 'Mere fiction', as Malone put it, is still rife in these biographies, all of which speculate about what Shakespeare was doing during those crucial lost years that took him from Stratford to London, from youth to maturity. The mix and match of fact and fiction has reached the point where one of Shakespeare's most recent biographers, Graham Holderness, divides each chapter of his *Nine Lives of Shakespeare* (2011) into discrete categories: first the handful of facts, then the traditions, next the speculation, and last, to cap it off, the fiction. Rather than dismissing the drift to fiction, Holderness recognizes its lure if not its inevitability. After dutifully showing how little we actually know for a fact or can surmise, Holderness embraces the fictional and goes on to retell each stage of Shakespeare's life in a different inventive mode—as Joycean stream of consciousness, as Sherlock Holmes detective story, as Hemingway riff, as Swiftian fable, and so on. Where, one wonders, can or should Shakespeare biography go from here?

I've been wrestling with the challenges of writing about Shakespeare's life for a long while, first in the course of researching my book about a single year in Shakespeare's life, *1599*, and then through the years I spent on the authorship controversy, engaging bizarre claims that other lives—Francis Bacon's? The Earl of Oxford's?—better suited the authorship of the plays than that of a glover's son from Stratford. Over time, I have found myself drawn to questions those writing (and reading) these 'Lives' tend not to address. One of these is what it means for a biographer to ask: 'How did Shakespeare *become* Shakespeare?' Underlying the way this question is usually approached is an unspoken assumption about a decisive and formative period in our lives: the years that straddle adolescence and early adulthood. Identity, this way of thinking goes, is indelibly forged in the complicated and often traumatic passage that leads from youth to maturity—and it is characteristic of writers to mine these fraught formative experiences in subsequent, and inevitably autobiographical, works. As convincing as this notion of how we become who we are may sound, other models are equally plausible: that who we are is determined much earlier than that, in early childhood, or by our ethnic or cultural heritage, or by our social station, or alternatively, that we reinvent ourselves many times over in the course of a complicated lifetime rather than spending our mature years playing out a part scripted for us in our youth.

What gives me further pause when this 'coming of age' model is applied to Shakespeare—besides the fact that it is better suited to describing modern lives than early modern ones—is that it fits the needs of his twenty-first-century biographers all too conveniently. Because we know nothing about what Shakespeare felt or experienced during his lost years between, say, nineteen and twenty-nine, it is easy to paint any kind of sexual, spiritual, familial, or professional crisis you wish—or elements of each of them—onto this blank space of the biographical canvas. Something, after all, must have led or driven Shakespeare from Stratford to London. And so, in recent biographies, we get the crypto-Catholic Shakespeare living in Lancashire, the Shakespeare with a fraught Oedipal relationship with his father, the Shakespeare fleeing from a hasty marriage gone sour into the arms of some Dark Lady or Young Man, or both, whose true identities, biographers proclaim, are at last revealed. All plausible. All resonant with modern preoccupations. And all difficult, if not impossible, to disprove.

All this leaves me wondering less and less about how Shakespeare became Shakespeare—I'm convinced we will never have a satisfying answer to that question—and more about *how*, *when*, and *why* Shakespeare biography became recognizable as the Shakespeare biography we read today. I'm interested then, in *unravelling* Shakespeare's life, in the sense of that word as first introduced in English writing by his fellow dramatist Thomas Dekker in 1603. 'Unravel'—originally a Dutch word (and Dekker was of Dutch descent)—not just as untangle but also in its now almost obsolete sense of 'reverse', 'undo', 'annul'.

Unravelling the tangled yarn of Shakespeare biography ultimately leads back to a pair of developments in the late eighteenth century that have shaped the story of how the playwright's life has been imagined ever since. Edmond Malone's own *Life* of Shakespeare was a shambles. He never published it. The son and namesake of Samuel Johnson's biographer, James Boswell, did his best to assemble the posthumous fragments Malone left behind. The first 118 pages of Malone's *Life* only go up to the year 1585, while Shakespeare is still living in Stratford. But with the arrival of the 'lost years' the trail goes cold and all Malone can do is entertain and reject the various and undocumented possibilities that then led Shakespeare to London. That, basically, is as far as Malone got. A hundred-page digression on whether Edmund Spenser was referring to Shakespeare when he speaks of 'pleasant Willy' in *The Tears of the Muses* (1591) is, sadly, padding. And the nine pages that follow that only take us up to Shakespeare the actor, at the verge of his London career. The rest is silence. Boswell's efforts to mask the problem by adding 400 pages of appendices and reprinting Malone's earlier and groundbreaking 'chronological ordering' of Shakespeare plays, can't hide the obvious. Too much information about Shakespeare's life had been irrevocably lost. As Malone learned the hard way, a cradle-to-grave biography based on documentary evidence was no longer possible—or could be done, as Stephen Greenblatt has shown in a dazzling act of compression in his essay 'The Traces of Shakespeare's Life', his highly recommended contribution to the recent *New Cambridge Companion to Shakespeare*, in just thirteen pages.[6]

It's all the more surprising, then, to find David Bevington recently claiming in his book *Shakespeare and Biography* that, by 'the end of the eighteenth century, Shakespeare's biography had taken its basic shape'.[7] That can't be true. Just a glance at any of these early biographical efforts confirms that these attempts, including Malone's, had no shape at all. What Bevington really means, I suspect, is that by the end of the eighteenth century nearly everything important that we now know about Shakespeare's life had already been discovered. Yet at the outset of the nineteenth century, what was still missing from Shakespeare biographies was a narrative frame that gave coherence and meaning to the traces of the life that had survived. How and why did that change?

While Malone was adamant in refusing to accept gossip or anecdotal evidence in setting forth Shakespeare's biography, when it came to interpreting or annotating the plays and poems, he didn't hesitate to draw on evidence from the life. Malone was the first writer to do so—but far from the last. So, for example, when Malone excitedly discovered in the Stratford archives that Shakespeare's son Hamnet had died in 1596, he thought it likely that Constance's 'pathetic lamentations' about the loss of her son

---

[6] Stephen Greenblatt, 'The Traces of Shakespeare's Life', in *The New Cambridge Companion to William Shakespeare*, ed. Margreta de Grazia and Stanley Wells (Cambridge: Cambridge University Press, 2010), 1–13.

[7] David Bevington, *Shakespeare and Biography* (Oxford: Oxford University Press, 2010), 30.

Arthur in *King John* (which he dated to this same year) was inspired by Shakespeare's own recent loss. It didn't occur to Malone to claim that Shakespeare would suppress this loss and wait for three or four more years until unpacking his heart in *Hamlet*. Why subsequent scholars rejected *King John* in favour of *Hamlet* as the play that really responds to this loss will soon become clearer.

Nowhere was Malone's practice of reading the works out of the life bolder or more influential than in the notes he first appended in 1780 to the opening lines of 'Sonnet 93', which begins with its speaker comparing himself to a cuckolded spouse: 'So shall I live, supposing thou art true, / Like a deceived husband.' Malone read these lines in light of Shakespeare's will, in which his wife Anne Hathaway was left the 'second best bed', a bequest that, for Malone, confirmed the poet's jealous resentment of her. And Malone found this corroborated in several of the dramatic works, for 'jealousy is the principal hinge of *four* of his plays', especially *Othello*, he writes, where 'some of the passages are written with such exquisite feeling, as might lead us to suspect that the author had himself been *perplexed* with doubts, though not perhaps in the *extreme*'. Knowing that using the life to explain the works crossed a boundary, one that had been respected by every previous editor and critic of Shakespeare's plays, Malone retreated a half-step, admitting that the case was built on 'an uncertain foundation', and explaining that all he meant 'to say is, that he appears to me to have written more immediately from the heart on the subject of jealousy, than on any other; and it is therefore not improbable that he might have felt it'. Malone refused to reword or remove what he had written, even when challenged to do so by his fellow editor, George Steevens, who pointed out that because 'Shakespeare has written with his utmost power on the subject of jealousy is no proof that he ever felt it'.

Struggling to extricate himself from charges that this was idle speculation, Malone further entangled himself in the intricacies of Shakespeare's love life. 'He might not have loved' Anne Hathaway, Malone adds, 'and perhaps she might not have deserved his affection.'[8] Malone was a bachelor when he wrote these words—in fact, he would never marry, though he

---

[8] For this and preceding quotations by both Malone and Steevens on Sonnet 93, as they exchanged blows in their footnotes to the poem, see Edmond Malone, *Supplement to the Edition of Shakspeare's Plays Published in 1778 by Samuel Johnson and George Steevens*, 2 vols. (London, 1780), vol. 1, 653–7.

wanted to (he seems to have wooed awkwardly and too aggressively).[9] Malone's note to 'Sonnet 93' introduced a new trend in Shakespearean biography: the infusion of autobiography, as writers projected onto Shakespeare their own personalities and prejudices.

German critics were among the first to recognize the rich biographical potential of Malone's approach. So, for example, August Wilhelm von Schlegel took the English to task in 1808 for never having 'thought of availing themselves of [Shakespeare's] sonnets for tracing the circumstances and sentiments of the poet', and, crucially, for failing to recognize that these works contained the 'confessions of his youthful errors'. Heine was equally convinced that the sonnets are 'authentic records of the circumstances of Shakespeare's life'. Ironically, Malone, who had opposed gossip and speculation in the writing of Shakespeare's life, had opened the floodgates for others to introduce just that. Within a few decades, critical heavyweights on both sides of the Atlantic—including the Schlegels, Wordsworth, Coleridge, Heine, and Emerson—had all reversed Malone's procedure of reading the work out of the life and were avidly reading the life out of the works, using at first the sonnets, then the plays.[10] By 1838 Shakespeare's fictions were called, for the first time, 'autobiographical' (a word that had only entered the vocabulary twenty-one years earlier) in *Shakespeare's Autobiographical Poems*. According to its author, John Keats' close friend Charles Armitage Brown, the sonnets were 'pure uninterrupted biography'.[11] Shakespeare's life was now an open book.

Crucially, at the same moment that Shakespeare biographers and critics had begun reading the life out of the works, there emerged, first in Germany, and soon in England and elsewhere, a new kind of fiction, the *bildungsroman* or 'novel of formation'.[12] Goethe's *Wilhelm Meister's Apprenticeship*, published in 1795–96, is generally acknowledged to be, if not the first, then

---

[9] Martin, *Edmond Malone*, 3–17.

[10] For the autobiographical responses to the sonnets by Heine, the Schlegels, Wordsworth, Coleridge, and Emerson, see Hyder Edward Rollins, ed., *A New Variorum Edition of Shakespeare: The Sonnets*, 2 vols. (Philadelphia: J. P. Lippincott and Company, 1944).

[11] Charles Armitage Brown, *Shakespeare's Autobiographical Poems. Being His Sonnets Clearly Developed: With His Character Drawn Chiefly from His Works* (London: James Bohn, 1838).

[12] Franco Moretti, *The Way of the World: The Bildungsroman in European Culture* (London: Verso, 1987).

surely the most influential early example of this genre.[13] It would have a profound influence on English writers from Thomas Carlyle (who translated it), Jane Austen, and Charles Dickens, to George Eliot and (the American) Henry James, who both wrote about it admiringly.[14] Though students of the novel are familiar with *Wilhelm Meister*, biographers and Shakespeare scholars are perhaps less so than they ought to be, for it is the *bildungsroman*, and, I would argue, Goethe's especially, that helped provide what had been missing until now: a narrative design that enabled biographers, in the absence of documentary evidence, to tell the story of how Shakespeare became Shakespeare.

Goethe's novel describes the formation of Wilhelm Meister, and its plot should sound familiar to anyone familiar with modern Shakespeare biographies: the search by a sensitive and artistic young man to find himself, find love, and overcome various obstacles that stood in the way of his coming of age and discovering his calling. He falls into various lovers' arms, deals as best he can with his melancholy nature, suffers physical and emotional wounds, turns to acting, and struggles with the demands of his father. Goethe, searching for a model for his hero, chooses Shakespeare's Hamlet—or rather a younger and more romantic and depoliticized version of him—who becomes the yardstick by which young Wilhelm Meister measures himself. Indeed, the notion of Prince Hamlet as a melancholic paralyzed by excessive thought, soon popularized by the German Romantic critics and then by Coleridge, was born here. Wilhelm Meister recognizes William Shakespeare as both his 'good friend' and, tellingly, as his 'godfather'[15]—and Wilhelm is, of course, William in German.

Wilhelm finds himself early in his journey 'behaving like Prince Hal', having 'spent some time with base and dissolute companions and despite his noble character, taken great pleasure in the rough, unseemly and foolish behavior of his earthy associates'.[16] But as he matures it is through Hamlet that he achieves a degree of self-awareness, and he closely studies his 'model through the strange labyrinth of so many different moods and

---

[13] Johann Wolfgang von Goethe, *Wilhelm Meister's Apprenticeship*, in *Goethe's Collected Works*, vol. 9, ed. and trans. Eric A. Blackall and Victor Lange (Princeton: Princeton University Press, 1989).

[14] For a recent overview of its influence, see Jeremy Adler, 'Towards Infinitude', *TLS*, 13 January 2012, 8.

[15] Goethe, *Wilhelm Meister*, 123.   [16] Goethe, *Wilhelm Meister*, 123–4.

peculiar experiences'. Wilhelm describes how he learned Hamlet's 'part and tried it out, feeling that I was becoming more and more identified with my hero . . . I searched for any clues of Hamlet's character previous to the death of his father. I observed what this interesting young man had been like without reference to that sad event and its terrible consequences, and considered what he might have become without them.'[17] Further study of Hamlet leads Wilhelm to grasp 'what Shakespeare set out to portray': a 'fine, pure, noble and highly moral person, but devoid of that emotional strength that characterizes a hero'.[18] Holding the mirror up to Hamlet, he sees himself.

Wilhelm joins an acting company, which enables him to act the part of Hamlet, merging his identity even more fully with his hero's. He even translates Shakespeare's play into German for his fellow actors, and edits the text—eliminating Fortinbras and the play's political frame—so that it focuses more on the Danish prince's familial struggle. The climax of his performance as Hamlet is the encounter with the Ghost, played by an actor who is disguised and unknown to Wilhelm. When this actor cries out, 'I am thy father's spirit', Wilhelm 'stepped back shuddering, and the whole audience shuddered. The voice seemed familiar to everyone, and Wilhelm thought it sounded like that of his own father.'[19] It is a key scene, one played out again at the end of the novel as a kind of coda. At that point Wilhelm has fully come of age, 'his apprenticeship' we are told, is 'complete', as the actor—now revealed as the Abbot who has overseen and guided Wilhelm in his spiritual journey—reappears as 'the old King of Denmark in full armor' and tells Wilhelm: 'I am your father's ghost . . . and I depart in peace, for all I wished for you has been fulfilled more than I myself could imagine . . . Farewell, and remember me.'[20]

Even as it became the pattern for the 'coming of age' story in European fiction, this *bildungsroman* offered an invaluable model for literary biographers, for Goethe had created a prototype for anyone trying to write a narrative about the journey of a sensitive young individual who faces sexual, social, spiritual, and professional crises. William Shakespeare's 'lost years' would soon be recast as a version of Wilhelm Meister's—perhaps we should think of these biographical portraits as 'Wilhelm Shakespeare's'—the struggles

---

[17] Goethe, *Wilhelm Meister*, 128.   [18] Goethe, *Wilhelm Meister*, 146.
[19] Goethe, *Wilhelm Meister*, 195.   [20] Goethe, *Wilhelm Meister*, 303–4.

with love, the early travels, the turning to an acting career, the guilt and struggle with his faith and his father—all, ironically enough, filtered through an adaptation of his own fictional creation. To complete the circle, Shakespeare's plays were then read autobiographically, as traces of this transformative journey. In Stephen Greenblatt's formulation, Shakespeare 'turned everything life had dealt him—the painful crisis of social standing, sexuality, and religion—into the uses of art'.[21] Once Malone had paved the way to reading the works through the life, what could be more natural than following in Goethe's footsteps and reimagining Shakespeare's own life through that of Hamlet, his most transparently autobiographical 'coming of age' character, in whom all these traumas are visible?

Over the next half-century, and certainly by the end of the nineteenth century, culminating in Edward Dowden's hugely influential biographical study of *Shakespeare's Mind and Art* (1875), the combination of reading the works as autobiography and describing Shakespeare's development as a kind of *bildungsroman* became enshrined, with *Hamlet* playing a key role. Dowden, who closely read and quotes approvingly from *Wilhelm Meister* in his biography, takes as given that '*Hamlet* seems to have its roots so deep in Shakespere's nature'.[22] Dowden's main contribution to Shakespeare biography was expanding the *bildungsroman* structure beyond Goethe's abbreviated move from Prince Hal to Hamlet, so that Shakespeare's life story could be seen as a longer and more fraught journey, through greater heights and depths. As Dowden neatly summarizes it: Shakespeare 'feared that he might become . . . a Romeo; he feared that he might falter from his strong self-maintenance into a Hamlet; he suffered grievous wrong, and he resolved that he would be a Timon. He ended by becoming Duke Prospero.'[23] The narrative through-line of Shakespeare biography was now essentially locked in place, despite the best efforts of critics like C. J. Sisson, in his devastating critique in 1934, *The Mythical Sorrows of Shakespeare*, to dislodge it.[24] For confirmation of the pervasive influence of Goethe and Malone on modern

---

[21] Stephen Greenblatt, *Will in the World: How Shakespeare Became Shakespeare* (New York: Norton, 2005), 377.

[22] Edward Dowden, *Shakespere: A Critical Study of His Mind and Art*, 3rd edn (1875; New York: Harper and Brothers, 1881), v, 132.

[23] Dowden, *Shakespere*, 32.

[24] C. J. Sisson, *The Mythical Sorrows of Shakespeare*, Annual Shakespeare Lecture of the British Academy, Proceedings of the British Academy, vol. 20 (1934).

Shakespeare biographies we need only quote from representative accounts of the autobiographical in *Hamlet*. Here, first, is René Weis:

Whatever spiritual debates or even disputes he and his father may have had in the privacy of the house in Henley Street, Shakespeare once more revisits them in a long play's journey into night, a play perhaps of old sorrows, writing Hamlet as his way of dealing with the loss of his father, a play in which a dead father's ghost appears to a son who is named after Shakespeare's own son in real life.[25]

And next, Stephen Greenblatt, who proves equally adept at writing a biographical account in this speculative tradition:

'To be or not to be': as audiences and readers have long instinctively understood, these suicidal thoughts, provoked by the death of a loved one, lie at the heart of Shakespeare's tragedy. They may well have been the core of the playwright's own inner disturbance . . . the coincidence of the names—the act of writing his own son's name again and again—may well have reopened a deep wound, a wound that had never properly healed. But, of course, in *Hamlet*, it is the death not of a son but of a father that provokes the hero's spiritual crisis. If the tragedy swelled up from Shakespeare's own life—if it can be traced back to the death of Hamnet—something must have made the playwright link the loss of his child to the imagined loss of his father . . . [T]he death of his son and the impending death of his father—a crisis of mourning and memory—constitute a psychic disturbance that may help to explain the explosive power and inwardness of *Hamlet*.[26]

It would be heartless to object that Shakespeare didn't make up the story of *Hamlet*, was updating an old and familiar play that had been on the boards for over a decade; that Shakespeare might not even have seen his son Hamnet more than a few times since leaving Stratford in the 1580s, may barely have known him, and in any case was on the road touring and distant from Stratford when Hamnet was buried; that Shakespeare's father was still alive when he wrote the play, and that we can't assume that the past and future deaths of his son and father necessarily produced what Greenblatt calls 'a crisis of mourning and memory' any more than, say, the past and future deaths of Shakespeare's unknown friends and lovers or siblings or of his aging mother might have, if indeed, there was any such crisis at all; and that if Shakespeare was really reacting to the death of his

---

[25] René Weis, *Shakespeare Revealed: A Biography* (London: John Murray, 2007), 272–3.
[26] Greenblatt, *Will in the World*, 311, 219.

son in his work, then *King John*, as Malone recognized, was a timelier play in which to do so.

But there's no denying that what Weis and Greenblatt offer is a deeply satisfying story that resonates with readers eager to know, 400 years later, in the absence of any other evidence, how Shakespeare *felt*. It should come as no surprise that the climactic reading of *Hamlet* comes remarkably late in their cradle-to-grave biographies—in Greenblatt's, fewer than 70 pages from the end of an almost 400-page account of the life, even though Shakespeare was only midway through his career, would write plays for another 13 years, and would live longer than that. This lack of balance in the biography is part of the price paid for reading the life out of the works and drawing so heavily on the narrative structure and emotional power of the *bildungsroman*. Modern Shakespeare biography is marked not by a turn to fiction, as some have suggested, but rather by a return to a fictional road first travelled two hundred years ago, whose foundations are now largely unacknowledged.

This lack of balance is not the only price paid. By overemphasizing his formative experiences and by having Shakespeare then obsessively revisit his past, modern biographies of Shakespeare end up portraying him far more as an Elizabethan writer than a Jacobean one, though he spent roughly as many years writing under a Stuart monarch as he did under a Tudor one. Giving short shrift to the Jacobean Shakespeare has also meant paying too little attention to the ways in which Shakespeare had to reinvent himself as a King's Man in 1603, find his footing in a new and different regime, endure the challenges due to plague that closed the public playhouses perhaps as much as two-thirds of the time from 1603 to 1610, meet the demands of playing at court a score of times a year instead of only two or three times, respond to the possibilities made available by playing indoors at the Black-friars playhouse, and, most of all, adjust to collaborating with up-and-coming younger writers.

For the Jacobean Shakespeare, far more than the Elizabethan one, collaborated extensively, working, in various ways, with George Wilkins on *Pericles*; with Thomas Middleton on *Timon of Athens* and perhaps *A Yorkshire Tragedy*; with John Fletcher on *Henry VIII*, *Two Noble Kinsmen*, and *Cardenio*; and with Robert Johnson, who wrote the music for Shakespeare's songs in *Cymbeline*, *The Winter's Tale*, and *The Tempest*. It goes without saying that a biographical approach so wedded to self-revelation can't begin to confront the challenges posed by the collaborative Shakespeare: If Timon is angry at the world, are we to read that as Shakespeare's or Middleton's rage? Should we trace the obsession with incest, or with father and daughter in *Pericles*, to Shakespeare or to Wilkins?

No play, other than perhaps *Hamlet*, has suffered more from the distortions forced upon it by biographers committed to reading the work out of the life than *The Tempest*. Shakespeare's career, after all, has to end in a fitting way, and what could be better than Prospero as Shakespeare writing his own final act—a self-portrait of the artist abjuring his rough magic. The image of Prospero leaving his island and returning to Milan as a transparent version of an aging Shakespeare leaving the world of London's theatres to retirement in Stratford has proved irresistible. It's a deeply satisfying narrative and a wonderfully sentimental way to bring the life to a close. As the normally sceptical David Bevington, who nonetheless promotes this story, puts it, 'Any biographer of Shakespeare finds it hard to imagine a more perfect ending, for a career, for a family story, for a life history of an incomparably great artist.'[27] Here's Peter Ackroyd's representative version: 'In the late plays, when Shakespeare himself was reaching the end of his life, an ageing father is reunited with a long-absent daughter; there may be feelings of guilt and shame associated with this absence, but all is forgiven.'[28] For Stephen Greenblatt, too, 'Shakespeare seems to have thought of himself as well struck in years and may have drawn from his own inner life Prospero's strange remark: "Every third thought shall be my grave." '[29]

This sounds convincing enough, until you realize that Shakespeare could not have known, as his biographers do, that he would not live for several more decades (to the ripe old age of his parents) but had only a half-dozen more years left. It's also worth noting that biographers who turn Shakespeare into Prospero can't help but prematurely age him, even though Shakespeare was only in his late forties when he wrote the play, far from old age, even by early modern standards. When you look back over the way his entire life is read through the works, such distortions become even more pronounced, for in the course of just fifteen years, Shakespeare

[27] Bevington, *Shakespeare and Biography*, 154.
[28] Peter Ackroyd, *Shakespeare: The Biography* (London: Chatto & Windus, 2005), 424.
[29] Greenblatt, *Will in the World*, 382.

must go from the romantic young lover of Romeo (though by then, he is already in his early thirties) to the aged Prospero.

The insistence that *The Tempest* is the very last play—which predictably originated in Malone, who didn't know that it was performed at court as early as November 1611 and almost surely at the Globe or Blackfriars theatres before that[30]—must ignore the fact that Shakespeare not only co-authored three other plays after *The Tempest*—*Henry VIII*, *The Two Noble Kinsmen*, and *Cardenio*—but may well have written *The Winter's Tale* or *Cymbeline*, perhaps both, after *The Tempest*.[31] And he was also freelancing, collaborating with Richard Burbage on the design and slogan of an *impresa*, a tournament shield, for the Earl of Rutland in 1613. This bears little resemblance to a writer drowning his books and breaking his staff. As for *The Tempest* as Shakespeare's autobiographical swansong: it doesn't take much ingenuity to choose *any* Jacobean play and read it as Shakespeare's farewell to the stage. Take your pick. Had Shakespeare died of the plague in 1605 after writing what we would now be calling his last work, *Timon of Athens*, you can be sure his biographers would be describing Timon as turning his back on the city, rejecting mankind, and writing his own epitaph as a dying and bitter Shakespeare's own dark leave-taking. Reading the life through the work leads not only to distorting that life, but also, and I think inevitably, to misreading the work.

It's not only distortions that should concern us, but omissions, for there are aspects of Shakespeare's career, aside from collaboration, that cannot easily be accommodated into the contours of the dominant biographical model I have described. Suppose I announced the discovery of a sixty-seven-line Shakespeare poem that I came across—found it buried in a book from 1601 of which only two copies survive, a discovery that transformed my understanding of what Shakespeare accomplished. And after finding that poem, I double-checked leading biographies to see if I had been scooped and was relieved that there was not a word about this amazing poem in Peter

---

[30] Malone, *An Attempt to Ascertain the Order in Which the Plays of Shakespeare were Written* (London, 1778). For the date of the play, see Stephen Orgel, ed., *The Tempest* (Oxford: Oxford University Press, 1987), 62–4.

[31] For an excellent account of distortions produced by reading *The Tempest* as a late play, see Gordon McMullan, *Shakespeare and the Idea of Late Writing: Authorship in the Proximity of Death* (Cambridge: Cambridge University Press, 2007).

Ackroyd or René Weis or Stephen Greenblatt's impressive biographies, or even in Samuel Schoenbaum's well-regarded *Compact Documentary Life*.[32]

Imagine that leafing through the volume that contained my newly discovered poem, I then found, to my great excitement, Shakespeare described as a 'modern' poet. In fact, the collection goes on to speak of him as one of a 'chorus' of contributors, including Ben Jonson, John Marston, and George Chapman, who responded to each other's work. My discovery offers something we don't see elsewhere in the canon: a mysterious allegory. And it was soon clear that, in writing this poem Shakespeare was involved in a patronage relationship with a little-known figure at Queen Elizabeth's court, Sir John Salusbury. Even more surprisingly, I discovered that it was one of the first metaphysical poems in English, if not the first; either John Donne influenced Shakespeare, or Shakespeare Donne.

This discovery threw me, for it called into question much of what I have read or been taught about Shakespeare's life and art: that Shakespeare had abandoned poetry in favour of drama after 1594, and that he had cut his ties to court patrons after dedicating *Venus and Adonis* and *Lucrece* to the Earl of Southampton. It made me think harder about what it meant for Shakespeare to be seen as a metaphysical and philosophical writer, as someone who collaborated with poets and not just playwrights, and as someone who had to position himself politically quite carefully in the wake of the Essex scandal of 1601.

Those of you familiar with the remarkable poem 'Let the bird of loudest lay'—better known as 'The Phoenix and Turtle'—will know that what I have described is no discovery on my part at all, that Shakespeare was the author of such a metaphysical conceit as 'So they loved as love in twaine, / Had the essence but in one, / Two distincts, Division none, / Number there in love was slaine', and that the poem has long been available to anyone who had delved into Shakespeare's contribution in 1601 to Robert Chester's collaborative volume, *Love's Martyr*. Yet for all the reasons I have set out so far, 'The Phoenix and Turtle' cannot easily be shoehorned into the

---

[32] S. Schoenbaum, *William Shakespeare: A Compact Documentary Life* (New York: Oxford University Press, 1977). Park Honan's excellent biography, *Shakespeare: A Life* (Oxford: Oxford University Press, 1998), devotes eight sentences to it, 289–90.

conventional narrative of Shakespeare's development—and so has dropped out of the life and the canon of works taught and discussed. Though I have long known and taught this poem and have found that students love its mysteries, it wasn't until I read James Bednarz's recent and brilliant book, *Shakespeare and the Truth of Love: The Mystery of 'The Phoenix and Turtle'*,[33] that the exciting biographical implications of the poem became clear.

Bednarz's book casts much fresh light on Shakespeare's world in 1601 and changes the ways in which we think about what Shakespeare was writing after *Hamlet*. Charles Nicholl's *The Lodger* does much the same for 1604, illuminating Shakespeare's life, surroundings, relationships, and work when he was living in Silver Street in Cripplegate.[34] These two books offer an alternative form of Shakespeare biography, one that is free of the constraints imposed by cradle-to-grave accounts. They are not the only examples. One of the best books on Shakespeare that I have read is J. Leeds Barroll's *Politics, Plague, and Shakespeare's Theater*.[35] Barroll painstakingly takes us through plague-ridden London in 1606 and wrestles with the question of how Shakespeare wrote, and what he wrote, in these dark days. His book would perhaps be better known if it were recognized as a forerunner of these micro-biographies—for like Bednarz's and Nicholl's books, and my own on the year 1599[36]—it offers a more historically informed way of thinking about Shakespeare's creative choices and challenges.

There are other, no less consequential moments in Shakespeare's life that would repay this sort of close attention: 1594, when he joined the Chamberlain's Men; 1603, when James succeeded Elizabeth and Shakespeare became a King's Man and Groom of the Chamber; and 1613, when the Globe burned down and he was actively collaborating with John Fletcher. Every year that Shakespeare wrote repays this close unpacking of the constantly shifting cultural, religious, political, and artistic worlds in which he lived and worked—and every year could usefully be read from many angles. I'm confident that this less rushed, more magnified view of

---

[33] James Bednarz, *Shakespeare and the Truth of Love: The Mystery of 'The Phoenix and Turtle'* (Basingstoke: Palgrave Macmillan, 2012).

[34] Charles Nicholl, *The Lodger: Shakespeare on Silver Street* (London: Allen Lane, 2007).

[35] J. Leeds Barroll, *Politics, Plague, and Shakespeare's Theater: The Stuart Years* (Ithaca, NY: Cornell University Press, 1991).

[36] James Shapiro, *1599: A Year in the Life of William Shakespeare* (London: Faber & Faber, 2005).

Shakespeare in different moments, in different circles, responding to unexpected challenges, will enrich not only how we understand his life but also how we read the works. While I admire the efforts of leading Shakespeare biographers who have sought out alternative approaches to writing the entire life—and I'm thinking here especially of the first-rate work of Katherine Duncan-Jones, who has no patience for the romantic Bard in her *Ungentle Shakespeare*, and who usefully offers 'scenes' from the life (though too heavily reliant on the anecdotal evidence), and Jonathan Bate's smart move to avoid the relentless chronological march and offer a biography of Shakespeare's mind in his *Soul of the Age*—writing from cradle to grave, as they do, makes it impossible to avoid the tendency to fill in the blanks, and then having that filler shape the subsequent life. To my mind, the future of Shakespeare biography is surely better served by studies that zoom in on key moments in the life, for which more context survives than is usually acknowledged.[37]

The strongest argument I can offer for abandoning conventional biographical approaches in favour of those that concentrate intensely on a slice of the life comes from the example of Shakespeare himself, who, we do well to recall, wrote the 'lives' of a dozen or so historical figures: King John, Henry VI, Henry V, Richard II, Richard III, Henry VIII, Julius Caesar, Macbeth, Lear, Timon, Coriolanus, and a joint biography of Antony and Cleopatra. In each of these biographical portraits Shakespeare focuses on the most consequential moments in these lives, sometimes limited to a few months, sometimes to a few years. Critics like to point out how closely he follows his main biographical model, Plutarch's *Lives* (turning prose into blank verse, say, in Enobarbus' description of Cleopatra on her barge). What you hear less often is how Shakespeare breaks from Plutarch's cradle-to-grave approach, how he circles these lives of Greeks and Romans looking for just the right entry point, landing on the part of the life that is worth writing about. He doesn't offer us the boyhood of Macbeth or the salad days of Cleopatra; these are left to our imagination. You would think that it's a lesson that Shakespeare's own biographers would have absorbed, but they

---

[37] Katherine Duncan-Jones, *Ungentle Shakespeare: Scenes from His Life* (London: Thomson Learning, 2001); Jonathan Bate, *Soul of the Age: The Life, Mind and World of William Shakespeare* (London: Viking, 2008). See, too, David Ellis, *The Truth about William Shakespeare: Fact, Fiction and Modern Biographies* (Edinburgh: Edinburgh University Press, 2012).

haven't, or haven't fully enough. I'm not at all sure why we care as much as we do about the half of Shakespeare's life that wasn't spent writing, acting, and responding to his creative and cultural moment. And I can't think of a better model for the future of Shakespeare biography than one favoured by Shakespeare himself.

2

A Boy from Stratford, 1769–1916: Shakespearean Biography and Romantic Nationalism

Michael Dobson

> We were, fair Queen,
> Two lads that thought there was no more behind
> But such a day to-morrow as to-day,
> And to be boy eternal . . .
> We were as twinn'd lambs that did frisk i' the sun,
> And bleat the one at the other.
>
> (*The Winter's Tale*, 1.2.63–6, 69–70)

Shakespeare's most idyllic and often-quoted evocation of boyhood, from the second scene of *The Winter's Tale*, is also one of his most powerful evocations of male friendship, and perhaps it is a sense that the boy depicted in this photograph (see Figure 2.1) is, by comparison, terribly isolated that gives the image something of its definite and agoraphobic pathos. Apart from a glimpse of a mysteriously unconvincing-looking building somewhere behind the trees, the entire universe this photo depicts seems empty. In the midst of nothingness, our gaze is met by that of an inexplicable child, his face at once challenging and anxious. If he had not been forced so

Figure 2.1 'Warwick Pageant—The Boy Shakespeare'. Postcard, 1906. Property of the author.

elaborately to wear historical costume, he might be a figure out of Beckett. The bland label at his feet, 'Warwick Pageant: The Boy Shakespeare', seems incongruous in at least two ways: firstly, in that pageants aren't usually performed in wholly vacant spaces by casts consisting solely of one juvenile, and secondly in that there is always something odd about a representation of someone from the 1570s which has clearly been made using a modern camera. The added inscription in Dickensian copperplate handwriting only makes the effect stranger: 'I thought this would please you.' Why would anyone think that?

I got very interested in shows such as the 1906 Warwick Pageant, in which this boy made a crucial and climactic appearance, while working on a book about the amateur performance of Shakespeare a little while ago, though, sadly for that book's list of illustrations, I only came upon this surviving postcard after it had gone to press.[1] Such massive outdoor community plays about local and national history, which flourished in Britain and the United States during the first three decades of the twentieth century, regularly incorporated passages from Shakespeare's histories in their scripts, and with their casts and audiences of thousands they represented some of the largest productions which the Shakespearean scenes they borrowed have ever had. It was not unusual, either, for their episodic parades of great names from the past to incorporate appearances by Shakespeare, but this one still seems

---

[1] See Michael Dobson, *Shakespeare and Amateur Performance: A Cultural History* (Cambridge: Cambridge University Press, 2011), 167–72.

remarkable. Why would a lavishly supplied twentieth-century spectacle wishing to offer a dramatic glimpse of the life of William Shakespeare choose to represent him, like Hercules in the pageant of the nine worthies, in his minority?

I propose to do what I can to explain this image over the remainder of this chapter, largely by placing it within a surprisingly rich and various history of depicting Shakespeare's childhood—of writing, in other words, about the bit of Shakespeare's life that came before he had done anything that would make him worth writing about. I think that these depictions are worth writing about themselves because all stories about the lives of writers, whatever their claims to historical impartiality, are first and foremost works of literary criticism. The desire for a life of Shakespeare is only ever a response to the works of Shakespeare, and a commentary on them: to explain Shakespeare by making facsimiles of Elizabethan legal documents, or to explain some of his plays by summarizing the events of the year in the life of William Shakespeare in which they were written, are equally ways of arguing for particular modes in which the works might be interpreted.[2]

Given how prominent ideas of Shakespeare's boyhood were to become, it is striking how far the early biographical traditions instead concentrate on the playwright's adolescence. In the seventeenth century, even while some of Shakespeare's Stratford family and acquaintances were still alive to be questioned about him, metropolitan writers about the playwright seemed perfectly content to retail and elaborate a small but expanding repertoire of hearsay. Such hearsay was considered valuable or convincing not so much for its certified correspondence to verifiable facts but for its perceived truth to the spirit of Shakespeare's plays. By the time Nicholas Rowe's edition of the Complete Plays was published in 1709, a canon of apocryphal anecdotes had emerged which made of Shakespeare's life exactly what neo-classical criticism made of Shakespeare's plays. As a result, Rowe's prefatory biography, though far from being mendacious or fraudulent, doubles as a critical introduction. Shakespeare's style was vulgar and over-exuberant, and his tragedies too bloody for refined Augustan tastes—hence the story about how he had been an apprentice butcher when young, and used to

---

[2] See Samuel Schoenbaum, *Shakespeare's Lives*, rev. edn (1970; Oxford: Oxford University Press, 1991), *passim*.

make bombastic speeches before killing calves. (Even in its first recorded form, in Aubrey's *Brief Lives*, the story looks like a garbled allusion to Hamlet's line about Polonius' student performance as Julius Caesar, 'It was a brute part of him to kill so capital a calf there', *Hamlet*, 3.2.101–2.) Shakespeare, a provincial without a degree, borrowed shamelessly from more courtly writers, as the first recorded criticism of his work, in *Greene's Groatsworth of Wit* (1592) had pointed out—and hence the persistent story of his stealing deer from a local aristocrat. But even so, his raw, unruly, populist talent made him a national treasure—and hence, again, the story of his stealing deer from a local aristocrat, which makes Shakespeare into an English folk hero, a latter-day Robin Hood. Indeed, the most indulged criminal in the plays, Falstaff, earned Shakespeare Queen Elizabeth's personal favour, at least according to John Dennis' preface to his 1702 adaptation of *The Merry Wives of Windsor*.[3] Tales of Shakespeare's own imputed Falstaffian drunkenness and petty crime have remained an important part of his mythos ever since. It is Shakespeare's unclassical misdemeanours as a writer which make him great, say these stories, his unrespectability which makes him respectable.

This paradox would be nicely picked up by a *Punch* cartoon from the days of the pageant boom, published while the Warwick Pageant was in preparation. In 'Mr Punch's Pageants. Stratford-upon-Avon. Number 1', a sheepish procession of aldermen are seen handing a scroll to a corpulent Shakespeare who sits contentedly on a bench, his legs confined in the stocks. 'Ye Mayor of Stratteford doth present ye Freedom of ye Borough to Master Will Shakespeare', reads the caption. 'Thatte Master Will did at ye moment occupy ye towne "stockes" for some light-heartede misdemeanoure didde lend a certain ironie to yre festive occas[ion].' On close inspection, there is more text within the image itself, in tiny capitals on a signpost nailed to the tree against which the playwright is leaning. 'Ye justices doe most mightlie regret to deale after this mannere with their most clevere townsman', it reads, 'but his naughtie ways compel.'[4] That is actually quite a good account of the effect Shakespeare's breaches of

---

[3] See John Dennis, *The Comical Gallant* (1702), dedicatory letter to George Granville, p. 2. On this anecdote and its subsequent progress see Michael Dobson and Nicola Watson, *England's Elizabeth: An Afterlife in Fame and Fantasy* (Oxford: Oxford University Press, 2002), 121–33.

[4] *Punch*, 30 January 1907, 87.

dramatic and poetic custom have on audiences and readers: his naughty ways compel.

In popular culture, then, Shakespeare was a juvenile delinquent well before he was a boy; and before he was a boy, similarly, he was a ghost too for good measure. For the Augustans, Shakespeare, despite his faults, was also a classic, the personification of a rougher but more heroic literary age. With the plays still undead in the theatrical repertory despite their stylistic obsolescence, Shakespeare made regular phantom returns to the stage from 1679 onwards, his ghost impersonated by actors as they spoke prologues lamenting the feeble decadence of his successors.[5] Shakespeare's spirit generally rose on these occasions, like the ghost of Hamlet senior, through a trapdoor, wearing clothes based on those of his posthumous depictions on the Folio title page and on his Stratford funerary monument. The earliest visual representation of this by-then well-established trope dates from 1728, in a satirical cartoon, *The Rival Printers*, commenting on the dispute between Richard Walker and Jacob Tonson over the right to publish Shakespeare's plays. The unregarded genius whose work is at the centre of their unseemly wrangling rises in horror in the middle of Covent Garden, to be confronted by a degenerate contemporary cultural scene of squabbling hacks, mercenary pugilists, and dancing dogs. The ghost of Shakespeare, according to the print's key, is 'intreating' the denizens of Grubstreet 'not to be so inhuman to his Ashes'. It is in just this guise and just this neighbourhood that Shakespeare would make his first appearance as a character in English fiction, in *Memoirs of the Shakespeare's Head in Covent Garden, By the Ghost of Shakespeare* (1755). Instead of being put in the stocks for his misdemeanours, as in the *Punch* cartoon, this book's Shakespeare has been posthumously condemned for all eternity to haunt the disreputable tavern that bears his name.

It is the fact that the Shakespeare-as-ghost trope was so prevalent and so influential that makes the appearance of a new image of Shakespeare in its place so striking and so important. From the mid-eighteenth century onwards, Shakespeare suddenly became not a ghost but a divinely spoiled

---

[5] See, for instance, the prologues to John Dryden's adaptation of *Troilus, Troilus and Cressida, or, Truth Found Too Late* (1679), or to George Granville, Lord Lansdowne's, adaptation of *The Merchant of Venice, The Jew of Venice* (1702), or John Dennis' 1707 prologue to *Julius Caesar* (in *A Collection and Selection of English Prologues and Epilogues*, 4 vols. (London, 1779), vol. 3, 1–2).

infant, a new way of imagining the author which first became visible in Joseph Warton's *The Enthusiast* (1744). This poem provides a rococo elaboration of John Milton's couplet in 'L'Allegro' (*c*.1635), in which theatregoers may hear 'Sweetest Shakespeare, Fancy's child, / Warble his native woodnotes wild.' Warton pictures a baby Shakespeare who, apparently left unattended by his negligent mortal parents despite the proximity of a deep river, gets abducted to a cave by Fancy, where he is subjected to genius-forming song recitals:

> What are the Lays of artful *Addison*,
> Coldly correct, to *Shakespear*'s Warblings wild?
> Whom on the winding *Avon*'s willow'd Banks
> Fair Fancy found, and bore the smiling Babe
> To a close Cavern: (still the Shepherds shew
> The sacred Place, whence with religious Awe
> They hear, returning from the Field at Eve,
> Strange Whisperings of sweet Music thro' the Air)
> Here, as with Honey gather'd from the Rock,
> She fed the little Prattler, and with Songs
> Oft' sooth'd his wondering Ears, with deep Delight
> On her soft Lap he sat, and caught the Sounds.[6]

Despite the tourist guiding which the poem attributes to its apocryphal shepherds, readers of Warton drawn to Stratford during the ensuing decades, as the habit of making pilgrimages to the birthplace and grave of the little Prattler gathered momentum, would have been disappointed had they asked after the cave. They might, however, have heard plenty more about the roles in Shakespeare's early life played by Fancy and, increasingly, Nature.

The painting by George Romney that is the source of the print reproduced as Figure 2.2, *The Infant Shakespeare attended by Nature and the Passions*, is now in the RSC's collection, dates from 1799, but it belongs to a subgenre of Anglicized, semi-secularized versions of the Nativity and of Mary and Elizabeth with the Infant Christ, which by then had been flourishing for thirty years. Romney himself, for example, produced a number of variations on the theme of 'The Infant Shakespeare Nursed by Tragedy and Comedy' and 'Nature

---

[6] [Joseph Warton], *The Enthusiast: or the lover of nature. A poem* (London, 1744), 12–13.

Figure 2.2 *The Infant Shakespeare attended by Nature and the Passions*, print (1840) after George Romney (1799). Property of the author.

Unveiling Herself to the Infant Shakespeare' from the 1760s through the 1800s.[7] (Compare too Angelica Kauffman's 'Allegory of the Birth of Shakespeare,' c.1796, now in the National Museum of Wales, and the grand chorus 'Be Shakespeare born!' in Thomas Linley the younger's 'Shakespeare Ode,' 1776). Clearly, such images aren't exactly biography: nobody looking at them, presumably, was supposed to wonder how Mary Shakespeare née Arden had been able to afford such a superior class of babysitters. But they would deeply colour biographies to come, since they articulate a new and enduring sense of what Shakespeare's genius meant and where it came from.

This new investment in Shakespeare—an investment every bit as important to the shape and indeed existence of biographies to come as any factual evidence for their contents—would crystallize most fully

---

[7] For an even more bizarre depiction of the infant Shakespeare's relationship with Nature, see William Godwin junior's poem 'Olympian Mulberry Leaves; or, The Offerings of the Gods to Shakespear', 1831, preserved among the papers of the Mulberry Club (*Mulberry Leaves*, Cadbury MS 631) in the Cadbury Library at the University of Birmingham:

> . . . 'Nought now remains', [Nature] cried, 'to grace my son,
> 'Save that which I, his mother, must put on:—
> 'Behold, ye Gods!'—As thus she spoke, she threw
> Her vesture open, & disclosed to view
> A chrystal mirror leading to her heart:—
> ''Tis here my Shakespear now shall learn his part . . .
> And like the bird who feeds her youngling nest
> With mother's blood extracted from her breast,
> 'So I my Shakespear's soul instil with food,
> 'In Nature's heart of hearts profound imbued.' . . . (16)

around a particular series of commemorative events in a particular town. Shakespeare's 200th birthday, in 1764, came only a year after Britain's worldwide victories over the French in the Seven Years' War—victories which secured British control of enormous new territories, notably in India and in North America—and the belated festival which eventually celebrated the former incorporated much which perpetuated the mood of the latter as well. Luring his metropolitan patrons to the town of Shakespeare's birth, David Garrick designed the Stratford Jubilee of 1769 as a glorification of the playwright's undilutedly native origins. In what we would now recognize as a definitively romantic move, Garrick backdated Shakespeare's genius to a point before the Bard had even discovered drink and deer-stealing. According to the poems Garrick composed for the occasion, most famously his Ode itself but also the song he composed for performance at the Birthplace on Henley Street, the playwright's imagination had sprung fully formed from the very soil of his nation's rural heartland.

> Here Nature nursed her darling boy
> From whom all care and sorrow fly,
>   Whose harp the Muses strung;
> From heart to heart, let joy rebound,
> Here, here, we tread enchanted ground,
>   Here Shakespeare walked and sung![8]

This is clearly another variation on Milton's couplet in 'L'Allegro' about Fancy's child warbling his native woodnotes. Milton, though, is off to hear those woodnotes in a London playhouse, where one can experience them whenever one of Shakespeare's plays happens to be on the bill: the location and time of their author's literal childhood are of no importance to this poem at all. From Warton and Garrick onwards, though, this trope would be changed forever—and so, in one instance at least, would Milton's words. In July 2012, after I had already completed one draft of this chapter, I made what turned out to be a vain attempt at getting away from work for a couple of days, on a brief family holiday. Since I needed to get back to Stratford the day the holiday ended, we chose to stay somewhere fairly local, Chipping Camden. In the main room of the house we rented, to my

---

[8] David Garrick, *The Jubilee* (1769), in *The Plays of David Garrick*, ed. Harry William Pedicord and Frederick Louis Bergmann, 6 vols. (Carbondale, IL: Illinois University Press, 1980–81), vol. 2, 97–126; 125.

great surprise, hung a crude copy of the Chandos portrait of Shakespeare, on a very solid piece of wood which looks like a pub sign and may well be one. Perhaps it even once adorned the Swan and Maidenhead on Henley Street, now better known as the Birthplace, since below the portrait are two lines of verse: 'Here sweetest Shakespeare, Fancy's child, / Warbled his native woodnotes wild.' It's the 'here', and the past tense of 'warbled', that gives a historical specificity to go with the local, that makes all the difference. In 1769 it suddenly mattered that sweetest Shakespeare had warbled here, in Stratford, a fact which enabled the general claim that he had been the child of Fancy and/or Nature to metamorphose into a piece of nationalist self-assertion. This celebration of Shakespeare as untaught son of his region permeated the festival, articulated most memorably, perhaps, in one of the songs Garrick composed for the occasion. 'Our Shakespeare compared to is no man', it rhymes, rather ungrammatically, 'No Frenchman, nor Grecian, nor Roman.' Tying this global superiority to Shakespeare's natal county, the local British Army regiment later adopted 'Warwickshire Lad', with its chorus of 'The Will of all Wills was a Warwickshire Will', as its marching song.[9]

Meanwhile, Garrick sought to link Shakespeare's creativity even more directly with his local roots by releasing his characters into the streets of Stratford, designing a procession through the town of his actors in costume, representing mobile tableaux vivants from the plays. This feature of the Jubilee proper had to be cancelled due to torrential rain, but it was incorporated, even so, into Garrick's dramatized account of the festival, *The Jubilee*, staged at Drury Lane after his return to London and destined to become his most popular play. Some version of this parade of Shakespearean characters has been included in most Shakespearean festivities in Stratford since 1829, notably the annual Birthday Procession, and, as we will see, it would provide a surprisingly convenient dramatic device for later scriptwriters determined to represent the boy Shakespeare's precocious genius on the stage.

According to the logic expounded at the Jubilee and by allegorical painters like Romney, Shakespeare had needed no education and no experience to become the immortal Warwickshire Will; he had just needed

---

[9] [David Garrick and Charles Dibdin], *Songs, Chorusses, &c., which are introduced in the new entertainment of The Jubilee* (London, 1769), 2–4.

to encounter Nature in his infancy, somewhere near the local river, and to retain the dreams she would impart for later use. Anthony Harrison, for instance, would describe this scenario in his poem 'The Infant Vision of Shakspeare':

> On Avon's banks, as Nature lay,
> And eye'd th'enchanting scene around;
> Transported at the rich survey,
> She smil'd, and bless'd the hallow'd ground...
>
> Now to her fond, maternal breast,
> Shakspeare, her darling child, she folds;
> Then gently lulls him into rest,
> And weaves the vision he beholds...
>
> For well she knew, her darling child
> Would nobly act a brother's part;
> And what he saw, in visions wild,
> Give man in cultur'd scenes of art.[10]

(I have missed out the seventeen stanzas which describe the vision itself, but you can probably imagine something of what they are like from this sample.) By 1794, when Harrison's poem was published, Edmond Malone's edition of Shakespeare, the first to include a chronology of the plays and the fruits of extensive fresh historical research into the circumstances of Shakespeare's career, had already been in print for four years. The same year would see Malone's triumph over the boy forger William Henry Ireland, supposedly the moment at which forensic Shakespearean scholarship defeated popular myth-making forever. Surely the public investment in Shakespeare as Nature's darling boy and Britain's acknowledged national treasure, developed so fancifully by Harrison, could not much longer co-exist with this new attention to documentary accuracy and historical fact? But 1794 saw another publication, too, which would in time allow national desire and documentary history to co-exist within a new mode of depicting Shakespeare's boyhood. In the preface to volume two of the fourth edition of his *Reliques of Ancient English Poetry*, Bishop Percy noted that Queen Elizabeth's famous visit to Kenilworth to enjoy the hospitality of the Earl

---

[10] Anthony Harrison, *The Infant Vision of Shakspeare: With an Apostrophe to the Immortal Bard, and other poems* (London, 1794), 3–4, 8.

of Leicester in 1575 had taken place only fifteen miles from Stratford, when Shakespeare was a darling child of eleven. Supposing the boy Shakespeare had been taken to see the spectacle by his father?

Whatever the old play, or 'storial show', was at the time it was exhibited to Queen Elizabeth, it had probably our young Shakespeare for a spectator, who was then in his twelfth year, and doubtless attended with all the inhabitants of the surrounding country at these 'Princely pleasures of Kenilworth', whence Stratford is only a few miles distant. [I]f our young bard afterwards gained admission into the castle to see a Play, which the same evening after supper was there 'presented . . .', we may imagine what an impression was made on his infant mind.[11]

This is simply the Warwickshire Will conveniently historicized: Shakespeare is again located in the county of his birth and represented as a sort of latently inspired tabula rasa, but now the visions which fire his infant mind are provided not by Nature but by Gloriana and her favourite. If you send the boy Shakespeare to Kenilworth, you can have your mythical infant genius and your picturesque historical record at the same time.

The conjunction of Shakespeare, Elizabeth, Leicester, and Warwickshire provided by Percy's suggestion turned out to be irresistible for the writer who did the most to establish historical fiction as a dominant mode for imagining famous lives over the ensuing century. Walter Scott, however, wanted the just-offstage Shakespeare who adorns *Kenilworth* (1821) to be not an unspoiled personification of English natural genius but a sample of enlightened royal patronage, and so he controversially adjusted Shakespeare's age, anachronistically representing him as already an established London writer and already the preferred dramatist of Elizabeth I at the time of the Kenilworth festivities. Others would correct Scott in due course, but meanwhile the notion of Shakespeare as Elizabeth's favourite writer would be reunited to the older tradition of depicting Shakespeare as naturally inspired Warwickshire Will in the first English play to represent a living Shakespeare as a character, Charles Somerset's *Shakespeare's Early Days* (1827). At the climax of Somerset's drama, which manages to be even more anachronistic than does *Kenilworth* in pursuit of its symbolic logic, the youthful Shakespeare has his first play, *Hamlet*, recognized as a work of

---

[11] Thomas Percy, *Reliques of Ancient English Poetry*, 4th edn, 3 vols. (1794; Edinburgh, 1858), vol. 2, 110.

genius by Elizabeth in person, just as she is about to hear of her navy's victory over the Spanish Armada. But despite the finale at court, the playbill's summary of the scene changes makes it clear that much of the action takes place in Stratford, from which Shakespeare only runs away to London to escape the consequences of his having stolen some deer with which to feed a starving cottager. The play's key scene is in fact an onstage re-run of Garrick's Jubilee procession or Harrison's poem, when Shakespeare falls asleep beside the Avon and enjoys an inspired vision of the works he will one day write, each represented by a tableaux vivant as per Garrick's procession. Once again, Shakespeare's genius comes direct from the (damp) Warwickshire soil.

Played by an adult actor, the Shakespeare of Somerset's play is a virtuous version of the teenaged delinquent of earlier legend, but such was the continuing ideological currency of the notion of Shakespeare as indigenous infant genius that the year after its premiere an anonymous poet reworked its most spectacular scene, this time carefully restoring the Warwickshire Will's youth. 'The Infant Shakespeare', published in *The Bijou; or, Annual of Literature and the Arts* (1828), finds the playwright-to-be once more dreaming on the banks of the Avon, in this distinctly saccharine incarnation sounding something like a more inspired premonition of Christopher Robin.

> By the living waterspring,
> By the grass-green fairy ring,
> Pillowed on the rathe primrose,
> Lies a boy in rich repose.
> Yet, though honey-dews of sleep
> All his crimson beauty steep—
> Though like languid lily-bands,
> Fall on earth his infant hands;
> And the veiling eyelids win
> From us all the light within;
> And, but for a passing glow,
> Sculptured stone might seem his brow.
> Yet that marble brow beneath,
> Dreams are born too strong for death;
> Thoughts, as with the stroke of lightening,
> Soul-pervading, smiting, brightening.
> Mighty visions are awake,

That shall yet the nations shake;
In that sleeping form enshrined,
Powers, and mysteries of mind;
That shall utter more than spell
Of a more than Oracle!

Now, on his enchanted sleep,
See the rich creations sweep;
Mark the lifting of his hand,

It has grasped a fancied wand;
Spirits, to its waving bowed,
Spring from the earth, and fire and cloud…

…Boy to witch the world—arise!
On that rose bank—SHAKESPEARE lies![12]

The poem is even illustrated, by Richard Westall, whose fetching likeness of Shakespeare when he was still just William (he would be completely unrecognizable as the future Bard were his prophetic dreams of future masterpieces not conveniently made visible) provides one of the most characteristic images we have of the susceptible child of Fancy cherished since the days of the Jubilee (see Figure 2.3).

From this point in the nineteenth century onwards representations of Shakespeare's boyhood, some tending as openly to the whimsical as this, some more historical, would proliferate. In 1847, for instance, Robert Folkestone Williams published his historical novel *The Youth of Shakespeare*, which re-runs a version of the plot of Scott's *Kenilworth* except with a happy ending. It further improves on Scott, crucially, by having Shakespeare, in the novel's most elaborate set piece, meet the Queen when he is taken to Kenilworth by his father as a precocious (and chronologically possible) eleven-year-old. But why this continuing fascination with Shakespeare before he had even become Shakespeare? Some of the publications which would follow Williams' lead, it is true, belong to the century's general interest in packaging the exemplary childhoods of exemplary figures for the edification of Victorian children: books such as W. J. Rolfe's *Shakespeare the Boy* (1896) and George Madden Martin's *A Warwickshire Lad: The Story of the Boyhood*

---

[12] 'The Infant Shakespeare', in *The Bijou; or, Annual of Literature and the Arts* (London, 1828), 15–17.

Figure 2.3 Richard Westall, *The Dreams of the Infant Shakespeare*, illustration to the poem 'The Infant Shakespeare', from *The Bijou, or, Annual of Literature and the Arts* (London, 1828). Birmingham University: courtesy of the Cadbury Research Library.

of William Shakespeare (1903). But the persistence of the nativist ideology hymned at the Jubilee was surely a factor too, and it was made the more resilient around Shakespeare by a more prosaic and material instance of survival. One building depicted in some key scenery of *Shakespeare's Early Days* was bought for the nation in the very year that *The Youth of Shakespeare* was published. With the cityscapes of Shakespeare's working life long ago destroyed by the Great Fire of London and the pace of urban redevelopment, and with the mansion to which he retired, New Place, long ago remodelled and subsequently demolished, the only key architectural relic of Shakespeare's earthly career which still stands is Shakespeare's Birthplace. (And whereas most shrines to writers preserve the author's writing desk, the only desk of Shakespeare's which one can visit in Stratford is the one at which he is supposed to have sat in the King Edward VI Grammar School when still a whining schoolboy.) The grave in which Shakespeare was buried after he was Shakespeare is still there, it's true, but the main thing that Stratford has to offer to the biographer is the house in which Shakespeare lived before he became Shakespeare. Ever since 1847, then, the Shakespeare Birthplace Trust has been obliged to go on evoking the circumstances of Shakespeare's boyhood, reading the plays for illustrative traces of his youthful experience, and thereby implicitly continuing Garrick's project of identifying the environs of Stratford before 1585 or so as the source of the playwright's genius. If the main thing you have to offer to the tourists is the rapt contemplation of what is called the Birthroom, then the shades of

Nature and the Passions cherishing the infant Shakespeare are not likely to stay far away. *The Youth of Shakespeare*, for instance, for all its carefully researched historical detail, succumbs to this standing temptation to allegory with glee, prefacing its account of Shakespeare's birth with an induction in verse whereby Oberon, Titania, and a train of Warwickshire fairies herald the arrival of their favourite genius.[13]

If Richard Westall's illustration to 'The Infant Shakespeare' had corrected the Shakespeare who meets Elizabeth I in *Shakespeare's Early Days* and *Kenilworth* back into native boyhood in the visual arts, and Williams had done so in fiction, it only remained for someone to complete the pattern in drama. The task was taken up by one Tresham Dames Gregg, who makes the investment in Shakespeare's boyhood and in its imagined high point at Kenilworth about as clear as it could be in the very title of his play: *Queen Elizabeth, or the Origin of Shakespeare* (1872). This mercifully unacted drama is perhaps the most ideologically explicit of all representations of Shakespeare's boyhood. Written by a rabidly anti-Catholic Church of Ireland vicar, it represents the reign of Elizabeth as marking at once the deliverance of England from the popish Antichrist and the instigation of a securely Protestant state culture, of which the boy Shakespeare, talent-spotted by Elizabeth when he comes to Kenilworth and enters a poetry competition alongside an equally precocious Francis Bacon, is the personification. Gregg, indeed, had a strong sense of destiny at work in world history in his own time no less than in Shakespeare's: the play is dedicated to the Kaiser, congratulating him on his recent victory over Catholic France in the Franco-Prussian War, and to Ulysses S. Grant, urging him to establish Protestant Christianity as the state religion of the USA. The play begins with a prologue about the threat posed to Tudor England by the Catholic

---

[13] Williams was, like William Godwin junior, a member of the Mulberry Club: its papers preserve his 'A Hymn to Shakespeare. Volunteered at the Shakespeare Anniversary. April 1832', in which he wonders whether the divine infant genius might not have been the result of a hitherto unrecorded Warwickshire encounter between Mary née Arden and the god Apollo:

> ... How know we not by Avon's waters bright
> Thy mother, full of woman's dazzling charms,
> Once held the God of Melody and Light,
> > Within her arms
> And thou inheritest the sacred fire
> Of thine immortal sire. (*Mulberry Leaves*, 48)

powers, written in the style of the Old Testament, and it culminates in a patriotic victory parade:

Q. ELIZABETH *(Here signifying to* LEICESTER, *they all surround* SHAKESPEARE, *and raise him aloft. He requires* BACON *to be similarly honoured, and they carry them in triumph around, singing—*
Chorus.
These prizes for truth to old England are given;
They're the warrant for hope in the blessings of heav'n—
Then for truth, joy and hope let the welkin be riven.
They're inspired by the light of her eye.[14]

With the boy Shakespeare being imagined like this in a version of the Kenilworth festivities which makes them into a communal celebration of the inevitable triumph of the English-speaking peoples, his participation in the boom in pageant-making per se which swept Britain and the United States in the early years of the twentieth century was assured. Orie Hatcher of Bryn Mawr, for instance, published a how-to guide during the run-up to the tercentenary of Shakespeare's death in 1916, *A Book for Shakespeare Plays and Pageants,* which shows an intriguing combination of academic scruples and imaginative licence on the subject. The cursory biography of Shakespeare included in the book discriminates as carefully as any Malone or Schoenbaum could wish between 'fact', 'tradition', and 'conjecture', and under the heading of 'Tradition' Hatcher declares that:

Nothing attests [Shakespeare's] attendance at the Kenilworth festivities in honour of Elizabeth in 1575, although it seems likely enough that, if conditions were even half favourable to his going the short journey of fifteen miles, he would not likely have missed the going, boy of eleven as he was.[15]

When it comes to designing a procession to represent Shakespeare's life, however, Hatcher includes groups representing both 'The Bidford Revellers' ('Shakespeare, a group of roistering companions, and the host of the Falcon Inn') and, preceding it, 'A group of Stratford people on the way to Kenilworth (1575)—among them Shakespeare, a boy of 11' (p. 219). Her one

---

[14] Tresham Dames Gregg, *Queen Elizabeth, or, The Origin of Shakespeare* (London and Dublin, 1872), 122–3.

[15] Orie Hatcher, *A Book for Shakespeare Plays and Pageants* (New York: Dutton, 1916), 80.

proviso is that these more apocryphal incidents should be signalled as such, possibly in a mildly uncomfortable manner:

The facts should march solidly forward and the traditions may run or limp on the side in somewhat incidental fashion, or floats may be used for them . . . In any case it will be best to have the title *Tradition* borne by some figure connected with each one. (p. 218)

No such inhibitions, however, had troubled the makers of the Warwick Pageant ten years earlier: the boy in the photograph, you will note, holds no such anxious subtitle. Instead he is placed at the symbolic centre of the entire day-long event, the slightly coy meeting between monarch and local child of destiny carefully marked as the pageant's key episode. Louis Napoleon Parker, the chief scriptwriter, originally planned to depict Shakespeare as an adult, quite independently of Elizabeth: in the address to the committee which marked his appointment as pageant master in October 1905, he envisaged, among much else:

Queen Bess alighting from her clumsy chariot to be welcomed by the magnificent Leicester . . . under the very trees which sighed to their whispers three hundred years ago . . . [and, separately, in an episode devoted to citizens rather than princes], you shall see one of middle height, with a great placid brow, and calm eyes, round which humour and sympathy and love and inscrutable wisdom have set their mark, and you shall say—There goes William Shakespeare.[16]

Perhaps it was the problem of finding anyone who answered this description which changed Parker's mind. In the finished pageant, in any case, the desirability of combining Elizabeth's visit to the area in 1575 with her 'traditional' meeting with the young Shakespeare won out, and the long set pieces in which the queen featured culminated with her introduction to a surprised Bailiff of Stratford, in Warwick quite by chance, and his son.

This extraordinary theatrical spectacle, staged by a cast of 2,000 amateur volunteers in front of audiences of 5,000 per show, was certainly the biggest thing to happen in Warwick since the episodes of medieval and Tudor history which it depicted, and its traces are now lovingly and extensively preserved in the Warwickshire County Record Office. These traces include boxes full of correspondence about seat bookings, minute accounts of

---

[16] 'The Warwick Pageant: Prospectus', Warwickshire County Record Office: Pageant Papers.

every penny spent on fabric and carpentry, and several bundles of unsold souvenir postcards. One of them depicts the arraignment of Piers Gaveston, an episode which simply recycled parts of Marlowe's *Edward II*; and another the defection of Warwick the Kingmaker, similarly borrowed from Shakespeare's *Henry VI*. Nothing, however, was quite as grand as the entry of Queen Elizabeth, who was even taken for a boating excursion on the Avon in a 60-foot-long state barge constructed for the occasion. Of all these postcards, one stands out (see Figure 2.4).

It stands out not so much for its picture—of Elizabeth kissing the boy Shakespeare—but for the fact that this incident was so clearly regarded as the script's key moment that the relevant dialogue is printed on the back of the card (see Figure 2.5).

Figure 2.4 'Warwick Pageant: Queen Elizabeth and the Boy Shakespeare', recto. Postcard, 1906. Property of the author.

Figure 2.5 'Warwick Pageant: Queen Elizabeth and the Boy Shakespeare', verso. Postcard, 1906. Property of the author.

Nor was this twee encounter between Gloriana and the poet of her golden age the end of the boy Shakespeare's role. At the close of the pageant, some additional, allegorical characters appeared: the Daughters of Warwick, for instance, representing towns named after it in the New World and the Antipodes; the Centuries; and Britannia and her Pages (each one representing a different province of the Empire). As in many specimens of the genre, all the characters of the successive episodes then processed onto the acting area together. At last, they all filed away, like this insubstantial pageant faded, leaving not a rack behind—and the last figure in the procession, whose puckish farewell bow signalled the ending of the show and the cue for applause, was the boy Shakespeare. The whole dramatic spectacle was thus signed as his: Warwick, Britain, the world, the past, and the future, all belonged to Nature's darling boy, the Will of all Wills, a Warwickshire Will.

When the celebrated Gwendolyn Lally staged a new pageant of Warwickshire for the Women's Institute in 1930, however, she reused a different familiar trope, and in a rather different way (see Figure 2.6). Her Shakespeare once more falls asleep on the Warwickshire turf and dreams his plays: but this time he is older and wiser, and the dreams he has are largely of the tragedies—the official photographer, for instance, chose to commemorate Ophelia's funeral, with Shakespeare apparently resting in peace on what might be Yorick's grave mound. Writing three years earlier, comparably, H. V. Morton, an enthusiastic disciple of Frank Benson in the

Figure 2.6 'Shakespeare's Dream', from Gwendoline Lally's pageant 'The Spirit of Warwickshire', 1930. From the special supplement to the *Royal Leamington Spa Courier*, 18 July 1930. Birmingham University: courtesy of the Cadbury Research Library.

pre-war years, makes a sadder and wiser return to Stratford in the culminating chapter of his classic travel book *In Search of England* (1927). Although he still regards the unfrequented woods alongside the Avon as the proper haunts of Oberon and Titania, he finds himself largely disillusioned along a Henley Street now crowded with transatlantic tourists. Stratford's success at selling itself as the originary ethnic heartland of the English-speaking peoples has produced both positive and negative effects, and hence Morton's account of revisiting Shakespeare's boyhood home incorporates a distinctly unreverential vision of the infant Shakespeare:

I went, of course, to the Birthplace, where, because Stratford seems to arouse all the instincts of the souvenir hunter, they keep a guardian in every room. I must have exhausted my Shakespeare worship years ago, for I found myself more interested in the moon-like faces of the pilgrims bent over the glass cases than in the fact that here, they say, was born the greatest poetic genius of the English race ... From his desk in the window Mr Wellstood, the curator, overlooks the garden in which Shakespeare was hushed to sleep, blew bubbles, tried to catch the clouds, and suffered, no doubt, from those alarming facial convulsions common to all infants. Another inspiration is the fact that from May till September every American girl in England passes in review before it.[17]

In fact by the middle of the twentieth century, as far as popular culture was concerned, Shakespeare's boyhood was largely over—at least as a way of describing Shakespeare's genius springing directly from the English soil. When H. Roland Evans composed a soon-forgotten novel for children called *The Boyhood of Shakespeare* in 1947, for instance, he depicted a dutiful schoolboy who only becomes a great playwright because he is effectively forced to by his elders and betters. The episodes it depicts are a far cry from those found in Williams' *Youth of Shakespeare* or Martin's *A Warwickshire Lad*. A solicitous vicar, having consulted Shakespeare's schoolmaster, gives the boy a blank book in which to write, and commissions a masque. A respectable strolling player trains him to recite a proclamation, and helps him with the masque: 'There, Will', he exclaimed, writing in a fresh title, 'we will call it "*Bottom, the Weaver, His Dream*". Hey?'[18] A benign aristocrat

---

[17] J. V. Morton, *In Search of England*, 6th edn (1927; London: Methuen, 1929), 212.

[18] J. Roland Evans, *The Boyhood of Shakespeare* (London: Hutchinson's Books for Young People, 1947), 93.

introduces Shakespeare to a ghost, providing all sorts of details that will later be used in *Hamlet*, and even the Autolycus-like peddler who passes through Stratford presents young William with a copy of Plutarch's *Lives*, thrusting his vocation upon him as he does so: 'England needs a playwright, son' (p. 16). (Actually, Shakespeare's juniors are just as bad—his younger brothers keep urging him to play a make-believe game with them called 'Wars of the Roses'.) William himself, when he speaks at all, sounds obsoletely and prissily Edwardian—the first line Evans gives him is 'What ho, my Fulk, let us to the Market, then!' (p. 7). He is much too much of a good boy for the received mythos: instead of stealing deer he rescues one, punishing the malefactors with a disgusted snort of 'Poachers deserve all they get!' (p. 36). He certainly doesn't sound like the child of Nature, through whom inspiration wells of its own accord. In subsequent children's fiction about Shakespeare, significantly, Shakespeare is nearly always a benign, avuncular adult instead, sexlessly looking after the adventurous boy actors who take over the role of protagonist.[19]

What happened? Perhaps the ultimate fate of the boy Shakespeare, and of the view about British destiny which he embodied, with or without biographical evidence, is tied up with the fate of the player who impersonated him in 1906. Such was Louis Napoleon Parker's commitment to a vision of history based on ethnicity that he insisted that the Warwick Pageant should be 'acted by the actual lineal descendants of the persons represented'.[20] In the case of Shakespeare, whose direct line died out with his granddaughter, this posed a problem, but Parker at least made a gesture in this direction, and though no surviving documents record a name for this actor some of the press reports at least give him a local habitation. Shakespeare, records the *Warwick Advertiser* for 6 July 1906, was played by 'A Boy from Stratford'.

So what happened to boys from Stratford who were 11 or so in 1906? For many of them, something that would start when they were 19. Coincidentally, accidentally filed among the postcards of the pageant in the Warwick

---

[19] On this trend see especially Kate Chedgzoy, Susanne Greenhalgh, and Robert Shaughnessy, eds., *Shakespeare and Childhood* (Cambridge: Cambridge University Press, 2007), 115–52.

[20] 'Warwick Pageant: Prospectus.'

archive I also came upon a rather different postcard, a stiff group photograph of ten men in khaki uniforms, sent from a base in France in December 1914. 'We've got to spend Xmas in this hole', writes one of the soldiers, fed up that the war, contrary to all the promises, would not be all over by Christmas. These were men of the Warwickshire Regiment. If our boy Shakespeare was among them, as is very likely, he would often have heard 'The Will of all Wills was a Warwickshire Will' played by the regimental band. If he lasted long enough at the Front to come home on leave, he might have stayed in the curious half-timbered rest and recreation centre which the YMCA built on the site which had been set aside for a national Shakespeare memorial theatre in London, the Shakespeare Hut. If he lasted as long as two years on active service, he might even have celebrated the 300th anniversary of Shakespeare's death there, in April 1916, when it was marked by recitations by volunteers— but then again, he might have been too busy at the time fighting the Battle of Verdun. Statistically, I'm afraid, the name of the unknown Shakespeare is most likely to be somewhere on Stratford's war memorial—originally placed at the top of Bridge Street, a matter of yards from the Birthplace on Henley Street, but later relocated to a site nearer to Shakespeare's own grave at Holy Trinity.

As a motif to abstract from the plays and project onto the biography, perhaps the figure of the boy was, in the end, as ill-omened as that of the ghost. We all know what happens to boys in Shakespeare: Young Macduff, the princes in Richard III, Arthur in King John, little Rutland in *Henry VI*, and, perhaps more to the point here, the boy in *Henry V*, destined to die on a French battlefield. Even in the play which waxes most lyrical on the subject of boyhood, *The Winter's Tale*, Mamillius only gets to be boy eternal by not surviving into adulthood. Inspired by the same notions of ethnic and national identity as was the Warwick Pageant, the First World War increased the territory of the British Empire, but together with that other memorable event of April 1916, the Easter Rising, it pretty much did for it as an idea. I suspect that the boy Shakespeare died with it.

Postscript

Since I wrote this chapter, Sylvia Morris of the Shakespeare Birthplace Trust, who heard an earlier draft given as a paper, has carried out further research in Warwickshire and other archives, and has tentatively identified the boy who played Shakespeare in the Warwick Pageant as one Malcolm Gordon Bland. He was killed in action in northern France in March 1918.[21]

---

[21] See <http://theshakespeareblog.com/2014/06/shakespeare-and-the-warwick-pageant/ http://theshakespeareblog.com/2014/07/from-warwick-pageant-to-theatre-of-war-the-boy-shakespeare/>.

3

Romantic Biography: Conveying Personality, Intimacy, and Authenticity in an Age of Ink on Paper

William St Clair

Romanticism is a loose and baggy category. So let me begin by saying that, in the following chapter, I propose to discuss attempts by biographers in the early nineteenth-century 'romantic period' to present to the readers of books and viewers of pictures an understanding of an individual biographee that approached as closely as possible to the way a unique life had been lived. Central, although not exclusive, to the chapter is Lord Byron, the most romantic figure, as well as the most romantic writer, of the age, who provides the best-documented case of a more general phenomenon. With the publication in 1812 of *Childe Harold's Pilgrimage, a Romaunt* (an archaic variation on 'romance'), Byron became instantly famous, and over the next few years he wrote prolifically in a romantic mode as the word was used at the time—stories of strong passion, exotic settings, and violence—not the tepid provincial English sense of the word that later became associated with Wordsworth. In 1816, as a result of an intrusive scandal, Byron went into voluntary exile and never returned. It was when in Italy that he wrote his comic, subversive, and certainly not romantic, epic masterpiece, *Don Juan*, first published in serial parts from 1819 until 1824, that, for reasons I need not discuss here, had a far larger readership than the romances. *Don Juan* was Byron's own attempt at presenting authenticity in a literary form.[1]

When Byron died in 1824 at the age of thirty six, in Greece, where he had gone to fight for Greek independence, he was already one of the most famous men in the world, celebrated not only for writing about, but for personally living, the virtues of romanticism by, for example, championing individual freedom, including sexual freedom, resisting political and ecclesiastical oppression, and despising hypocrisy ('humbug') in all its many forms. And it was all done with the stylish panache of an aristocrat who presented himself as not giving a damn for what other people thought. After his death Byron quickly became a rallying symbol, across the whole Europeanized world, of romanticism widely defined.

Byron, therefore, offers us two for the price of one: the romantic life presented by those, including Byron himself, who wished to convey across time and distance some understanding of the uniqueness of that romantic life. In addition to the romantic subject and the romantic biographer there is, therefore, also a third party, the romantic reader who receives the presentation, and has to cooperate if it is to be accepted. As you will have noticed, I am extending my ambit of the word 'biography' away from its traditional usage as a description of a literary genre. The life-presenter-cum-conveyers of the age of romanticism, as we could call them, were also able to offer visual images, sometimes within the covers of a printed book that was mainly words, and to experiment with newly invented mixed forms. And besides these three main parties, biographee, biographer, and reader/viewer, there were many other agents whose role the mainstream romantic discourses of 'genius' and 'creativity' traditional literary history has, until recently, largely ignored or downplayed, such as publishers, printers, designers, engravers, and manufacturers, who together constitute a fourth party who also participated in the invention and deployment of new ways of presenting and conveying a romantic life. All operated within the economic limitations of the time, and within legal and other constraints, including censorship, self-censorship, libel,

---

[1] The extraordinarily large numbers of copies and editions, a direct result of the absence of an enforceable copyright, are quantified from archival sources in William St Clair, *The Reading Nation in the Romantic Period* (Cambridge: Cambridge University Press, 2004), ch. 15 and appendix 11.

and copyright that limited the forms that the conveying of a sense of a life could take. And all agents operated within the technological opportunities of the age, that, give or take a few portraits in oil or watercolour, were limited essentially to ink on paper.

The convention of arranging the history of literature and art, including that of life-writing and portraiture, as a chronological parade of moments of first publication or production is itself imbued with romantic assumptions to which we should be alert and which we should try to offset. When, by contrast, we tell the history of romantic biography as a series of transactions and of temporary outcomes, the chronological trajectories are very different from those of parade histories. Furthermore, the texts themselves, both the verbal and the visual, were often changed a great deal after the moment of first production, as producers responded to feedback, and adapted them for new readerships and viewerships.

If, as I suggest, we think in terms of dynamic systems, it is impossible to separate the cultural from the material, the production from the consumption. And an understanding of the operation of the system within which books and pictures were produced and consumed in material form can not only help to release historic readers and viewers from the passive role that has been allotted to them by the conventions, but enable us to gain a fuller understanding of the processes of cultural formation and of mentalities.

Next let me offer a few generalities that emerge from thinking of romantic life-writing as a distinctive project within a tradition. First, even if we confine ourselves to first publication, as we should not, it is not useful to think of 'romantic' as a chronological category. Many biographies of the time, notably Lockhart's *Scott*, that first appeared in 1837–38, are in the non-romantic tradition of exemplary lives based on counter-romantic assumptions about a moral self that is consistent over time. Works, such as that by Lockhart, while claiming to be truthful, were mainly concerned with celebrating and recommending mainstream ideologies, and we know from the work of John Sutherland how inauthentic was the resulting book.[2]

The romantic biographer, while not going as far as modernists in distrusting narratives of a unified self offered by an all-knowing outsider,

---

[2] John Sutherland, *The Life of Walter Scott: A Critical Biography* (Oxford: Blackwell, 1995).

tolerates contradiction, indeed often celebrates it. Thomas Moore, for example, himself a romantic poet and biographer, begins his attempt to present the great champion of liberal egalitarianism with a paradox that he, no mean snob himself, admits was true: 'It has been said of Lord Byron that "he was prouder of being a descendant of those Byrons of Normandy, who accompanied William the Conqueror into England, than of having been the author of Childe Harold and Manfred".'[3] Nor do romantic biographers wholly abandon the moralizing that was central to the aim of earlier biographical traditions, but even the most censorious usually claim to present a truthful account of the life as it was lived even if they disapprove or they want it to serve as a warning. Perhaps the most romantic on a wide spectrum was William Godwin in *Memoirs of the author of A vindication of the rights of woman*, first published in 1798, who proclaimed in his opening words that truthfulness to the lived life was not only an obligation and a duty to the dead but a bigger contribution to the public good than the alternatives.

So how did life presenters go about showing and conveying personality, intimacy, and authenticity? First of all, they aspired to offer a sense of knowing what the subject looked like as an individual person. Portraiture is supposed by some to allow a viewer an access to the inner self as well as the outer. Thomas Carlyle, who helped found the National Portrait Gallery, declared that a portrait could convey more 'real instruction' than a biography or could be 'a small lighted candle by which the Biographies could, for the first time, be read'.[4] So a portrait could, according to one of the rhetorics of romanticism still prevalent today, enable access to an authenticity by using an entirely visual, non-verbal, language, although in practice portraits that are not accompanied by some words are almost non-existent.

So, in the case of Byron, we can ask, what portraits were available to be looked at? The period of time when he lived in Britain after he became famous was quite short, and the number of people who had the opportunity to see him personally was limited, as are the written reports of how he appeared to his friends. We know, for example, that he sometimes put his hand over his

---

[3] Thomas Moore's *Letters and Journals of Lord Byron with Notices of his Life*, which was first published under that title in 1830 and 1831, remained unsuperseded until the publication, in 1956, of Leslie A. Marchand's three-volume *Byron, A Biography*—which remains the standard work, and is, to a large extent, drafted within the conventions that Moore pioneered.

[4] Quoted by Annette Peach in Christine Kenyon Jones, ed., *Byron: The Image of the Poet* (Newark: University of Delaware Press, 2008) 58.

Figure 3.1

mouth when he spoke, apparently an involuntary act of self-effacement. To conceal his misshapen foot and his limp, he wore loose and baggy trousers, not the tight-fitting breeches of modern costume romance. Figure 3.1 shows a nineteenth-century photograph of a miniature, now lost, that once belonged to Byron's local publisher, in Newark in Nottinghamshire. I came across it in the library vaults of Trinity College in Cambridge where Byron had studied.[5]

This is the young Byron, before he was famous, before he was Byronic, before he was romantic. As post-romantic viewers ourselves, we may not immediately recognize him. But there is no reason to doubt the claims of this picture. It even shows the ears without lobes, a feature which one of his lovers, Lady Caroline Lamb, said she had only encountered in two other men.

Today the most famous portrait of Byron shows him in his Grecian costume wearing a moustache. The picture was later bequeathed to Byron's daughter Ada on condition that she was not allowed to see it until she was twenty-one, and after that only with her mother's permission under supervision. For years, the picture was covered by a green curtain. Ada's mother was worried that the picture of her father was too far from the truth, too inauthentic, too romantic, and that it would encourage her to fantasize. Although the picture is today probably the most commonly seen of all images, it was not engraved until 1841 and was rarely seen even as an engraving. That picture played almost no part in the construction of romantic Byronism and I do not reproduce it here.

[5] Reproduced in Thomas Matthews Blagg, *Newark as a Publishing Town by T. M. B.* (Newark: S Smiles Printer, 1898).

Instead, I offer the fact of its absence as an example of a more general point. Byron's visual fame did not accompany his literary fame, as is often assumed, but followed it after a gap. *Childe Harold*, the Eastern tales, the plays, and *Don Juan* did not contain even one picture when they were first published.

Nor is this pattern unique to Byron. Indeed, it is the normal pattern of the time. Of the tens of thousands of newly-published books from the period from 1770 to 1835 only a tiny number had any pictures at all. Only those literary works that have achieved large sales or were likely to do so are illustrated, and then usually only with a portrait frontispiece. This phenomenon is a result of the economics of the engraving industry in the age of copper, that can be demonstrated with financial figures drawn from manuscript archives. Only if a newly printed book could be confidently expected to sell at least a few thousand copies, rather than the five hundred or less that was more normal, could the extra cost be sufficiently widely spread across the print run for a picture to be included. The political economy structures, we can also say, required that if the investment in a frontispiece or portrait was to be risked by the book producers, it had to earn its place. In order to perform its paratextual role in setting expectations, a visual image had to be dense with signs.[6]

So let me next turn to the first portraits of Byron that were made in 1814, when his fame was increasing. How did Byron and his publisher present him? They could have followed the tradition of showing him as a writer, as in the engraved portrait of his contemporary, Walter Scott, as shown in Figure 3.2.

Scott is shown surrounded by the instruments of his trade. Shakespeare the master is looking on. A Grecian urn given him by Byron shows the distinguished company Scott keeps, and the room is full of the paraphernalia of the violent history of the Scottish and mediaeval pasts that Scott romanticized. Among the objects in the room are the keys to the Tolbooth as imagined in *The Heart of Midlothian*, Montrose's sword, Claverhouse's pistol, and Rob Roy's sporran. Scott the author is presented as a modern gentleman, separated decisively from the works of his imagination.

The first portraits of Byron are quite different. Figure 3.3 reproduces a mezzotint engraving of what has come to be called the cloak portrait by Thomas Phillips, exhibited at the Royal Academy in 1814.

[6] My essay, entitled 'Word and Image, towards a Political Economy of Book Illustration', forthcoming.

Figure 3.2

There are no indications either in the portrait or in the accompanying words, that the subject is a writer. In the exhibition catalogue the sitter was not even named. The picture was *Portrait of a Nobleman*.

Christine Kenyon Jones and Germaine Greer have shown how the cloak portrait exploited traditions of theatrical costume, as used particularly in *Hamlet*, and Figure 3.4 shows a little engraving of Edmund Kean, that I thought was a bad pirated picture of Byron, with his book.

Since Byron presented real life as a masquerade, costume may be appropriate, but authenticity and dressing up do not fit well together. The combination is only possible when the viewer collaborates with the

Figure 3.3

artist or engraver in the performance of an illusion whose systems of signs the parties already know, but that we in our time do not know unless we actively recover them by historical investigation.

A cloak portrait of Byron, even when described, as it was in advertisements, as 'a spirited and faithful Likeness', was, of course, a presentation, rather than a representation. As Phillips explained in his lectures at the Royal Academy, one of the professional secrets he had learned from his study of the old masters was to invent a sideways light falling on the folds of drapery. By using the possibilities of chiaroscuro on drapery, he says, the portraitist can 'captivate the most

Figure 3.4

unlearned'.[7] The unlearned are viewers, among whom, until my visit to the 2014 Veronese exhibition in London, I included myself, who wrongly assume that the art of the portraitist lies in depicting the face. Mezzotint engraving, which cannot be adequately reproduced by other media, catches the tactile feeling of soft cloth even more vividly than oil. One of the commonest terms of praise for a mezzotint is 'velvety'. It was, I would suggest, in order that his clothes, as well as his pale skin, appear attractive to the touch when engraved that Byron was painted in a cloak. The medium, formal though it is, invites intimacy.

The mezzotint print was made after the oil painting, but it is just as true to say that the oil was composed as a preliminary for the mezzotint just as sketches were preliminary to the oil. And it took far more time and skill and expense to make a mezzotint, than to make a copy of an oil painting in oils. In Byron's time, good artists were cheap and plentiful, and apprentices

[7] Thomas Phillips, *Lectures on the History and Principles of Painting* (London: Longman, 1833), 328, footnote.

even more so. The rhetoric of romanticism regards the painting as the 'original' and the engravings as copies, but the distinction conceals hierarchical assumptions that we should resist. Walter Benjamin's essay on the mechanical reproduction of works of art, and the 'aura' given off by some, we can surely now see, is a modern affirmation of a romantic ideology that, if we are to understand and not just submit, we should try to offset.

And besides the engraving in mezzotint, suitable for hanging on a wall, the oil was intended to lead on to another, technologically different, but cheaper and faster, form of engraving, line and dot, suitable for binding into a book. Figure 3.5 shows an engraving made by the simpler process of line and dot that was more often encountered than mezzotint.

Figure 3.5

Figure 3.6

In order for the engraving to be fitted into a book, Byron had to lose the soft girlish hand, a change not driven by artistic considerations but by the material trade-off between size and visibility, between a picture encountered hanging on a wall and one viewed in a book held on the lap.

With one of the other cloak portraits, the master engraver Charles Turner did not simply copy the oil painting—he added to it—making a strong feature of the scenic rocks and the daylight breaking through, as shown in Figure 3.6.

This too was a professional secret. As Phillips said in his lectures, repeating the standard teaching of the Royal Academy: 'Our minds are powerfully excited by quantity in nature, the sea, the mountain, the plain, the lake, or the forest.' By this device the image of the poet is linked to the conventions of the romantic sublime, another set of conventional signs shared between producers and consumers of the time, but not necessarily known to us. And the image was also linked to psychological metaphors of character—tempestuous, volcanic, untamed nature, and so on. Was Byron 'A head all fine, a heart all ice' as his estranged wife Lady Byron is said to have written?[8] Or, as Letitia Landon wrote about another print, did the outward Byron conceal 'the lava of the imagination'?[9]

Byron, when engraved, is increasingly shown seated uncomfortably on a rock, with the sea raging at his feet. In Figure 3.7 he is shown as the solitary romantic cut off by his genius from the concerns of ordinary men. In the print of 'The Misanthrope', an illustration in a piece of conduct literature warning against the perils of irreligion, there is no need to name him.[10]

Byron is unperturbed, neither himself nor his clothes ruffled by the wind and the rain.

Figure 3.8, a frontispiece to a much reprinted, inexpensive, book, and amongst the most commonly encountered images for half a century, adds other features, including references to the writings.[11]

The cloak image had become what today is called a brand, instantly recognizable in numerous contexts. And it is not a brand that can be adequately explained by notions of cultural emanation or emergence, or the spirit of the age. It was the result of a deliberate choice by author and publisher in the specific circumstances of 1814.

Already in 1812, when sales of Byron's books were booming, his publisher Murray had wanted to sell an image of a realistic Byron wearing a fur-collared coat—these were some of the coldest years in British history—as an engraving for customers to bind into the books. But when Byron was shown the proof, he refused his consent, insisted that all proofs except one should be burned and that the copper plate be destroyed.

And you will notice that, like many such portraits, the one shown has Byron's signature engraved underneath.[12] A signature on a cheque or a

---

[8] 'Portrait of Lord Byron written by his Wife', in a lady's commonplace book, private collection.

[9] In 'Stanzas Written beneath the Portrait of Lord Byron painted by Mr. West', *Literary Souvenir*, 1827.

[10] Steel engraving painted by H. Howard, engraved by H. Cook, in Sarah Stickney, *Pictures of Private Life*, second series (London: Smith Elder, 1834).

[11] Frontispiece, J. Stewart delt. W.H. Lizars sc. steel engraving, in *Select Works of Lord Byron* (William Milner, Halifax), first printed around 1837 and kept in print for most of the rest of the century.

[12] Many of the Murray later editions and all the Galignani editions contained a portrait and a signature, as have even the cheapest pirated editions.

Figure 3.7

Figure 3.8

legal document has traditionally been the ultimate proof of personal authentication. And shortly after Byron's time we see the beginnings of the cult of the autograph collection, and of attempts to devise semi-scientific ways of discerning the essentials of an individual self from studies of handwriting.[13] A signature copied by somebody else sits uncomfortably

[13] An article on Autographs as a way of judging character in the *Literary Souvenir*, 1825, with facsimiles of the Living Poets of England, including Byron.

with notions of authenticity. It is generally known as forgery. But for many years it was a common presentational device.

The brand could then be used to amalgamate the branded author with the fictional characters of his works, a process Byron and his publisher had encouraged. In Figure 3.9 he is presented as Childe Harold.

Figure 3.9

Figure 3.10

And, in Figure 3.10, he is Don Juan.

Although there are examples of other authors and actors being presented in theatrical costume, the practice of amalgamating the biographized author with his fictional literary characters appears to be unique to Byron. I know of no image of Walter Scott dressed up as Rob Roy nor of a leech gatherer made to look like William Wordsworth. Only in the case of Byron do we find an innumerable series of playful collaborations between the pictures and their viewers, offering and conveying the intimacy of a shared irony.

Meanwhile, alongside portraits made in the studio, an ancient genre that long predates romanticism, we see another way of presenting the biographical subject unmediated by learned conventions. The sketch, that presents itself as spontaneous, immediate, and realistic, purports to be dashed off, a preparation for something more complete, an intermediate stage for an 'original' oil painting that the artist never completed. It appears to offer a direct romantic transfer from the perceived reality to the representation of that reality. Surely this is taking us nearer our quest for authentic? And indeed the neuroscience of cognition confirms that it matches how we actually see, the eye involved in a conscious choice of what to focus on and interpret, with some peripheral vision tailing away at the edges. But a reproduced sketch, like a reproduced signature, only escapes contradiction if the viewer/reader cooperates in the illusion, as he and she evidently had little difficulty in doing, as appears in Figure 3.11.

In this presentation the subject offers not only his bodily appearance, but also his actual words. By using the signoff 'yours faithfully', as well as his

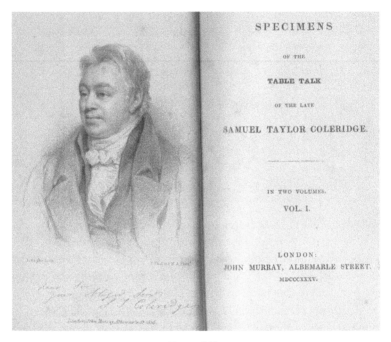

Figure 3.11

signature, the image of Coleridge guarantees the authenticity of the words. The reader/viewer is invited to the dinner table. The intermediating biographer, by excluding all mention of his name or identity from the title page, has ceased to exist within the book. In such books of 'table talk' the reader/viewer is invited to eavesdrop directly on the subject's words.

But the romantic biographer could also invite him to listen in on other people's conversations, another convention in which he pretends not to exist, as in Figure 3.12.

Just as the sketch appeared to capture the immediacy of seeing, the anecdote offered the illusion of being present. By reading a selected collection, an anthology, the reader/viewer was invited to believe that he or she could appreciate the essence of the subject's character in a more concentrated form than any one of his friends. But although anecdotes appeared to be more authentic than narrative, they often had to be edited to avoid libel or offence. Sometimes the tantalizing omissions and asterisks themselves

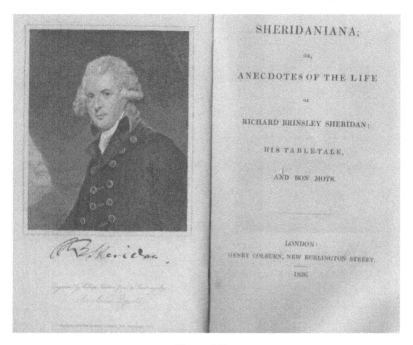

Figure 3.12

contributed to the illusion of being invited into a forbidden private space, an effect beautifully parodied by Theodore Hook in a spoof memoir of which Figure 3.13 is an extract.

Part of the romantic intimacy projected by Byron as a writer was that many readers, especially young women, felt that he was writing especially for and to them as individuals, and that they knew him personally. For example, Isabella Stanley wrote a letter to Byron: 'I have a print of you to which I talk every day, and I make your answers, and I should like you to fancy me as a friend.'[14] It was, I would guess, a fear that something like this form of projection would happen to Byron's daughter Ada that led to the green curtain. And just as some readers conversed with images, some conversed with the printed words. Numerous books exist in which personal friends of a biographized subject have written in marginal comments in the

---

[14] Many are transcribed in George Paston's *To Lord Byron: Feminine Profiles, Based upon Unpublished Letters, 1807–1824* (London: Murray, 1936).

> " He told me one night that —— told —— that if
> —— would only —— him ——, she would ——
> without any compunction; for her ——, who, though
> an excellent man, was no ——, and that she never
> ——; and this she told ——, and ——, as well as
> Lady —— herself. Byron told me this in confi-
> dence, and I may be blamed for repeating it; but
> —— can corroborate it if he happens not to be gone
> to ——."

Figure 3.13

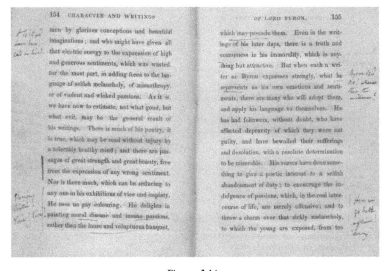

Figure 3.14

voice not of an annotator, but of a conversationalist. Figure 3.14 is from a book annotated by Richard Sharp who knew Byron personally, and whose nickname was 'Conversation' Sharp.

In his marginalia Sharp addresses the printed words in the book as if he were in a three-way conversation with the dead Byron as well as with the unnamed author, and, on the last page, he ends with a farewell as if to a dying friend 'Vale. R.S.'.

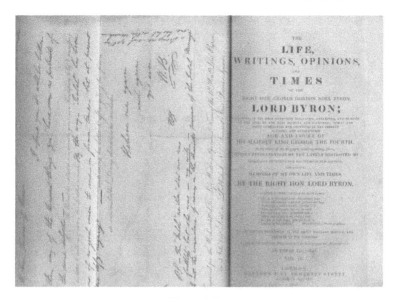

Figure 3.15

Even more intimate and authentic than a report of a conversation is the subject's own voice, as he himself translated it immediately on to paper. In romantic biography the supreme document is the letter. And Byron was a most extraordinary letter writer, witty, ironic, teasing. He jumped from topic to topic, he wrote all over the paper, he underlined, used Capitals for emphasis, and added one afterthought PS after another, and hardly ever used any punctuation other than the dash or two dashes. When his letters were read aloud to parties of friends, and passed around, it must have seemed as if he was in the room. Many of the romantic biographers of Byron obtained an autograph letter and reproduced it as a facsimile engraving. This could give an illusion of authenticity to a cut and paste compilation of old newspaper cuttings, as in Figure 3.15. The densely worded title page, which repeats many of the claims to credibility and authority that we see in those romantic biographies that do not set out to deceive, is therefore worth transcribing plainly and in full.

The life, writings, opinions, and times of the Right Hon. George Gordon Noel Byron, lord Byron; including anecdotes, and memoirs of the lives of the most eminent and eccentric, public and noble characters and courtiers of the age and court of His Majesty King George the Fourth. In the course of the biography is also separately given, copious recollections of the lately destroyed ms. originally intended for posthumous publication, and entitled: Memoirs of my own life and times, by the Right Hon. Lord Byron. 'Crede Byron.' Motto of the Byron family.

> I have, in this rough work, shaped out a man
> Whom this beneath world doth embrace and hug
> With amplest entertainment: my free drift
> Halts not particularly, but moves itself
> In a wide sea of wax: no levelled malice
> Infects one comma in the course I hold.
> But flies an eagle flight, bold and forth on,
> Leaving no tract behind. Shakspeare-Timon of Athens.

By an English gentleman, in the Greek military service, and comrade of his Lordship. Compiled from authentic documents and from long personal acquaintance. In three volumes, Vol. III. London: Mathew Iley, Somerset Street. Portman Square. MDCCCXXV.

In many romantic biographies we are offered a scrap of writing that has no relevance to the contents. Shelley, whose notebooks are marvellously revealing of the stages of romantic composition, was unlucky. His first biographer was only able to obtain a highly untypical, carefully written, business letter, although it did have an autograph signature, as shown in Figure 3.16.

But even the boldest producers of romantic biographies were unable to break the tyrannies of print. No biographer that I know of allowed his subject, or was allowed by the book industry, to use his subject's own punctuation. Vivid dashes and personal spellings were tidied into standard rule-based conventions, and edited to avoid trouble with readers.

And of course it was by no means certain that even modified, self-censored, tidied-up authenticity would be welcomed. Godwin and his family paid a heavy price for his trust in sincerity and honesty when he wrote about Mary Wollstonecraft. Felicia Hemans, who had worn a lock of Byron's hair in a brooch, and thought of herself as a romantic author, gave it away when she read what she called the 'inexpressibly disgusting' biography by Thomas Moore.[15]

---

[15] Henry F. Chorley, *Memorials of Mrs. Hemans: With Illustrations of Her Literary Character from Her Private Correspondence* (Philadelphia: Carey, Lea, & Blanchard, 1836), 161.

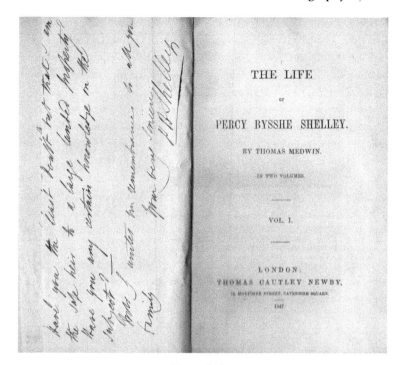

Figure 3.16

As the stream of newly discovered letters by Byron has reduced to a trickle, I offer, in conclusion, just a few of his own words that you are unlikely to have heard. The first is a torn-off note to Moore that was transcribed by a nineteenth-century autograph dealer: 'Dear M with ye greatest pleasure—I will send the carriage at half past 5—and for you at your own time—by the time you have all drunk your bottle of port (one bottle between all [breaks off].' This can be linked with another fragment of a letter to Moore, which, although already self-censored, was removed at a late stage from his book.

" If ever you see * * *, ask him what he means by telling me, * Oh, my friend, inveni portum. ?' [Latin for I have found a safe haven] — What ' portum ?' Port wine, I suppose — the only port he ever sought or found, since I knew him."

The literary and visual devices that I have outlined can be regarded as attempts to shrink the gap between the reader and the subject, to reduce the role of the middleman, to exclude outsiders from what they wanted to make and keep as a personal and an intimate relationship. If reader/viewers can see Byron plain, read his letters, listen to his conversations, and even posthumously participate in them, who needs intrusive, judgemental, and opinionated mediators? Who needs biographers?

And here we risk entering the realm of speculation. What occurred in the minds of romantic reader/viewers, that is, the series of temporary mental outcomes, is hard to recover. By the very nature of the relationship they are condemned to be receivers and interpreters of materialities designed and manufactured by others, and whether they accepted, declined, or negotiated, we cannot usually know. However, just occasionally, we can glimpse a reader/viewer taking control of the mental process. Figure 3.17 reproduces a recently discovered portrait miniature of an unknown English young man made some time around 1820.[16]

How such miniatures were looked at and by whom, and with what aims and results, can only be guessed at. But one probable viewer, the young man himself, we can see, has imagined himself as Byron, adopting a nonchalant

Figure 3.17

---

[16] Private collection.

posture, wearing the clothes associated with one of Byron's fictional Grecian heroes, the Corsair, even a dagger, but he is also himself. He is in a cave, such as was made familiar by the engravings of the portrait. And above the image are the words: 'He Sways the Soul with that Commanding Art / Lord Byron's Corsair'.

The adapted quotation, that refers to Conrad, the fictional corsair, and was applied to Byron, who presented Conrad's life, has been adapted to address the reader/viewer.

> That man of loneliness and mystery,
> Scarce seen to smile, and seldom heard to sigh—
> Whose name appals the fiercest of his crew,
> And tints each swarthy cheek with sallower hue;
> Still sways their souls with that commanding art
> That dazzles—leads—yet chills the vulgar heart.

This is probably as near as we can get materially to the shrinking of the gap between the subject and reader/viewer that romantic biography aspired to close or at least to leap across with the help of the imagination.

4

Prosopography and Crowded Attention in Old and New Media

Alison Booth

It is a commonplace that there are only a handful of plots, and no one regards this as a sign that literature is impoverished. The idea that narratives about real lives similarly have only a few plots is much less comfortably and widely conceded. Modern individualism favours the idea that one writes a script of one's own. A written life that conforms to expected scenarios or motifs seems inauthentic and somehow naive or childlike. Though literary historians recognize that medieval and early modern lifewriting tends to prescribe typical narrative patterns, often presented in groups as in hagiography, they favour those works that most suit recent preferences for close-ups on distinctive, variable selves, and focus on monographs with a single subject. Yet, in fact, life-writing since the seventeenth century continues to adhere to plots and forms that resist the notion of unique autonomy. A closer look reveals that such texts as Benjamin Franklin's *Autobiography* (1791) or Thomas Moore's *Letters and Journals of Lord Byron with Notices of His Life* (1830) entail collaborations of first-person and third-person auto/biographers, and are intertextual reconstructions. One form of life-writing that has persisted without much notice is collective biography: a set of short narratives in one volume; another term for this form is prosopography. In this genre, the biographical subjects may be thematically related but not related to each other in life, as in *Great Jewish Women of History* (1939).[1] This chapter considers the implications of prosopography, or representations of cohorts (sets of persons), and introduces my digital study of collective biographies of women. In the context of print and digital, old and new media, many forms of life narratives are presented in sets and networks of association.

Life-writing shapes personal details into the overall pattern. 'Attention must be paid', we hear in *Death of a Salesman* (1949); Willy Loman cries, 'I am not a dime a dozen'. But a tragedy or a biography plays upon the person as representative type, a *salesman*—he must at least seem to fit with the dozen. With the Internet, we face a run on the bank of attention, which puts a premium on what has been inherent in biography for millennia: it must shape some specifics about a named person into intelligible patterns. Otherwise it is noise, trivialities about nobodies. Categories and connections, however, can also reduce the individual. Generalizations are dull, and when it comes to people and cultures, they often seem tyrannical or unethical (though there are urgent generalizations such as human rights). Yet representation of marginal groups, as well as national traditions, lends itself to collections of portraits, as in George Ballard's *Memoirs of Several Ladies of Great Britain* (1752), with incremental effects on prevailing social norms. Collective Biographies of Women (CBW), the digital project on prosopography that I introduce in this chapter, reveals trends in representation of women as measured in a genre of books that was printed in Britain and North America in increasing numbers after 1830.

Although life-writing in many forms is radically multiple in the sense that any individual is imbedded in social relations, I call for more critical attention to the many texts and genres that make an explicit theme of this multiplicity by taking the form of a collection of short narratives. CBW's genre makes the social tropes of biography explicit and ripe for interpretation; we assign types to the personae and collections, but the presenters have anticipated this categorization. The prosopographies of women in printed books in English have antecedents long ago and far afield, not only in Christian hagiography but also in vernacular French and Italian

---

[1] A *group biography* presents subjects who are relatives or associates in a period or location. Reference works multiply and often alphabetize the subjects, and minimize narration. As I will elaborate, prosopography is a debatable term.

neo-classical compilations: Boccaccio's, Chaucer's, and Christine de Pizan's prosopographies of women, for example.[2] Long lists of renowned women were available to the humanists in the fourteenth and fifteenth centuries, but, in that revival of learning, new women emerged who could be added to the traditions that had been compiled over centuries. Women recognized in the courts of Europe, as royalty, courtesans, beauties, or writers, tended to have more standing than the realist persons of recent memory on home soil. By the mid-seventeenth century, translations of Scudéry's, Brantôme's, and others' collections of *femmes fortes* or illustrious ladies began to shape English efforts to assemble female worthies as well, spurred by increasing middle-class literacy, a kind of delayed-action Renaissance. Wars and religious conflicts as well as reform causes brought forward new female protagonists to gradually supplant heroines of legend, antiquity, or sacred history. Nineteenth-century books' contents may be a 'world history sample' (*World-Noted Women, or Types of Womanly Attributes of All Lands and Ages* (1857)) or may select person types (*Noted Negro Women* (1893); *Mothers of Great Men* (1859)). And distinctions, increasingly, could be drawn between women of different affiliations, as it became less exceptional for a woman to have any biography at all.

Before I enter into the designs and methods of the CBW project, I should introduce prosopography as a useful framework for attending to the crowded representations of persons (names, narratives, faces, or other profiles) in print, in online databases, and social media. *Prosopography*, derived from Greek *prosopon*, face or person (similar to the Latin *persona*), and *graphia*, writing, can be understood as personae-writing. The *OED* traces early modern usage in English as a description of an individual's appearance, a sense of the term that persisted through the later nineteenth century. All forms of life-writing have sought to substantiate their subjects with portraiture, especially when technology made it practical to include more than a woodcut frontispiece. Many forms of life-writing are collections of multiple personae. Rhetorically, prosopography is commemorative and suggests communal rites to collect and reanimate dead ancestors. Prosopography entails the figure of speech, *prosopopoeia*, the rhetoric of elegy and epitaphs as well as autobiography and dramatic monologue. Michel

---

[2] See the first four books in the pre-1830 chronological list at Collective Biographies of Women <http://womensbios.lib.virginia.edu/browse?section=1>.

Riffaterre regards prosopopoeia as an insatiable figuration of absence, hence the tendency to build plural personae in an elegiac series or list. *Parataxis*— the list or web or pantheon or anthology—is the formal and rhetorical orientation of prosopography.[3]

CBW can be understood as a prosopography of prosopographies: a relational database of historical women, a study of the short narratives of their lives, and a bibliography of the books that collected those narratives; a site for research on persons, texts, and trends of representation of historical women within the horizon of English-language book publishing. The project began as an annotated, searchable version of the bibliography in my book, *How to Make It as a Woman: Collective Biographical History from Victoria to the Present* (2004), which challenged the consensus that biographies of women had been suppressed until the mid-twentieth century. CBW studies all English-language collective biographies of women, representing many different periods, nationalities, and occupations. It provides a digital platform for research on over 8,600 persons and 13,700 narratives collected in 1,270 books published primarily between 1830 and 1940.[4] Whereas encyclopaedias and reference works outline historic facts, or family or other relationships, these narratives offer versions intended to entertain and instruct general readers.[5] In collections that offer multiple versions of individuals in comparative arrangements, and that flesh out the narratives beyond reference works, the presenters unwittingly contribute to a measurable, extended debate about a variety of social differences and roles, including gender and

---

[3] Lorna Clymer, 'Graved in Tropes: The Figural Logic of Epitaphs and Elegies in Blair, Gray, Cowper, and Wordsworth', *ELH* 62:2 (1995), 347–86, disputes de Man's focus on apostrophe; the traveller or reader rather than the graven words may bestow the voice. Paul de Man, 'Autobiography as De-Facement', *Modern Language Notes* 94 (1979), 919–30. Michel Riffaterre, *Semiotics of Poetry* (Bloomington: Indiana University Press, 1978). How does prosopopoeia become the collective representation of prosopography? Thanks to Walt Hunter for discussion of prosopopoeia and its inherent plurality in classical rhetoric. See Pierre Fontanier and Gérard Genette, *Les Figures Du Discours* (Paris: Flammarion, 1993), on figures of speech in abstracted personifications that become collective. On the collectivity of *fictio personae*, see Heinrich Lausberg, *Handbuch der literarischen Rhetorik: eine Grundlegung der Literaturwissenschaft* (Stuttgart: Franz Steiner Verlag, 1990), 412–13.

[4] CBW's English-language publications, mostly written by men, are collections of three or more biographies of women. Our bibliography excludes dictionaries and encyclopaedias. Since 2003, the University of Virginia Library has hosted the online annotated bibliography: <http://womensbios.lib.virginia.edu>.

[5] The administrative workflow is accessible at <http://cbw.iath.virginia.edu/cbw_db>. A new Web interface is in progress, <http://cbw.iath.virginia.edu/public/index.php>.

class.[6] In 2007, CBW joined the peer-reviewed Networked Infrastructure of Nineteenth-Century Electronic Scholarship (NINES),[7] and moved towards biographical studies, a database, and new visualizations.[8] Among the thousands of rare and obscure names there are some persons associated with forty-seven short biographies published across 200 years.

To approach the challenge of the computational 'reading' of hundreds of books and multiple versions of individual lives, CBW began with sample corpora. A sample corpus in CBW consists of page images and text files of all the books that include a specific woman; this *nodal persona* epitomizes certain types of women likely to be grouped together. The names that co-occur in a single book are called *siblings*, who often coincide in several books. CBW currently focuses on six nodal personae: (1) the saintly nurse Sister Dora (who is a subject in 20 books, with 141 siblings); (2) the 'Spanish' dancer Lola Montez (14 books, 151 siblings); (3) the traveller, writer, and mother Frances Trollope (10: 306); (4) the astronomer Caroline Herschel (25: 268); (5) the classical queen and lover Cleopatra (32: 815); (6) the French assassin Charlotte Corday (22: 341). I offer some examples relating to Sister Dora and Lola Montez, but the richness of their narratives in many versions would invite much more extensive treatment. To analyse the structure of collected biographical narratives, CBW designed a stand-aside XML schema that editors follow in creating standardized outlines of the features of each text.[9] Complete analysis of all the narratives about 'sibling' women in a sample corpus will reveal the conventions of biographies of women within certain explicit and implicit roles and social codes. This close attention to

---

[6] Both persons and collections can be organized into types, some 57 varieties of collection such as women of the Bible, wives of leaders, actresses, etc.; and more than 100 person types.

[7] This consortium has generated the umbrella Advanced Research Consortium (ARC), uniting digital humanities (DH) studies in different historical periods. ARC will share metadata (DTDs) of CBW and many other projects with Digital Public Library of America, among others.

[8] CBW has grown through indispensable collaboration with Bethany Nowviskie, Joe Gilbert, Wayne Graham, Jeremy Boggs, Purdom Lindblad, and others in the Scholars' Lab, and Worthy Martin, Daniel Pitti, Doug Ross, Rennie Mapp, and others in the Institute for Advanced Technology in the Humanities, and several generations of research assistants.

[9] Biographical Elements and Structure Schema, or BESS, analyses aspects of non-fiction narratives within prosopographical networks. With a controlled vocabulary, we tag the type of each element that appears in a specific portion of text—to the level of the paragraph, not the word or sentence. Each BESS XML file becomes a kind of abstract associated with the numbered paragraphs of a single chapter in one of these books.

cohorts and versions allows multi-level interpretation that would not be practicable for the entire genre (many of the texts are not yet digitized). Just as it would require many pages to do justice to the lives of Sister Dora and Lola Montez, it would consume more than a brief chapter to demonstrate the design and application of the BESS schema. My purpose instead is to stir reflection on the possibilities of digital studies of biography and the prevalence of prosopography in print and online.

CBW assigns types to the personae of historical women and to the all-female collective biographies that include these personae, for the purpose of tabulating trends in gender representation across centuries. No biographical collection holds both a biography of Sister Dora and one of Lola Montez, two antithetical contemporaries who escaped Victorian domestic life and gave themselves Catholic-sounding pseudonyms. By today's lights, Montez is the better-known and far more compelling figure: a riot of outrageous variety, sparking scandals on several continents: 'Wherever she went, things began to happen', as an admiring biographer puts it.[10] Dora is a revered local saint of repetitive, gruelling service to suffering patients. Think Lady Gaga vs. Mother Teresa. Dorothy Wyndlow Pattison (1832–78), a clergyman's daughter from Yorkshire, gained international renown as a version of Florence Nightingale. An expert in surgery and treating wounds, Sister Dora ran small hospitals for victims of industrial accidents or smallpox epidemics in Walsall, near Birmingham, in the 1870s. The *Dictionary of National Biography* labels Lola Montez (1821–61) with the occupational term, 'adventuress' (see Figures 4.1a and 4.1b).[11] A beauty also known as Elizabeth or Marie Dolores Gilbert and the Countess of Landsfeld, she was born in Ireland, raised in India, whipped up the public from Europe to Australia, accumulated lovers and husbands (she was charged with bigamy), inspired a revolution in

---

[10] Edmund d'Auvergne, *Adventuresses and Adventurous Ladies*, a221A.bio07 par. 3. <http://cbw.iath.virginia.edu/exist/cbw/dual/a221A/bio07>.

[11] She is one of five women so designated in the online ODNB, though the word appears twenty-one times, not counting the name of a ship. More women could bear this label. Mary Nesbitt, for example, is 'courtesan and adventuress', and there are sixty-eight returns for a search of 'courtesan' in the ODNB; 'mistress' 1,479 (including the 'demi-mondaine' Montez); 'adulteress' is a term applied seven times (including to Montez). 'Dancer' is an appellation used 481 times, and it includes a high proportion of men and gay lovers as well as women or wives of famous men. 'Performer' appears 578 times but is not used in reference to Montez. Some men appear under the vocational type 'rogue' or 'adventurer'. The ODNB counts date from 29 June 2015. Archivists and information specialists are still far from establishing global standards for occupational terms.

Figure 4.1a Detail taken from *Lola Montez*, unknown artist, in Albert Payson Terhune, *Superwomen* (New York: Moffat Yard, 1916), 2.

Figure 4.1b *Lola Montez*, after Joseph Stieler, 1848, Munich Museum, in Frances A. Girard, *Some Fair Hibernians* (London: Ward & Downey, 1897), 255.

Munich, and ended her days in piety in New York. In the era of newspapers and photography, both Sister Dora and Lola Montez exploited the power of legend, the archetypes of saint or vixen.

Typecasting and genre conventions shape even modern, fact-based narratives, and we can show this machinery at work by studying brief but documentary biographies in aggregates. In addition to full-length biographies, Sister Dora appears in nineteen collections ranging from queens and writers to missionaries, from 1880 to 1930, and a twentieth in 1993. Many of her 141 siblings (including several who occur with her multiple times) took charge of the souls, bodies, appetites, or discipline of the poor, often with an attachment to regimentals such as the Salvation Army (see Figure 4.2). Heroines of this sort become obsolete with women's access to the professions; Sister Dora drops out of sight.[12] Lola Montez joins fourteen

---

[12] She garnered a couple of full-length biographies almost a hundred years apart: Margaret Lonsdale, *Sister Dora, a Biography* (Boston: Roberts Brothers, 1880), and Jo Manton, *Sister Dora: The Life of Dorothy Pattison* (London: Methuen, 1971), as well as a TV mini-series. See Alison Booth, 'Recovery 2.0: Beginning the Collective Biographies of Women Project', *Tulsa Studies in Women's*

Figure 4.2 Sister Dora with Others in One Collection: Clockwise from upper left: Agnes E. Weston, Catherine Booth, Sister Dora, Frances E. Willard. Frontispiece, Jennie Chappell, *Noble Workers* (London: Partridge, 1910); rpt. from *Four Noble Women and their Work* (London: Partridge, 1898).

collections also published in decades surrounding 1900, with 151 siblings, with somewhat less co-occurrence (this sort of book can be more eclectic). In the eighteenth century, numerous English-language collections featured 'bad' women of high society (French and English); this collection type goes under ground until the 1890s. The 1920s were a heyday of such Montez collections as *Gallant Ladies* (from Mata Hari to Calamity Jane).[13] Lola

Literature 28:1 (Spring 2009), 15–35. The versions of her life in collective biographies show little interest in Victorian social context and never focus on her brother, Mark Pattison, the Oxford don associated with George Eliot's *Middlemarch*.

[13] The author Cameron Rogers observes, 'The very term "Gallant Ladies" connoted carnal misdemeanors and bawdy overtones', yet, regarding his own heroines, 'the word "gallant" denotes not sexual aberration, but courage, resource and character'. The issue of chastity is 'no

Montez's notoriety outlasts Sister Dora's renown; the dancer appears in film and in two 1950s musicals, and her type of sexual adventurer gets into second-wave feminist collections: books or websites with titles that echo 1920s titles, such as *Hell's Belles and Wild Women* (1998) or *Women Who Dared* (2009). The sample corpus of Sister Dora we call 'Noble Workers', and that of Lola Montez we call 'Women of the World'.

CBW shares with many digital projects a desire to interconnect persons and documents, and to visualize data about historical trends to support fresh insights into the past. In DH, the methodology and scope of such investigations are in ferment. The diverse possibilities for large-scale textual analysis, including topic modelling and stylometrics, are beyond the scope of this chapter and, thus far, of CBW. CBW designs a mid-range approach, between distant and close reading. CBW will collaborate with various comprehensive studies of historical women, of Victorian publishing, and of archives in order to link our interpretative studies with available evidence.[14] The discoveries of our mid-range readings of sample corpora and our prosopographical database may be tested and enhanced using other sorts of resources, approaches, and tools. Dan Cohen, Fred Gibbs, and others have experimented with the data of book titles across Google Books' digitized archives, but even such data as titles and publication dates can be unstable indicators of the text's contents or a publication's characteristics.[15] CBW has obtained digitized texts of some of the 123 volumes in our sample corpora through HathiTrust, by agreement with Google Books. Google's Ngram Viewer can yield impressions of Google's

---

more consequential' in their lives than it is for Odysseus or John Paul Jones. Rogers objects to a double standard for male and female adventurers. Cameron Rogers, *Gallant Ladies* (New York: Harcourt, Brace, 1928), 11–12.

[14] A grant from NEH Office of Digital Humanities funds collaboration between CBW and Social Networks and Archival Context (SNAC) Prototype History Research Tool <http://socialarchive.iath.virginia.edu/snac/search>. We begin to share data with Susan Brown, Patricia Clements, and Isobel Grundy, *Orlando: Women's Writing in the British Isles from the Beginnings to the Present* (Cambridge: Cambridge University Press, 2006); University of Alberta <http://www.arts.ualberta.ca/~orlando>.

[15] Dan Cohen, 'Searching for the Victorians', *Dan Cohen's Digital Humanities Blog*, 4 October 2010. <http://www.dancohen.org/2010/10/04/searching-for-the-victorians> (accessed 12 May 2015). Patricia Cohen, 'Victorian Literature, Statistically Analyzed with New Process', *New York Times*, 3 December 2010. http://www.nytimes.com/2010/12/04/books/04victorian.html (accessed 12 May 2015).

millions of books, bearing in mind the imprecision of word forms in page scans en masse (the Viewer merely says 'lots of books' and the first name–last name form does not cover all references to a person). On a graph from 1830–2008, a search in the Ngram Viewer for rates of occurrence of the phrases 'Florence Nightingale', 'Sister Dora', and 'Lola Montez' produced three rising and falling lines. Nightingale climbs with various peak rates at periods of military nursing, through the 1940s, and then recedes to her fin-de-siècle rate. Lola Montez rises to a respectable rate of mention after her death in 1861 and again in the 1920–40 era. For a short time after her death in 1878, Sister Dora appears to have been written about more frequently than Nightingale; by 1920 she has decidedly dropped below Montez and almost sinks below the horizon of the Viewer. Within CBW's human curation of sets of books, similar comparisons of representations over time can be traced with precision, amplified by our qualitative as well as quantitative analysis of the complex narratives in many versions of Nightingale and various cohorts (Nightingale is featured in sixty-one books, nine with Sister Dora and none with Lola Montez).

Digital projects have sought ways to mine data from many texts without losing recognition of the details that are the forte of interpretative scholarship. CBW remains grounded in a meticulous bibliographical study, but with increasingly available digitized texts in this genre we could expand and automate the interpretation of specific words such as 'noble' or 'worker' in book titles, concepts, or features of the texts and their narratives. The books as physical objects and the paratexts such as chapter titles, headers, prefaces or indexes, and advertisements are rich sources of contextual data across this collection of books. Currently, CBW has instead designed functions to compare cohorts of women formed by tables of contents, as a complement to the approach to narrative analysis of sample sets of books. Albert Payson Terhune's *Superwomen* (1916), for example, has the following table of contents:

1. Lola Montez, the Dancer Who Kicked Over a Throne
2. Ninon de l'Enclos, Premier Siren of Two Centuries
3. Peg Woffington, Irish Heart Conjurer
4. Helen of Troy, Model for All the Sirens of the Centuries
5. Madame Jumel, New York's First Official Heart Breaker
6. Adrienne LeCouvreur, the 'Actress Heart Queen'
7. Cleopatra, 'The Serpent of Old Nile'
8. George Sand, the Hopelessly Ugly Siren

9. Madame du Barry, the Seven-Million-Dollar Siren
10. Lady Blessington, 'The Most Gorgeous Lady Blessington'
11. Madame Recamier, the Frozen-Hearted Angel
12. Lady Hamilton, Patron Saint of Dime-Novel Heroines

Any reader will recognize a femme fatale on this list. A reader might also correctly infer that any superlative female transgression will be outdone by another avatar. This easy misogynist romp (fashionable in 1916) was reissued as *Famous Hussies of History* in 1943, and again in 2005 and 2007. Montez's peers are 'sirens' of differing levels of historical eminence. Another collection of adventuresses, *Enchanters of Men* (first published in 1909) mixes Montez with the sixteenth-century Italian poet Tullia d'Aragona, the singer Jenny Lind, and Napoleon's younger sister Pauline Borghese, in a largely Franco-Italian list of twenty-three. In another cohort, *Calamity Jane and the Lady Wildcats* (1927), a parade of notorious women of the American West, Montez appears alongside suffragette Carrie Nation and convicted horse thief Belle Starr, among others.

In CBW, a user may search for a particular woman, such as the astronomer Caroline Herschel, and find her biography in A. J. Green-Armytage's *Maids of Honour* (1906), along with one of Sister Dora. This volume gathers together twelve short biographies (with portraits) to illustrate the premise that unmarried women have succeeded in a range of careers (as the subtitle *philanthropy, nursing, poetry, travel, science, prose* suggests) that may be subsumed under the rubric 'honour'.

In such a book, narratives by the same author share certain features and cross-reference each other, while building comparisons with other eminent women or men. A reader of the whole sequence of lives collates typical characteristics and experiences in addition to the features of each person. Copying of all kinds is frankly encouraged in this discourse. Whereas the portraits of the same woman differ across her lifetime and between images by different artists or in different media (see Figure 4.1a and 4.1b), images in collections tend to make different women look more alike (see Figure 4.2). Just as the women emulate each other's careers and readers are recruited to adopt these roles, texts about them are reproduced, usually as digests of previous texts. We can demonstrate how various versions select, omit, or arrange the typical and the unique, from actions and plots to traits and tropes.

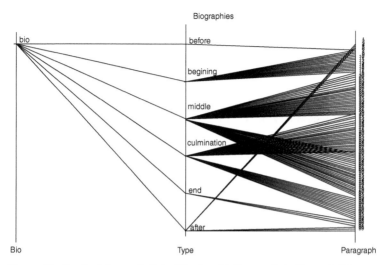

Figure 4.3 Graph of Stage of Life in 'The Spanish Dancer: Lola Montez', (99 paragraphs) in Edmund d'Auvergne, *Adventuresses and Adventurous Ladies* (London: Hutchinson; New York: Sears, 1927).

An understanding of these cohorts is enriched by our mid-range reading with the BESS schema. For understanding the 'plot' of biographies, Stage-OfLife is a key element, derived from millennia of poetics; we name the stages *before, beginning, middle, culmination, end*, and *after*. Biographies, especially in shorter forms, rely heavily on chronology, and very often place birth in the first paragraph, death in the last. Modern biography tends to narrate a journey towards 'triumph over adversity' rather than conversion and salvation. Suffice it to say that the chronology of a person's life may be rearranged or omitted in a particular version; as in fiction, the discourse may follow a different order than the story.[16] Some biographies are *all* culmination—the story of the 'deed' that made a name for that person; Lola's biographies usually have more than one passage that narrates culmination (see Figure 4.3). In this version, the first three and last three

---

[16] In a020/bio04, *Calamity Jane and the Wildcats* (1927), there's no *end*, as happens when the subject of the narrative is still alive. But Montez died in 1861. Its theme is the Wild West of early days, and hence only the California phase of Montez's life. The narrative concludes with Lola Montez's abrupt abdication from ruling California, whereupon 'California heard of her once more' in defiant testimony in a lawsuit in the East (par. 97 out of 102 paragraphs).

paragraphs narrate *after* her death, which is covered in the penultimate three paragraphs (*end*). Lola's *middle* career of professional performance and romantic and political intrigue is interrupted by two culminations: the revolution that she sparked in Munich, and then the phase of her violent encounters as a star in the Australian gold rush, followed by conversion in New York. Arguably, her life was seldom out of crisis mode. Different narrative designs as well as lifestyles will reveal different configurations of the story and the discourse. By the end of the nineteenth century, more and more books feature living members of societies or causes, without *end* or *after*. Still other kinds of chapters represent groups such as anonymous Women of Africa or aristocratic sisters in French society, with multiple chronologies. The digital tagging of textual details across a genre can test, on a body of non-fiction, some long-standing concepts of narrative theory such as pace, frequency, and order. The smooth chronological trajectory may be typical of good models but not wayward women. We will be able to display patterns of discourse in different social types and collections addressed to different implied audiences.

Lives of contrasting women such as Sister Dora or Lola Montez will not only reveal different structures but also very different events, discourse, and other elements, as measured by the values that we give each element in our interpretations of the texts. Edmund d'Auvergne includes a short biography of Lola Montez in *Adventuresses and Adventurous Ladies* (1927)—Montez undoubtedly belongs in the first of these two types—that narrates events utterly incompatible with lives of Sister Dora and her ilk. Thus paragraph six:

```
<event>
        <textUnitReference>6</textUnitReference>
        <type>escape</type>
        <type>wedding</type>
        <type>elopement</type>
        <agentType>officer, military</agentType>
        <agentType>lover, male, named</agentType>
        <locationSetting>Ireland</locationSetting>
        <locationSetting>city</locationSetting>
        <dateSingle standardDate='1837-07-23'>23 July 1837</dateSingle>
</event>
```

In bold are event types that never appear in the short biographies about a woman who renounced marriage and family for Christ-like service to the poor and suffering. And of course the date and location exclude a nurse born in 1832 who committed herself to one town in the Black Country. (Lola's association with Ireland places her in a cohort of wild Irish beauties.) The frequency of 'wedding' in Lola's life, especially when there is no intervening 'divorce' or 'death or loss of spouse', in itself flags a Woman of the World; Lola lives up to her role by appearing in courtroom scenes, riot, and revolution in keeping with adulterous or bigamous frequency of union with men. As we mark up all versions of one person's life and all the parallel lives in the social networks of these printed collections, we can query and visualize patterns and correlations. These texts can be curious mixtures of unexpected historical evidence, variations upon biography's usual tendentiousness (pointing to signs of talent in childhood or the fateful turning point), effective storytelling, and expressions of contemporary models for women's lives. With their blend of realist characterization and action with a certain amount of explicit instruction, these texts, singly and as an archive, require human interpretation, yet they offer qualities measurable by the new quantitative tools of digital studies. Our analysis draws out the conventions in one historical strain of prosopography, with implications for all modes of biographical representation in different media.

Literary studies recently have debated the value of different scales of reading or interpretation.[17] Quantification of data always runs into the limits of human perception, as in visualizations that become crowded with indistinguishable details. In 'R-graph' displays (see Figure 4.4), we can show kaleidoscopic relationships among all the subjects in biographical collections. A single cohort in a sample corpus includes too many names to be read in a screenshot, especially in representing fourteen books with Montez's 151 siblings or twenty books with Dora's 141 siblings. Online, such visualizations are interactive; the spider webs of relationships can be

---

[17] See Stephen Best and Sharon Marcus, 'Surface Reading: An Introduction', *Representations* 108:1 (2009), 1–21. Franco Moretti, *Distant Reading* (New York: Verso, 2013). Alison Booth, 'Screenshots in the Longue Durée: Feminist Narratology, Digital Humanities, and Collective Biographies of Women', in *Narrative Theory Unbound: Queer and Feminist Interventions*, ed. Robyn Warhol and Susan S. Lanser (Columbus: Ohio State University Press, 2015), 169–93.

rearranged to focus on any individual. Another illustration of the problem of crowded attention appeared in a 2012 ad for the career network, LinkedIn: an aerial photograph of hundreds of standing people clad in shades of blue, looking up towards the camera; the crowd stands apart from white spaces forming lower-case letters spelling 'in'.[18] In such a represented network, the scale prevents us from focusing on the actual life stories of each person in the crowd. Similar issues of the loss of details in the big picture occur in a digital project, when the biographies of thousands of individuals are interlinked in a database. Worthwhile as it is to drill down into the individual narrative—and our studies of narrative structure using BESS are designed to extract some of the ore of these narratives—there also may be sublime perspectives and tangible discoveries across horizons of the landscape.

Biography must be the least interesting of all genres of writing. It seems, in any case, to have been the least studied and theorized. There is remarkably little exploration of third-person forms of life-writing compared to autobiography, memoir, and life-writing online. A notable recent exception is Hermione Lee's *Biography: A Very Short Introduction* (2009), and from time to time a scholar comes to terms with permutations of biography in one historical context, as in Juliette Atkinson's *Victorian Biography Reconsidered* (2010). Published criticism on biography usually expresses surprise, as I do, at the genre's critical neglect. In trade publishing, after all, 'biography' does quite well, though not as well as might be assumed.[19] A book about a president or a famous writer has a good chance of being reviewed in major print venues, and lives of celebrities, ghosted or third person, can bring sales.[20] In 2012, Amazon's online list of bestsellers had a lone biography at #26 in the top 40, Walter Isaacson's *Steve Jobs*. Founding fathers of a new era

---

[18] Corporations often use this sort of group photograph to evoke the personality of their team, but this makes the people resemble pixels. See *LinkedIn Sizzle Reel 2012.* <https://www.youtube.com/watch?v=tzaSrnpdKU4&feature=youtube_gdata_player> (accessed 12 May 2015).

[19] According to Julie Rak, *biography*, the term booksellers use for 'personal non-fiction' of all kinds, has maintained its single-digit share of book sales, approximately 5,000 books per year, the fourth largest market share at around 7% (personal email communication). Biography appears to be a relatively good way for a scholar to reach a broad educated readership.

[20] In life-writing, the memoirist or autobiographer need not be famous, but some authenticating trauma or triumph over adversity is called for. James Hall, 'Celebrity Biography Sales Slump', *The Telegraph*, 16 March 2012.

command public attention. Otherwise, the bestsellers that season offered fiction, food, lifestyle, religion, easy at first glance to mistake for each other—*The Hunger Games* and *The Blood Sugar Solution*, *The Power of Habit* and *The Walking Dead*.

Literary studies mirror the market's proportions: novels take the lion's share of critical attention, followed by autobiography and memoir, with biography an afterthought. In academic circles, biography is everywhere in disciplinary histories and in many research methods but it might almost be transparent for all the critical attention it receives. After some forays in higher education in the early twentieth century, biography encountered resistance in the humanities, with theoretical turns against the author and against heroic history. Autobiography has done better since the 1970s; attention is paid to emergent voices and subjectivities, in various modes. In feminist studies of all sorts, life-writing has been central because of the premise that women have encountered gender bias that shapes their careers, yet feminist research has often relied on a history of biography that misrepresents the actual depictions of women's lives over the centuries. The misreading comes from traditional preoccupation with the full-length monograph, above all the homosocial bonding between writers, Boswell and Johnson, Gaskell and Brontë, that comes with the rise of the professions. A great deal of biography across millennia doesn't take the one-person-one-book format but collects brief 'parallel lives', as the English title of Plutarch's Greco-Roman collection has it.

I argue that life narratives in any form both reveal networks of persons and distribute authorship or agency. Collective or multiple forms of life-writing, which make these networks of association explicit, are surprisingly pervasive in print, acknowledging people in groups or categories such as martyrs of Methodism or Australian engineers.[21] The boundaries are blurred between first- and third-person or even second-person forms, when we consider the agency of production.[22] Who is shaping or sharing

---

[21] No one has attempted statistics on collective biographies or biographies of all kinds. By the mid-nineteenth century, a single year often produced five–ten collections of women only (in English); I estimate that five times as many collective biographies were all-male or mixed male–female. Victorian publishers' advertisements suggest that the numbers of collections of men rival or even exceed monographs about individual men.

[22] Alison Bechdel's *Fun Home*, like other graphic memoirs, represents intersecting lives of a family (traumatized by homophobia and suicide), blending a focal, first-person

the narrative? Full-length, documented biography may seek to immerse a reader in the experience of a self-reflective, influential person, someone who, like Virginia Woolf or Charles Dickens, collaborated with future lives written about her or him in a vast archive of writings, and who is immersed in circles of famous friends and family. More and more people are able to publish autobiographical narrative, but it is not difficult to see ways that first-person testimony has been shaped by third-person voices or parties. Social media seem to present extremes of unfettered self-expression under tight prescriptions. Facebook or Twitter resemble piecemeal ghosted memoirs in their collaborative production of what appear to be first-person testimonials. This activity in short-form personal narrative is as mesmerizing as industrial music in a crowded bar; it is fascinating to 'follow' and 'like' and 'comment', to capture some of the attention measured in 'hits', 'page views', 'visits', or 'traffic'. There are increasing numbers of studies of everyday narrative practices (e.g., blog communities among the deaf; YouTube videos of pre-teen fashionistas—millions of voluntary subjects for an emergent ethnography). Many branches of online media present features that resemble prosopography, in the sense of retrieved, commensurate data about persons in groups. Prosopography dominates social networks, biographical databases, and websites representing national, local, and social histories.[23] Social media put prosopography to work, a massive, crowd-sourced life-writing project. The study of prosopography in the CBW project can help us recognize the effects of ubiquitous life-writing today.

I indicated that prosopography has been understood as a research method quite distinct from the form and rhetoric that collective biographies and social media share. By the later nineteenth century, German classical scholarship had influenced English-language prosopographies of named persons in ancient documents. In the early twentieth century, Lewis

---

character-narrator who is also the artist-writer, who represents phases of her earlier self and family in a visual equivalent of third person.

[23] See, for example, Mapping the Republic of Letters, <http://republicofletters.stanford.edu/>, or African American Women Writers of the Nineteenth Century, <http://digital.nypl.org/schomburg/writers_aa19/>. My approach to prosopography has taken into account multiple media and popular reception, as in the study of monuments and festivals: Mount Rushmore, halls of fame, Women's History Month, forms that evolved from the early twentieth-century passion for preserving and measuring cultural achievements.

Namier and other historians adopted the method of prosopography, in such studies as the life histories of Members of Parliament in a certain era, with statistical analysis of standardized data. Some historians have shown renewed interest in the method and the form in the years since the historian Lawrence Stone called attention to it in 1971. Computation has invited more attempts at exhaustive derivation of person data from documents or remains, as in People of the Founding Era, a study of the lesser-known correspondents indicated in the digitized papers of early Presidents and Signers of the Declaration of Independence. Today, the Prosopography of the Byzantine World at King's College, London, is a good example of the large collaborative scholarly databases that derive data about individuals from documentary traces and that create profiles for quantitative analysis.

In 2003, Paul Magdalino, contributing to the conference proceedings *Fifty Years of Prosopography*, insisted rightly that prosopography is more than 'simply the plural' of biography; he considers prosopography 'most useful in the study of societies where the number of recorded individuals is relatively modest, and where the records do not lend themselves to the construction of major biographies'.[24] This seems to imply that individuals in developed countries in the print era all receive the full-length individuation of 'major biographies', and prosopography is only warranted in conditions of scarcity. Katherine S. B. Keats-Rohan emphasizes prosopography's 'focus . . . upon the total collection of individuals in aggregate', and separates their method from belletristic biography and from collective biographies including the *Dictionary of National Biography* (*DNB*).[25] Certainly, printed biographical collections are created by a different process than a prosopography of the persons named in the Domesday Book. But it is important to recognize the form and rhetoric of prosopography in a discursive database such as the printed and online *DNB*. Prosopography's rhetoric and form are found in *existing* printed texts and emerge all the more energetically in the age of the Internet, under

---

[24] Magdalino, in Averil Cameron, ed., *Fifty Years of Prosopography* (Oxford: Oxford University Press, 2003), 42–3.

[25] K. S. B. Keats-Rohan, 'Biography, Identity and Names: Understanding the Pursuit of the Individual in Prosopography', Prosopography Research, Modern History Research Unit, Oxford University, <http://prosopography.modhist.ox.ac.uk/prosopdefinition.htm>.

conditions of superabundance rather than scarcity. Each person warrants a full-length life narrative, but each is an animated node of many intersecting edges in the vast networks of representation—some 'found', in the published records, and some reconstructed by the prosopographical collection or database.

Many concepts of identity and auto/biography are less stable, less personal and inalienable, than we might suppose. It is worth considering the basic elements that establish a persona, identity, and life story in a standardized, collectible form, whether first or third person. A 'life' or identity in print, online, or in other social registers requires at least a name, events, and appearance.[26] Secondary identifiers may be the most valuable, from ID numbers to documented choices we have made, our purchases and likes. But these especially *must* be standard or transferable, from the point of view of host sites.

Biography hinges on the name, which might seem to be the easy part of biographical data. Classic prosopography is closely allied with onomastics: names are often all one has. The practical challenge quickly becomes a theoretical one: What is a person? As a database for research on the individuals who surface in cohorts, CBW encounters the challenges of any prosopography, whether in conditions of scarcity or plenitude of data. In some contexts, from fables to the Bible, a proper name is almost sufficient for an audience to infer a life story of great significance. But historical researchers encounter widely variable naming systems in different cultures and eras. Even in modern, well-documented times, name records, especially of women, are redundant or slippery, as in the example of the woman who gave herself the stage name Lola Montez. For analytic purposes, on the one hand, the lack of a name isn't always an obstacle; Keats-Rohan reminds us that research can be conducted on 'Anonymous 1, Anonymous 2, and so on'.[27] For identification, on the other hand, a legal name is seldom enough; other biographical information is needed to 'disambiguate', as Wikipedia says. CBW's database has encountered multiple identities that appear to refer to the same individual, as biographers use

---

[26] Apart from the public 'ID' components such as passwords and National Insurance numbers, there are other identifiers like fingerprints or voice or smell—the discussion could expand.

[27] Keats-Rohan, 'Biography, Identity and Names', 151. She insists that '*establishing personal identity . . . individualization . . . identification*' are separate processes (152).

different styles of naming. The problem of naming increases with historical distance, as spellings become less standardized and a 'family' name may be a place of origin or an epithet. Women are a special challenge in biographical databases because, according to custom, they adopt married names. They have often been undocumented or lied about their age, have often been less literate than their brothers (though there are pockets of history in which they reverse this), and only in recent centuries have many of them had legal standing to hold property and leave legacies or other historical documentation.

The expected attributes that confirm the biography of an individual turn out to be fraught with indeterminacy. Even in reputable reference works or official records the facts are confounded. Motivated or inadvertent errors begin at the source—the say-so of the person or family—and magnify with transmissions. The dates and location of birth, marriage, and death have become an expected cluster of public facts—reinforced, on application forms and resumes, alongside education, employment, skills, or hobbies—documenting an individual with a proper name. Beginning with gendered names, people are resolutely identified as male or female in documents and databases, yet that binary designation has been inadequate to represent gender and sexuality across lifetimes, in earlier eras as well as today. The names of women in CBW are disrupted by status or rank. A large portion of the women who did march into any national records were noble or royal, and titles obscure given names and blend individuals of different generations who hold the same title. Disambiguating persons is crucial for making use of prosopography.

When we have eliminated duplicate entries, there is still the challenge of interconnecting the many repositories' ways of tabulating that individual identity, to make it easier for our biographical studies to lead a user to records in Library of Congress, Virtual International Authority File, and other parallel or intersecting systems. How do you designate names and attributes in ways standard enough for recognition, distinct enough to be unique? Name and basic biodata determined, we feel an even stronger identification in the person's appearance, as on passports we insist on seeing the face and shoulders and signature of the traveller.[28] Printed biographies

---

[28] Both portraiture and biography predate modern individualism, of course; visual and verbal representations begin to conform to the idiosyncratic features of the sitter at around the same period in the age of print reproduction.

since the mid-nineteenth century almost invariably include at least one portrait, often a frontispiece with a facsimile signature, to locate the real subject of the prose text.[29] Of course portraiture, like names and events, can be unreliable identification. Even as photography increased the expectation of seeing 'warts and all', Victorian collective biographies might offer imaginative engravings of captive Zenobia or repentant Magdalene, or—even where historical portraits exist—exotic Pocahontas. As noted, the same person looks different in different images over time, particularly in different media such as painting or photography. Further, representation by the same artist or text reduces individual differences to a kind of adaptive resemblance. A portrait or a face can provide the basis for a detective reconstruction of a person, as in forensic archaeology that attempts facial reconstruction from skeletal remains, or historical research identifying the subject of an anonymous photograph of a Civil War soldier.[30] Yet like the name, the *prosopon* or face is alienable rather than inherent in identity. This goes beyond the matter of fake photo IDs. Accident victims or wounded veterans have long received reconstructive surgery, and face transplants may soon become more common.

When we fill out surveys and application forms in the USA today, we are less likely to be asked about religious affiliation than in the past, but religion was ahead of nationality in distinguishing women in the historical record. Users of CBW who are interested in religion may find the Quaker preacher Elizabeth Fry in 54 books, including *Quaker Women* (1915), or discover 12 books with titles similar to *Heroines of Methodism* (1857); 34 collections are labelled 'sectarian (religious group)'. CBW enables a reception history of types of women and the ways that groups of women were represented relative to each

---

[29] Handwriting as forensic or psychological evidence coincides with other tools of identification established by the late nineteenth century. Biography uses the autograph (facsimile) as a token of actual signatures collected from the correspondence of famous people and pasted into amateurs' albums or sold on the market.

[30] A National Public Radio piece retraces the identity of a young northern soldier through clues such as his uniform, musket, initials, and height. Ramona Martinez, 'Unknown No More: Identifying a Civil War Soldier: NPR', *NPR.org*, 11 April 2012. http://www.npr.org/2012/04/11/150288978/unknown-no-more-identifying-a-civil-war-soldier (accessed 12 May 2015).

other. Consider one Mrs John Livingstone. She appears in only three CBW collections, forming a cohort (a set of associated names in a sample corpus) with 40 other women.[31] To visualize this network, Figure 4.4 is centred on Mrs Livingstone, with the three collections positioned on the innermost circle and the other women of those collections around the second circle. A third of her siblings also appear in these same three collections and nowhere else in CBW, confirming some consensus on the names that represent 'Notable Women of the Scottish Reformation', a specific historical episode in one location. Delving into the books that include her siblings, we encounter 329 documentary 'cousins' of a more diverse network: some of the Scottish heroines of religious conflict intersect with a multinational set of women widely recognized today, including writers such as Harriet Beecher Stowe and heroines of war such as Joan of Arc or the Countess of Montfort.[32]

The heroines of religion also represent national differences, which are high on the list of attributes for an individual today but which took some centuries to gel. The challenges of identifying nationality, like names, reveal the effects of historical change and class. Depending on various alliances among royal or noble houses, some of the women who fit into an Italian Renaissance picture, for instance, were born or died beyond the borders of modern Italy. The concept of nationality is a modern attribute associated with birth certificates and the nation state. Today, as in the past, such supposedly definitive attributes of identity can change mid-life, with or without the person's agency, through exile or changing borders; consider the passports of various countries of the former Soviet Union, within the

---

[31] Janet Fleming Livingstone or Mrs John Livingstone surfaces in a cohort of late seventeenth-century Scottish Protestant Dissenters; many are wives of Presbyterian ministers or widows of martyrs or exiles. This relatively persistent cohort includes noblewomen, but most are historically obscure (life dates or first names unknown). Two collections have versions of the same list of persons: a029, Rev. James Anderson, [of Edinburgh], *The Ladies of the Covenant: Memoirs of Distinguished Scottish Female Characters, Embracing the Period of the Covenant and the Persecution* (London: Blackie, 1850), with reprints through 1880; a157, William Chapman, *Notable Women of the Covenant: Their Lives and Times* (London: Swan Sonnenschein, 1883). The third book including Mrs Livingstone is a068, Rev. Donald Beaton, *Scottish Heroines of the Faith: Being Brief Sketches of Noble Women of the Reformation and Covenant Times* (London and Glasgow: Catt and Adshead, 1909).

[32] One cousin of Livingstone is Sister Dora, who illustrates the exponential possibilities: Dora has a prodigious 3,763 'cousins' who share a volume with a 'Noble Worker' woman but not Dora herself.

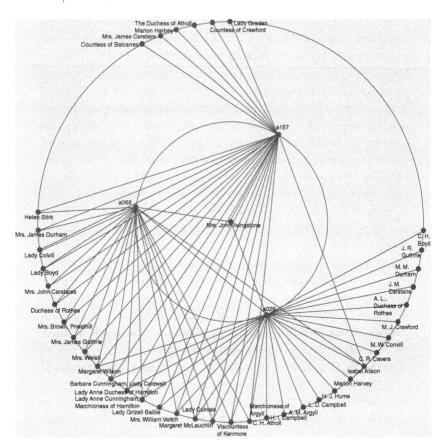

Figure 4.4 Mrs John Livingstone and Siblings in Three Books (R-graph).

twentieth century. Names are destabilized by national differences: English transliteration or translation of names leads to variations that produce separate person IDs that need to be reconciled as alternate names for the same person. Book titles in CBW may be patriotic or take note of national character, sometimes uniting 'Britain and America': 'Engl' (England or English, 64 books); 'British' (12 books); 'Britain' (8); 'America' (incl. American, 88 books); four additional titles indicate the 'United States'. Yet in these collections, written and published in English for American and British audiences, the traditions passed down from the humanists persist: selections of women of classical, biblical, medieval, and early modern Europe enrich many lists of recent queens or First Ladies, with less focus on national difference. Like gender and like occupational roles, association with a country must be designed to accommodate multiple 'values', types, or attributes (e.g. Christine de Pizan is French, is Italian). Frenchwomen pervade the database: fifty-three books announce a group of Frenchwomen or 'France' as their titular theme, compared to fourteen books indicating Italy or Italian matters in their female biographies.[33] Fortuitous as the specific numbers may be in a comparatively limited genre, the aggregated trends offer some indication of the reception of individuals and types over time that is unavailable in reference resources or descriptions in libraries and archives.

If there is comparatively little academic interest in biography in its conventional sense, I would hardly expect there to be more in standardized outlines of lives constructed for prosopographical research. Short versions of lives do command public attention, from journalism to documentaries, and collective and group biographies are often published, yet little systematic criticism considers the form and rhetoric of life-writing that interconnects and aligns multiple personae.[34] It's a modern orthodoxy that we each possess exclusive rights in a self, although identities may be stolen or shared. But what if all life narrative is immersed in social networks and all personhood is, in a sense, corporate? (The Supreme Court has recently confirmed that corporations are persons.) And what if a *bios* or life narrative follows a template or set of raw elements to be filled in? We're not a dime a dozen, surely. It often seems that new media make it possible for each person to publicize every detail of experience; nothing can waste its sweetness on the desert air. This can be deplored as a free-for-all of self-recognition, but from another perspective the scale is so vast that

---

[33] Currently, 204 persons appear in a search for the type 'French', and of these, many have high rates. Joan of Arc has 68 short biographies, the most of one person in CBW; Marie Antoinette, 60; Empress Josephine (the wronged wife of Napoleon), 31. Revolutionary times promoted women to public history: Madame Roland (in 35 CBW books); the celebrated beauty Madame Récamier (16); George Sand (14). Italians are less dominant in the Anglo-American books in CBW: 140 persons we now identify as Italian, of whom 11 are male. Italian names are less likely to rise above single-digit rates in the tables of contents.

[34] Alison Booth, 'Books Full of Women', Review of Alice Kaplan, *Dreaming in French* and Lisa Cohen, *All We Know*, in *Public Books*. 20 June 2013. <http://www.publicbooks.org/fiction/books-full-of-women>.

individuals become indistinguishable. Commercially, our life narratives can only be worth megabucks en masse.

Unstable data—from name, to event, to appearance—serve to represent one life, whether I do it myself or it is done to me, whether I am alive or dead. In film and television as well as on websites, standard formulae circulate today, expanding beyond the minimal identification I have just considered. The discourse of celebrity 'lives' is so ubiquitous it may seem to have nothing in common with a literary genre, but this mediation of identity draws its formulae from earlier constructions. Biography online is a kind of difference engine reproducing eminent lives, adding character and anecdote to 'basic facts (education, work, relationships, and death)' concerning presidents, athletes, justices, entertainers, Nobel laureates.[35] Much discussion in the media focuses on privacy, ethics, pseudo-intimacy, and deficits or surfeits of attention in today's social media.[36] Researchers are seizing the opportunities in the metadata that reveal revision and user histories in social networks such as Facebook and LinkedIn. I would invite formal interpretations of these representational platforms as models of life-writing in groups. Names, faces, lists (the prosopographical rhetoric of parataxis) of milestone events assemble one's 'profile'. All these forms of online life-writing warrant sustained attention, but I conclude with some remarks associating new media with CBW's experiments.

Facebook is a new mode of prosopography—in rhetorical and formal ways. Obviously, it favours names tagged upon portrait images. It has been utterly traditional in assuming that the course or 'curriculum' of a life can be registered by tagging the values for certain elements, with the addition of relationships (key to the logic of extensible networks) and consumer habits. Vast networks like social media favour 'lists', the paratactical series that omit conjunctions. A few years ago (2009) there was a flurry of '25 Random Things About Me'.[37] Some of these lists were imaginative ways of disrupting

---

[35] These definitions appear in entries on 'Biography' on Wikipedia.org and infoplease.com. A systematic critique of the website Biography.com would reveal much about the genre codes of life-writing.

[36] Pamela Haag, 'Death by Treacle', *The American Scholar*, 17 April 2012. <https://theamericanscholar.org/death-by-treacle/#.VVKwi2ZDlnQ> (accessed 12 May 2015).

[37] Claire Suddath, '25 Things I Didn't Want to Know About You', *Time*, 5 February 2009. <http://content.time.com/time/arts/article/0,8599,1877187,00.html> (accessed 12 May 2015); Jane Devin, 'In Defense of Facebook's Hated "25 Random Things" Writers', *The Huffington Post*, 6 February 2009.

the flattening, nearly anonymous format of name, pictures, events, likes, and comments. Predictably, people responded to the 'random' idiosyncrasies as clichés or impertinences. Who could be curious about millions of telegraphic memoirists? A feature introduced in 2012, Timeline, makes explicit the life-writing that Facebook engineers for its users. Those components of biography, name, event, appearance, are collapsing, as Timeline makes pictures 'events', and if anyone tags your name to one, it's an event on your Timeline, equally weighted with any other. This is extreme collective narration. But Facebook invites you to reclaim authorship of your narrative, overcoming the functions of the site itself; Timeline will allow you to flesh out the basic information of your profile and preserve the history of your participation. You can now tell the big as well as the little picture. 'What will you create? We can't wait to find out'.[38] These pronouns are not entirely reassuring. Again, personhood is easily troped as corporate or collective, for better or worse. LinkedIn advises, 'How to Invest Wisely in the Start-Up of You'. But they have tellingly dubbed their 'publish-subscribe system' Kafka, with its capacity for surveillance of a billion messages per day.[39]

A culture that values autonomous narration of one's own life nevertheless practises schematic collecting of personal narrative with an insatiable passion for *sharing* in every sense. Perhaps it is reassuring to recognize print-era ways to represent individuals in a collective way. I devote many person-hours to the various and surprising and somewhat prescriptive lives of women in printed books. These narratives, all overtly written by third parties, take the trouble to persuade readers that they represent real individuals with unique experience in defined time and place.[40] The conditions

<http://www.huffingtonpost.com/jane-devin/in-defense-of-facebooks-h_b_164538.html> (accessed 12 May 2015).

[38] Slater Tow, 'Tell Your Story with Timeline', 22 September 2011. <https://www.facebook.com/notes/facebook/tell-your-story-with-timeline/10150289612087131> (accessed 12 May 2015).

[39] Azarias Reda, Sam Shah, Mitul Tiwari, Anita Lillie, and Brian Noble, 'Social Networking in Developing Regions', *Proceedings of the International Conference on Information and Communication Technologies and Development* (March 2012), 96.

[40] An effective biography for readers today must adapt techniques from fiction for a realistic, individuated characterization of a person beyond the public facts or the typical roles, as many of these brief narratives do. When the techniques are too liberally used, critics may balk at the invention, from Edmund Morris's *Dutch* to James Frey's *A Million Little Pieces*.

of non-fiction tend to be observed, as any known facts cannot be bent to the instructive purpose, though many may be omitted or glossed. When the format, or the implied author, such as an advocacy group or corporation, are too overt in their aims upon the audience, we lose our trust, among Victorian readers as now. For all these reasons, I propose that social networks in old and new media deserve sustained attention, even a new theory of biographical narrative in the digital age.

5

Writing Real People

Adam Foulds

In a review of E. L. Doctorow's novel *The March*,[1] John Updike declared that 'A number of reviewers, including this one, had a problem with E. L. Doctorow's best-known and best-selling novel, *Ragtime* ... the book not only mingled the American celebrities of 1902 (Harry Houdini, J. P. Morgan) with the typical and the obscure ... but had the historical figures do things and achieve conjunctions that never transpired ... It smacked of playing with helpless dead puppets, and turned the historical novel into a gravity-free, faintly sadistic game.'[2]

This is strongly put. The objection notably is moral rather than aesthetic; Doctorow is arraigned for his cruelty and mendacity. Implicit in Updike's position is the notion of a fiction writer's duty of care towards people who have actually lived and the facts of their lives. That those facts exist in a fairly stable category of the knowable is likewise implied. Updike speaks from the centre of the shared ground of historical consensus. There, the anarchist agitator Emma Goldman is not to be found decorseting and massaging with oil the famous demi-mondaine beauty Evelyn Nesbit while an entirely fictional character masturbates in the wardrobe. Updike's

---

[1] E. L Doctorow, *The March* (New York: Random House, 2005).
[2] John Updike, *Due Considerations* (London: Hamish Hamilton, 2007), 293 (first printed in *The New Yorker*, 12 September 2005).

historical conservatism recoils from Doctorow's pop-art collisions, his gleefully abrupt and vivid dialectical montage, pieced together from cut-ups of early twentieth-century American iconography.

Doctorow's intent is indeed radical. In an essay first published two years after the publication of *Ragtime*, Doctorow contrasts the free play of literary language, which he argues represents 'the power of freedom', against the language of facts, 'the power of the regime'.[3] Evidently for Doctorow, all literary writing is an act of opposition against (or at least a determined evasion of) the prevailing power structure. He then goes on to explore the literary tradition of 'false documents', those works that appear at the inception of the modern literary novel—*Don Quixote, Robinson Crusoe*—that present themselves deadpan, as genuine artefacts of reportage discovered and reprinted. Doctorow argues that they may well have convinced their first readers of their veracity. And the point of this deception? To return fiction to the state of the tale, the myth, before fact and fiction became ontologically differentiated, when story, fact, and wisdom were all alloyed in one mode of telling the truth about the world. Here Doctorow is drawing on Walter Benjamin's essay on Nikolai Leskov, 'The Storyteller',[4] which contrasts the tale's capacity to deliver wisdom, the epic version of truth, with the novel's many scattering, centrifugal facts. The novel, according to Benjamin, is 'the epic of confusion'. So Doctorow's project, it would seem, is to recover a more robust kind of narrative meaning; it is to make sense, to be deeply, perversely truthful.

For Doctorow to achieve this in a demystified world, he must challenge the exclusive truth claims of historical fact, thus making reality malleable, something he can invent and esemplastically shape as much as perceive. He quotes the historian E. H. Carr quoting Carl Becker: 'The facts of history do not exist for any historian until he has earned them.'[5] He returns to that central source of relativism and cites Nietzsche: 'There are no facts in themselves. For a fact to exist we must first introduce meaning.'[6]

Doctorow himself argues that 'history is a kind of fiction in which we live and hope to survive, and fiction is a kind of speculative history, perhaps a

---

[3] E. L. Doctorow, 'False Documents', in *Jack London, Hemingway and the Constitution* (New York: Random House, 1993), 152.

[4] Walter Benjamin, *Illuminations* (New York: Schocken, 1998).

[5] Doctorow, 'False Documents', 161.   [6] Doctorow, 'False Documents', 160.

superhistory by which available data for composition are seen to be greater and more various in their sources than the historian supposes',[7] a statement that recalls and elaborates Gide's statement that 'fiction is history which *might* have taken place, and history is fiction which *has* taken place'.[8]

After this vigorous shove at the monolith of objective truth, Doctorow runs up again and topples it: 'I am thus led to the proposition that there is no fiction or nonfiction as we commonly understand the distinction: There is only narrative.'[9]

It's an interesting essay, jumpily argued, that ultimately rests its case at this apogee of the relativist position. Frustratingly, it fails to explore what other kinds of facts or truth claims are in play in the construction of the sort of historical critique performed in *Ragtime*, the analysis of social forces and discourses that Doctorow gathers his cast of the famous dead to enact for us. What comprises the radical storyteller's wisdom that Doctorow has wrestled back into his art? The essay, however, does have a good go at clearing the ground of intellectual objections to the undertaking as a whole and, it would seem that, for Doctorow, once the intellectual objections are removed, the moral licence must be granted and the carnivalesque show can go on.

Not so for Updike. At least, not so for Updike and *Ragtime*: those objections obtained before the conversion experience of the book that Updike presently is reviewing:

His splendid new novel, *The March*, pretty well cures my Doctorow problem... Reading historical fiction, we often itch, our curiosity piqued, to consult a book of straight history, to get to the facts without the fiction. But *The March* stimulates little such itch; it offers an illumination, fitful and flickering, of an historical upheaval which only fiction could provide. Doctorow here appears not so much a reconstructor of history as a visionary who seeks in time past occasions for poetry.[10]

Updike shares some examples of this poetry, moments of dazzling aesthetic success, on his way to declaring in the final line of the review that 'Doctorow's impertinent imagination holds fast to the reality of history

---

[7] Doctorow, 'False Documents', 162.

[8] André Gide, *Les Caves Du Vatican*, Livre Troisième, Chapitre 1, 'D'avisés critiques ont considéré le roman comme de l'histoire qui aurait pu être, l'histoire comme un roman qui avait eu lieu.'

[9] Doctorow, 'False Documents', 163.   [10] Updike, *Due Considerations*, 294.

even as he paints it in heightened colours.'[11] The sadist is now merely impertinent, handling honestly what Updike takes to be the truth of history, and the artistic achievement ratifies the undertaking.

Neither the writer of the essay nor the review really addresses what I think ought to be a crucial factor in this argument: the sophistication of readers and the commercial generic framing of these works as fiction. Perhaps charged with confidence in his own superb manipulative power as a novelist, Updike assumes that the reader is quite vulnerable to a writer's distortions or inventions, as though a novel might have the final lapidary word in constructing the reader's understanding of history. But surely this late in the long literary day we are beyond imagining that there are any definitive histories out there, books that establish a final and incorrigible truth about a person and time. The very fact that multiple biographies of major historical figures exist suggests that there aren't any such definitive versions. The reader approaches the section for biographies of Napoleon in the bookshop and is confronted by shelf-loads of competing, overlapping, mutually reinforcing but also often contradictory accounts. And that's in the category of non-fiction. Readers who have wandered over to 'Fiction D' and are taking to the till a copy of *Ragtime* by E. L. Doctorow know that they are buying a novel set in 1903 that was written in 1975, and that for it to exist at all there a good deal of imagination and guesswork must be involved. Furthermore, we know that elision, simplification, and stylization are in the nature of fiction per se. No work of art can capture the complexity of lived life, either in its myriad encounters, interactions and connections, or in the inner complexity of consciousness. Even the most ambitious attempts at the latter, James Joyce's *Ulysses* being the obvious example, present only a good simulacrum, internally logical but far from comprehensive, if only because so much of consciousness is non-verbal. And that's fine. We don't want fiction to be as incoherent as lived experience. Nor, for that matter, do we want our own lived experience to be as incoherent as lived experience. Instead, we narrate ourselves, we edit and schematize, we manufacture post facto rationalizations, causal chains of events and people that led us from any given earlier point in our lives to the

---

[11] Updike, *Due Considerations*, 299.

present moment.[12] Moreover, the arguments of psychoanalysis, that the stories we tell ourselves about ourselves are always, for varieties of overt or occluded reasons, partial and often quite wrong, are widely accepted. We falsify ourselves in order to live out the stories of our lives that we are inventing as we live them. We narrate and falsify our friends and families, often mistaking their motives and perceptions. And we know that we do this, by and large, in good faith, while trying to get things right.

The good faith of literary novelists rendering real people can also, by and large, be presumed upon. (Leo Tolstoy perhaps offers an interesting counterexample that we will come to later when discussing a different aspect of this enterprise.) The tradition of the literary novel that I would suggest flows on from the confluence of *Don Quixote* and *Hamlet* and is channelled in its particular modern and realist direction by Flaubert, is in some sense inimical to the kinds of flattening and distortion that would be required seriously to defame and misrepresent a historical figure. The modern novel is a machine for the dismantling of cliché and for the production of subtlety, nuance, doubt, and empathy. Its writers sometimes take time out to declare war on cliché, like Martin Amis, or to anatomize the crude stupidities of common, journalistic certainties about the world, as in Flaubert's dictionary of received ideas.

Let us entertain the possibility that literary novelists are decent, clever, well-intentioned people who, when rendering historical figures, try hard to get them right, to be rich and subtle about disclosing them as embodied human beings. It could be argued that this makes any distortions or misunderstandings that they do perpetrate all the more adhesively plausible but that thought should return us to my earlier point about the sophistication of literary readers and can be straightaway contradicted. We are used to negotiating the different kinds of truth claims of different kinds of writing—artistic, historical, or the two blended together—and contemporary psychological discourse has alerted us to an ultimate untrustworthiness in all kinds of narrative while simultaneously affirming narrative as a crucial, possibly *the* crucial and defining human intellectual activity. Literary readers are used to stepping back and forth through these mirrors and still knowing where they are. I'm reminded here of an account

---

[12] At the time that this chapter was first conceived, Facebook had recently industrialized this process with its new 'Timeline' feature, to 'help tell your story'.

of a bit of research into child psychological development. An earnest scientist interrogated a number of children about their imaginary friends. How old is the imaginary friend? How did you meet him? What does he eat? What does he do when you're asleep? What does he wear? and so on and so on. Each child responded enthusiastically at first, then patiently, then finally snapped with words to the effect of, 'You do realise my friend is imaginary, don't you?' You do realize that Tolstoy was born seven years after the death of Napoleon, that E. L. Doctorow never met Houdini, don't you? We do. We realize. I think that our gradings of reality and fiction are rather like our bipedal locomotion—learnt naturally, our second nature—but when analysed by roboticists or literary critics found to be dismayingly complex and subtle. Nevertheless, we persist in remaining upright and walking about.

No, whether or not one follows Doctorow to his extreme relativist position, I do not think that the moral objections to the portrayal of real people within fiction are really serious. The potential serious objections are artistic. The problem is that literary fiction needs to be written freely, irresponsibly, gratuitously, and handling any kind of historical material makes this more difficult, as does handling any kind of researched material. Two problems arise. One is that the learnt facts break the surface of the prose, are visible to the reader as strenuous acquirements of the author not fully incorporated into the body of the work. Many of us, I suspect, have encountered that moment in a novel when the research notes of a writer, nicely gussied up in continuous prose, pour down onto our heads as from a garbage chute: so heavy, so much factual bric-a-brac that is only contingently related to the evolving fate of the characters.

The other disturbing possibility overlaps with the first, and that is the fetishization of this historical material for its own sake. The excellent critic James Wood has written of historical fiction that becomes a kind of science fiction in reverse, with parchment replacing laser weapons or sedan chairs spaceships. It offers, therefore, a kind of materialist escapism, an antiquarian's fantasies, not the urgency of a literary writer's perplexed encounters, her griefs and rhapsodies, her formally beautiful distillations of experience. The challenge then is for the writer to absorb and internalize the researched material so deeply that it emerges in the creative act with a plasticity and spontaneity that is indistinguishable from that of the invented elements of the work. Here it might be noted that this is of course true of elements drawn from other sources, from life or other fiction. *Ragtime* offers an example of the latter.[13] The long and ultimately murderous struggle for justice of the African American character Coalhouse Walker is a rewriting of Heinrich von Kleist's novella *Michael Kohlhaas*.[14] This too must be smelted into the single alloy of the novel. Shakespeare did nothing but absorb and reimagine earlier works, including histories. Furthermore, in an extreme formulation it might be suggested that there are no elements in fiction not drawn from somewhere else, even if that somewhere else is the writer's own past experience. I is another, the self is a social construct, there is no purely originated, and so on. The materials for fiction, no matter their source, might then be held to comprise a single category that could be graded on a scale of their readiness for fictionalization, their volatility, their chemical reactivity, with, let us say, single observations or lines of description in a notebook, pertaining to no particular character or situation, being the most reactive, the most easily assimilated into a new work of fiction, while real historical figures and events, huge aggregated compounds of facts and possibilities, would be at the other end of the scale: the heaviest and most challenging materials to work with.

I imagine that some readers, still holding to a naive and Romantic notion of creativity, would resist this notion. They perhaps include some otherwise highly sophisticated readers. In an essay called 'Enigmas and Homelands', occasioned by a previous conference at the Huntington under the same auspices, Michael Wood writes of being disquieted by the strong circumstantial evidence that V. S. Naipaul was using elements of his own life experience, barely if at all reimagined, in the novel *The Enigma of Arrival*.[15] He asks 'Is it possible to fictionalize lightly?' And went on, 'Perhaps it is. I'm inclined to believe that fiction is like flying: you're either doing it or you're not.'[16] Michael Wood is, here at least, hesitant and open to persuasion, his theory of the production of fiction something that he is no more than 'inclined to believe'. I might suggest to Michael Wood that the sensation of continuous flight is more important for the reader to experience than the

---

[13] E. L. Doctorow, *Ragtime* (New York: Random House, 1975).

[14] Heinrich von Kleist, *Erzählungen* (1810), vol. 1.

[15] V. S. Naipaul, *The Enigma of Arrival* (London: Penguin, 1987).

[16] Michael Wood, 'Enigmas and Homelands', in *On Modern British Fiction*, ed. Zachary Leader (Oxford: Oxford University Press, 2002), 89.

writer. Writers spend a lot of time in turbulence with their engines cutting out, as well as joyfully looping the loop or banking into the rising sun. It is not, in my experience, a particularly smooth ride and you often aren't sure whether you're flying or crashing or just taxiing endlessly around the airfield. So the novel really works for and is ultimately legitimated by the pleasure of the reader. And in that reckoning, where the assembled materials of the novel originated from doesn't much matter. It matters that it works, it flies, it pleases.

What then is the particular pleasure to be had from reading fiction about people we know to have actually lived? For me, I think the answer to that question lies principally in the notion of embodiment.

Knowing the company I would have the privilege of keeping in this volume prompted me to reread Saul Bellow's *Ravelstein*.[17] Very early in the novel, we find Chick, the narrator, urged to consider writing a biography by Ravelstein with the sidelong intent of encouraging Chick to write his biography. Considering this and the varieties of ways to approach biography, Chick thinks first of all of Macaulay's essay on Boswell's Johnson, something he was made to read in high school:

Reading it put me into a purple fever. Macaulay exhilarated me with his version of the Life, with the anfractuosity of Johnson's mind. I have since read many sober criticisms of Macaulay's Victorian excesses. But I have never been cured—I never wanted to be cured of my weakness for Macaulay. Thanks to him I still see poor convulsive Johnson touching every lamppost on the street and eating spoiled meat and rancid puddings. [...] Johnson, despite his scrofula, his raggedness, his dropsy, had his friendships, wrote his books ... [18]

Here it is in a nutshell: the anfractuous mind in the convulsive body. Biography allows the reader to locate the subject in a single human form, to see the lotus blossoms of the works anchored by twisted roots in the mud of worldly physicality. This pleasure for the reader—and it definitely is a pleasure—is heightened by extreme contrast such as that here between Johnson's brilliance and his helpless Tourettic behaviours. The most famous such contrast must be the older Beethoven, malodorous in his sordid apartment, eating great bowls of scrambled eggs, composing the Ninth

---

[17] Janis Freedman Bellow is another of the contributors.
[18] Saul Bellow, *Ravelstein* (London: Viking Press, 2000), 6.

Symphony at a wrecked piano and then, at its premiere, being so deaf that he had to be turned around to *see* the applause he was receiving. Why this contrast is pleasurable to readers is interesting to speculate about. I think in part its extremity gives an emphatic quality to the readers' sense of an encounter with a real person. I think it also provokes a kind of wonder and compassion that perhaps helps reconcile us to our own painful bodies. And I think that somewhere beneath the surface is active the cultural inheritance of the Christian Passion narrative, Jesus' exemplary suffering body.

In the following great passage from Boswell, the body is everywhere, even when it is not in question. Boswell physically allegorizes thought in an extended image of the body in combat and Johnson himself insists on introducing the body to test the truth claims of the asserted ideas. To borrow a phrase from Keats, Johnson wants philosophy 'proved upon our pulses'.[19] It is a passage suffused with suffering and compassion, its imagery drawn from Christian martyrdom:

When we were alone, I introduced the subject of death, and endeavoured to maintain that the fear of it might be got over. I told him that David Hume said to me, he was no more uneasy to think that he should *not be* after this life, than that he *had not been* before he began to exist. JOHNSON. 'Sir, if he really thinks so, his perceptions are disturbed; he is mad; if he does not think so, he lies. He may tell you, he holds his finger in the flame of a candle, without feeling pain; would you believe him? When he dies, at least he gives up all he has.' BOSWELL. 'Foote, Sir, told me, that when he was very ill he was not afraid to die.' JOHNSON. 'It is not true, Sir. Hold a pistol to Foote's breast, or to Hume's breast, and threaten to kill them, and you'll see how they behave.' BOSWELL. 'But may we not fortify our minds for the approach of death?' Here I am sensible I was in the wrong, to bring before his view what he ever looked upon with horrour; for although when in a celestial frame, in his 'Vanity of human Wishes', he has supposed death to be 'kind Nature's signal for retreat', from this state of being to 'a happier seat', his thoughts upon this aweful change were in general full of dismal apprehensions. His mind resembled the vast amphitheatre, the Coliseum at Rome. In the centre stood his judgement, which, like a mighty gladiator, combated those apprehensions that, like the wild beasts of the Arena, were all around in cells, ready to be let out upon him. After a conflict, he drove them back into their dens; but not killing them, they were still assailing him. To my question, whether we might not fortify our minds for the approach of death, he answered, in a passion, 'No, Sir, let it alone. It matters not how a man dies, but

---

[19] John Keats, Letter to J. H. Reynolds, 3 May 1818.

how he lives. The act of dying is not of importance, it lasts so short a time.' He added, (with an earnest look,) 'A man knows it must be so, and submits. It will do him no good to whine.'[20]

Saul Bellow is, of course, one of the great noticers of human physicality in literature. In *Ravelstein* we see the brilliant and garrulous intellect housed in a body as humanly faulty as Johnson's:

> The Japanese kimono fell away from legs paler than milk. He had the calves of a sedentary man—the shinbone long and the calf muscle abrupt, without roundness. Some years back, after his heart attack, the doctors told him he must exercise, so he bought an expensive sweat suit and elegant gym shoes. He shuffled around the track for several days and then gave it up. Fitness was not his cup of tea. He treated his body like a vehicle—a motorbike that he raced at top speed along the rim of the Grand Canyon.[21]

The mind and body contrast is noted and celebrated by Chick, impresario for his friend: 'You couldn't imagine an odder container for his odd intellect.' Elsewhere we see his great internal, intellectual energy discharged in a clumsiness of the fingers, a muddled contact with the world. We see profuse and absent-minded smoking, spilled drinks, and ultimately the body helpless and dwindling, suffering oedema and muscle wasting. It is Ravelstein's Passion.

In Tolstoy's *War and Peace*, the physical being of Napoleon Bonaparte is invoked for reasons other than to elicit empathy and compassion:

> Bonaparte meanwhile began taking the glove off his small white hand, tore it in doing so, and threw it away. An aide-de-camp behind him rushed forward and picked it up.
>
> 'To whom shall it be given?' the Emperor Alexander asked Koslovski, in Russian in a low voice.
>
> 'To whomever Your Majesty commands.'
>
> The Emperor knit his brows with dissatisfaction and, glancing back, remarked: 'But we must give him an answer.'
>
> Kozlovski scanned the ranks resolutely and included Rostov in his scrutiny.

---

[20] Boswell, *The Life of Samuel Johnson, LL.D.* (London: Baynes and Son, 1826), vol. 2, 92. This passage must surely be an influence on Larkin's late poem about death and the fear of dying, 'Aubade' (*Times Literary Supplement*, 23 December 1977), with its assertion that 'death is no different whined at than withstood'.

[21] Bellow, *Ravelstein*, 10.

'Can it be me?' thought Rostov.

'Lazarev!' the colonel called, with a frown, and Lazarev, the first soldier in the rank, stepped briskly forward.

'Where are you off to? Stop here!' voices whispered to Lazarev who did not know where to go. Lazarev stopped, casting a sidelong look at his colonel in alarm. His face twitched, as often happens to soldiers called before the ranks.

Napoleon slightly turned his head, and put his plump little hand out behind him as if to take something. The members of his suite, guessing at once what he wanted, moved about and whispered as they passed something from one to another, and a page—the same one Rostov had seen the previous evening at Boris'—ran forward and, bowing respectfully over the outstretched hand and not keeping it waiting a moment, laid in it an Order on a red ribbon. Napoleon, without looking, pressed two fingers together and the badge was between them. Then he approached Lazarev (who rolled his eyes and persistently gazed at his own monarch), looked round at the Emperor Alexander to imply that what he was now doing was done for the sake of his ally, and the small white hand holding the Order touched one of Lazarev's buttons. It was as if Napoleon knew that it was only necessary for his hand to deign to touch that soldier's breast for the soldier to be forever happy, rewarded, and distinguished from everyone else in the world. Napoleon merely laid the cross on Lazarev's breast and, dropping his hand, turned toward Alexander as though sure that the cross would adhere there. And it really did.[22]

Here the historical titan is cut down to size. Tolstoy is very keen to let the reader know that Napoleon's mighty hands were in fact small, white, and plump. In the essay passages of *War and Peace*, Tolstoy writes against the idea that the single great individual agent shapes history. Napoleon being laughably small and delicate adumbrates this abstract point.[23] Napoleon has only a walk-on part in *War and Peace*. He walks on on his little legs or those of his horse Marengo, and Tolstoy doesn't attempt to render in any extended way the emperor's consciousness beyond now and again register-ing particular discreet thoughts. With some circularity, the reality of Napoleon's body as described by Tolstoy endorses Tolstoy's politics. In

---

[22] Tolstoy, *War and Peace*, trans. Louise and Aylmer Maude (London: Macmillan & Co. Ltd, 1943), 447–8.

[23] Incidentally, Tolstoy here, although in accord with consensus history, is actually perpetu-ating an inaccuracy: Napoleon was not particularly small. At five foot seven he was actually tall for the period. Nelson, at five foot four, was closer to average. Napoleon's diminutive stature was an invention of British caricaturists, Gillray in particular.

this way, the full embodiment of a real person in fiction is used to allow a refreshed analysis of historical events. Real historical characters can be constricted for the author and the reader by their usual meanings and agreed trajectories. Placed back inside their bodies and their physical environments they get to breathe again, to sense the world and make their decisions for the first time. The dividend for the reader is to experience the historical moment as open and flowing forwards rather than stilled by retrospect.

In E. L. Doctorow's other great novel of the 1970s, *The Book of Daniel*,[24] a version of the historical trial and execution of Julius and Ethel Rosenberg, a Communist couple found guilty of conspiracy to commit espionage, physical embodiment is politically charged. Their bodies, ultimately imprisoned and destroyed, are exemplary of the fates of bodies under authoritarian state power. Their story—or rather that of the novel's version of them, the Issacsons—is told by their graduate student son, Daniel. More than simply a telling of the story, it is an anguished lament and a furious work of historical analysis throughout which Daniel interpolates a history of physical punishments visited on the lower classes: knouting in Tsarist Russia, hanging, drawing, and quartering under an English monarchic government, and so on. Enduring these punishments, subject people are reduced to nothing but their suffering bodies, sites of pain. This could be said to be a catastrophic version of something that fiction often more benignly entertains through characters' embodiment—the presence in our lives of the meaningless as well as the meaningful. Through the recording of physical sensation, the accidental, the contingent, and actual crowd up to the surface of a text and allow it to respire free of thought. The world flattens to an absolute present. This is lifelike. Part of everybody's life is just this complex and iridescently shifting multiplicity of raw sensation. Often in fiction it is celebrated for its incidental pleasure, as when Stephen Dedalus, on a warm beach in James Joyce's *Ulysses*, looks up beyond his hat brim with half closed eyes: 'Under its leaf he watched through peacocktwittering lashes the southing sun.'[25] But in *The Book of Daniel*, the physical gratuitousness degrades the body to nothing but a body to procure its destruction. Here is how Daniel describes his father's electrocution, a description closely based on accounts of the execution of Julius Rosenberg:

---

[24] E. L. Doctorow, *The Book of Daniel* (New York: Random House, 1971).
[25] James Joyce, *Ulysses* (Paris: Shakespeare and Company, 1926), 48.

My father smashed into his straps as if hit by a train. He snapped back and forth, cracking like a whip. The leather straps groaned and creaked. Smoke rose from my father's head. A hideous smell composed of burning flesh, excrement and urine filled the death chamber. Most of the witnesses had turned away. A pool of urine collected on the cement floor under the chair.

When the current was turned off my father's rigid body suddenly slumped in the chair and it perhaps occurred to the witnesses that what they had taken for the shuddering spasming movements of his life for God knows how many seconds was instead a portrait of electric current, normally invisible, moving through a field of resistance.[26]

The historical body is then finally a field of resistance and individuals' physical fates can be argued to be a bottom line in the auditing of history, the ultimate accounting of who did what to whom and how they all lived. In this light, the body is the one ungainsayable reality of a person's life, and it is as essential for the writing of real people in fiction as it is in biography. The etymology of the word 'biography' makes this perfectly clear.

---

[26] Doctorow, *The Book of Daniel*, 297–8.

6

Rosamund and *Ravelstein:* The Discandying of a Creator's Confection

Janis Freedman Bellow

Saul Bellow's *Ravelstein* (2000) is about the friendship between two men. A once-in-a-lifetime friendship. Two men who laugh, and argue, and disagree about almost everything. Take death, for instance. Abe Ravelstein thinks the end is the end. ('To lie in cold obstruction and to rot.') He doesn't believe in an afterlife. Chick claims, 'I was not about to get into the ring with this Sumo champion representing Platonic metaphysics. One bump of his powerful belly and I'd be out of the brilliant ring and back again in the noisy dark.'[1] However, Chick jumps straight into the ring:

He...asked me what I imagined death would be like—and when I said that the pictures would stop he reflected seriously on my answer, came to a full stop, and considered what I might mean by this. No one can give up on the pictures. The pictures must and will continue. If Ravelstein the atheist-materialist had implicitly told me that he would see me sooner or later, he meant that he did not accept the grave to be the *end*. Nobody can and nobody does accept this. We just *talk* tough.

---

[1] Saul Bellow, *Ravelstein* (New York: Viking, 2000), 222 (henceforth cited within the text by page numbers).

So when I made my remark about the pictures, Ravelstein had given me his explosive laugh-stammer: 'Har har'. But he had some regard—some respect for the answer. But then he let himself go so far as to say, 'You look as if you might by and by be joining me.'

This is the involuntary and normal, the secret, esoteric confidence of the man of flesh and blood. The flesh would shrink and go, the blood would dry, but no one believes in his mind of mind or heart of hearts that the pictures *do* stop. (pp. 222–3)

Chick, left behind to mourn, and to memorialize his friend, speaks the novel's last sentence: 'You don't easily give up a creature like Ravelstein to death' (p. 253).

Pre-publication buzz had it that Bellow's book was a vicious attack on Allan Bloom, author of *The Closing of the American Mind* (1987). Rather than wait for critics to out the writer who had scandalously outed a dear friend, Saul agreed to speak to a reporter. He was quoted briefly towards the end of a lengthy article about *Ravelstein* in the *New York Times* on 16 April 2000:

'There are few people who are trained in their souls, so to speak, to do something extraordinary, and I think Bloom was such a person.' Such models present themselves only rarely in a writer's life, and he couldn't resist the challenge. 'Bloom was in some sense a great man', [Bellow] . . . said, 'and I wanted to get him down on paper'.[2]

A handful of words, and instead of protecting himself, his friend, and his book, the author demolished the wall separating novel from memoir. Saul threw his own dynamite stick at the *roman à clef*. How delicious: these weren't characters, they were people, and more to the point, famous people with dirty secrets and compromising illnesses. No one felt obliged to wear grey kid gloves when mining the wreckage for juicy bits.

A decade passes, and these names—both the fictional and the real—are forgotten. The books go the way of all books that shine in store windows, smoulder on remainder tables, and then darken in the infinite outskirts of cyberspace. I have been invited in this chapter to revisit these friends, and wish to focus on Rosamund in *Ravelstein*. Rosamund, Chick's wife, a minor character, delivers me to you, in my capacity as—as what? Not as academic, and certainly not as writer. Perhaps as the person I once trippingly called Saul's late wife.

---

[2] The title of the article was 'With Friends like Saul Bellow'; the author was D. T. Max.

Dissection would be the nasty way to describe writing about someone who is dead. Following this grisly line, to pin a living person on the page would require the skills of a vivisectionist. Excruciating—for the one being seen, or not seen. I asked Saul to remove his minor character Rosamund from *Ravelstein*. Pull one thread and be rid of the prissy girl. Nothing would unravel. No scar would be visible in the fabric. What could so slight a character add to a story already teeming with vibrant human types? A specific pain attached to this request. Don't do this to me. You misrepresent me. I'm not that woman: servile, prim, obedient. Is that the way you see me? Wounded vanity might be endured. But to be invisible to the person you love?

What whiny distraction such comments must have seemed. Small comfort to remember that, like Rosamund, I kept my feelings largely to myself. When I did not, the rejoinder was brief: Rosamund is a character. A minor character. The book is about the friendship between two men. Go argue.

Ungrateful! To earn a place in the story, find yourself fixed in words, candied by a master craftsman! The craftsman known for exquisite notation had turned his all-seeing eyes on me. Strange moment to lament being unseen. I knew it was foolish to be stung. That I hadn't a literary leg to stand on side-stepped the fact that he had set aside our delicious intimacy and substituted Rosamund for me.

I never resolved my feelings about these matters to my satisfaction. During Saul's lengthy illness, and in the years immediately following his death, I found little time to revisit them. The numb person who scribbled poems, privately mourned in the shower, and cared for our five-year-old, Rosie, was decidedly post-Rosamund. To remember the intense flavour of those days, I looked up one of my poems, in which a broken woman goes unrecognized by her fashionable, condescending female interlocutor. The interlocutor had expected to meet Rosamund, but finds a bitter old woman in her place. Curious, and more than a touch amused, I reread more of these poems. Again, self-pity, and contempt for Rosamund. But oddly, a note of longing as well. Rosamund, after all, had been innocent, and young.

I intended, eventually, to write about my life with Saul Bellow. But as I mined the thousands of journal pages scribbled over those twenty years, they seemed written by someone else. My life had been recorded by Rosamund, not by me.

Insofar as life-writing is, or will someday be, about our dead, we need to lend them words. How we feel about them is no less important than our invented language.

A small aside: in Nathan Englander's novel, *The Ministry of Special Cases* (2007), a girl in the bowels of an Argentinian prison discovers a series of gummed up notes or 'caramels' written by the previous occupant of her cell. She swallows the incriminating bits of paper, (they are inside her as she meets her end), but not before memorizing their contents. What Englander does here, is at the centre of his fictional enterprise. He allows us to ingest, and to see thoroughly what would otherwise remain unseen. Here, as elsewhere in his writing, he delivers the last written words of someone who has been erased, or 'disappeared'. Englander creates these caramels, he imagines the words, and puts them in the mouths of these voiceless individuals, thereby resurrecting the dead. This particular novel describes the futile efforts of an Argentinian boy's parents to find their son. They never read the notes secreted in his terror-soaked cell. They never learn anything about what happened to him. But we know. We are in the belly of the girl who swallows the notes that reveal the boy, and with them, we lie at the bottom of the icy river.

These caramels opened up for me a new way of thinking about my dead. What a task to find the words to effect a resuscitation. Might it be done simply? You offer up a sweet. Something the reader might never otherwise taste. Much more attractive than the idea of dissection. Why not oblige our dead through resurrection, through candying.

When Abe Ravelstein dies, Chick readies himself for this task: 'Ravelstein's legacy to me was a subject—he thought he was giving me a subject, perhaps the best one I ever had' (p. 14). 'What line to take in writing a biography', Chick tells us, 'became the problem' (p. 6). But only a very small part of the problem. Chick has a fairly clear notion of where to go with his project. It will be 'freewheeling', 'laidback' (p. 129). Any attempt at rigid chronology will be jettisoned: 'In approaching a man like Ravelstein', he tells us, 'a piecemeal method is perhaps best' (p. 16). Chick knows he will 'write short', he will concentrate *not* on the ideas of Ravelstein as educator but on his personal life. Neither shameful details nor compromising facts need be omitted. But no 'psychobiography'. Chick writes as a friend who sees. The eye he trains on his subject, the seeing eye of the writer, allows him to serve up 'exquisite notation'—caramels.

The enterprise seems straightforward. Ravelstein, dying, spoke these words to Chick, 'You could do a really fine memoir. It's not just a request... I'm laying this on you as an obligation' (p. 129). Obligation's long tendrils bud and flower into heavy burden. Chick cannot locate the 'right position' for launch:

But as the months—years—went by, I couldn't for the life of me find this starting point. 'It should be easy. 'Easily or not at all', or as what's-his-name said, 'If it isn't like birdsong, it ain't right.' (p. 162)

Chick settles in for some serious torment, stewing in guilt syrup of the kind we lesser mortals—we of the unanswered emails, unopened letters, and unwritten papers—burn our tongues on daily. His writer's block scalds—a broken promise to a friend, a batch of uncandied caramels. He has ware-housed Ravelstein in a cell of sorts, confining him to an afterlife in which the pictures have stopped.

Early on, hints that he was not up to the task of portraiture assigned him by his friend troubled Chick. Ravelstein had often teased him about something too soft in his character. Or at least in his self-presentation. Beneath Chick's 'darling doll' (p. 13) act, Ravelstein claimed to detect signs of a sharper awareness. In fact the two men endlessly analysed Chick's desire to be non-confrontational. An *amour-propre* heavily invested in inno-cent display might suit a man of lazy or abstracted intelligence. But there was an oxymoronic ugliness to Chick's knowing-naiveté. Ravelstein attempted to uproot it. Unsuccessfully.

A doubleness to the project enjoined upon Chick by Ravelstein emerges. Chick must square off against the second task before he can turn to the first: '[Ravelstein]...wanted me to write his biography and at the same time he wanted to rescue me from my pernicious habits' (p. 9). But with Ravelstein in the grave, who will Chick talk to about his killing kindness? Odd that in all my prior readings of *Ravelstein*, I had not registered that it is Rosamund who steps up. I'd noticed that she whisks Chick off the island when he gets sick. But saving his life does not ready him to write. Conversation does. Talking to Rosamund, Chick gets unstuck. Pedestrian Rosamund, noticed, if at all, for her well-brought-up ways, speaks boldly. She ignites in Chick the seeing requisite to the telling of the tale. And this silly girl, as I thought her, whose one notable transgression had been to swipe some truffles (no doubt neatly folded in a doily) from a fancy French restaurant, then elbows death aside so that her husband can write down what he has seen.

Chick talks to Rosamund at length about his tendency to feign innocence: 'I do shut off my receptors sometimes and decide, somehow, not to see what there is to be seen. Ravelstein noticed that, naturally. I was the one who failed to notice' (p. 163). He tells her that Ravelstein winced at the company he kept. He mocked him for hanging out with characters like Radu Grielescu, and wasting his storytelling powers. Radu, a man who had belonged to the Romanian Iron Guard. There was Chick, dining with Grielescu, listening politely to his French patter, his jokes, his courtly conversation without paying any 'particular attention', Chick confides. 'I didn't get the drift, and that bothered Ravelstein' (p. 164). Radu Grielescu used Chick for cover. Being seen in public with a prominent Jew who didn't feel moved to expose him as a fascist meant a lot to the man. And at the time Chick had his own less than courageous reasons for giving Radu a pass: the pleasure of studying his quirks, and avoiding confrontation with the volatile Vela, his wife at the time. Rosamund understands Chick's distress, but speaks candidly: 'Well, you were [Ravelstein's] . . . appointed biographer. That you were slow on the uptake couldn't have pleased him' (p. 166). If Chick is to write the Ravelstein memoir he has to locate in himself the source of his unwillingness to examine certain essential questions, chief among them, 'the Jewish question' (p. 167).

Long before Chick and Rosamund became man and wife he had taken up these matters with her. His unwillingness to assume full wakefulness was not a failure of knowledge, he had said, but rather a refusal to take in matters of greatest importance. A kind of colossal stubbornness. Ravelstein, he explained to her, attempted to cut through this stubbornness: 'He turned your face again toward the original. He forced you to reopen what you had closed' (p. 180). Chick had been surprised when Rosamund, then his soft-spoken secretary, offered 'an unusual personal comment'. She had said, 'I think I understand what you are talking about.' And Chick muses, 'I was persuaded by and by that it was really so' (p. 180).

In my original take on the Rosamund character, I missed the role she played as sparring partner to Chick. Introspection always took the shape of dialogue with him. Bellow invites Rosamund to listen as Chick turns his face towards what he elsewhere calls the central event of our time: the destruction of European Jewry. This event is inseparable, in Bellow's analysis, from what he writes of as 'the long crisis of the West' and 'the arrival of nihilism'.[3] There remains no better place to taste the flavour of this agonized reckoning than *Ravelstein*. Bellow does not need pages of discursive argument to deliver his character to the centre of a new awareness. Others may exercise the option not to see, Chick tells Rosamund, but 'for "the chosen" there is no choice' (p. 179). A Jew cannot avoid wrestling with murderous hatred:

Such a volume of hatred and denial of the right to live has never been heard or felt, and the will that willed their death was confirmed and justified by a vast collective agreement that the world would be improved by their disappearance and their extinction. (p. 179)

Chick now keeps company with several Bellow characters who berate themselves for staying too long in the fog. In fact, Bellow repeatedly levels this accusation against himself. In a letter to Cynthia Ozick, Saul writes:

I was too busy becoming a novelist to take note of what was happening in the Forties. I was involved with 'literature' and given over to preoccupations with art, with language, with my struggle on the American scene . . . with anything except the terrible events in Poland. Growing slowly aware of this unspeakable evasion I didn't even know how to begin to admit it into my inner life.

Critics have pounced upon this mea culpa as a Bellovian admission of non-involvement. They fail to mention that, for both characters and author, such self-laceration leads to heightened awareness. Bellow admits error, and spends a lifetime reckoning with the extremity and horror of nihilism. Chick, in conversation with Rosamund (and Saul in his letter to Ozick), have barely introduced their subject. The 'unspeakable evasion' launched by the murderers (who absolve themselves of responsibility because they were 'carrying out orders') infects us all. Who in their right mind stares into the void, or concentrates their energies on plumbing the maddest forms of nihilism? Chick says to Rosamund:

[T]here was a general willingness to live with the destruction of millions. It was like the mood of the century to accept it. In combat you were covered by the special

---

[3] This quotation comes from Saul Bellow to Cynthia Ozick, 29 August 1989, in Benjamin Taylor, ed., *Saul Bellow: Letters* (New York: Viking, 2010), 456. The reference to the destruction of European Jewry as the central event of our time comes from an earlier letter to Ozick, 18 July 1987, in *ibid.*, 438.

allowances made for soldiers. But I'm thinking of the great death populations of the Gulag and the German labor camps. Why does the century—I don't know how else to put it—underwrite such destruction? There is a lameness that comes over all of us when we consider these facts. (p. 169)

A lameness Chick chose to combat. Saul read everything from Thucydides to Nietzsche, from Lucy Dawidowicz to Primo Levi, from Mandelstam to Maccoby. Attempting to see everything seeable about human viciousness, about murderous nihilism, Saul carried his books from city to country, carted large volumes on 'pleasure trips' and borrowed massively from every library that gave him a card. In the twenty years I lived with him, only once did the books on the Holocaust disappear from the bedside. I remember this time, because I enforced the ban. I told him that we would not have Hitler in bed with us while I was pregnant. That did not stop us from talking in the middle of the night, or over breakfast, or after a morning's work. That ban would have been too large to enforce. These conversations began when I was Saul's graduate student, and deepened while Saul was writing *The Bellarosa Connection* (1989) and the essay that was born with it, the recently published, 'A Jewish Writer in America'.[4] One of the first books Saul gave me to read was Varlam Shalamov's *The Kolyma Tales* (1982). Next he handed me Tadeusz Borowski's short story, *This Way for the Gas, Ladies and Gentleman* (1959), with a warning: go slowly with poison, swallowing a bit at a time, and only as much as your soul can bear.

On holiday in their island paradise, Chick and Rosamund lack a remedy for ingested poison. Whenever people talk about 'the banality of evil' (a phrase Saul abhorred), I wonder how many seconds pass before something banal jack-knifes into its opposite. You might smell it immediately. The smell of filth, blood, human fear. You'd have to be far away not to catch a whiff. After Chick eats the poisoned fish, and succumbs to ciguatoxin, he abhors ordinary cooking smells. Knocked flat by the stench of his neighbour's dinner, he fares no better on his daily diet of books—in particular, an account of cannibalism in the New Guinea rainforest, where blood and crimson orchids mix, and the smell of roasting human thigh turns out to be particularly savoury. Failing, Chick reads on: during the siege of Leningrad

---

[4] 'A Jewish Writer in America', originally a talk given by Bellow in 1988, was first published in two parts in the *New York Review of Books* (27 October and 10 November 2011).

by the Nazis, people ate human flesh. Examples of cannibalism abound. He tells Rosamund, 'And surely our own nihilists who tell you that everything is permitted would have to agree that cannibalism is perfectly logical' (p. 194).

In his feverish state, Chick's thoughts return to Grielescu, but with none of the old amusement. Now he wonders whether or not the man had been 'in league with killers' (p. 202)—and no ordinary murderers these, but, as Ravelstein had once reminded Chick, murderers who butchered Jews and hung them on meat-hooks. In his defenceless condition Chick no longer shirks a head-on look at the 'will to viciousness' (p. 204). This awareness had been missing from what Ravelstein described as Chick's natural gift—the capacity to take a reading of reality—'to put your loving face to it and press your hands against it' (p. 203). But why must this hideous extra measure of seeing be demanded of Chick? Why on earth would Jews, who were the victims of nihilism, have the additional duty to turn their faces towards it? A strange understanding of 'chosenness', this: 'the Jews had been used to give the entire species a measure of human viciousness' (p. 174), and continue to be used in this way. We as Jews don't have the option of pretending not to know that measure.

When Chick emerges from his intensive care ordeal the measure remains, and once released to write his story, he doesn't say he has come close to dying, but rather that he has 'died and risen again'. He tells Rosamund of a 'curious distance in my mind between the old way of seeing (false) and the new way (strange but liberating)' (p. 216). A rather tortured path to ridding yourself of writer's block! But Chick sought radical revision. On the island he had put it this way to Rosamund:

I don't suppose that when he directed me to write an account of his life he expected me to settle for what was characteristic—characteristic of me, is what I mean, naturally. (p. 186)

In casting off what was characteristic, Chick can now sing, along with Handel's Solomon, 'How vain were all I knew.' His new birdsong has not come easily.

Chick needed Rosamund: first for conversation, then for understanding, and finally for love. He recognized her strengths early; I confess to being late. I completely overlooked this passage:

Only Rosamund, normally flexible, ladylike, deferential, and genteel now revealed (no question about it) an underlying hardness and the will that showed how prepared she was . . . (p. 199)

Prepared for what? Prepared to save his life, and to continue to sing Handel's 'Live Forever!' though Chick lay dying. Chick's hospitalization, described briefly in *Ravelstein* by way of the dreams and hallucinations of the sufferer, had also to be endured by Rosamund, who was fully awake.

Rosamund suffers from a surfeit of 'humane impulses', she is 'tender-minded' (p. 184), overwhelmed by the pain of others, '—she is like that' (p. 183), Chick sums up, not altogether disapprovingly. Life has its own way of delivering a woman from her 'girlish queasiness' (p. 185), but Ravelstein's remedy for delayed ripening was to invite laughter. Nothing a little *immenso giubilo* (p. 118) wouldn't cure. What to do about those poor red salamanders in the middle of the road? Throw them into a spaghetti sauce, says Chick. Did I smile at his joke then? I certainly laugh when I read it now, but characteristically, relapse into seriousness. I'm back on the parched beach with the shiny lobsters, swung by their antennae under the hot sun. Served up in sauces of their own. And who am I kidding—I still ferry the salamanders to the side of the road. Chick's ribbing—Rosamund, how do you know you're putting them where they want to go—only increased my solicitude.

From Chick's perspective, the fact that Rosamund feels the suffering of others proves essential to his survival. As he sees it, the application of the 'humane tape measure' more often serves as evasion, as 'a cover for our heartlessness' (p. 185), than proof of a more rigorous or scientific outlook. Delicate, decidedly short on confidence, Rosamund may seem squeamish, but by book's end she uncovers massive reserves of untapped toughness: 'Yes, I was tempted to drop out', Chick admits, 'but she had concentrated her soul entirely on my survival' (p. 227). Her hardness endures: 'Rosamund was determined that I should go on living. It was she, of course, who had saved me—flew me back from the Caribbean just in time, saw me through intensive care, sleeping in a chair beside my bed' (p. 225).

Rosamund in *Ravelstein* was never a slender figure. In the last pages of the novel, the author singles her out for a stunning tribute, one that made me squirm every time I read it:

Rosamund kept me from dying. I can't represent this without taking it on frontally and I can't take it on frontally while my interests remain centered on Ravelstein. Rosamund had studied love—Rousseauan romantic love and the Platonic Eros as well, with Ravelstein—but she knew far more about it than either her teacher or her husband. (p. 251)

Rosamund did not know more about love than her husband or her teacher. It wasn't about knowing. She was in love, and had limitless expectations about its endlessness—more oceanic, certainly, than her fine education ought to have allowed. Singing 'Live Forever', as she carries Chick through the water she inhabits the world of pictures. And when the idyll transforms itself into nightmare, her strength increases exponentially, fuelled not by hardness, but by love.

After losing a round or two to Time and Death, I bear little resemblance to that girl, but I have been moved by her story. My situation is peculiar: here I am, writing about a character who helped her husband tell his tale, but then found herself unable to tell her own. Chick with his empty notebooks; me with my black screen. His softness delayed his introspection—I may have hardened myself against mine.

Opening my *Ravelstein* I read this inscription: 'Beyond Rosamund there is Janis herself to whom I turn almost hourly for navigational data, for explanations—from her grateful husband S.B. April 2000.' To whom should Janis turn? If I am to move towards creation I need my own revolution in the direction of laughter, lightness, brio—more of Saul's, 'easily, or not at all'. During my own long nights of unravelling I reread Bellow, and was often drawn to this sentence in *Mr. Sammler's Planet* (1970), 'we watch these living speed like birds over the surface of a water, and one will dive or plunge, but not come up again and never be seen any more'.[5] I wrote then that when it was Saul's turn, he simply disappeared, taking with him what I knew of soaring. Unless. Unless I could carry things back to the surface—words, stories, songs about Saul. The fictional Rosamund deserves her rest. My task remains to write that book of caramels.

A voice warns: leave creation to the novelists. After all, it was Saul who returned Ravelstein to Chick, resurrecting him in the book's final pages:

Ravelstein, dressing to go out, is talking to me, and I go back and forth with him while trying to hear what he is saying. The music is pouring from his hi-fi—the many planes of his bare, bald head go before me: in the corridor between his living room and his monumental master bedroom. He stops before his pier-glass—no wall mirrors here—and puts in the heavy gold cufflinks, buttons up the Jermyn Street Kisser & Asser striped shirt—American Trustworthy laundry-and-cleaners deliver

---

[5] Saul Bellow, *Mr. Sammler's Planet* (New York: Viking, 1970), 236.

his shirts puffed out with tissue paper. He winds up his tie lifting the collar that crackles with starch. He makes a luxurious knot. The unsteady fingers, long, ill-coordinated, nervous to the point of decadence, make a double lap. Ravelstein likes a big tie-knot—after all, he is a large man. Then he sits down on the beautifully cured fleeces of his bed and puts on the Poulsen and Skone tan Wellington boots. His left foot is several sizes smaller than the right but there is no limp. He smokes, of course, he is always smoking, and tilts the head away from the smoke while he knots and pulls the knot into place. The cast and orchestra are pouring out the *Italian Maiden in Algiers*. This is dressing music, accessory or mood music, but Ravelstein takes a Nietzschean view, favorable to comedy and bandstands. Better Bizet and *Carmen* than Wagner and the *Ring*. He likes the volume of his powerful set turned up to the maximum. The ringing phone is left to the answering machine. He puts on his $5,000 suit, an Italian wool mixed with silk. He pulls down the coat cuff with his fingertips and polishes the top of his head. And perhaps he relishes having so many instruments serenading him, so many musicians in attendance. He corresponds with compact disc companies behind the Iron Curtain. He has helpers going to the post office to pay customs duties for him.

'What do you think of this recording, Chick?' he says. 'They're playing the original ancient seventeenth-century instruments.'

He loses himself in sublime music, a music in which ideas are dissolved, reflecting these ideas in the form of feeling. He carries them down into the street with him. There's an early snow on the tall shrubs, the same shrubs filled with a huge flock of parrots—the ones that escaped from cages and now build their long nest sacks in the back alleys. They are feeding on the red berries. Ravelstein looks at me, laughing with pleasure and astonishment, gesturing because he can't be heard in all this bird-noise. (pp. 252–3)

Saul's pictures don't stop. Even after death.

7

'From Memory': Literary Encounters and Life-Writing

Hermione Lee

Life-writing is a useful and suggestive turn of phrase. It was used by Virginia Woolf when she came to start her autobiography, 'Sketch of the Past', towards the end of her life in 1939, when she speaks of the importance of 'invisible presences' in a life story: the memory of a dead parent, the consciousness of what other people do or say, public opinion, all those magnets 'which attract us this way to be like that, or repel us the other and make us different from that'. Those are the 'invisible presences' which play such a large part in everyone's lives: 'Well, if we cannot analyse these invisible presences, we know very little of the subject of the memoir; and again how futile life-writing becomes. I see myself as a fish in a stream; deflected; held in place; but cannot describe the stream.'[1]

The term suggests, too, how various and mixed are the narratives which tell a life story. Autobiographers often stray into fiction, and infiltrate the lives of others into their own stories. Biographers too may find themselves straying into fiction in their writing of life stories, as they make use, and try to make sense, of a great mass of autobiographical, biographical, and

---

[1] Virginia Woolf, 'Sketch of the Past', in *Moments of Being*, ed. Jeanne Schulkind and Hermione Lee (London: Pimlico, 2002), 92.

historical data. Biographies deploy memoirs, retrospects, letters, diaries, journals, witness testimony, film, newspapers, legal contracts, bills, post-cards, photographs, wills, and, in the future, by means yet to be established and regularized, the vast virtual hoard of communications via social media.

At the heart of these impure, multilayered and multisourced narratives, is always the desire to get a vivid sense of the person, or people, who are the subject. The reader's first question of a biographer is always going to be, what was she, or he, like? Other questions (like why, or how do you know, or do we approve, or does it matter?) may follow. But 'likeness' must be there. Whatever form of 'life-writing' we are drawn to, we always greedily want moments of intimacy, revelation, immediacy, and inwardness. We are like the readers Elizabeth Gaskell was thinking of when she noted to herself, as she started her life of Charlotte Brontë, 'Get as many anecdotes as possible, if you love your reader and want to be read, get anecdotes!'[2]

The particular kind of anecdote this chapter is going to deal with is the moment of an encounter which changes a life, and the remembering and telling of such moments. The chapter asks how such stories are remembered, how they get told, and what a biographer can do with them. Most of the examples I will use here are literary encounters between great writers. But a legendary musical encounter provides a useful starting point.

The composer Alexander Goehr once told me the story of the legendary encounter between Puccini and Schoenberg. He told me that Puccini, very ill and composing *Turandot* in the 1920s, encountered Schoenberg, who was conducting the first performance of *Pierrot Lunaire* at Florence. Puccini went to the performance and was then sent a score by Schoenberg. On reading it, he said, 'This is the music of the future. I don't understand it, but I know it will prevail—and I will never write another note.' Shortly thereafter he died, and *Turandot* was completed by someone else.

Pursuing this story with interest, I found this version in Julian Budden's 2002 book on Puccini:

An event that Puccini was determined not to miss was the first performance of Schoenberg's *Pierrot Lunaire* in Florence on 1 April 1924 under the master's direction. Through the composer Alfredo Casella he obtained an introduction to Schoenberg himself, who received him cordially and provided him with a score with which to follow the performance.

<hr/>

[2] Jenny Uglow, *Elizabeth Gaskell: A Habit of Stories* (London: Faber & Faber, 1993), 406.

Puccini's reaction was noted by a witness, as follows:

To arrive at a conception of such a musical world one must have gone beyond a normal sense of harmony, that's to say one must possess a nature quite different from what one has at present. Who can say whether Schoenberg may not be a point of departure for a goal in the distant future. Just now—unless I understand nothing—we are as far from a concrete realization of it as Mars is from Earth.

The biography then tells the story of how Puccini continued to work on *Turandot*, though very ill with throat cancer. On one occasion the conversation turned to Wagner, and Puccini played the Prelude to *Tristan* on his piano. Then, as Budden describes it, he suddenly 'threw down the score' and 'burst out': 'Enough of this music! . . . Heaven help us if we get caught up in it! This terrible music annihilates us and makes us unable to achieve anything!' On 29 November 1924 he died on the operating table, leaving *Turandot* unfinished.[3]

The differences between these two versions of the story are intriguing (and suggest, too, how such stories are always changing shape). Alexander Goehr had, perhaps, conflated the Schoenberg and the Wagner anecdotes; and he had made Puccini's end more operatic. But the essence of the story, in both versions, is Puccini's sense that he had encountered, in Schoenberg, the man of the distant future, and that he was being left behind in the past.

One of the famous stories of encounters between literary figures I will mention in this chapter is that between the political philosopher Isaiah Berlin and the poet Anna Akhmatova, in Leningrad, in November 1945. The encounter is narrated, many years later, in Isaiah Berlin's *Personal Impressions*, alongside other accounts of remarkable men and women Berlin had known. In his 1980 introduction to this volume, Noel Annan notes Berlin's interest in human beings, rather than abstract ideas:

Like Hamlet he stands amazed at what a piece of work is man; unlike Hamlet he delights in man . . . His thought, his theories, always refer to people . . . To see Shelley plain, to meet as Berlin has done men and women such as Pasternak or Stravinsky, Virginia Woolf or Picasso, Russell or Einstein, he finds greatly exciting.[4]

---

[3] Julian Budden, *Puccini: His Life and Works* (Oxford: Oxford University Press, 2002), 441, 443.

[4] Isaiah Berlin, *Personal Impressions* (London: Hogarth Press, 1980), introduction by Noel Annan, xxx, xiv.

As Berlin himself said, in 1958, of his friendship with Chaim Weizmann: 'To know a great man must permanently transform one's ideas of what human beings can be or do.'[5]

Noel Annan refers there to the much-cited poem by Browning, 'Memorabilia' (1855), which was inspired by an accidental meeting in a bookshop with someone who had known Browning's early hero, Shelley. The poem famously begins:

> Ah, did you once see Shelley plain,
> And did he stop and speak to you
> And did you speak to him again?
> How strange it seems and new!

This chapter is about those moments of 'seeing Shelley plain', moments which 'permanently transform one's ideas of what human beings can be or do'. These are not encounters which lead to long friendships or to numerous further encounters, but encounters which remain isolated in the memory, as turning points or key moments in a life. For a biographer, such moments can reveal a great deal about the people involved. But what is also of interest is how these momentary encounters are remembered and narrated. So much depends on who the witnesses are, how soon and by whom the record is written down, to what extent the memories are hardened, distorted, and revised in the telling, and what use is made of the encounter by memoirists and biographers.

Memory, we all know, can play us false. Memoirists, fiction writers, autobiographers, and biographers are always telling us so, even while they are busily engaged in acts of remembering. As the fine American writer William Maxwell wisely remarked:

What we refer to confidently as memory . . . is really a form of story-telling that goes on continually in the mind and often changes with the telling. Too many conflicting emotional interests are involved for life ever to be wholly acceptable, and possibly it is the work of the storyteller to rearrange things so that they conform to this end. In any case, in talking about the past, we lie with every breath we draw.[6]

---

[5] *Ibid.*, 32.
[6] William Maxwell, *So Long, See You Tomorrow* (1980; London: Vintage, 1996), 27.

A more technical account of the same idea is given by Ciaran Benson in *The Cultural Psychology of Self* (2001),[7] drawing attention to the importance of an audience or interlocutor in the process of remembering. Theorists of memory, going back to Frederick Bartlett, in *Remembering* (1932), frequently argue that memory retains 'a little outstanding detail', while the remainder of what we remember represents an elaboration that is merely influenced by the original event. Bartlett referred to this key characteristic of memory as reconstructive, as opposed to reproductive: 'We are so good at this sort of reconstruction ... that we are often consciously unaware that it has happened. This seems especially likely to happen when a memory is told and retold ... In such situations the "reconstructed" memory often seems as real as the "recollected" memory.'[8]

The relationship between the event itself and the reconstruction of the event is central to these 'encounter narratives'. Other people, too, will take hold of and alter a story in the process of its being told. When the two people involved in the encounter are of great fame, interest, and distinction, these meetings can often be the subject of rival versions, disputes and, controversies.

The British satirist Craig Brown published a comic anthology of 101 such curious and coincidental meetings in 2011 called *One on One*, which includes such intriguing pairings as Harpo Marx and G. B. Shaw, Marilyn Monroe and Khrushchev, Edward Heath and Sickert. There are some excellent anecdotes here, for instance of the biographer Michael Holroyd sitting next to Princess Margaret at dinner. Everyone felt they had to indulge her, so when she started doing terrible impersonations of famous people, for instance of Edna O'Brien with 'a heavy Irish brogue', he 'laughed dutifully at the first two, which he vaguely recognised', and again at the third—'a high pitched nasal squeak'—which he did not. ' "If I may say so, ma'am, that's your funniest yet!" he remarked. The moment he did so, it occurred to him that the Princess had, in fact, reverted to her own voice.'[9] Brown is more interested in the comedy of the anecdotes than in the ways

---

[7] Ciaran Benson, *The Cultural Psychology of Self: Place, Morality and Art in Human Worlds* (London: Routledge, 2001).

[8] Jonathan K. Foster, *Memory: A Very Short Introduction* (Oxford: Oxford University Press, 2009), 12, 14.

[9] Craig Brown, *One on One* (London: Fourth Estate, 2011), 106.

they have been remembered. But he does mention the unreliability of witnesses, giving seven different versions, for instance, of Proust's only encounter with James Joyce. He prefers Walt Disney's version to Igor Stravinsky's of their meeting over *Fantasia* (which cannibalized the *Rite of Spring* for its score). Stravinsky remembered hating it, Disney remembered him liking it. 'Whose memory are we to trust?' asks Craig Brown. 'There may be a temptation to favour the highbrow over the lowbrow...but self-delusion rains on all, high and low.'[10]

The remembering of remarkable meetings often follows certain patterns, common to the genre of what might be called 'encounter narratives'. These features show up, particularly, in accounts of meetings which do not mark the start of lifelong friendships, but which remain singular, striking memories in the two peoples' lives, not blurred or muddied by regular later encounters or long-term changes of feelings.

If any of us thinks back to the moments in our life when we have met a remarkable man or woman, it is likely that certain features will stand out more than others. Probably we will remember who introduced us, how the meeting came about, something about the room or setting where it took place, something of what we ate or drank there, and one or two things the person said. But, unless we are detailed diary-keepers or blessed with total recall, we might not remember the whole conversation, or what clothes we were wearing, or who else came and went, or what we said ourselves during the meeting. What we retain from the encounter is probably what we said about it to others soon afterwards, and what we continue to say. We keep our nugget of the encounter, we treasure it and polish it, and we produce it when we can, when the moment for the story is right.

What are the common features of the narratives of such encounters? They are often a mixture of comedy, excitement, bathos, or disappointment, with feelings of high emotion cut across by banal details of food and drink, physical discomfort or social embarrassment. They are often a meeting between a younger person—the visitor—and an older—the visitee. They often contain within them that sense, as when Puccini met Schoenberg, of the past encountering the future. They often mention the gatekeeper, the introducer, the person through whom the intense encounter became

---

[10] *Ibid.*, 56.

possible, and this person is often a minor or even irrelevant character (someone whose own vantage point on the event would be of interest, but is hardly ever registered). Other 'minor' characters may appear, interrupting or obstructing or terminating the meeting. Isaiah Berlin's legendary meeting with Akhmatova, as he recalls it, is particularly rich in such minor figures, rather like a scene in a Russian play. The narratives usually include some description of place. Most often the meeting will be indoors, and will depend on the famous person being fixed in their home, visitable, known to be at that address. Famous people have often suffered from their visitability: Tennyson in famous old age loathed the fact he had become a 'social curiosity' and that people would line up along his garden wall at Farringford with their heads sticking over the wall to try and catch a sighting of him. The novelist Evelyn Waugh, in the words of the novelist Penelope Fitzgerald, would emerge from his study to meet visitors 'threateningly aloof... with the message: I am bored, you are frightened'.[11]

There are many 'encounter narratives' in the history of major figures in Anglo-American literature, and they share some common features. Oscar Wilde, on his attention-grabbing American lecture tour of 1882, wearing his brown velveteen knee breeches, went, like all the world, to Camden, New Jersey, to meet the bearded, white-haired Walt Whitman. He was given a glass of elderberry wine made by Walt's sister-in-law. Wilde (trying perhaps to sound a touch like Jesus) said, looking back on the encounter: 'If it had been vinegar, I would have drunk it all the same, for I have an admiration for that man which I can hardly express.' He sat at Whitman's feet on a low stool, with his hand on the older poet's knee. Whitman was entranced, and described him as 'a great big, splendid boy, so frank, and outspoken, and manly'. 'And he had the *good sense* to take a great fancy to *me!*', Whitman added. Wilde said he was 'the grandest man I have ever seen', and boasted in later years that 'the kiss of Walt Whitman is still on my lips'. So the encounter between the old bohemian sage of Camden and the young Irish aesthete and dandy became a symbolic validation and benediction.[12]

[11] Penelope Fitzgerald, *A House of Air* (London: Flamingo, 2003), 330.

[12] Gay Wilson Allen, *The Solitary Singer: A Critical Biography of Walt Whitman* (1955; Chicago: Chicago University Press, 1967), 502–3; Richard Ellmann, *Oscar Wilde* (London: Hamish Hamilton, 1987), 160–3.

Transatlantic crossings worked the other way when famous English authors were visited by their American admirers. The author as visitable pilgrimage site, a literary tourist destination like Hampton Court or St Paul's, was a phenomenon which had grown up during the nineteenth century. British literary visitors to America 'took in' Emerson or Whitman, as part of their grand tour; American devotees, acquaintances, and fans regularly went to introduce themselves to Wordsworth or Carlyle or Dickens, as part of their cultural pilgrimage.

When the transatlantic visitor was entirely unknown to the famous literary icon, the encounters often did not go well. Edith Wharton, making herself at home in England in her forties, from 1908 onwards, her path smoothed by the fame of *The House of Mirth* (1905) and her friendship with Henry James, enjoyed being welcomed by grand English hostesses in their ancient country seats and their big London houses. Here she could be, as writers most like to be, at once an insider and an outsider, a welcome guest who was also a sharp observer of the English upper classes. She would make unforgiving use of this material, many years later, in her unfinished novel *The Buccaneers* (1937). But she was less at ease with the quest for literary lions in their homes, where she felt awkward, and intrusive.

She never forgot the day, in November 1908, when Henry James insisted on taking her to Box Hill to visit George Meredith. Wharton was, at heart, a shy person, and extremely reluctant to be introduced. She wanted to stay in the car; she hated 'human sight-seeing'. James bullied her into the house to meet the deaf and immobilized author, in a small room that seemed full of people, including Meredith's daughter, and a nurse eating her supper. At first all was embarrassment and discomfort. This changed to delight when Wharton found that Meredith was in the middle of reading her most recent book, *A Motor-Flight through France* (1908). So, in this encounter, one form of transatlantic life-writing, the elite travel narrative, paved the way for another, the cultural encounter between older and younger writer.

Their exchange, though, was a failure. She could not respond to his courtly, generous questions about her book, because he could not hear anything she said. Instead she stepped back to let 'the great bright tide of monologue' flow on in James' direction. Watching the 'nobly confronted profiles of the two old friends', she said in her reminiscences, 'I felt I was in great company, and was glad.'[13] Both Wharton and Wilde retrospectively idealized their visits to their literary heroes, and turned them into a moment of benediction from older to younger writer.

A much less successful encounter between a young woman American writer and an older, venerated English author took place a few years before Edith Wharton's meeting with Meredith. The keynote of this encounter is disappointment. In 1902, a twenty-nine year-old Nebraskan journalist, Willa Cather, who was writing poems and stories and was full of raw, passionate ardour for English and European culture, went abroad for the first time, with two young women friends. As for so many American writers, her European experience felt to her as much like a homecoming as a discovery: the landscape and architecture and social panorama acted as confirmations of well-loved, long-known books and paintings.

She and her friends took the usual American cultural tourist's itinerary in England, exclaiming like Hawthorne over the Liverpool slums, admiring by contrast Chester's medieval charm, recognizing Hogarth and Dickens and Kipling in the seedy inhabitants of London's streets, seeking out painters' studios and the theatre. But as a cultural tourist she had a specialism, a deep love of the poetry of A. E. Housman. Cather's Housman quest took her to Ludlow and Shrewsbury in search of Shropshire Lad settings, and resulted in some wistful, romantic, neo-pagan Housmanesque verses. If that had been all, no damage would have been done to her romantic hero worship. But unfortunately her pilgrimage to England also involved an unsolicited visit to the poet's house. She extracted his address from his publishers, and she and her two friends turned up at the front door of what turned out to be a dreary little Highgate boarding house. An embarrassed and reluctant Housman, faced with three strange mid-Western American girls, one of them enthusing about his poetry, took refuge in a long conversation with another of them about her thesis on French literature and about Latin manuscripts. Cather was mortified by the encounter, which deflated her ideal of the poet and punctured her romantic quest for him. In later years the episode would come back to haunt her. Ford Madox Ford made up an embellished version of it. In the 1940s, by

---

[13] Edith Wharton, *A Backward Glance* (New York: Scribner's, 1934), ch. 10; Edith Wharton to Sarah Norton, 18 November 1908, in *The Letters of Edith Wharton*, ed. R. W. B. and Nancy Lewis (New York: Simon & Schuster, 1988), 165.

which time she was as renowned and self-protective as Housman had been, importunate Housman scholars badgered her with questions about their meeting.[14]

That comical and poignant example of a disappointing literary encounter suggests the problems that can arise when there are transatlantic differences at play, as well as differences of temperament, gender, and age. The famous first meeting (there were a few more to follow) between Charlotte Brontë and Thackeray, on 4 December 1849, was also an uneasy encounter. Charlotte had published *Jane Eyre* and *Shirley* under the name of 'Currer Bell'; the fact that Currer Bell was a woman and that the woman was Charlotte Brontë was just becoming an open secret, but Brontë still did not want it widely known. She went to London to stay with her publisher, George Smith, and the high moment of the visit was the night her hero, the great Thackeray, came to dinner. Unfortunately, she had had no breakfast and no lunch and by dinner time she was, she reported, 'thoroughly faint from inanition . . . excitement and exhaustion together made savage work of me that evening. What he thought of me—I cannot tell.' She cast a sharp eye on him:

He is a very tall man . . . with a peculiar face—not handsome—very ugly indeed—generally somewhat satirical and stern in expression, but capable also of a kind look . . . It is better—I should think to have him for a friend than an enemy—for he is a most formidable looking personage. [I listened to him as he conversed with the other gentlemen]—all he says is most simple but often cynical, harsh and contradictory.

Thackeray went off to his club and told everyone he had been dining with Jane Eyre, thereby unmasking her. He described 'the trembling little frame, the little hand, the great honest eyes', and said that 'an impetuous honesty seemed to me to characterise the woman'.

On their few later meetings, Brontë found him cynical, unserious, and worldly, he found her stiff, over-idealistic, and 'high-falutin'. It's a fine example of a brief encounter between two great writers who could not be more different—physically, socially, intellectually—and who could not

---

[14] Hermione Lee, *Willa Cather: A Life Saved Up* (London: Virago, 1989), 60–1; Willa Cather to Carl J. Weber, 31 January 1945, Willa Cather to Ferris Greenslet, 9 May 1945, in *The Selected Letters of Willa Cather*, ed. Andrew Jewell and Janis Stout (New York: Knopf, 2013), 637–8, 642–3.

find common ground. Yet they admired each other, and fundamentally wished each other well.[15] So such encounters are often about awkwardness or resistance, rather than sympathy or high emotion.

One of the most eloquent and vivid, though not always kind, narrators of literary encounters is Virginia Woolf, whose diaries and letters make rich stories out of her meetings with remarkable men and women. These are almost always written very close to the time of the event, so they have the raw, quick detail of instant recollection. Indeed she makes jokes to herself about her need to turn people she meets, instantaneously, into narrative. 'When people come to tea I cant [sic] say to them, "Now wait a minute while I write an account of you."'[16] She is always acutely aware, in writing these meetings down, how fast one starts to make a selective, settled shape out of an encounter. She talks about this in her record of meeting Thomas Hardy, whom she and Leonard went to visit in his house in Dorchester, Max Gate, on 23 July 1926.

Woolf was forty-four, Hardy was eighty-six, and would die two years later. The reason for meeting was that Hardy had known Woolf's father Leslie Stephen well. The gatekeeper of the visit was Mrs Hardy; the minor, but important character was Hardy's dog Wessex, 'who bites people'. In a long diary entry written two days later, Woolf puts down everything she could recall, circling back over the encounter with as much detail as possible. It is evident that she partly has in mind that this record of Virginia Woolf's only meeting with Thomas Hardy may be of interest to posterity. First she 'does' the parlourmaid, bringing in the silver cake stands, and Mrs Hardy—resigned to yet another lot of visitors, more interested in Wessex the dog than anything else. Then Hardy, trotting in (she uses the verb several times), 'a little puffy-cheeked cheerful old man, with an atmosphere cheerful & businesslike in addressing us, rather like an old doctors or solicitors, saying "Well now—" as he shook hands'.

He took his tea, 'extremely affable & aware of his duties', later offering Leonard a whisky and water—evidently a competent host. He talked about

---

[15] Juliet Barker, *The Brontës* (London: Weidenfeld & Nicholson, 1994), 618, 620–1; *Selected Letters of Charlotte Brontë*, ed. Margaret Smith (Oxford: Oxford University Press, 2007), 150–1, 165; *The Oxford Companion to the Brontës* (Oxford: Oxford University Press, 2003), 494.

[16] Virginia Woolf, Diary, 18 April 1918, *The Diary of Virginia Woolf*, vol. 1: *1915–1919*, ed. Anne Olivier Bell (Harmondsworth: Penguin, 1979), 139.

her father, a little bit about his books, about mutual friends, and about the dog. Meanwhile Mrs Hardy, Woolf noted, 'was leaning upon the tea table, not eating gazing out'. Woolf tried to get him to say which of his books he would choose to read on a train, but 'he was not going to be drawn'. She said *she* had brought *The Mayor of Casterbridge* with her to read on the train. 'And did it hold your interest?' he asked. He 'trotted off' to sign a copy of a book for her, and came back with *Life's Little Ironies*, with her name spelt 'Wolff', which, she thought, must have 'given him some anxiety'. She asked him to pet Wessex, who 'went on wheezing away'. Summing him up she noted his impressive simplicity, his 'freedom, ease & vitality', his interest in facts, his 'setting no great stock by literature', his bright eyes. She felt how he would be 'naturally swept off into imagining & creating without a thought of its being difficult or remarkable; becoming obsessed; & living in imagination'. The visit made a great impression on her. When she came to write about Hardy on his death she called him a 'great unconscious writer'. The simplicity, the lack of self-consciousness which she noted in him in person also seemed to her to apply to his work—and, by implication, contrasted with her own arduous struggle to find the right form and shape for her own fiction.

For weeks after her visit to Hardy she talked to all her friends about it, and was aware that she was shaping it as an encounter narrative as she retold it to herself and to others, using a musical language for how this process works: 'I was telling myself the story of our visit to the Hardys, & I began to compose it: that is to say to dwell on Mrs Hardy leaning on the table, looking out, apathetically, vaguely; & so would soon bring everything into harmony with that as the dominant theme. But the actual event was different.'[17] *But the actual event was different*: it is a strong warning note for all readers of 'encounter narratives'.

That warning note has to be kept firmly in mind for one of the most famous of twentieth-century literary encounters, Berlin's with Akhmatova. His essay on 'Meetings with Russian Writers' was written, in English, in 1980 of a meeting which took place, in Russian, in 1945. He makes a point of saying that he did not keep a diary and that he has relied on his very intense

---

[17] Virginia Woolf, Diary, 25 July 1926, *The Diary of Virginia Woolf*, vol. 3, ed. Anne Olivier Bell, 96–102 ; Hermione Lee, *Virginia Woolf* (London: Vintage, 1997), 529–31.

memories of the event. Yet this moving 'encounter narrative' is historically vivid and dramatically convincing.[18]

In 1945, Isaiah Berlin, taking time out of his life as an Oxford don, was employed by the British Embassy in Washington to write a despatch from Moscow about post-war American–Soviet–British relations. His visit to Russia in 1945 was his first return since his childhood. (He was born into a Russian-Jewish family in Riga in 1909; the family moved to Petrograd, as St Petersburg then was, in 1916, and then to England in 1921.) He talked to politicians, writers, composers, critics, and bureaucrats. He wanted to know what had happened to the great flowering of talent and genius which had briefly flourished after the Revolution and then been ruthlessly crushed under Stalin. He met Pasternak and other writers, and in Leningrad was put in touch, almost by chance, with Anna Akhmatova.

Akhmatova was one of the great quartet of writers (the others were Mandelstam, Marina Tsvetaeva, and Pasternak) who had come to adulthood in the early twentieth century at a time of war and revolution. Her close friend Mandelstam had been killed during Stalin's years of terror. Tsvetaeva had committed suicide. Akhmatova's first husband, the poet Gumilyov, was killed on Lenin's orders in 1921. Her second husband would die in prison in 1953. Her son had been in prison since 1938, and had only just been released. Her work had been banned for publication for decades. She had not been to Europe for thirty-four years. She lived in bleak

---

[18] Isaiah Berlin [IB], 'Meetings with Russian Writers in 1945 and 1956', Maurice Bowra Lecture, Wadham College Oxford, 13 May 1980, published in *New York Review of Books*, 20 November 1980, then revised and published in *Personal Impressions* [PI] (London: Hogarth Press, 1980), 156–209. IB's two contemporary accounts of his visit to Leningrad are 'A Visit to Leningrad', 1945, first published in *Times Literary Supplement*, 2001, then in *The Soviet Mind* [SM], ed. Henry Hardy (Washington, DC: Brookings Institution Press, 2004; 2011), 21–8, and 'The Arts in Russia under Stalin', a formal report written 23 March 1946, published in edited form in *New York Review of Books*, 19 October 2000, first published in full in SM. See also: Michael Ignatieff, *Isaiah Berlin* (1998; London: Vintage, 2000), ch.11; Anatoly Naiman, 'Akhmatova and Sir', in *The Book of Isaiah*, ed. Henry Hardy (Woodbridge: The Boydell Press, 2009), 62–81; and comments by IB in *Flourishing: Isaiah Berlin, Letters 1928–1946* (London: Chatto & Windus, 2004), and *Enlightening: Isaiah Berlin, Letters 1946–1960*, ed. Henry Hardy (London: Chatto & Windus, 2011). For Akhmatova's version of the encounter, see György Dalos, *The Guest from the Future: Anna Akhmatova and IB*, trans. Anthony Wood (London: John Murray, 1998); Anatoly Naiman, *Remembering Anna Akhmatova*, trans. Wendy Rosslyn (1989; New York: Henry Holt, 1991); Amanda Haight, *Akhmatova: A Poetic Pilgrimage* (Oxford: Oxford University Press, 1976); Josephine von Zitzewitz, 'That's How It Was', *Times Literary Supplement*, 9 September 2011, 14–15.

and deprived circumstances in a room in the crumbling Fountain House, by the Fontanka Canal, with nothing on the wall except a drawing of her done by Modigliani in Paris in 1911, little furniture, little privacy, and little to eat. Here she was writing her long, epic 'Poem without a Hero'.

Their encounter almost did not happen: it was set about with awkward interruptions, obstructions, and false starts, at once comic and sinister. A number of 'gatekeepers' (most of whom turned out, according to later commentators, to be KGB spies) had to be broached. But eventually, at about midnight, they were left alone, and talked all night. They talked about Russia, friends, writers, music, their lives, the terrible fate of those close to her, and her tragic history. She recited some of Byron's *Don Juan* to him, in an unintelligible accent, which at once moved and embarrassed him. Interspersed with tears, she read him the unfinished 'Poem without a Hero'. 'Even then', he noted, 'I realised I was listening to a work of genius.' It was a memorial to her life as a poet and 'to the past of the city, St Petersburg, which was part of her being'—and of his. She described the years of Stalin's terror, the 'fate of loved ones', the 'torture and slaughter of millions of innocents'. In the middle of the night, they shared a dish of boiled potatoes brought to them by her son—it was all there was to eat. Then they began to speak of other writers, including Chekhov, whom she disliked for his absence of 'heroism and martyrdom', Tolstoy, whom she criticized for his philistine morality and egocentricity, and Dostoievsky, whom she worshipped. They disagreed over Turgenev, whose delicate subtlety attracted Berlin much more than it did her.

The conversation became increasingly intense and personal. She talked at length about music, especially Beethoven. She described her 'loneliness and isolation' and said that her 'sustenance' came from 'literature and the images of the Past', and from translating. She spoke, he said, 'without the slightest trace of self-pity, like a princess in exile'. As the night wore on, Berlin smoked his miniature Swiss cigars, and the cigar smoke filled the room. He was longing to pee, but did not want to go down the hall to the lavatory in case it stopped her talking. Outside they could hear the frozen rain falling onto the Fontanka Canal. For him, it was (as his biographer describes it) an intense passage of validation: 'Here was the greatest living poet of his native language talking to him ... as if he knew everyone she knew, had read everything that she had read, understood what she said and what she meant.' For her it was meeting 'a messenger between the two

Russian cultures—one in external exile, the other in internal exile—which had been split apart by the revolution'.[19]

He was thirty-six, she was fifty-nine. He was a privileged visitor from the West; she was living at an extreme of impoverishment and oppression. To her, he was 'the Guest from the Future', and that was how she wrote him into her 'Poem without a Hero', and into other poems, after their meeting. To him, it was like meeting a legendary 'tragic queen'. They met once or twice more, very briefly, and again some years later when he arranged for her to get an honorary doctorate from Oxford. But it was this night-time meeting which had a profound effect on them both.

He wrote up his visit to Russia at once, without describing this encounter, but drawing on it implicitly to make impassioned statements (in 'The Arts in Russia under Stalin' and 'A Visit to Leningrad') about the appalling situation for writers under Stalin.[20] In private, he talked endlessly about the encounter, sometimes to the wrong people. He called it 'one of the most moving experiences of my life', and said that it 'affected me profoundly and permanently changed my outlook'.[21] Berlin's dedication to liberalism, his commitment to individuals as the agents of history, his profound horror of tyranny and coercion, were fuelled by his meeting with Akhmatova.

For her—though she did not blame him—the results were disastrous. The visit came to Stalin's attention, who commented 'So now our nun is consorting with British spies, is she?' Her room was bugged and she was continually spied on, vilified by the Party, expelled from the Writers' Union, her poems pulped, her son rearrested. In 1949 she burnt all her manuscripts, after learning all her poems by heart. She thought, probably rightly, that these catastrophes were the result of Berlin's visit, which she continued to turn into rhapsodic poetry. More grandiloquently, she was persuaded that their encounter marked the beginning of the Cold War. He felt some guilt about what happened to her after his visit, but resisted her mythologizing, world-changing versions of the encounter.[22] Meanwhile, their encounter began to become legendary. Poems, a play, memoirs, biographies, rewrote the

---

[19] Ignatieff, *Isaiah Berlin*, 156–7. [20] SM, 27.

[21] IB to Frank Roberts, 20 February 1946, in *Flourishing*, 619; IB to Arthur Schlesinger, 27 August 1953, in *Enlightening*, 387.

[22] Dalos, *The Guest from the Future*, 64. IB to Gleb Struve, 19 July, 24 September, 1971, 6 November 1972, in *Building: Isaiah Berlin, Letters 1960–1975*, ed. Henry Hardy (Chatto & Windus, 2013), 460, 467, 505–6 respectively.

story; questions continue to be asked about the meeting and about Berlin's business in Leningrad.[23]

Isaiah Berlin himself did not write his account of this encounter until thirty-five years afterwards; yet he reports Akhmatova's opinions as if he had a tape recorder in the room with him, or has a complete memory of what she said, and has then translated it. He prefaces his essay on 'Meetings with Russian Writers' with this warning:

Every attempt to produce coherent memories amounts to falsification. No human memory is so arranged as to recollect everything in continuous sequence. Letters and diaries often turn out to be bad assistants.

The first footnote to the essay reads: 'I have never kept a diary, and this account is based on what I now remember, or recollect that I remembered and sometimes described to my friends during the last thirty or more years.' 'Recollect that I remembered': the phrase subtly sums up the dangers of memory. Yet, for all these warning notes, the anecdote has the intensity and dramatic presence of something vividly recollected. The encounter took place at a moment when Berlin had just gone back to Leningrad for the first time since leaving it as a child, when he was in a state of heightened recall. Both he and Akhmatova belonged to a national culture that was used to communicating through oral tradition, particularly at a time of censorship, when the memorizing of poetry was often the only way of preserving it. Akhmatova made a profound impression on Berlin. And he was a remarkable, eloquent storyteller with intense powers of memory. It is not improbable that he retained this encounter in his mind, over so many years, so clearly.

A few months before his death, in April 1997, Isaiah Berlin was interviewed by Anatoly Naiman, a Russian friend who had also known Akhmatova well. Isaiah said of her: 'She made me up, I wasn't the person she saw in me ... She constructed me in some way.'[24] The remark sums up the mystery that often underlies encounter narratives. The protagonists—as in any love story— make each other up. What the reader latches on to in the narrative are the traces of something real: the boiled potatoes, the sound of the frozen rain falling on the canal, the cigar smoke, the sound of voices. Whenever he

---

[23] von Zitzewitz, 'That's How It Was'; unpublished letter from Henry Hardy to TLS, September 2011.

[24] The Book of Isaiah, 78.

read Akhmatova's writings Berlin said that he remembered the sound of her voice.

The sound of a voice thrums through one of the most haunting of all literary encounter narratives, that between two poets, Keats and Coleridge. Unusually, this did not take place indoors, but on Hampstead Heath, on the rural northern edge of London, where both poets used to walk. They knew about each other, but this was their only meeting. It took place on 11 April 1819. Keats was twenty-three, and had two more years to live. Coleridge was forty-seven. He was the great, senior, famous man in the encounter. The gatekeeper of the encounter was Coleridge's friend Joseph Green, with whom Coleridge was walking. Keats knew Green from being a medical student at Guy's Hospital, so felt able to go up to him and introduce himself. Both poets recorded the encounter, but very differently. Coleridge produced two accounts of it, both with the benefit of hindsight, over ten years later, one in conversation in 1830, one written in 1832. He described Keats as a 'loose, slack, not well-dressed youth', who talked with them for a few minutes, then came back and said: 'Let me carry away the memory, Coleridge, of having pressed your hand.' Coleridge shook hands and, as Keats walked away, he turned to Green and said: 'There is death in that hand.' Or, as he embellished it in conversation: 'Heavens, said I, when I shook him by the hand there was death!'

In Keats's version, which has the persuasive advantage of being written four days later in a letter to his brother and sister-in-law, the two poets, with Mr Green, take a two-mile walk on the Heath together, while Coleridge talks, in his notorious and inimitable style, brilliantly rendered by Keats in his letter:

In those two Miles he broached a thousand things—let me see if I can give you a list—Nightingales, Poetry—on Poetical sensation—Metaphysics—Different genera and species of Dreams—Nightmare—a dream accompanied by a sense of touch—single and double touch—A dream related—First and second consciousness—the difference explained between will and Volition [...] Monsters—the Kraken—Mermaids—southey believes in them [...] a Ghost story—Good morning—I heard his voice as he came towards me—I heard it as he moved away—I had heard it all the interval—if it may be called so.[25]

[25] John Keats to George and Georgiana Keats, 15 April 1819, *The Letters of John Keats 1814–1821*, ed. J. K. Rollins, vol. 2 (1958; Cambridge, MA: Harvard University Press, 1976), 88–9. See also:

Keats's and Coleridge's biographers all pounce on this famous and touching encounter, though they treat it in different ways. Some remark on Coleridge's condescension and inaccuracy, some on Keats's spellbound amusement at the comedy of Coleridge's talk. Some note that Coleridge didn't remember their walk together because it was he, as usual, who was doing all the talking. Some point to the closeness in time of the conversation to Keats's writing of his dream–nightmare poem 'La Belle Dame Sans Merci' and his 'Ode to a Nightingale'. Nicholas Roe writes: 'What an interval! Keats's first and only encounter with the Sage of Highgate could not have come at a better moment. Poetry, poetical sensation and different kinds of dreams were all among his recent preoccupations, and in many ways this famous record of Coleridge's extraordinary, thousand-thinged voice foreshadowed Keats's own remarkable resurgence of creativity during May.'[26] All are struck by the spell-binding sound of Coleridge's voice, what Virginia Woolf, writing about Coleridge, would call 'a swarm, a cloud, a buzz of words, darting this way and that, clustering, quivering and hanging suspended'.[27] For Keats, the story of the encounter—which in time, like all encounter narratives, has become a ghost story—is one haunted by a voice. 'I heard his voice as he came towards me—I heard it as he moved away—I had heard it all the interval . . . '

Andrew Motion, *Keats* (1997; London: Faber, 1998), 366–7; Walter Jackson Bate, *John Keats* (Oxford: Oxford University Press, 1967), 469; Robert Gittings, *John Keats* (Harmondsworth: Penguin, 1968), 443; Richard Holmes, *Coleridge, Darker Reflections* (London: HarperCollins, 1998), 496–8.

[26] Nicholas Roe, *John Keats* (New Haven, CT: Yale University Press, 2012), 308–9.

[27] Virginia Woolf, 'The Man at the Gate', 1940, first collected in *The Death of the Moth* (1940), *Virginia Woolf: Collected Essays*, ed. Leonard Woolf (London: Chatto & Windus, 1967), vol. 3, 217.

8

Medieval Life-Writing and the Strange Case of Margery Kempe of Lynn (c.1373–c.1440)

Karen A. Winstead

In 1934, Colonel William Butler-Bowdon brought to the Victoria and Albert Museum an old manuscript that, as he later told a *Times* interviewer, had lain in the library of his Derbyshire manor for as long as he could remember. Hope Emily Allen, an American scholar of late medieval spirituality then researching in London, was invited to assess the colonel's document. Her reaction, scribbled on a postcard to a friend about two months into her examination: '[the manuscript] is too thrilling for words'.[1]

Allen had recognized the manuscript as the unabridged source of a brief devotional tract printed by Wynkyn de Worde in 1501 and labelled 'a shorte treatyse of contemplacyon taught by our lorde Ihesu cryste, or taken out of the boke of Margerie kempe of lynn';[2] Henry Pepwell reprinted the tract in

---

[1] Marea Mitchell, *The Book of Margery Kempe: Scholarship, Community, and Criticism* (New York: Peter Lang, 2005), 16. John C. Hirsh provides a detailed account of the discovery of the manuscript, its reception, and the events leading to the publication of the first scholarly edition in 1940 in his *Hope Emily Allen: Medieval Scholarship and Feminism* (Norman, OK: Pilgrim Books, 1988).

[2] The extracts comprise Appendix 2 (pp. 353–7) of *The Book of Margery Kempe*, edited by Sanford Brown Meech with a prefatory note by Hope Emily Allen and Notes and Appendices by Sanford

1521 as part of a devotional anthology. These printed extracts consist mostly of Christ's teachings about how to please him, prompted by the questions of a devout woman whom Pepwell assumed to be an anchoress. They give no indication of being part of a life story; one might, rather, have expected this 'boke of Margerie kempe of lynn' to be akin to the contemporary *Showings* of Julian of Norwich, a series of visions and meditations that remains a classic of medieval English spirituality.

As Allen found, the 'Margerie kempe of lynn' revealed in her complete *Book* was anything but the 'deuout ancres' Pepwell supposed. Indeed, the *Book* fleshes her out in ways nobody could have anticipated. It relays the story of a flamboyantly singular woman—a failed entrepreneur, a wife who aspires to a born-again virginity after mothering fourteen children, a religious seeker and pilgrim who has knocked around England and ranged as far as Jerusalem on her spiritual quest, and who now, at God's command, records her experiences.

Margery's story is presented in two parts. An extended prologue introduces the first and longest part, which carries the story up to circa 1430, beginning with her marriage at the age of twenty. It recounts her pregnancies, her business failures as miller and brewer, her mid-life religious epiphany, and her struggle to persuade her husband to forswear marital sex. It further describes her travels around England and her pilgrimages to the Holy Land, Rome, and Compostela. Margery's eccentric brand of piety excites controversy: among other things, she weeps loudly and uncontrollably at the thought of Christ's Passion, and she dons the white apparel associated with virgins. Some people—among them bishops, archbishops, and theologians—commend and encourage her devotion, while others resent her lectures on religion and reprimands for moral shortcomings. Some even agitate to have her imprisoned and burned for heresy or sedition. In addition to these 'real world' experiences, part one of the *Book* reports Margery's many conversations with Jesus, encounters with the Virgin Mary and other saints, and visions of biblical events.

Brown Meech and Hope Emily Allen. Early English Text Society, Original Series 212 (Oxford: Oxford University Press, 1940). Studies of the extracts include Sue Ellen Holbrook, 'Margery Kempe and Wynkyn de Worde', in *The Medieval Mystical Tradition in England: Exeter Symposium IV*, ed. Marion Glasscoe (Cambridge: Boydell and Brewer, 1987), 27–46; and Allyson Foster, '*A Shorte Treatyse of Contemplacyon: The Book of Margery Kempe* in its Early Print Contexts', in *A Companion to The Book of Margery Kempe*, ed. John H. Arnold and Katherine J. Lewis (Cambridge: D. S. Brewer, 2004), 95–112.

The second part of the *Book* is shorter and simpler. Begun in 1438, it is a selective continuation of Margery's life story, mostly recounting her perilous journey, undertaken when she was about sixty years old, to escort her merchant son's widow to her home in Germany. Though visions, spiritual dalliances with Jesus, and miracles are fewer here, Margery persists in her boisterous mode of worship and alienates her fellow travellers thereby. Her return to England and a sampling of her prayers conclude this second part and the *Book*.

The discovery of *The Book of Margery Kempe* caused an even greater stir than that of the sole surviving manuscript of Malory's *Morte Darthur*, which turned up the same year in Winchester College Library.[3] Indeed, it ranks with the discovery of the *Beowulf* manuscript as one of the most important events in English literary history. Thanks to Colonel Butler-Bowdon's 1936 modernization, the *Book* immediately captured the imagination of the English-speaking public. Reviewers enthused about the remarkable life it relayed.[4] *The Times* ranked it 'among the English Classics', 'a spiritual autobiography, a travel-book, and a domestic chronicle' of a 'fearless East Anglian fifteenth-century mystic'. The *New York Times* called it the 'life tale' of a 'pioneer militant feminist and evangelist who lived 500 years ago'. To the *Children's Newspaper*, Margery was 'an indomitable old tramp', the 'first known woman to write her story in English'. This warm reception reflected, in part, Butler-Bowdon's reshaping of the *Book* to align it with contemporary understandings of (auto)biography by relegating not only its concluding prayers but also thirteen chapters of 'wearisome' 'mystical matter' to an appendix.[5]

---

[3] For a comparison of these two literary events, see Mitchell, *The Book of Margery Kempe*, 55–60.

[4] Mitchell, *The Book of Margery Kempe*, 57–9, from which are drawn the headlines that follow.

[5] *The Book of Margery Kempe* (London: Jonathan Cape, 1936), 16. Butler-Bowdon makes his text more accessible, too, by providing chapter titles. The American edition, published in 1944 by the Devin-Adair Company, sets 'chapters entirely devoted to mystical matters . . . in a smaller type to keep them distinct from the narrative text' rather than putting them in an appendix. The impulse to excise features of *The Book of Margery Kempe* that might alienate modern readers and to render the *Book* a more recognizable autobiography has persisted. Two 'translations' have changed the *Book*'s third-person narration to first-person: *The Autobiography of the Madwoman of God: The Book of Margery Kempe*, trans. Tony D. Triggs (Tunbridge Wells: Burns & Oates, 1995); and *The Book of Margery Kempe*, trans. John Skinner (New York: Doubleday, 1998). Justifying this radical departure from the original, Triggs writes that he made a 'confident choice in favour of allowing Margery to speak for herself throughout; we hear her account in the first person, just as her scribes must have heard it themselves' (p. 12). Skinner silently changes all the third-person references to first person.

Scholarly reception of *The Book of Margery Kempe* was less effusive. Hope Emily Allen was herself profoundly ambivalent. Though the manuscript might have been 'too thrilling for words', Margery herself was obviously a disappointment. As Allen admitted in her preface to the Early English Text Society's 1940 edition, which she prepared with Sanford Brown Meech, she at first considered *The Book of Margery Kempe* 'as merely the naïve outburst of an illiterate woman, who had persuaded two pliant men to write down her egotistical reminiscences'.[6] Upon due consideration, she allowed that Margery is 'devout, much travelled, forceful and talented', despite being 'petty, neurotic, vain, illiterate, physically and nervously over-strained'.[7] Allen trusted that her annotations to the edition would help the 'professional psychologist' make sense of Margery's 'neuroticism'.[8] For decades thereafter, the consensus among readers was that the *Book* was an invaluable mine of information about everyday life in fifteenth-century England, despite its egotistical, neurotic protagonist and lack of literary merit.[9]

The disdain that characterized the first decades of the *Book*'s reception by literary scholars has yielded, since the 1980s, to more positive readings from practically every theoretical persuasion—historicist, Marxist, feminist, psychoanalytic, and queer, to name but a few.[10] As of 2014, the MLA Bibliography lists over three hundred scholarly publications on the *Book*. Editions, translations, and modernizations have appeared, and extracts are now found in the most widely used teaching anthologies of English literature. A website developed with a National Endowment for the Humanities grant is devoted to Margery Kempe and her world.[11] The *Book* has inspired at least two novels.[12] A Kempe Society is surely forthcoming.

Though *The Book of Margery Kempe* now has an undisputed place in the canon of English literature, virtually everything else about it is hotly

---

[6] See the 'Prefatory Note', *The Book of Margery Kempe*, ed. Meech, lvii.

[7] *Ibid.*, lxiv.   [8] *Ibid.*, lxv.

[9] For succinct surveys of Kempe scholarship, see Mitchell, *The Book of Margery Kempe*, 73–93; and Barry Windeatt, 'Introduction: Reading and Re-reading *The Book of Margery Kempe*', in *A Companion to The Book of Margery Kempe*, 1–16.

[10] *A Companion to The Book of Margery Kempe* provides a good sample of approaches, with special attention to the work of historians.

[11] *Mapping Margery Kempe: A Guide to Late Medieval Material and Spiritual Life* (<http://college.holycross.edu/projects/kempe/>), developed by Sarah Stanbury and Virginia Raguin.

[12] Robert Glück, *Margery Kempe* (New York: High Risk Books/Serpent's Tail, 1994); and Mark Schroeder, *The Book of Margery Kempe* (Amazon Digital Services, 2012).

contested. Not least among the controversies is its genre. In his introduction to the Butler-Bowdon modernization, Chambers was unsure what to call the *Book*, but the choice was, for him, dichotomous: 'The book is a biography, or autobiography.'[13] His hesitation between these two categories is understandable. On the one hand, *The Book of Margery Kempe* claims, at least, to comprise reminiscences that Margery dictated to two scribes, and it stresses the control that Margery exercised in shaping the *Book*: she dictated the events of her life as she remembered them, and she had her scribes read their transcriptions back to her. Yet, with just one exception, the *Book* is narrated in the third person and refers to Margery simply as 'this creature'.[14] Moreover, her original scribe (a layman, probably her son) produced a text so garbled that it could barely be deciphered, and her second scribe (a priest) resolved to 'copy it out and write it better' (p. 5). Does 'write it better' refer merely to polishing the phrasing and penmanship, or does it imply something more, perhaps even heavy revision? Attempts to identify which portions are Margery's more-or-less unadulterated memories and which have been reshaped by her priestly amanuensis are bound to be speculative and to rely, in the absence of any similar (auto)biographies of middle-class Englishwomen, on modern assumptions about what and how such a woman might have written about her life.[15]

Chambers' classification of *The Book of Margery Kempe* as either 'autobiography' or 'biography' has persisted, albeit with caveats and qualifications. Some have objected that the terms, particularly 'autobiography', do not apply to *any* medieval text. 'The word "autobiography" has been traced no

---

[13] 'Introduction', *The Book of Margery Kempe*, ed. Butler-Bowdon, 1.

[14] After Margery and John Kempe petition the Bishop of Lincoln to allow them to enter into a 'chaste marriage', the text states, 'the Bishop did no more to us on that day, save he made us right good cheer and said we were right welcome' (p. 26). I am using *The Book of Margery Kempe*, trans. Lynn Staley (New York: Norton, 2001), henceforth cited within the text by page numbers. Elsewhere in the text, others address 'the creature' as Margery Kempe. For example, the bishop of Worcester says, 'Margery . . . I know well enough you are John Brunham's daughter from Lynn' (p. 80).

[15] John C. Hirsch attempts such a distinction between scribe and author in his 'Author and Scribe in *The Book of Margery Kempe*', *Medium Ævum* 44 (1975), 145–50. It is useful to compare *The Book of Margery Kempe* with another 'collaborative project', the twelfth-century *Life of Hildegard of Bingen* by Theodoric of Echternach. Theodoric includes often extensive passages from Hildegard's writings in his narration of her life; however, those passages are always clearly signalled by such markers as 'she says' or 'she wrote'. For a translation of this work, see *Jutta and Hildegard: The Biographical Sources*, trans. Anna Silvas (Turnhout: Brepols, 1998), 118–210.

further back than the late eighteenth century', A. C. Spearing observes, and nobody in the Middle Ages claims to be 'writing an autobiography'.[16] Some contend that *The Book of Margery Kempe* is better viewed as a book *about* Margery Kempe written by her clerical scribe.[17] Most, however, view it as fundamentally Margery's account of her experiences, though many suggest designations such as 'autohagiography' or 'spiritual autobiography' to signal its difference from 'modern' understandings of the genre.[18] More radically, Lynn Staley has argued that *The Book of Margery Kempe* is more properly considered a work of fiction; and indeed, though there are traces of a Margery Kempe of Lynn in historical records, there is no documentary evidence that any of the events described in the *Book* ever took place.[19] Underlying these debates about genre and terminology are fundamental questions about selfhood, identity, authorship, audience, and purpose.

---

[16] A. C. Spearing, *Medieval Autographies: The 'I' of the Text* (Notre Dame, IN: University of Notre Dame Press, 2012). As the title implies, Spearing views 'autography' as more appropriate to the forms of first-person narration that found expression during the Middle Ages. Robert C. Ross contends that because *The Book of Margery Kempe* 'makes no pretense that the narrative encompasses the entire life of its subject' we cannot call it autobiography 'unless we choose to distort the range of that word's meaning beyond recognition'; Ross prefers to treat the text 'as a form of oral life-history'. See his 'Oral Life, Written Text: The Genesis of The Book of Margery Kempe', *Yearbook of English Studies* 22 (1992), 226–37; 226.

[17] John C. Hirsch 'confidently' states that 'the second scribe, no less than Margery, should be regarded as the author of *The Book of Margery Kempe*, in 'The Author as Scribe', 150. Spearing proposes, 'our understanding would surely be improved by an experimental envisaging of *The Book of Margery Kempe* as *The Book of Robert Spryngolde about Margery Kempe*, in his 'Margery Kempe', in *A Companion to Middle English Prose*, ed. A. S. G. Edwards (Cambridge: D. S. Brewer, 2004), 93. Likewise, Joel Fredell posits that the *Book* 'as we have it may be substantially a male construction' in 'Design and Authorship in the *Book of Margery Kempe*', *Journal of the Early Book Society for the Study of Manuscripts and Printing History* 12 (2009), 19.

[18] Caroline Dinshaw calls *The Book of Margery Kempe* 'above all a spiritual autobiography', but hastens to add, 'it does not closely resemble what we call autobiography today'. See her 'Margery Kempe', in *The Cambridge Companion to Medieval Women's Writing*, ed. Carolyn Dinshaw and David Wallace (Cambridge: Cambridge University Press, 2003), 224. Richard Kieckhefer defines 'auto-hagiography' in his *Unquiet Souls: Fourteenth-Century Saints and their Religious Milieu* (Chicago: University of Chicago Press, 1984), 6–8.

[19] Lynn Staley, *Margery Kempe's Dissenting Fictions* (University Park: The Pennsylvania State University Press, 1994). Sarah Rees Jones proposes that *The Book of Margery Kempe* was most probably authored by a reform-minded cleric determined to castigate 'moral laxity' among the clergy in her ' "A peler of Holy Cherch": Margery Kempe and the Bishops', in *Medieval Women: Texts and Contexts in Late Medieval Britain*, ed. Jocelyn Wogan-Browne, Rosalynn Voaden, Arlyn Diamond, Ann Hutchison, Carol M. Meale, and Lesley Johnson (Turnhout: Brepols, 2000), 389.

'Life-writing' offers a useful lens through which to examine this perplexing text. Although much about *The Book of Margery Kempe* is unknowable, although we cannot know which, if any, of the incidents it reports were the lived experiences of the historical Margery Kempe, we *can* examine how the *Book* goes about constructing the 'life'—real or imagined—that it indisputably *writes*. That is my goal here. I will avail myself of the latitude offered by the designation 'life-writing' to leave aside the thorny issue of agency in order to examine how Margery's life is presented, and, in particular, how its presentation intersects with and departs from some powerful models for writing the lives of holy people during the Middle Ages. Though *The Book of Margery Kempe* bears little resemblance to lives being written today, I propose that it illustrates a literary adventurousness, an interest in exploring ways of narrating human experience, and a flexible approach to 'reality' that is quintessentially medieval and that we are better poised now, than in intervening centuries, to comprehend and appreciate.

The Book of Margery Kempe endows its subject with privileges that had for centuries been associated with saints.[20] Christ promises that he will take Margery directly to himself following his death—she will never see Purgatory, much less Hell (p. 14). In Heaven, she will enjoy a place of honour among the saints (pp. 16, 39). On earth, Christ appoints her an intermediary between himself and sinful humanity, authorizing her to speak in his name and telling her that 'those who worship you, they worship me; those that despise you, they despise me' (p. 18). Margery's holiness is certified with the types of miracles routinely found in saints' lives. For example, she discerns the secrets of others; her prayers heal the sick and obtain God's mercy for sinners; those who scorn her are punished; and she survives an accident that would have killed an ordinary person.

Yet these conventional indicators of sanctity certify a most unusual kind of saint and occur, moreover, in a life story that eschews many of the then-prevalent conventions for narrating the lives of holy people. These narrative conventions existed to attest to a saint's conformity with the *vita sanctorum*—the universal life story of the saints, rooted in the lives of Christ and the early martyrs and confessors of the Church—and it is odd that

---

[20] For a useful overview of *The Book of Margery Kempe*'s hagiographical qualities, see Katherine J. Lewis, 'Margery Kempe and Saint Making in Later Medieval England', in *A Companion to the Book of Margery Kempe*, 195–215.

they should be disregarded (indeed, consciously violated) even as *The Book of Margery Kempe* respects other hagiographical conventions. Little wonder that the *Book* is one of the most controversial works of English literature: there is quite simply no other narrative like it.

Unlike most lives of late medieval holy women, which immediately name their subjects and proclaim their singularity—'the unforgettable virgin Christina' or 'the gracious virgin Lutgard'[21]—the *Book* announces itself as a 'short' and 'comfortable' 'treatise' wherein 'sinful wretches' may understand the grace God 'works in any creature' by learning of 'how charitably he moved and stirred a sinful caitif unto his love' (p. 3). The prologue does not immediately specify even the gender of this 'caitif', introducing her rather as an 'Everyman' figure who had long tried, sincerely but unsuccessfully, with 'fastings with many other deeds of penance', to follow Jesus. During the course of the entire *Book*, the 'caitif' is only twice referred to by name.

Prologues to lives of late medieval holy people typically establish the credentials of those who wrote and/or commissioned them, but *The Book of Margery Kempe* claims no sponsor and names neither of its scribes.[22] In fact, the prologue recounts the trouble Margery had in getting anybody to record her experiences. Twenty years earlier, we are told, when she first shared her 'movings and stirrings' with respected clergymen—archbishops, bishops, and theologians—many of them urged her to have them written down, some even offering to do the job themselves (p. 4). God, however, told her to wait. Two decades later, he has charged her to 'have written her feelings and revelations and the form of her living', but she cannot find a scribe; at length, one who knows of her (probably, as mentioned earlier, her son) travels from Germany to assist her. When he dies, she persuades a priest to carry on his work, but he loses his nerve in the face of the 'evil' (p. 5) spoken in the community about Margery and her weeping, and he

---

[21] Thomas of Cantimpré, *The Collected Saints' Lives* (Turnhout: Brepols, 2008), 123, 215. For examples of other lives of late medieval saints translated into modern English, see Anneke B. Mulder-Bakker, ed., *Living Saints of the Thirteenth Century* (Turnhout: Brepols, 2011). For an edition of three lives of late medieval holy women that were translated into Middle English, see Jennifer N. Brown, ed., *Three Women of Liège* (Turnhout: Brepols, 2008).

[22] On the close relationship between medieval women and their confessors and biographers, see John W. Coakley, *Women, Men, and Spiritual Power: Female Saints and their Male Collaborators* (New York: Columbia University Press, 2006).

procrastinates for years before conscience moves him to fulfil his promise. Thus, in lieu of the usual endorsements by reputable clerical authors and patrons, *The Book of Margery Kempe* offers only the *remembered* endorsements that Margery claims to have obtained twenty years or more in the past; in lieu of the usual hagiographer eager to glorify his subject, we have only amateur scribes recruited to the work with great difficulty and delay.

Lives of late medieval holy people typically recount events in roughly chronological order, often beginning with prenatal portents of sanctity and concluding with accounts of posthumous miracles. Childhood in the lives of female saints typically emphasizes the saint's early virtue—she prefers prayers to games, she fasts, and she hopes to consecrate her virginity to Christ. Most female saints achieve their desire to remain unwed, while those who cannot escape marriage perform their marital duties joylessly. The account of Margery's life, by contrast, begins by identifying Margery as a wife, mother, and sinner—identities that set her apart from most female saints. We are told little of Margery's life before her marriage at the age of twenty, and that little contains no indication that she was remarkably pious—rather the opposite.[23] There is, furthermore, no indication that she had any objection to marriage; the only problem with wedding John Kempe appears to have been that marriage to this 'worshipful burgess' (p. 6) meant a step down the social ladder for the daughter of John Brunham, five times mayor of Lynn and alderman of the prestigious Trinity Guild.[24] Margery's desire for a chaste marriage appears to have arisen during her thirties. In fact, she recalls the 'great delectation' that she and John *both* took in 'using' each other's bodies: 'In her young age [she] had full many delectable thoughts, fleshly lusts, and inordinate loves for his person' (pp. 76, 132).

Repentant sinners were, of course, well represented in the ranks of the saints, and the *Book* repeatedly alludes to two of the most famous, Saints Paul and Mary Magdalene.[25] Yet Margery's penitential experience departs

---

[23] Margery's summary of her childhood suggests that she was anything but a child prodigy of holiness: 'how unkind she had been against our Lord Jesus Christ, how proud and vain she had been in her bearing, how obstinate against the laws of God, and how envious against her fellow Christians' (pp. 29–30).

[24] On the importance of this step down to Margery's self-conception, see Nancy Partner, 'Reading *The Book of Margery Kempe*', *Exemplaria* 3 (1991), 29–66.

[25] On the importance of the Apostle Paul and Mary Magdalene as models for Margery Kempe, see Sarah Salih, 'Staging Conversion: The Digby Saint Plays and *The Book of Margery Kempe*', in *Gender*

fundamentally from theirs. Paul and Mary Magdalene—indeed, to the best of my knowledge, *all* of the penitents whose lives were widely known in late medieval England—pass suddenly and dramatically from sinfulness to sanctity.[26] Margery Kempe's path to holiness begins much as theirs did, with a religious epiphany. A difficult childbirth deprives her of her wits. She lashes out at her husband and friends, renounces God and the saints, and 'desire[s] all wickedness' (p. 7). This state lasts almost a year, until a vision of Jesus, 'in the likeness of a man, most seemly, most beautiful, and most amiable' (p. 8), restores her to her senses. This 'wonderful changing' (p. 3) convinces her that she is now 'bound to God and that she would be his servant' (p. 8). She goes 'obediently to her ghostly father, accusing herself of her misdeeds', and afterwards does 'great bodily penance' (p. 3). So far, her story seems to follow the usual track of the penitents; yet, unlike them, she has not arrived at holiness but only begun a journey towards it that continues for many years and never, in fact, reaches entire freedom from temptation.

The Book of Margery Kempe frankly recounts its protagonist's backslidings. After the period of penance immediately following her conversion, she resumes gaudy dress, unable to bear the thought that any of her neighbours should be better arrayed than she; she also tries her hand at business 'for pure covetousness and to maintain her pride', because 'all her desire was to be worshipped by the people' (pp. 8–9). Most distressingly, she cannot repress her sexual desires. Years after her conversion, she is tormented by visions of exhibitionist priests (p. 107). Though her husband's embraces repel her, she desires other men. When a certain 'man whom she loved well' propositions her for sex, she consents to the assignation, only to have him reveal that he was merely testing her (pp. 12–13).

As these examples suggest, the *Book* makes it clear that Margery is no saintly superhero. The saints' lives that she would have heard in church cast saints as intrepid soldiers of Christ scoffing at those who seek to

and Holiness: Men, Women and Saints in Late Medieval Europe, ed. Samantha J. E. Riches and Sarah Salih (London: Routledge), 121–34.

[26] Augustine of Hippo famously recounts his prolonged conversion process in his *Confessions*, but that process was radically abbreviated in the versions of his life that were most readily available in late medieval England. See, for example, the account in Jacobus de Voragine's 'bestselling' hagiographical collection, *The Golden Legend*, trans. William Granger Ryan, 2 vols. (Princeton: Princeton University Press, 1993), vol. 2, 116–25.

intimidate or harm them. The martyrs could, perhaps, afford their bravado; often their legends attest that they were extended heavenly protection from the pain that their tormentors sought to inflict, and they were always saved from threatened rape. Margery Kempe evinces no such confidence that God will intervene on *her* behalf. Accused of heresy in York, she tucks her hands into her sleeves so that her inquisitors will not see her tremble (p. 91). Though God may call her his 'singular lover' (p. 39) and dally in her soul, she does not expect him to save her from rape as he did Saint Cecilia and so many other virgins of old. For that, she must rely, ironically, on the earthly husband whose embraces she had spurned. Arrested in Leicester and in Beverley, she entreats her captors not to imprison her with men because 'she was a man's wife' (pp. 82–3, 98). When an angry mob in Canterbury calls for her death ('Take and burn her'), she 'stood still, trembling and quaking full sorely in her flesh, without any earthly comfort, and knew not where her husband was gone' (p. 23). Only when she cannot find her husband does she think to pray for God's help.

The *Book* presents Margery Kempe as one who knows what is expected of a saint but also knows she cannot live up to those expectations. Female saints, from the 'desert mothers' and the myriad martyrs of the early Church to the nuns, anchoresses, and beguines of her own day, were overwhelmingly virgins—yet Margery is a wife and mother of fourteen who, as we have seen, cannot fully extinguish her sexual urges.[27] Though she eventually negotiates a chaste marriage with her husband, she knows that she cannot recover her virginity, and she continually laments its loss, which she feels makes her unworthy of God's special favour. At one point, she wishes she had been killed just after her baptism, for then God would have 'had my maidenhood without end' (p. 38). Her despair moves Jesus to declare, 'I love wives also', and 'I love you as well as any maiden in the world' (pp. 36–7). Spiritual chastity counts as much as physical intactness: 'forasmuch as you are a maiden in your soul . . . you [shall] dance in heaven with other holy maidens and virgins' (p. 39).

---

[27] On the importance of virginity in medieval saints' lives, see Karen A. Winstead, *Virgin Martyrs: Legends of Sainthood in Late Medieval England* (Ithaca, NY: Cornell University Press, 1997); Jocelyn Wogan-Browne, *Saints' Lives and Women's Literary Culture: Virginity and its Authorizations* (Oxford: Oxford University Press, 2001); and Sarah Salih, *Versions of Virginity in Late Medieval England* (Cambridge: D. S. Brewer, 2001).

Similarly, Margery 'knows' that those dearest to Jesus have expressed their love through willing submission to torments; the martyrs of old were flayed, flogged, beaten, boiled, mutilated, and mangled.[28] Margery, however, cannot even imagine herself doing the same:

She imagined to herself what death she might die for Christ's sake. She thought she would have been slain for God's love, but dreaded the point of death, and therefore she imagined for herself the softest death, as she thought, for dread of her lack of endurance—that was to be bound by her head and feet to a stock and her head to be smote off with a sharp axe for God's love. (p. 23)

Fortunately, God assures her that she need not be martyred for his sake: 'as often as you think so, you shall have the same reward in heaven as though you suffered the same death' (p. 23). In Margery's case, at least, God values 'martyrdom by slander' over martyrdom of blood.[29]

Jesus further assures Margery that she does not need to emulate the extreme asceticism found in so many of the lives of late medieval saints, especially women. Mary of Oignies (d. 1213), whose life is alluded to in *The Book of Margery Kempe*, took a knife to her own flesh.[30] Mary's contemporary, Christina 'the Astonishing' (d. 1224), whose life also circulated in England, flung herself into fiery ovens and cauldrons of boiling water, hanged herself from gallows, and submerged herself in freezing river waters; she tortured herself on the racks used to interrogate criminals, and bloodied herself with thorns and brambles.[31] Bridget of Sweden (d. 1373), whom Margery seems to have viewed as something of a rival for Jesus' affection, lacerated herself with her fingernails, dripped the wax from a burning candle onto her bare skin, and wore hard knots next to her skin so that they would chafe at her continuously.[32] *The Book of Margery Kempe*, by contrast, construes

---

[28] On the popularity in Margery's England of saints who died violently, see Lewis, 'Margery Kempe and Saint Making', 206–7.

[29] Gail McMurray Gibson, *The Theater of Devotion: East Anglian Society and Drama in the Late Middle Ages* (Chicago: University of Chicago Press, 1989), 47.

[30] Mary's life, indeed, was translated into Middle English. See Brown, ed., *Three Women of Liège*, 85–190 (for instances of self-mutilation, see book 1, chapter 7 and book 2, chapter 7).

[31] For the Middle English translation of Christina's life, see Brown, ed., *Three Women of Liège*, 51–84 (the account of her self-inflicted torments can be found in chapters 6–14).

[32] For a Middle English life of Bridget, see *The Liber Celestis of St Bridget of Sweden*, ed. Roger Ellis, Early English Text Society, Original Series, 291 (Oxford: Oxford University Press, 1987), 1–5. Bridget's feats of asceticism are described on p. 1.

self-inflected harm as at best ineffective and at worst a sign of spiritual depravity. When Margery loses her mind and denounces God and the Virgin Mary, 'she bit her own hand so violently that it was seen all her life afterward [and] tore the skin on her body against her heart grievously with her nails' (p. 7). The acts of 'great bodily penance' that she undertakes after regaining her sanity lead to vainglory, followed by gruelling temptations, followed by despair, until Jesus finally calls a halt: 'You have a hair cloth upon your back. I want you to take it away, I will give you a hair cloth in your heart that shall please me much better than all the hair cloths in the world' (p. 14).

Whereas many late medieval holy women were said to be nauseated by food and to subsist on little more than the Eucharist, Margery Kempe loves to eat, and the *Book* is full of meals with friends, family, fellow travellers, and acquaintances.[33] Nor does Jesus lightly demand that she give up what she loves 'best in the world', namely 'eating of meat' (p. 14). Fasting, he avers, is an exercise for beginners (p. 65). When he does order her to forgo food, it is as a means to other, more important, ends.[34] *Eating* for his love is as important as fasting for his love; indeed, in order to love and serve him properly, Margery must take care of herself (pp. 118–19). 'Forget me not at your meals' (p. 134), Jesus says.

As we have seen, Jesus does not want Margery to prove her devotion through suffering and deprivation, or even discomfort and inconvenience. Instead, he endorses a form of virtual holiness. *Willingness* to suffer and die is as valuable as doing so; *longing* to be a virgin is as good as being one. Likewise, contemplating the Holy Land is as spiritually efficacious as visiting it (p. 55); wishing to endow abbeys or sponsor priests is as good as laying out actual funds (pp. 148–9). God even assures her that wishing to pray is as good as praying, when she laments that the writing of her *Book* has distracted her from her prayers (p. 157).

Jesus thinks little of the prayers one learns by rote and recites by heart (p. 14). He instructs Margery to engage actively with him in 'dalliances'

---

[33] On the importance of fasting for medieval holy women, see especially Caroline Walker Bynum, *Holy Feast and Holy Fast: The Religious Significance of Food to Medieval Women* (Berkeley: University of California Press, 1987) and Rudolph M. Bell, *Holy Anorexia* (Chicago: University of Chicago Press, 1985).

[34] For example, he demanded that she fast so that she could more effectively bargain with her husband about taking a vow of chastity (pp. 19–20).

within her soul, where she converses with him 'as clearly as one friend should speak to another' (p. 156). Moreover, he enjoins her to participate in his life through meditation. A life of meditation, he explains, is a 'holy life' that 'pleases me more than wearing of the jacket of mail or the hair shirt or fasting on bread and water, for if you said every day a thousand Pater Nosters, you should not please me as well as you do when you are in silence and suffer me to speak in your soul' (p. 65). Good deeds she imagines while meditating are, he assures her, as valuable as if she had performed them with her 'bodily wits outwardly' (p. 148).

Margery's meditations were clearly influenced by the 'bestselling' *Meditations on the Life of Christ*, composed in the fourteenth century and available in an English translation by Nicholas Love. The *Meditations* provide more fully detailed accounts of events described in the Gospels, and the author exhorts the reader to 'place yourself in the presence of whatever is related as having been said or done by the lord Jesus, as if you were hearing it with your own ears and seeing it with your own eyes, giving it your total mental response'.[35] The author often prompts his reader not only to witness but to participate in the episodes he describes: she should hold the baby Jesus, kiss his feet, and help his mother take care of him; she should travel with the Virgin, carrying the holy infant, and accompany the Holy Family into Egypt—'help carry the child, and serve in whatever way you can'.[36]

Margery Kempe does all of this and more as she engages and embellishes the templates provided in the *Meditations*, enthusiastically rescripting events narrated in the Gospels, both canonical and apocryphal.[37] Margery essentially raises the Virgin Mary: following Mary's birth, 'she busied herself to take the child to herself and keep it until it was twelve years of age with good food and drink, with fair white clothes and white kerchiefs' (p. 15). When the time comes, Margery, not Gabriel, informs Mary that she will become the mother of God. Margery, not Joseph, arranges for Mary's accommodation when the holy family travels first to Bethlehem and then into Egypt, and Margery begs food for mother and child (Joseph is presumably left to fend for himself). Margery accompanies Mary to visit her

---

[35] John of Caulibus, *Meditations on the Life of Christ*, trans. Francis X. Taney, Anne Miller, and C. Mary Stallings-Taney (Asheville, NC: Pegasus Press, 2000), 4.

[36] *Ibid.*, 28, 40, 45.

[37] See Gail Gibson's discussion of this refashioning in *The Theater of Devotion*, 47–65.

cousin Elizabeth, who declares herself as impressed with Margery's service as Mary herself is (p. 15). Margery appears later to support Mary through the horror of Christ's Passion, practically displacing John the Evangelist, whom Jesus appointed his mother's son and guardian (pp. 142–3).

Through meditation, Margery enters a virtual world far more satisfying than the world she inhabits bodily. She is a cherished member of a supportive community centred on the Holy Family. Saints, male and female, come to converse with her, and she more than holds her own among men. Paul apologizes for all the grief his disparaging pronouncements about women have caused her (p. 118), and when the Apostles tell her to cease crying at the Virgin Mary's deathbed, Margery scolds them for their insensitivity (p. 128). Unlike her husband John, who criticizes her for wearing flamboyant clothing that antagonizes the neighbours (p. 8), Jesus orders Margery to wear the white garments of a virgin even over Margery's protests that people will ridicule her for doing so (p. 60). Wholly indifferent to malicious gossip, Jesus compares himself to the husband who truly loves his wife and makes her wear fine clothes regardless of what others might think. She even enjoys a guilt-free sex life, as Jesus commands that he must 'be homely with you and lie in your bed with you . . . you may boldly, when you are in your bed, take me to you as your wedded husband' (p. 66). Like any man and wife, they can 'go to bed together without any shame or dread' (p. 155).

Margery's virtual life often intrudes into her 'bodily' life. The sight of candles on feast days or of a priest celebrating the Eucharist triggers visions that cause uncontrollable weeping. The sight of weddings elicits meditations on Mary's marriage to Joseph or Jesus' marriage to the human soul (p. 145). An infant crying or somebody beating an animal transport her instantly and completely to the biblical world, prompting meditations on Jesus as a baby or as the suffering saviour. When a priest tells her, 'Jesus is dead long since', she replies that, for her, 'his death is as fresh . . . as if he had died this same day' (p. 109).

Given these accounts of an interior life more vivid and more valued than the exterior, one cannot help but wonder whether at least some of the events that Margery seems to experience in 'bodily wits outwardly' were in fact part of her virtual life. Should we trust the account of a pilgrimage to the Holy Land that mostly records her emotional responses to famous sites, rather than their physical features? Her interrogations by clerical authorities, which are absent from scrupulously kept episcopal registers?[38] The scorn suffered from her contemporaries, or perhaps even the flamboyant religiosity that elicited such scorn? After all, the only surviving records pertaining to Margery Kempe's life document her admission, late in life, to the prestigious Trinity Guild of Lynn, somewhat undercutting her representation as a social pariah.[39]

The author of the *Meditations* claims that it is perfectly appropriate to embellish Jesus' life story with details, incidents, and conversations that are not attested in Scripture, so long as they are not 'contrary to faith or good morals'.[40] He urges his reader: 'Make your meditation on the Lord Jesus as if he said or did thus and so.' Could Margery have been applying the same principles when she recounted the events of her own life—as well as Christ's and the Virgin Mary's lives—to her scribes? In short, could the *Book* represent the life that Margery Kempe would have *liked* to have lived for Christ's sake—the triumphs and the slanders, the hurdles, and even the failings?

However it may have come about, *The Book of Margery Kempe* is a bold experiment in life-writing. It is radical in its rejection of the centuries-old model of sanctity as manifested through a life of celibacy and suffering. It is radical in its projection of sanctity as attainable through a life of contemplation and meditation. And it is, thus, radical in its broadening of the definition of a saint. When a man entreats Margery, 'Damsel, if ever you are a saint in heaven, pray for me', she responds 'Sir, I hope you shall be a saint yourself and every man who shall come to heaven' (p. 96). The radical paradigm of sainthood it conveys is articulated in a radically different *form* of life-writing—a hybrid that borrows from many genres but sits uneasily in any of them.

Though the extracts printed by Wynkyn de Worde, which may have been compiled shortly after the *Book*'s completion, are usually regarded as a conservative rendering of a controversial text, I would argue that they distil its radicalism.[41] They begin with Margery wishing that she could demonstrate

---

[38] Lynn Staley discusses the absence of such corroborating documentation in *Margery Kempe's Dissenting Fictions*, 173–4.

[39] The relevant entries in the Account Roll of Trinity Guild are given in Appendix 3 of the Early English Text Society's *Book of Margery Kempe*, 358–9.

[40] John of Caulibus, *Meditations on the Life of Christ*, 4.

[41] See Holbrook, 'Margery Kempe and Wynkyn de Worde', and Foster, 'A Shorte Treatyse of Contemplacyon'. For me, an indication that the redactor did not intend a conservative rewriting of

her love of God as the martyrs did—'She desired many times that her head might be smitten off with an axe'—and with Jesus gently but firmly refusing her offer, stating, 'as often as you think so, you will have the same reward in heaven as if you suffered the same death, and yet no man shall slay you'.[42] Margery requests elaboration, demanding to know 'how she should love him best and how she might best please him'.[43] Jesus explains that he prefers contemplation to fasting. In the ensuing pages, he further declares that he would rather converse with her in her soul than listen to her recite Pater Nosters. Thinking of the places he suffered is as valuable as visiting the Holy Land; practising patience is better than performing miracles; suffering slander is better than being struck with a sword, however many times a day. Thought is what matters: 'you shall be rewarded in heaven for good intentions and desires, as if you had done them in deed', Jesus avers, and he immediately iterates, 'you shall have as much reward with me in heaven for your good service and your good deeds that you have done in your mind as if you had done them bodily'.[44]

The extracts thus highlight Jesus' articulation of a new form of saint's life, a life forged in the fires of the imagination. The everyday world so vividly conjured in the *Book* is reduced to fleeting allusions and to moments that trigger devotion—the sight of someone beating a child or whipping a horse, an encounter with a leper. The 'years of her youth and of her prosperity' rate barely a mention as the extracts recount a progress that is wholly spiritual: 'the more she increased in love and in devotion, the more she increased in sorrow and contrition, in lowliness and meekness, and in holy fear of Our Lord Jesus and in the knowledge of her own frailty'.[45] Yet details of Margery's imaginary life are retained: 'I would be laid naked upon a hurdle . . . for all men to wonder at me and cast filth and dirt on me and be drawn from town to town every day', offering a model that the reader might use in envisioning his or her own alternative life.[46]

---

the *Book* is the preservation of Jesus' elevation of his 'daughter' above the clergy, a pronounce-ment that concludes the text. When Margery remonstrates, 'you should show these graces to religious men and to priests', Jesus replies, 'No, no daughter, for I love best what they love not, and that is shames, reproves, scorns, and despites of the people, and therefore they shall not have this grace, daughter, for he who fears that shames of this world may not perfectly love God' (p. 357).

[42] 'Printed Extracts from the Book of Margery Kempe', in *The Book of Margery Kempe*, ed. Meech, 354. Here and elsewhere, the translations are mine.

[43] *Ibid.*, 354.   [44] *Ibid.*, 355–6.   [45] *Ibid.*, 355.   [46] *Ibid.*, 356.

Distilling the *Book*'s radicalism entailed taking out the details that most make the *Book* (auto)biographical in the usual sense of that term—the details, that is, mostly extracted in modern anthologies. The medieval anthologizer, however, provided not a singular life, but a template for constructing singular lives. The *dis*embodied subject of the extracts could be *em*bodied by *anybody*—man or woman, clerical or lay, low or high born. (Though Margery is obviously female, referred to throughout as 'she' and 'daughter', nothing marks her experience as specifically feminine.) The resulting 'life' *may* have inspired a more conservative piety than Margery's— but not necessarily; the extracts also authorize pieties as flamboyant as Margery's, if not more so. We cannot know, alas, how these extracts were read, but the very fact that they were made—and explicitly associated with Margery Kempe—suggests that Kempe's life, performed or written, was more warmly received than the survival of her *Book* in a single manuscript might suggest.[47]

Medieval texts have long been marginalized in, or even excluded from, studies of biographies and autobiographies. To many historians of these genres, the Middle Ages sacrificed individuality to exemplarity and eschewed innovation for formulation. Reluctance to speak of medieval 'biography' or 'autobiography' sometimes derives, as I noted earlier in this chapter, from the view that the terms, and by extension the genres, did not exist in the Middle Ages.[48] It derives, too, from the view that medieval people did not share the sense of 'self' that underlies these genres. *The Book of Margery Kempe*, to be sure, bears little resemblance to lives being written today—nor, more generally, do lives composed during the Middle Ages evince values, interests, and tastes like our own.

Yet those surface differences belie deeper commonalities. As we enter this twenty-first century, to many of us the nature, or even the existence, of 'selfhood' is far from clear. As Clarissa Atkinson avers, 'the medieval "self" is not the modern "self"',[49]—but our postmodern self is not the modern self, either. The boundary between fiction and non-fiction has been destabilized,

---

[47] On this point, see also Foster, '*A Shorte Treatyse of Contemplacyon*', 112.

[48] The *Oxford English Dictionary* dates the use of 'biography' to 1671 and of 'autobiography' to 1797.

[49] *Mystic and Pilgrim: The Book and the World of Margery Kempe* (Ithaca, NY: Cornell University Press, 1983), 23.

and an omnipresent Internet has made 'virtual experience' integral to many, perhaps most, quotidian lives in the developed world. As this volume attests, we are less likely to have crisp notions of the ambit of (auto)biography and are increasingly prone to prefer the more flexible term of 'life-writing'. It is thus high time to look more closely at the lives that were being written in Middle Ages, when boundaries between fiction and non-fiction were fluid and authors both entertained multiple realities—spiritual, bodily, virtual, visionary, and imagined—and creatively negotiated the relationships among them. *The Book of Margery Kempe* is an instance of a flexibility that we are perhaps better equipped to comprehend and appreciate now than ever before. Though it may not be representative of the lives of holy people that were composed in its day, it *is* representative of a deep interest in the narration of lives that is evident throughout the medieval period, and of a willingness to both follow and transgress conventions—social, religious, and literary.

9

The Materiality of Early Modern Life-Writing: The Case of Richard Stonley

Alan Stewart

On 23 April 1973, the Folger Shakespeare Library announced a momentous Shakespearean discovery. While perusing a recent acquisition of three volumes of a manuscript diary belonging to an Elizabethan Exchequer official named Richard Stonley, curator Dr Laetitia Yeandle had come across the earliest known record of a purchase of a book written by William Shakespeare.[1] On Tuesday, 12 June 1593, Stonley had laid out twelvepence, recording the transaction in this entry:

Bookes	for the Survey of ffraunce with	
	the Venus & Adhonay per	xij d
	Shakspere————————————[2]	

---

[1] Anon., '[Illustration]: Diary of Richard Stonley', *Shakespeare Quarterly* 24 (1973), unnumbered pages [3–4]; Samuel Schoenbaum, *William Shakespeare: A Compact Documentary Life* (Oxford: Clarendon Press, 1977), 176 n. * The three volumes are now Folger Shakespeare Library [Folger], MS V. a.459–61.

[2] 12 June 1593. Folger MS V.a.460, fo. 9^r.

From this it appears that Shakespeare's recently published erotic poem *Venus and Adonis* was sold alongside a very different volume, John Eliot's *The suruay or topographical description of France*, published in the previous spring of 1592.[3] Thanks to this entry, Stonley wins the prize, or as Samuel Schoenbaum puts it, 'the minor distinction of being the first recorded purchaser of Shakespeare's first publication'.[4]

That single entry helped to bring Stonley's diaries to public attention—but it also obscured many other aspects of the Folger's remarkable purchase. In what follows, I shall look again at these diaries, not by pursuing *what* they contain—the 'rifling for data' to which historians routinely subject diaries[5]—but by asking instead *how* Richard Stonley wrote about his life. The first step must be to challenge that term 'diary' that I have been using. 'Diary' is the generic label by which the Folger routinely describes these volumes, yet the Folger's catalogue records testify to a (proper) confusion about how the volumes might be understood, variously classified under the rubrics 'Manuscripts', 'Diaries', 'Journals (accounts)', and 'Journals'.[6] In part, this confusion arises because Stonley is writing in a period which is generally viewed by scholars as preceding the advent of the modern diary as we know it. In his 1950 catalogue of 'British Diaries Written between 1442 and 1942', William Matthews designates all the pre-1600 'diaries' under other categories that qualify their diary status: daily notes of embassy, diplomatic diary, family diary, travel diary, public diary, military diary, astrologer's diary, religious diary, private diary, prison diary, medical diary, war diary, theatre diary, ecclesiastical diary, yeoman's diary, legal diary, country diary, farming diary.[7] Typically, these diaries record only a limited period of time (a military campaign, a journey, an embassy), public events, a professional life (astrologer, farmer, doctor, theatre owner), or a private or spiritual life. The unspoken assumption of such qualified definitions is that it is not until the legendary diary of Samuel Pepys, written

---

[3] William Shakespeare, *Venus and Adonis* (London: Richard Field, 1593); John Eliot's *The suruay or topographical description of France* (London: John Wolfe, 1592), entered in the Stationers' Register on 29 April 1592.

[4] Schoenbaum, *William Shakespeare*, 176.

[5] The phrase is from William Matthews, *British Diaries: An Annotated Bibliography of British Diaries Written between 1442 and 1942* (Berkeley: University of California Press, 1950), vii.

[6] See CLIO record <http://shakespeare.folger.edu/cgi-bin/Pwebrecon.cgi?BBID=231286>.

[7] Matthews, *British Diaries*, 1–7.

in the 1660s, that we find a work that merges the private and the public, the professional and the domestic in a satisfyingly modern manner. In pursuing this 'pre-diary' period, some scholars have placed great emphasis on the rise of personal financial accounting as the necessary precursor for the rise in journal-keeping: P. A. Spalding, for examples, argues that the majority of early diaries 'developed, almost unawares, as the amplification of account-books or other domestic records'.[8] Others have focused on the rise of the puritan spiritual journal, which proliferated in the seventeenth century.[9] But neither of these traditions adequately explains what we read in Richard Stonley's diaries, which are neither wholly financial, nor remotely puritan.

Adam Smyth, in his groundbreaking 2010 book *Autobiography in Early Modern England*, also assumes that 'the diary or autobiography began to dominate attempts to arrange a written life' in 'the later seventeenth century'. But Smyth opens his study with a useful new question: '*How* did individuals write about their lives, before a tradition of diaries and autobiographies was established?' He suggests that before that later seventeenth-century moment, 'individuals seeking to produce textual records of their lives experimented and improvised with other available genres', pre-existing formats belonging both to manuscript culture (financial accounts, the commonplace book, parish registers) and to print culture (the almanac with its blank spaces to which writers added their own autobiographical notes). Working through his pre-existing genres, Smyth convincingly portrays a complex life-writing 'culture of innovation and development' in seventeenth-century England.[10] But his model does not explain what Richard Stonley is doing, since Stonley's diary does not adhere to the rules of any one 'available genre'. Stonley himself titles each volume 'Receptes and payments', suggesting that these books are primarily financial account books—hence the record of the purchase of *Venus and Adonis*—but the volumes contain much more than receipts and payments. As I'll show, Stonley appears to be elaborating his own

---

[8] P. A. Spalding, *Self-Harvest: A Study of Diaries and the Diarist* (London: Independent Press, 1949), 64.

[9] For an influential account, see William Haller, *The Rise of Puritanism* (New York: Columbia University Press, 1938), 30. Important recent contributions include Tom Webster, 'Writing to Redundancy: Approaches to Spiritual Journals and Early Modern Spirituality', *Historical Journal* 39 (1996), 33–56; and Andrew Cambers, 'Reading, the Godly, and Self-Writing in England, circa 1580–1720', *Journal of British Studies* 46 (2007), 796–825.

[10] Adam Smyth, *Autobiography in Early Modern England* (Cambridge: Cambridge University Press, 2010), 2, 3, and *passim*.

genre of life-writing, one that we can appreciate best if, rather than attempting to understand it through the prism of a pre-existing genre, we work outwards from the ways in which Stonley writes.

Stonley's diaries constitute a helpfully accessible case study. Despite the fanfare in 1973, the entry containing Stonley's purchase was not in fact news—it had been known by Shakespeare editors Edmond Malone and George Steevens in the mid-1790s, when the relevant volume was in the possession of collector Francis Douce—but the source of the information was lost, as the diaries remained in private hands for the next 175 years.[11] As a result, Stonley's journals do not feature in twentieth-century scholarship on early modern diaries,[12] and, more importantly, they avoided the fate of being edited and published for a scholarly audience. During the nineteenth and early twentieth centuries, historical societies, led by the Camden Society and various religious, county, and local associations, displayed a healthy appetite for publishing historical diaries, journals, and other notebooks. But they tended to extract for publication only certain portions of text that recorded, in a narrative fashion, the events of the day—that same 'rifling for data'. In so doing, they ignored, and effectively effaced, the original format of each document. It is widely known that what is today published as Samuel Pepys' diary is in fact a deciphering or expansion of a document that Pepys wrote in shorthand. But casual readers of the Camden Society's 1868 edition of John Dee's *Private Diary* would be unaware that the so-called 'diary' is in fact a transcript of the notes Dee wrote in printed 'ephemerides', tables showing the predicted movements of heavenly bodies; by lifting the notes out of this context, the edition entirely stripped them of what Dee took to be the recorded events' astrological significance.[13] In 1933, when the American Society of Church History presented the important early puritan diary of Richard Rogers, the editor

---

[11] Owners included the architect William Niven of Kingwood, Berkshire (then living in Marlow Place, Great Marlow; Niven died in 1921) (bookplate in vol. 1) and John Adair Hawkins (bookplate in vol. 2). The three volumes were purchased from Stanford, CA, collector William Wreden in 1972.

[12] Spalding, *Self-Harvest*; Matthews, *British Diaries*; Robert A. Fothergill, *Private Chronicles: A Study of English Diaries* (London: Oxford University Press, 1974); Élisabeth Bourcier, *Les Journaux privés en Angleterre de 1600 à 1660* (Paris: Publications de la Sorbonne, 1976).

[13] John Dee, *The Private Diary and Catalogue of His Library of Manuscripts*, ed. James Orchard Halliwell (London: Camden Society, 1868).

was confounded by 'the writer's habit of making frequent changes in the text at dates subsequent to that of the original writing', and his tendency 'to make preliminary marginal notes, which he expanded in the body of the text, and also marginal comments when he reread his diary'. In his desire 'to present only the original form of the body of the text', the editor 'simplified and abridged the text',[14] producing a readable text; but as he eliminated the marginalia, he also eliminated what was to Rogers the most important feature of his journal—its role as a record of his life on which he could meditate, and compare his spiritual estate in the present to that of the past.

With Stonley's diaries, however, there is no such legacy of editorial intervention, no accessible print edition to lure and confuse us. We are forced to approach Stonley's diaries directly, either in person at the Folger, or through their open-access digital platform, Luna (<http://luna.folger. edu>). Since their re-emergence in the 1970s, the diaries have received some scholarly attention beyond Shakespeare studies: Christopher Coleman mentioned them in an important article in 1986 on the Exchequer of Receipt,[15] and John Guy, Joad Raymond, Christopher Haigh, and Alex Ryrie have alluded to them.[16] The Folger's present curator of manuscripts, Heather Wolfe, has described the volumes for an exhibition,[17] and most recently, in 2010, Jason Scott-Warren published an excellent article on Stonley's extensive book collection—an inventory of which survives at the National Archives in Kew—that had much to say about the diaries.[18]

[14] M. M. Knappen, ed., *Two Elizabethan Puritan Diaries* (Chicago: The American Society of Church History, 1933), viii–ix.

[15] Christopher Coleman, 'Artifice or Accident? The Reorganization of the Exchequer of Receipt, c.1554–1572', in *Revolution Reassessed: Revisions in the History of Tudor Government and Administration*, ed. Christopher Coleman and David Starkey (Oxford: Clarendon Press, 1986), 163–98; 191 n. 101. Coleman here wrote that 'I hope one day to publish' the diaries.

[16] John Guy, *Tudor England* (Oxford: Oxford University Press, 1988), 393–5; Joad Raymond, *Pamphlets and Pamphleteering in Early Modern England* (Cambridge: Cambridge University Press, 2003), 4–5, 6, 37, 93; Christopher Haigh, 'The Character of an Antipuritan', *Sixteenth Century Journal* 35 (2004), 671–88; 686; Alex Ryrie, *Being Protestant in Reformation Britain* (Oxford: Oxford University Press, 2013), 299.

[17] H[eather] W[olfe], 'Richard Stonley (ca. 1520–1600)', in *'The Pen's Excellencie': Treasures from the Manuscript Collection of the Folger Shakespeare Library*, ed. Heather Wolfe (Washington, DC: Folger Shakespeare Library, 2002), 75–6.

[18] Jason Scott-Warren, 'Books in the Bedchamber: Religion, Accounting and the Library of Richard Stonley', in *Tudor Books and Readers: Materiality and the Construction of Reading*, ed. John N. King (Cambridge: Cambridge University Press, 2010), 232–52; for the inventory, see The National Archives, Kew [TNA], E159/412/435.

But to date, there has been no work on what we might describe as the 'materiality' of the volumes, their physical characteristics—precisely the kind of information that got lost in many editions of early diaries; in this chapter, I shall attempt to start such a reading. In so doing, I am borrowing an approach used by recent criticism on early modern letters, which has radically redefined our understanding of epistles by showing how much information was contained not only in the text of a letter, but in various material aspects: the use of paper, choice of hand, layout of text, super-scription, and valediction, its folding and sealing.[19] In examining Stonley's diary, as I shall demonstrate, the visual layout of the page is particularly revealing.

The Folger's Stonley diaries constitute three volumes, which presumably derived from a longer run, since they are not chronologically consecutive. The first volume (now Folger MS V.a.459), of 100 leaves, runs from 15 June 1581 to 31 December 1582; the second (V.a.460), 92 leaves long, from 14 May 1593 to 24 May 1594, and the third (V.a.461), some 77 leaves, from 14 March 1596/97 to 18 May 1598. All three are small paper books, purchased already sewn, but blank and unformatted. Stonley writes in them in a remarkably consistent manner. In the first volume (1581–82), there is no evidence of fumbling to find a format, which may suggest that Stonley had been keeping diaries for some time. On the first opening of this first volume, for example (see Figure 9.1), Stonley adopts a very clear layout, in which each page is effectively divided into two columns. The second column, which takes up about three quarters of the space, contains the body of the text; the first column serves as a kind of marginal indicator of what is in that text. Each new day is signalled with the date in Latin centred on the page as if it were a title, so the top of the left-hand page reads 'Die Solis 18. Iunij' (Sunday 18 June)—or rather, 'Die ~~Iunii~~ Solis', because Stonley slipped and wrote the month before the date. Monday 19 June 1581 starts further down the left-hand page, with Tuesday 20 June five lines into the right-hand page and Wednesday 21 June seven lines further down.

---

[19] See, most fully, James Daybell, *The Material Letter in Early Modern England* (Basingstoke: Palgrave Macmillan, 2012).

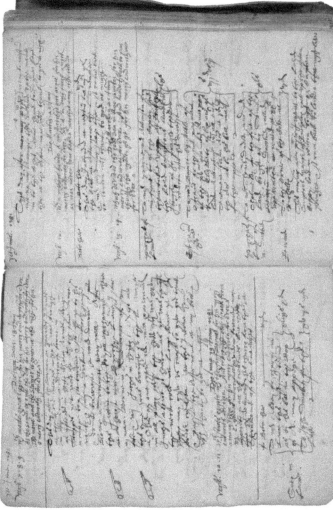

Figure 9.1 The first opening of Folger MS V.a.459, fos. 3ᵛ–4ʳ, containing Stonley's entries for 18-21 June 1580. By permission of the Folger Shakespeare Library.

Following the date, each day's entry begins with a sentence or two of text. On Sunday 18 June, this text reads 'Which made great lightes for his mercy enduryth forever As the sonne to rule the day for his mercy endureth for ever The mone and the stares to gouerne the night for his mercy endureth for ever.' A marginal note points out that this is 'verse .7.8.9'. of something, but does not specify what: it is, in fact, Psalm 136. At the beginning of the entry for Monday 19th, we get verses 10 and 11 of the same psalm; verse 12 follows on Tuesday 20th, with verses 13 and 14 on Wednesday 21st—in other words, each day Stonley copies out a verse or verses consecutively from the same scriptural text. On some days, however, he goes further. On Monday 19th, he copies out verses 10 and 11: 'Which smote egipte with ther first Borne for his mercy endureth for ever. And c browght out Israel from among them for his mercy endureth for ever.' But then Stonley continues, 'vz. c. goddes mercyfull providence towards man appereth in all his creatures. but chefly in that he delyuered his church from the ꝉ Thralwdome of the enemyes.' Clearly this addition is a commentary on or explication of the verses Stonley has just quoted. One might expect that this commentary is his own, but no: Stonley is not only copying the psalm verses from his Bible, he's also copying out the marginal commentary from his Bible, going so far as to copy out the cross-referencing cue 'c', which makes little sense in his transcription. The translation, the gloss, and the cross-referencing cue reveal this Bible unequivocally as the English translation of the Geneva Bible.

The first portion of each day's entry, therefore, is an act of verbatim copying. It is after the copied passage that Stonley rules a line, and embarks on an account of his day. On Monday, Tuesday, and Wednesday (but not Sunday, the Lord's Day), this involves financial expenditures. On Monday, for example, Stonley lists: 'for Bote hire—viijd [8 pence]; To Mr Abdey for charges in Lawe this mydsumer terme as by his bill in the Box of A. may appere—xlixs xd [49 shillings and 10 pence] To John dawtrey for the Law— xviijs ixd [18 shillings and 9 pence]'; the three latter charges are bracketed together as 'Sutes in Lawe', denoting Stonley's legal expenses. ('Box of A' presumably denotes one of the boxes in which Stonley keeps his financial papers.) These financial outgoings are followed by a narrative of the day, which on Monday reaches only two sentences: 'This day after morning prayers I went to Westminster cast vp my Accomptes ther Delyuerd vp the money in to the Chest. came home to Dyner kept ther all the After none with thankes to god at night.'

This entry follows a formula that becomes very familiar as the manuscript progresses. But within that format, as should already be apparent, there are multiple different ways of writing Stonley's life on display. One might be called spiritual, as suggested by the scriptural quotations and the emphasis on prayer. Another is financial, in the form of his itemized outgoings. Another reaches towards narrative, with the sequential account of the day, split up into regular portions and activities: morning prayer; morning work, quite often at Westminster; dinner (a midday meal in the period) at home; activities at home—most often 'with my books'; and then 'thanks to God at night'. But does one of these dominate? Is the point of keeping the diary to record his expenses, or to document his activities? Is the quoting of Scripture merely a rote activity of copying? And, most fundamentally, what is the relationship between these three?

Let's take the spiritual first. As we've seen, Stonley starts each day's entry with a verse or verses from Scripture, and includes prayer at the beginning and end of his narrative entries. And indeed, his piety seems to be more than a daily habit, as Stonley shows himself highly sensitive to matters of doctrine. St James' Day, 25 July, fell in 1581 on a weekday. Stonley clearly expected a church service to be offered, but the local minister (presumably of a more puritan cast of mind) did not offer one. Stonley improvised, recording that 'This day for lacke of seruice at our parishe Churche by our obstinate Curate I red the seruice at home to my familie. And spent the day in viciting the sicke.'[20] The doctrinal differences between Stonley and his parish minister return as a significant theme later in the year. On Sunday 10 September, he complains that at his parish church, 'At this morning seruice was first rede serten Psalmes & lessons contrary to to [sic] the Order of the book of Common prayer . . . neyther preyed for the Queen in the beginning nor end of the Sermon enveyed agenst Busshops & doctors prayd in his prayer to haue the Church restored to the Auncient order of Elders & deaknes &c.' Following the service, presumably to make up for this unsatisfactory nature, Stonley 'kept home all the holeday reading the Scriptures'.[21] Two weeks later, on 24 September, he once again heard

<hr />

[20]   25 July 1581. Folger MS V.a.459, fo. 10ᵛ.
[21]   10 September 1581. Folger MS V.a.459, fo. 19ʳ.

morning service 'at my parishe Churche wher the minister refuzinge the service for the day According as yt is appointed in the <co> booke of Common preyer did reade the Psalmes iiij xj [40:11] iii xij [30:12] & iiij xiiij [40:14]: A Lesson owt of deowtronomie v^{to} A lessen out of S^t Jo: gospel 11 ca. Afterwardes made a Sermon without preyer at all for the quenes maiestie, & vsinge for the week dayes no service at all.'[22] This kind of specificity about the order of service, and its deviation from the set readings, suggests that Stonley was invested in preserving orthodoxy in his parish church; in his telling, the minister's infractions move seamlessly from mixing up the order of the Book of Common Prayer to implying an insulting lack of respect to the Crown. From this one might imagine a quite strong antipathy to the heterodox prelate, but on the first of these days, Stonley 'had with me to dyner our minister'.[23]

Turning to financial reckoning, there can be no doubt that this is a central component of Stonley's diaries, which are titled, as we've already seen, 'Receptes and payments'. The financial aspect goes beyond the kind of notation we have already encountered in the entries, and beyond what we can glean from viewing a single opening. In the top left-hand corner of that first opening, Stonley writes 'yet June 1581' [i.e. still June 1581], to let himself know the month and the year in which he is writing his entries. That detail suggests that Stonley expected to come back to these entries, and required a quick reminder of where certain years and months were in his books. Similarly, the marginal notes on these pages constitute a quick guide to the contents of the main text. The three symbols pointing in the left-hand column are examples of what is now usually called a 'manicule'[24]—a little hand—but might also be understood as a pointing index finger that serves literally to *index* the entries in the right-hand column. These marginal pointers relate primarily to two areas: first, the text that opens each day's entry, and second, outgoing expenses—we find fingers indicating 'Purchase of land', 'Reward', 'Owt rent', 'Reparacions', 'Servantes wages', 'Apparrell', 'watching', 'Stable charges', 'Barber', 'Scollers Charges' (at Oxford, where

---

[22] 24 September 1581. Folger MS V.a.459 fo. 21^r. The lessons are on Moses, and the raising of Lazarus.

[23] 10 September 1581. Folger MS V.a.459, fo. 19^r.

[24] William H. Sherman, 'Toward a History of the Manicule', in Used Books: Marking Readers in Renaissance England (Philadelphia: Pennsylvania University Press, 2008), 25–52.

Stonley paid for his stepsons' education), 'Bokes', 'Iren work', 'Vittell', and so on. Stonley apparently used these index descriptions to facilitate the calculation of totals of expenditure in certain categories. At the end of the earliest volume, for example, we find a tally entitled 'The Some of the Totall Charge of the Book', which runs from 1 January 1581 to 1 January 1582 (1 January 1582 to 1 January 1583 in modern terms). Returning to the start date in the diary, 1 January 1581/82, we find that Stonley has gone through each marginal note and scored it out—presumably as he transferred the individual amounts to a running total.

Recent critical work has pointed to the plethora of popular book-keeping manuals that aimed to instil long-established mercantile practices among the population at large, and shown how the language, habits, and mindset of mercantile accountancy can be found in forms of life-writing in the period, as the writer tallies incomings versus outgoings.[25] When confronted with this sort of evidence, the temptation is to assume that these documents are *primarily* financial in nature: that the record of certain purchases might prompt a brief narrative account of the day, but that at heart the function of these diaries was to keep track of money. So for Alex Ryrie, for example, despite its evident piety Stonley's diary is 'less a spiritual journal than an account-book containing brief notes of Stonley's actions and devotions'.[26] For some critics, the ostentatious piety of a diary writer like Stonley can seem bogus. Jason Scott-Warren suggests that, in mercantile ledgers, the 'sometimes elaborate religious formulas ... aimed to demonstrate the piety and probity of the merchant and to redeem their profits from the taint of usury'. In this case, Scott-Warren continues,

Stonley's rote use of moral and scriptural excerpts to frame his daily accounts suggests that he too saw the utility of contemporary book-keeping practice in sublimating the worldliness of his everyday experience. Put simply, a massive tailor's bill looks less sinful when it is prefaced by a biblical excerpt about the calamities that God sent to his church in order to test his children.

In this reading, 'Stonley's diaries are an accountant's fictions, a means for securing creditworthiness in the wider community'.[27]

---

[25] Smyth, *Autobiography*, esp. ch. 2.   [26] Ryrie, *Being Protestant*, 299.
[27] Scott-Warren, 'Books in the Bedchamber', 249.

Scott-Warren's argument here implies that the 'wider community' might be reading these volumes, which seems doubtful; there is no evidence that anybody else saw Stonley's diaries. I would also be wary of prioritizing the financial over the spiritual here, as if the latter simply serves as a cover for the former. Far from being in opposition, these two registers often met, with the language of accountancy permeating even the most pious writings. William Perkins, perhaps the most popular English Calvinist writer, explicitly calls for the godly to 'take a fore-hand reckoning of our selues in the time of this our life' ahead of the final reckoning:

First, we must draw out the bill of our receipts and expences. The bills of receipt are framed thus: we must call to remembrance what graces, blessings, and gifts we have received of God, whether temporall or spirituall . . . This done, we are next to frame our bills of expences: which are nothing els, but large considerations of our sinnes . . . Tradesmen for their temporal estates, keepe in their shoppes bookes of receipts and expences: shall we not then much more doe the like for our spirituall estates?

Ultimately, 'we shal appeare before the great God of all the world, to give vp our account'.[28] Is Stonley, then, balancing his books, both spiritual and temporal, in one document?

I have deliberately refrained from introducing the writer of these diaries, for good reason. Even before his diaries were rediscovered by historians, enough was known about Richard Stonley to furnish a detailed biographical account by Nora Fuidge for the History of Parliament Trust.[29] Born around 1520, Stonley lived in Aldersgate Street in the parish of St Botolph's without Aldersgate in London. He owned property in several counties, although his primary country estate seems to have been Doddinghurst in Essex. He was well connected in City circles thanks to his marriage to Anne Branche Dun,

[28] William Perkins, *A treatise of the vocations, or, Callings of men* ([London]: John Legat, 1603), STC 19751.5, I1^v, I2^r, I2^v.

[29] N. M. F[uidge], 'Stoneley, Richard (c. 1520–1600), of Itchington, Warws., Doddington, Essex, and London', in *The House of Commons, 1558–1603*, ed. P. W. Hasler, 3 vols. (London: HMSO for the History of Parliament Trust, 1981), vol. 3, 450–1. The following account is based on Fuidge's biography, supplemented by information from K. W. Cameron, 'John Heywood and Richard Stonley', *Shakespeare Association Bulletin* 14 (1939), 55–6; Leslie Hotson, 'The Library of Elizabeth's Embezzling Teller', *Studies in Bibliography* 2 (1949–50), 49–61; Scott-Warren, 'Books in the Bedchamber'.

the widow of Robert Dun, who died in 1552 or 1553. Anne's brothers, John and Thomas Branche, were both prominent London drapers (John became Lord Mayor in 1580); she brought three sons into her second marriage, including Dr Daniel Dun (or Donne), who became Master of Requests and the principal of New Inn,[30] and the physician William Donne. Together the Stonleys had two daughters: Anne, who married William Heigham of East Ham, and Dorothy, who married William Dawtrey of More in Sussex (d. 1589).

In his professional life, Richard Stonley was an official of the Exchequer, one of four tellers whose responsibilities included the receiving of monies owed to the Crown. Stonley became a teller in his early twenties, in 1554 during the reign of Mary I, and remained in post until the late 1590s, a remarkable fifty-year career. The longevity is all the more remarkable given that, for the last fifteen years of that career, Stonley was under investigation for defrauding the Crown. Apparently, when he 'went to Westminster cast vp my Accomptes ther Delyuerd vp the money in to the Chest', Stonley did not deliver all the money. Like other Exchequer officials, Stonley saw one of the unofficial perks of his job as the ability to use the cash he was holding—and he claimed to be handling about £300,000 per annum—in order to speculate in property, and to lend money at interest. In 1584, Thomas Lichfield, auditing the Exchequer, alleged that Stonley 'had defrauded the Crown by concealing fines and by other means, [and] that his denial of the charges, and demands to be allowed to answer them in a court of law, were subterfuges'.[31] In February 1588, Stonley attempted to explain the shortfall with a litany of excuses, and to sell off his lands to make up about £14,000 of what he owed. Somehow, he salvaged the situation, and remained in post until May 1597, when his luck finally ran out, his property was sequestered by the Crown, and Stonley himself was gaoled in the Fleet Prison. He died there on 19 February 1600.

Knowing this fascinating life story is something of a poisoned chalice for the reader of Stonley's diaries. Although Stonley's professional woes are amply documented in various state papers, the diaries bear almost no trace of them.[32] The single exception is an entry on 21 January 1593 (i.e. 1594),

---

[30] Ralph Houlbrooke, 'Dun, Sir Daniel (1544/5–1617)', in *Oxford Dictionary of National Biography* (Oxford: Oxford University Press, 2004).

[31] Fuidge, 'Stonley, Richard', vol. 3, 450.

[32] *Pace* Guy, *Tudor England*, 394, who claims optimistically that 'his diaries illuminate the range and extent of his dealings'.

when he notes that 'This day after morning prayer I kept home at my bookes preparing to Answer all persons agenst this terme especially my Lord Treasorer who sercheth earnestly my dealings in my office as reason for his owne discharge';[33] Stonley apparently believed that Lord Treasurer Burghley was fingering him as a scapegoat to cover up his own tracks. From this perspective, it would seem, then, that these diaries provide only a slim slice of the life that Stonley led. For those wishing to investigate Stonley's conduct in his Exchequer role, the diaries are either: (a) pretty much useless, or (b) a compelling piece of negative evidence to show that Stonley was a thoroughgoing dissembler who lied even to his diary. For Scott-Warren, for example, there is an irresistible continuity between Stonley's embezzling at work and his account-keeping at home: 'just as his public account-keeping unraveled...so (one senses) might these "privy purse" accounts have been a fragile façade'.[34]

I would like to suggest a third scenario. These diaries are an important record of a way in which Stonley attempted to make sense of his daily life. They represent what he wanted to record and to remember, perhaps simply for himself. Certainly they do not include the details of his professional financial dealings. But that omission may suggest that Stonley was able to, or at least attempting to, separate out parts of his life. In order to pursue this, we might look more closely at Stonley's page—but rather than reading the text, analysing instead how he places his text on the page.

The spiritual, financial, and narrative jostle for room on the page—or rather, they try not to jostle, because Stonley is clearly attempting to impose some order and separation on the aspects of his life he has brought together. While the text is divided into days, as one would expect, blocks of text are also divided by ruled lines that do not coincide with the move from one day to the next; instead, those ruled lines bisect the entry of a single day. So while Stonley groups together his scriptural quotations, financial accounts, and narrative through the unit of the day, he works against that day-unit in his use of ruled lines, which separate the scriptural quotation (and commentary) from the next item, be it the accounts or the narrative. Similarly, it might be said that the left-hand column serves to index Stonley's disparate activities on a single plane, so that 'verse .7.8.9' registers

---

[33] 21 January 1593/4, Folger MS V.a.460, fo. 58^r.
[34] Scott-Warren, 'Books in the Bedchamber', 249.

as comparable to 'Bote hire'—indeed, Scott-Warren suggests that 'the form of the diary puts the evidence of reading and of shopping on a par'.[35] But while the spatial layout of the diary might support that reading, it is contradicted by another aspect of the diary's materiality, namely, the fact that Stonley deliberately writes in two different hands: the scriptural quotations and the marginal notes against them are in a Roman, italic hand, whereas the rest of the entries are in the more common secretary hand—a move that serves visually to highlight the verses. Does this mean that we should not relegate the scriptural verses to a secondary, 'copied' status, but instead see them as importantly constitutive of Stonley's day?

Even within the 'narrative' element of each day, there emerge some insistent patterns and separations. It is not difficult to perceive a correlation between the shape of Stonley's day (in his relating of it), and the daily entries in the manuscript. Each entry starts with a scriptural quotation, echoing the morning prayer; it then moves to business; and lastly to what is effectively a short narrative account of the day, which finishes with 'thankes to god at night'—both a record of the thanks Stonley offers to God in prayer, and a reiterated 'thanks' in written form. But the entry also distinguishes between what happens in his house (morning prayer, time spent with his books, dinner, supper, evening prayer) and what happens elsewhere (at Westminster, at church, at the Lord Mayor's house). Even within the house, we are made aware of irruptions into the domestic scene, as Stonley painstakingly lists the names of 'Strangers at dyner and supper', with 'Strangers' denoting those not of his household.

Other aspects of the diaries are thrown into relief when one focuses attention on the layout. Returning to that first opening of the 1581 volume, perhaps the most striking feature of the layout is the excessively long narrative entry on Sunday 18 June, in which Stonley writes:

This day after the Sarmon at Paules I dyned at the Lord Mayers where was brought in after dyner a dwarf borne in [lacuna] of ij fote ded in heyth [i.e. height] without Armes savinge Stomppes yet wold he with the same daunce a cuppe top set turvie and set yt to his mowth & sing a drunken dowch songe and drinke Carowse & wold daunce & blowe a Trumpet very well After this I went to the Royall exchaunge where at a house nere Byrchyn Lane I saw a man Borne in Andwarpe of vij fote & vij

---

[35] Scott-Warren, 'Books in the Bedchamber', 250.

Inches in hyeth Also at this tyme was brought to the L Mayor a Child of one yere old, well proporcioned in all places save the hedd which was xxviij Inches abowt so heavie as yt was thought the necke cold not longe beare yt Thes sightes may gyve vs cause to gyve god thankes for our creason [creation]. After this I went home & passed the Afternone at my bookes with thankes to god at night.[36]

In stark contrast to so many of Stonley's terse entries, this offers a wonderfully vivid evocation of early modern London's foremost venues: the Sunday sermon at Paul's Cross in the churchyard of St Paul's Cathedral; the Lord Mayor's residence (a visit not as remarkable as it might seem, since Lord Mayor John Branche was Stonley's brother-in-law); and the merchants' meeting place, the Royal Exchange, opened ten years earlier. The entry is not alone in recording what we might describe as 'public events': on Friday 30 June 1581, for example, Stonley notes 'a disorder abowt Smythfeld in taking a way of one Butcher from the Cart that was ponyshed ther for sturringe vp the people to make a rebellion about gentlemen & Servingmen', and on 21 July, records the pillorying of those who had rescued Butcher.[37] On 23 July, he notes how the Jesuit Edmund Campion was paraded through Cheapside to the Tower, and later notes his arraignment (16 November) and execution (1 December).[38] But such occurrences are the exception. Then why this emphasis on Sunday 18 June on what we might see, in comparison, as rather inconsequential sideshows?

In this entry, Stonley brings together three sightings of sensational human figures: a 'dwarf', a very tall man, and a baby with an oversized head. Interestingly, a month later, the 'dwarf' and the tall man appear in the chronicles of Raphael Holinshed and John Stow, by which time they have formed a double act of somewhat limited versatility—they sit side-by-side, and the smaller man walks between the legs of the taller while wearing a feathered hat.[39] But for Stonley, these sights have a specific purpose: they are to 'gyve vs cause to gyve god thankes for our creason': they serve as a salutary contrast to Stonley's state, an interruption to the order that

---

[36] 18 June 1581. Folger MS V.a.459, fo. 3^v.

[37] 30 June 1581, 21 July 1581. Folger MS V.a.459, fos. 6^r, 10^r.

[38] 23 July 1581, 16 November 1581, 1 December 1581. Folger MS V.a.459 fos. 10^v, 31^r, 33^v.

[39] Raphael Holinshed, *The first and second volumes of Chronicles* ([London]: John Harrison, George Bishop, Rafe Newberie, Henry Denham, and Thomas Woodcock, [1587]), 3: 6L6^r (p. 1322); John Stow, *A summarie of the chronicles of Englande* (London: Ralph Newberie and Henrie Denham, [1587]), 3A8^v (p. 704).

Stonley is so keen to find in his life and in his life-writing. The sheer length of this Sunday's entry—longer than any other in the diaries—serves to make it pop out of the page as something uncommon and outsized, echoing the monstrousness of the information it contains. By contrast, Stonley's entries for Monday, Tuesday, and Wednesday evince a reassuring sense of proper balance and order.[40]

Strikingly, Stonley's layout and format remain the same throughout the three volumes, despite a radical change in the author's circumstances. By the time Stonley embarks on the final volume in 1598, he is a prisoner in the Fleet Prison. Relieved of his duties at the Exchequer, his daily routine is, of necessity, radically altered—and yet his diary's account of each day is notably similar to what it has always been. Each day is still headed by a Latin quotation and its English commentary—although by now, having presumably worked through the Bible, the text is not scriptural, but from a collection of apophthegms by Erasmus, with English commentary by Richard Taverner.[41] Stonley continues to record his outgoings: once a week, his 'flete charges' are registered, usually with an entry written by Stonley, for example, 'To John Hore deputie to the warden of the fleete for one fortnights Chamber rent endinge this daye', thirty shillings. The recipients then countersign his book in proof of payment (it is here that the book truly becomes a record of 'Receipts and payments').[42] There is then usually a one-line account of the day, either 'I kept my Chamber' or 'I occupied my self abrode in the Citie', the latter betraying the fact that Stonley was not required to remain in prison twenty-four hours a day. This too was for a price: there are entries 'To the same [John Hore] for my libertie abrode duringe that tyme', six shillings and eightpence with a further payment 'To m^r wever my keeper for that tyme' of five shillings. And Stonley keeps up the practice of listing 'strangers' at dinner—usually his son-in-law Heigham, grandson Henry (Harry) Dawtrey, and 'the boy', presumably his servant—although the scene is no longer his household,

---

[40] I am indebted to Margreta de Grazia for this observation.

[41] In the second volume, Stonley is copying from *Catona disticha moralia*, ed. Desiderius Erasmus, trans. Richard Taverner (London: Nicholas Hill for Robert Toy, 1583). In the third he moves to Richard Taverner's *The garden of wysdome* (London: Richard Taverner, 1539), based on Erasmus' *Apophthegmata*.

[42] 29 April 1598. Folger MS V.a.461, fo. 74^v.

and the strangers are listed no doubt partly as a way of keeping track of Stonley's gaol expenses.

In other words, the same set of groupings and demarcations are still in evidence, and the shape of the day remains the same. There is, however, one late entry which speaks to a heightened awareness of the way in which the diary is crafted. We have already seen how Stonley uses his diary as a ready reckoner to calculate annual expenses, but on 29 June 1597 he proposes that, starting on that day, his system would become more complex:

> [F]rom this day ther is a nother booke which I terme the weekboke or kytchin book wherin I notte all thynges & somes of money laid out all kynde of weyes. what ys spent besides of provicion what presentes & what stranger resort to me that in the end of the yere I may voyd owt euery thing in ther proper places.[43]

Stonley introduces a preliminary book, into which 'all thynges' (including all expenses, all visitors, etc.) would be noted, to allow for the end-of-year calculations, in which he 'voyd[s] owt euery thinge in ther proper places'. (A 'week book' is the weekly version of a 'daybook' 'in which the occurrences or transactions of the day are entered', and a 'kytchin book' provides an inventory of victuals bought for the household.[44]) This shows that Stonley's 'diary' is in fact one document in a series of 'multiple, interconnected notebooks', a phenomenon which Adam Smyth has shown to be a feature both of early modern accountancy and early modern autobiography.[45] But it also reveals the extent to which the diaries now at the Folger are *not* a week book or a kitchen book, not the first 'catch-all' manuscript in which 'all thynges' are jotted down, but a meditated redaction of those things, 'in ther proper places'.

In the diaries, there may not be a trace of the thousands that passed through Stonley's hands as a teller—but not necessarily because Stonley was hiding those transactions, which were of course recorded in their own 'proper place'. Instead, we might consider the diaries as a telling exploration of what was important to Stonley, what he wanted to record, and how he wanted to understand the elements of his own life. The evidence of the

---

[43]   29 June 1597. Folger MS V.a.461, fo. 36^r.

[44]   Neither term has yet found its way into the *OED*.

[45]   Smyth, *Autobiography*, 63, and ch. 2, *passim*.

diaries' pages suggests that Stonley had found a way to conceive of his spiritual, financial, and domestic lives together as part of his day; but the insistent separating out of those elements—by ruled lines, by a change in hand—equally suggests that the utter absence of his Exchequer activities was not necessarily the devious deception of a criminal mastermind, but rather the textual effect of a man who was keen to separate his domestic and professional lives. And I would tentatively suggest that what may have mattered most to Richard Stonley, according to this, was not his post at the Exchequer, nor his embezzlement, but his morning prayer, his dinner with the Lord Mayor, his rare indulgence in an erotic pamphlet 'per Shakespere', and his thanks to God at night.[46]

[46] I am grateful to Andy Boyle, Jason Scott-Warren, Heather Wolfe, and Laura Lehua Yim for conversations about Stonley; and to the audiences at the *Life-Writing* conference at the Henry E. Huntington Library (February 2012), the London Renaissance Seminar at Birkbeck College, London (June 2014), and the Wolfe Institute, Brooklyn College, New York (March 2015) for their comments and suggestions.

10

The Autobiographies
of Benjamin Franklin

Joyce E. Chaplin

It underestimates Benjamin Franklin, and impoverishes the history of life-writing, to assume that the famous American managed to produce only one 'Autobiography'. And yet the document typically given that title is thought to be a singular production. It has been part of the canon of American literature since the nineteenth century and has thus been nationalized, regarded as the pre-eminent early example of the transfer of life-writing to the new world and in particular to the United States. But that characterization of Franklin's memoirs, however precious to scholars of American culture (and patriotically inclined readers), is too narrowly conceived and makes Franklin look too uninventive. Franklin's autobiographies, in the plural, did not passively adopt ideas of a self that had already been defined in Europe, but actively rehearsed options for personal identity that have been overlooked in scholarly definitions of the modern self. Even before Franklin wrote a set of conventional memoirs, he had produced autobiographical texts under pseudonyms and in the form of scientific essays. The pseudonymous writings showed how human identity could be a creative construction; the scientific ones established personal subjectivity through physical experience and obser-vation of nature. Franklin's life-writings must be situated between these two possibilities—indeed, his example indicates that all modern life-writing should be.

In making these claims, I challenge the idea that Franklin's penchant for pseudonyms is a problematic sign of personal inauthenticity and I restore his science to the centre of his life, which is certainly where he thought it belonged. Because of Franklin's array of pseudonymous selves—Silence Dogood, the Busybody, Anthony Afterwit, Richard Saunders, Miss Polly Baker, a Tradesman, a Citizen, Father Abraham, and so on until his final fictional projection as Sidi Mehemet Ibrahim—several scholars of literature, above all Michael Warner, have argued for a hollowness or impenetrable blank at the centre of Franklin's self, as if his protean multiplicity was achieved at the cost of his ever being a consistent and credible character.[1] Historians of science, for their part, have tended to be suspicious of the biographical approach altogether, though new attention to the epistemology of the 'scientist's' personal identity has begun to modify this suspicion. Even so, analysis of scientific efforts as iterations of autobiography has not included Franklin. Instead, recent studies of Humphrey Davy and Charles Darwin, for example, have ignored how Franklin would have been a prior example for both of these figures. And, overall, the tendency is to separate Franklin from his science, all the better to emphasize his status as an American Founding Father, for which his 'Autobiography' is usually read as a prehistory.[2]

Franklin's memoirs are in fact strikingly anomalous, more difficult to place within his corpus than has previously been acknowledged. A sustained first-person narrative written under his own name, the form of Franklin's memoirs, was not his usual style. Rather, he tended to author narratives under pseudonyms or else write personal letters signed by himself, including correspondence intended for wider circulation or publication, as with his scientific reports. The 'Autobiography' must be read in

---

[1] Michael Warner, 'Franklin: The Representational Politics of the Man of Letters', in Michael Warner, *The Letters of the Republic: Publication and the Public Sphere in Eighteenth-Century America* (Cambridge, MA: Harvard University Press, 1990), 73–96.

[2] Thomas L. Hankins, 'In Defence of Biography: The Use of Biography in the History of Science', *History of Science* 17 (1979), 1–16; Thomas Söderqvist, ed., *The History and Poetics of Scientific Biography* (Aldershot: Ashgate, 2007); Janet Browne, 'Making Darwin: Biography and the Changing Representations of Charles Darwin', *Journal of Interdisciplinary History* 45 (2010), 347–73; Jan Golinski, 'Humphry Davy: The Experimental Self', *Eighteenth-Century Studies* 45 (2011), 15–28.

relation to these two other kinds of life-writing, not least because those publications had established Franklin as a specific character long before he contemplated his memoirs. The earlier texts had created a Franklin whose life story was of interest in the first place—through them, he had defined himself as an individual of note. He had presented himself, that is, either in semi-fictional form under a pseudonym, or else as a person firmly embodied in a series of physical experiences. The latter form of character-ization seemed to supply greater authenticity, above all in the letters in which Franklin described his famous experiments with electricity. And yet these were episodic experiences, done within an interactive context of eighteenth-century sociability, in which the narrated self existed in relation to correspondents.

Altogether, the sense of a 'Franklin' imparted through his multiple life-writings is different from the unique unitary self, the inward-looking consciousness severed from the external social and physical worlds, that has dominated scholarly discussion of modern life-writing. Franklin's example indicates not a static condition that did or didn't occupy a point on a teleological progression towards that inward-looking personhood, but instead a modern self that existed in two states of tension: imagined yet also empirical; socially interactive yet also sensorily interactive with the natural world. These tensile states of being should be regarded as constitutive of the modern self, as set out in writings that described Benjamin Franklin's life, from 1706 to 1790.[3]

Franklin and his contemporaries had at their disposal two established genres of life-writing, the oldest of which was the religious confession. This took the form of the criticism of the self as a means to spiritual redemption and reconciliation with God, and as such was of great use to many of the spiritually orientated American colonists. Many Christian saints' lives, whether autobiographical or biographical, used this classic spiritual narra-tive, which was intended to show believers the value of an exemplary life and to make them imitate it. Franklin must have known St Augustine's famous *Confessions* (and possibly of Jean-Jacques Rousseau's *Confessions*, a complicated modern variation within this tradition). And he was deeply

---

[3] Charles Taylor, *Sources of the Self: The Making of the Modern Identity* (Cambridge: University of Cambridge Press, 1987), esp. 185–98; Dror Wahrman, *The Making of the Modern Self: Identity and Culture in Eighteenth-Century England* (New Haven, CT: Yale University Press, 2004).

familiar with New England puritan elegies to individuals who had led exemplary Christian lives—these were Protestant variations on the longer tradition of spiritual confessions. In his own memoirs, Franklin's emphasis on his religiously inclined New England family, his reflections on his ethical lapses or errata, and his 'bold and arduous Project of arriving at moral Perfection' all show indebtedness to the spiritual tradition in life-writing.[4]

But his narrative is quite different from the many other colonial examples that are far more invested in piety. It is by now a standard practice to compare Franklin to Olaudah Equiano, the former slave who also wrote a memoir. Although Equiano was younger than Franklin and a convert to Christianity, so in a sense twice-removed from Europe's spiritual traditions of life-writing, his narrative is far more conventional as a story of redemption. Franklin's disbelief in a Christian sense of self is apparent in many of his other writings, including those in which he adopted a pseudonym. He parodied puritan self-examination, as in his famous 'Silence Dogood' letters, in which he wrote as a self-regarding puritan widow who was as inclined to praise as to criticize herself. Indeed, in his constant references to secular literature, and in his ironic, near-comic admission of his flaws, Franklin took strategic steps away from the Christian genre of the confessions. He distanced himself from conventional piety even as he praised that quality in other people and recommended it, particularly in letters to female members of his family. (It is not clear whether he did so out of personal conviction or because he feared that women could not reject this cultural norm without worse consequences.)[5]

Franklin balanced these religious remnants with secular traditions of self-improvement that had prevailed since the Renaissance, the second genre of life-writing that he and his contemporaries had inherited. In this tradition, an individual tracked a constantly evolving self as displayed to other humans (not necessarily to God). The creation and presentation of a

[4] Sacvan Bercovitch, *The Puritan Origins of the American Self* (New Haven, CT: Yale University Press, 1960); Daniel B. Shea, *Spiritual Autobiography in Early America* (Princeton: Princeton University Press, 1968); Ruth A. Banes, 'The Exemplary Self: Autobiography in Eighteenth-Century America', *Biography* 5 (1982), 226–39.

[5] Vincent Carretta, *Equiano the African: Biography of a Self-Made Man* (New York: Penguin, 2007); Joyce E. Chaplin, '1722: Benjamin Franklin's Silence Dogood Letters', in *A New Literary History of America*, ed. Greil Marcus and Werner Sollors (Cambridge, MA: Harvard University Press, 2009), 74–9.

polished persona were goals of early modern conduct manuals, guides that were usually written to advise young aristocrats and monarchs-to-be, who needed to learn how to project authority. Niccolò Machiavelli was notorious for subverting this mirror-for-princes genre in *The Prince* (1532); Machiavelli's book recommended cunning and the naked use of force in instances where more traditional conduct manuals advocated mercy and justice.[6]

By Franklin's lifetime, the elite ideal of self-improvement had become a credible goal for people at lower social ranks. Self-help guides were published to assist the ever-rising middle classes. The manuals told people how to polish themselves as simulacra of members of the ruling orders, by acquiring a battery of graceful habits and expensive consumer goods: polite table manners, proper ways of speaking in public, fashionable dancing, wide reading, the acquisition of foreign languages, and appropriate dress and house furnishings. The development of guides to good living ran parallel to a general profusion, by the fourteenth and fifteenth centuries, in first-person narratives. Indeed, while life-writing continued to be dominated by the stories of elite or exemplary persons, by the Renaissance, literate members of the artisanal classes (men usually, though sometimes women) increasingly kept diaries and other personal explanations of themselves.[7]

This improving genre of life-writing arrived in the eighteenth-century British colonies in copious quantities. Franklin was not unique in his enthusiasm for self-help literature, which was imported, read, and reprinted widely throughout the British Atlantic. Like many of his contemporaries, including George Washington, Franklin drafted an ambitious programme of self-improvement. He went further than others, nonetheless, by writing self-help literature for publication, both in the form of sincere recommendations ('The Way to Wealth', 1758) and as parodies ('How to Make

---

[6] Felix Gilbert, 'The Humanist Concept of the Prince and the Prince of Machiavelli', *Journal of Modern History* 11 (1939), 449–83.

[7] Norbert Elias, *The Civilizing Process*, trans. Edmund Jephcott (Oxford: Blackwell, 1994); Karl J. Weintraub, *The Value of the Individual: Self and Circumstance in Autobiography* (Chicago: University of Chicago Press, 1978); Stephen J. Greenblatt, *Renaissance Self-Fashioning: From More to Shakespeare* (Chicago: University of Chicago Press, 1980); Natalie Zemon Davis, *The Autobiography of a Seventeenth-Century Venetian Rabbi* (Princeton: Princeton University Press, 1988); James Amelang, *The Flight of Icarus: Artisan Autobiography in Early Modern Europe* (Stanford, CA: Stanford University Press, 1998).

Oneself a Disagreeable Companion', 1750). When some friends suggested that he complete and publish an essay called the 'Art of Virtue', he instead decided to incorporate his moral programme into his life's story. Around a mountingly busy public career, made all the busier by the American Revolution, he tried to compose a clear narrative of himself, from birth until the public service that, in a vicious circle, kept him too preoccupied to actually document how and why he had become so prominent.[8]

How and why indeed? Franklin had become financially successful and modestly influential through his activities as a printer in Philadelphia. He acknowledged that his writings under a pseudonym, Richard Saunders, had been particularly lucrative, and that an impressively large sphere of readers knew and followed him under this name—unsurprising, given that it was the longest-running of all of Franklin's pseudonyms, deployed by him for a full quarter of a century and eventually familiar to readers on both sides of the Atlantic Ocean. Saunders was the putative author of *Poor Richard's Almanac*, launched in 1733, in which Franklin followed convention by adopting the persona of a fictional astronomer/astrologer, an invented self who spoke in the insistent first person. A personal pronoun, 'I', was the third word of this, the most famous American almanac: 'Courteous Reader, I might in this place attempt to gain thy Favour, by declaring that I write Almanacks with no other View than that of the publick Good.' This declaration placed a vivid self in public view (however artlessly introduced in terms of humble service to the common good) and supplied him with a backstory. Poor Richard was particularly memorable for his lucklessness and his exasperated wife, who demanded that he take his meagre assets, his mathematical and astronomical instruments, and use them to support the family, very possibly an in-joke for those Philadelphians who knew Franklin and his wife, Deborah Read Rogers Franklin, at this early stage of their marriage.[9]

The almanac was so successful that Franklin expanded it in 1748 under the title *Poor Richard Improved*, improved because longer and because tailored

---

[8] Richard L. Bushman, *The Refinement of America: Persons, Houses, Cities* (New York: Knopf, 1992), 30–99; Joyce E. Chaplin, ed., 'Benjamin Franklin: A How-to Guide', *Harvard Library Bulletin* (special double issue) 17 (2006).

[9] *Poor Richard* (Philadelphia, 1732), in Leonard A. Labaree et al. (eds.), *The Papers of Benjamin Franklin*, 41 vols. to date (New Haven, CT: Yale University Press, 1959–), vol. 1, 311; hereafter *PBF*.

to three markets, New England, the middle colonies, and the southern ones. This work, alongside the *Pennsylvania Gazette*, government printing contracts, and various stand-alone works, was the foundation of Franklin's public identity for fiscal wisdom, political leadership, and civic usefulness. Franklin calculated that 10,000 readers were eventually following 'Poor Richard' in his almanacs, each of which had a preface to the reader composed in the first person and charting Saunders'—meaning Franklin's—rising wealth and prominence.[10]

When he retired from the printing business, Franklin wrote a comic farewell to his faithful readers. His 'Speech of Father Abraham' appeared in his final almanac, of 1758. Franklin ended as he had begun, with a direct personal address (through Richard Saunders) to his audience: 'Courteous Reader, I have heard that nothing gives an Author so great Pleasure, as to find his Works respectfully quoted by other learned Authors.' In this case, Saunders was respectfully and repeatedly quoted by Father Abraham, a village elder who delivers a long speech copiously salted with instances of 'as Poor Richard says'. The result was a comic (because ridiculously long) compendium of the sayings of one of Franklin's aliases as quoted by yet another. Published independently, and running into hundreds of editions, this amusing essay was called 'The Way to Wealth', in English, and 'La Science du Bonhomme Richard', in French, and was translated into at least fourteen other languages. In slightly different ways, the English and French titles made clear the expectation that the constantly self-improving Franklin was himself speaking to the reader, under his best-known alias. It was to honour the US diplomat that John Paul Jones named his warship the *Bonhomme Richard*, who was Benjamin Franklin, and vice versa.[11]

Not only had Franklin narrated a version of himself in his almanac, recognized as such (under the name Richard Saunders/Poor Richard/ Bonhomme Richard) on both sides of the Atlantic, but that very kind of publication was a common vehicle for the individual subjectivities of its readers. Almanacs were essentially calendars and therefore very convenient

---

[10] James N. Green and Peter Stallybrass, *Benjamin Franklin: Writer and Printer* (New Castle, DE: Oak Knoll Press, 2006), 101–43.

[11] *Poor Richard Improved* (Philadelphia, 1757), *PBF*, VII, 326–50; 340; Sophus A. Reinert, 'The Way to Wealth around the World: Benjamin Franklin and the Globalization of Capitalism', *American Historical Review* 120 (2015), 61–97.

containers for diary entries. Surviving examples with manuscript annotations show that their possessors could also be authors. More to the point, they were autobiographers, who noted their mental, physical, or financial states over time and in specific circumstances. In that way, almanacs might function as private diaries or as personal records that, because they tended to be shared within households or even in public places, were accessible and visible to others, as performances. That practical use for almanacs suggests that, if readers imagined themselves into being within their pages, and were prepared to display those selves to others, they were likely to recognize the pseudonymous almanac-maker as the manifestation of a similar creative impulse, rather than as a meaningless deception.[12]

And yet to say that Franklin was best known as Poor Richard, and famous because at least semi-pseudonymous, would be to ignore the masterwork that made him internationally famous under his very own name, and through his documented and multiply witnessed historical actions: *Experiments and Observations on Electricity, Made at Philadelphia in America, by Mr. Benjamin Franklin* (1751; four expanded editions in English to 1774). The volume was composed of Franklin's personal letters that related his and three friends' experiments with an electrical machine. That device, which generated what would now be called an electrostatic charge, had been sent by a benefactor in London. Franklin's letters were composed to that patron, Peter Collinson. In the first document, basically a thank-you note (not published until the fourth edition of the work, in 1769), Franklin briefly summarized the initial experiments in 162 words, including the letter's date ('March 28, 1747'), salutation, and signature. Of these words, nine are first-person pronouns in the singular (*I, my*), compared to four that are second-person pronouns, referring to Collinson (*you, your*), and a mere three that are first-person plurals (*we, us*), summarizing the role of Franklin's collaborators. Basically, the letter documented that its author was an emerging man of science. It established an identity for 'Franklin', the recurring 'I', that was witnessed by others and carefully dated.[13]

---

[12] Adam Smyth, 'Annotators, Almanacs and Life Writing in Early Modern England', *English Literary Renaissance* 38 (2008), 200–44; Michael J. Eamon, '"Don't Speak to Me, But Write on This": The Childhood Almanacs of Mary and Katherine Byles', *New England Quarterly* 85 (2012), 335–52.

[13] Franklin to Collinson, 28 March 1747, *PBF*, III, 118–19.

In the succeeding letters, Franklin continued to narrativize and personalize a set of specific experiences in science in the form of experiments. For that reason, his scientific writings were formally autobiographical—there was a generic resemblance between them and his formally designated 'Autobiography'. To be sure, they did not narrate an entire life, or even a very long section of one. But they made visible and memorable certain critical episodes of a life, with precise details as to the timing of these moments, their duration, the other people involved in them, and their perceptual dimensions and intensity. These inhabited instantiations existed within a short period of momentous historical importance: the definition of electricity as a specific physical phenomenon. That the relation of personal experience and interpretation mattered to this science was apparent in the first letter published in the first edition of the work, where Franklin initially stated (as a personal observation) his most momentous insight, that electricity existed in two opposing conditions: 'So wonderfully are these two States of Electricity, the *plus* and *minus* combined and ballanced . . . situated and related to each other in a Manner that I can by no Means comprehend!' In a subsequent letter, Franklin used a well-rehearsed posture of mock humility to establish his personal authorship of the theories about electricity that he was actually generating with three collaborators. 'My Hypothesis', he admitted, did not match all the experimental results; no other discovery about electricity was as valuable, he quipped, as 'that it may *help to make a vain Man humble*'.[14]

By designating the *Experiments and Observations on Electricity* as an example of life-writing, I obviously want to make a claim that we think of science as more significant to the modern history of individual subjectivity than we have done so far. Just as historians of science are beginning to consider this possibility, so too should scholars of literature. If modern selfhood is defined according to a unique and authentic inner self, removed from interaction with others and from the natural world, Franklin looks pre-modern, dependent on Christian and Renaissance notions of the person. But if modernity must take science into account, which it surely does, then Franklin is not an eventually outmoded adopter but instead an innovator.[15]

---

[14] Benjamin Franklin, *Experiments and Observations on Electricity* (London, 1751), 3; Franklin to Collinson, 14 August 1747, *PBF*, III, 171.

[15] Wahrman, *Making of the Modern Self*, discusses the *ancien régime* of identity and the transition to a modern sense of unique and interior personhood; Taylor, in *Sources of the Self*, 185–98, 355–90,

Franklin's personal approach to experimentation was in fact conventional for much of the science of his era, with the observer offering immediate testimony about what he (more rarely she) had perceived with one or more of his senses. As Jessica Riskin has pointed out, Franklin's narrative of his electrical experiments was especially vivid in its depictions of what electricity did to his body, all the better to give the reader a sense of electricity and of the author, the specifically embodied experimenter. Although Franklin used plural pronouns to convey the existence of his experimental associates, his language betrayed personal familiarity with electricity's painful data: 'the shock was as violent' from electrified water as from a metal conductor, for instance. Franklin was quite literally an auto-experimenter who testified about what nature did to his body, though this was not unique to him.[16]

Moreover, the genre of the personal letter was likewise an accepted medium for scientific communication. It formed the bulk of publications in the *Philosophical Transactions* of the Royal Society of London, the era's premier scientific journal; it would be used in other freestanding contributions to natural knowledge, including Gilbert White's *Natural History of Selborne* (1789). In this way, science participated in the eighteenth-century's culture of sociability, the expectation that humans were at their most human when interacting with others. That gave personal identity a relational cast. Life was social; life-writing had to be as well. Personal letters are the best documentary evidence of those contemporary convictions. If anything, Franklin used letters not compiled in his *Experiments and Observations* to consolidate his personal association with electrical experiments. In a letter to Collinson published in 1750 in the *Gentleman's Magazine* (London), he presented as his own 'opinion' the idea that pointed metal rods could protect buildings from lightning strikes. It was this technology, the lightning rod, that would remain tightly connected to Franklin, the man who had tamed fire from heaven.[17]

---

emphasizes nature as a source for a sense of self, but without exploring the physically sensate experiences characteristic of science in Franklin's day—an overly cerebral and misleading analysis.

[16] Jessica Riskin, *Science in the Age of Sensibility: The Sentimental Empiricists of the French Enlightenment* (Chicago: University of Chicago Press, 2002), 69–103; Franklin, *Experiments and Observations*, 24.

[17] From a large literature on Enlightenment sociability, see Edward A. Bloom and Lillian Bloom, *Joseph Addison's Sociable Animal: In the Market Place, on the Hustings, in the Pulpit* (Providence, RI: Brown University Press, 1971); John Dwyer and Richard B. Sher, eds., *Sociability and Society in*

Over the several editions of the *Experiments and Observations*, Franklin's experiential and therefore personal claim to natural knowledge was augmented by the inclusion of other letters. Some of these were on non-experimental subjects, as with a letter in which he encouraged a timid friend to learn how to swim, and some of them were on politically partisan matters, as with his 'Observations on the Increase of Mankind', which speculated, as the American Revolution smouldered and then caught fire, that the Americans could simply outbreed their British overlords.[18]

Franklin's scientific persona, as an author with an engaging individual personality and significant physical experiences, was heightened in the longest edition of the *Experiments and Observations* to appear in France, under the title of the *Oeuvres de M. Franklin*, produced in 1769 by a French acolyte, Jacques Barbeu-Dubourg. As editor of the work, Barbeu-Dubourg had the major sections of the most recent English edition of the *Experiments and Observations* translated into French and he solicited some previously unpublished essays from Franklin. He also wrote an introduction with personal details about Franklin, something found in no English edition of the scientific letters—he was in essence the author's biographer. He included new material on Franklin's bodily experiences, as with the American's proclivity for swimming and for nude 'air baths' which he thought good for health. That people gained a sense of Franklin as a particular (and embodied) individual from this French edition is clear from the mistaken belief, in France, that the American man of science was a Quaker. He was not, but Barbeu-Dubourg had implied that he was, fostering a widespread misapprehension that continues today, and emphasizing the power of contemporary scientific genres to shape public apprehension of individuals engaged in science.[19]

Eighteenth-Century Scotland (Baltimore, MD: Johns Hopkins University Press, 1991). Letters have been considered as forms of autobiography, though typically for figures in literature, not science; see Trev Lynn Broughton, *Men of Letters, Writing Lives: Masculinity and Literary Auto/Biography in the Late Victorian Period* (London: Routledge, 1999). Quotation from Franklin to Collinson, [2 March 1750], *PBF*, III, 472–3.

[18] Joyce E. Chaplin, *Benjamin Franklin's Political Arithmetic: A Materialist Conception of Humanity* (Washington, DC: Smithsonian Institution, 2009).

[19] Joyce E. Chaplin, *The First Scientific American: Benjamin Franklin and the Pursuit of Genius* (New York: Basic Books, 2006), 224–6.

All of this is to say that Franklin was accustomed, by 1771, when he began writing his memoirs, to placing himself before the public in a series of interrelated, first-person documents, mostly, but not entirely, written by him, from which a reader could construct a single narrative, if he or she chose to do so. That is what his first *international* best-seller, *Experiments and Observations on Electricity*, had done, with its unfolding story of the identification of electricity as one material force that had two material manifestations, positive and negative. And by presenting himself (as 'Franklin of Philadelphia') through science, Franklin was continuing to call attention to the pursuit that had made him of international interest in the first place. The epistolary construction of the work would not be unfamiliar as an example of life-writing, especially in the eighteenth century. Nor would the inclusion of an occasional letter or other contribution by another author, such as Barbeu-Dubourg, in order to augment the sense of correspondence or conversation that typified eighteenth-century sociability.[20]

Still, the Franklin of Philadelphia who had experimented with electricity was not exactly the same as Richard Saunders. True, both are men of science, if on different levels, and this too emphasizes how Franklin had long used natural knowledge as the connection between himself and his readers. But the two personae are otherwise different and were meant to be, one hapless, amusing, and fake; the other masterful and absolutely real in his unreal genius, as Immanuel Kant registered in his dubbing of Franklin as the 'Prometheus of the modern age'. Sustained and comic fictional narrative versus interactive and highly serious personal correspondence: do the memoirs reconcile those two ways of being and of explaining oneself?[21]

While Franklin's memoirs narrate a long section of his life, they were not composed that way. He wrote four sections of his life's story at four different times during the last quarter of his life. He drafted the memoirs on large sheets of paper, folio sized, folded in half to form pages that measured about 25 by 38 centimetres, roughly the dimensions of a coffee-table book or laptop computer. He divided each page lengthwise and composed an initial narrative on one half, leaving the other side blank so he could make

---

[20] Clare Brant, *Eighteenth-Century Letters and British Culture* (New York: Palgrave Macmillan, 2006).

[21] Gabriele Rabel, tr. and ed., *Kant* (Oxford: Clarendon Press, 1963), 30. Kant wrote the description, 'Prometheus der neuern Zeiten', after the Lisbon earthquake of 1755. From the German in Immanuel Kant, *Gesammelte Schriften* ... (Berlin: George Reimer, 1902), vol. 1, 472.

notes to himself to add or alter material later, or to compose changes to what he had already written.[22]

Most of the pages, 200 out of the 230, include alterations of some kind or other, either made shortly after Franklin had composed the original text, or when he had moved on to later events and reconsidered his original composition. The page with the densest alterations is the first one, as Franklin, who knew very well that the first appeal to the reader mattered most, struggled to craft just the right opening to his story. He began with an overview of the Franklin family's history. That must have seemed too remote from his true interest, himself, because he jotted in the margin several personal comments: his progress 'from the Poverty and Obscurity in which I was born and bred, to a State of Affluence and some Degree of Reputation', his belief that he 'should have no Objection to a Repetition of the same Life from its Beginning' if given the chance to correct its errors, and his admission, meant to disarm, that writing his memoirs would gratify his '*Vanity*'. He made decisions about how to shape the story as he went. For example, all but one of his famous 'errata', the major mistakes of his youth, were at first marginal additions, afterthoughts that he inserted later into the narrative flow. Those little confessions add greatly to the story, preventing it from being a merely self-congratulatory recitation of Franklin's succeeding triumphs.[23]

Franklin's reasons for writing his memoirs changed over the nearly nineteen years during which he worked on them. He wrote the first of the four sections (eighty-seven manuscript pages) in the summer of 1771, during a two-week visit to his friend Jonathan Shipley, Bishop of St Asaph. Franklin addressed this opening piece to his only (and illegitimate) son, William Franklin, but by the time he wrote the next section he had broken with William, who remained loyal to Great Britain while his father sided with the American revolutionaries. Friends urged Franklin to continue his memoirs. When he resumed writing, he dedicated his life's story to a wider audience, the rising generation of independent Americans. Franklin was at that point in France and, released from his duties as American plenipotentiary to that country in 1784—once Great Britain recognized the

---

[22] J. A. Leo Lemay and P. M. Zall, eds., *The Autobiography of Benjamin Franklin: A Genetic Text* (Knoxville: University of Tennessee Press, 1981), xix–xx.

[23] *Ibid.*, 1–3, 20, 34, 43, 45, 65, 71.

independence of the United States—he was finally able to write part two of his memoirs, a total of twelve pages, including the list of the thirteen virtues he tried to pursue. ('1. TEMPERANCE. Eat not to Dulness./ Drink not to Elevation ... 12. CHASTITY. Rarely use Venery but for Health or Offspring; Never to Dulness.') The famous virtues appeal equally to those readers who see them as serious goals and to those who think Franklin was yet again mocking earnest self-improvement.[24]

Franklin made an interesting decision, when he returned to Philadelphia in 1785, to use his time at sea to draft a few scientific theses, rather than continue with his memoirs. He did this to the dismay of scholars of literature but to the delight of historians of science, including the eminent I. Bernard Cohen, who argued that the memoirs should not be ranked above the essays: 'I am glad that he spent the voyage in the fashion that he did. For science was very dear to his heart ... This voyage was his last opportunity.' Indeed, public service distracted Franklin yet again when he returned to Philadelphia in 1785 and was swept into politics, as head of the government of Pennsylvania and as a Pennsylvania representative at the Federal Constitutional Convention in 1787.[25]

In 1788, Franklin retired from public office for good and was finally able to write his narrative's third part, 119 pages, the longest of the text's sections. But, aged eighty-two, his rapidly declining health interrupted. It was impossible for him to compose more than a very short part four before his death in 1790. He was too weak to hold the pen himself, and probably dictated these final seven pages to his younger grandson until, his breathing increasingly laboured, he was unable to continue even that. The narrative simply ends in the middle of 1758, without a final piece of punctuation. Fortunately, Franklin had sketched an outline for the entire work, probably when he was writing the first and second parts of it, so we have good evidence of what he had wanted to include, at least down through his departure from America in 1776: 'to France, Treaty, &c.' That retrospective filling-in does not take into account, however, whether Franklin would have been satisfied either with the existing narrative, or with the list of

---

[24] *Ibid.*, xx–xxi.

[25] I. Bernard Cohen, ed., *Benjamin Franklin's Experiments: A New Edition of Franklin's Experiments and Observations on Electricity* (Cambridge, MA: Harvard University Press, 1941), 12.

topics he had hoped to cover. The corrections and alterations inscribed in the manuscript might only have been the first of a series of revisions.[26]

When Franklin died, he bequeathed the manuscript of his autobiography (unfinished, unrevised) to the older of his two grandsons, William Temple Franklin, the illegitimate son of his estranged son William for whom the memoirs had originally been intended. Having taken 'Temple' from his loyalist father, the grandfather had made an effort to finish the young man's education and launch him in life. He tried to make a good marriage for him in France and then to get a good position for him in the United States government, neither of which worked out. The manuscript was yet another attempt to give Temple something of value which, when printed, might afford him a small income. But Franklin had asked his other and younger grandson, Benjamin Franklin Bache, to make two copies of the first three parts of the autobiography to send to friends in England and France for their criticism and thoughts for revision. Although Temple inherited the fullest text, and the implied right to publish it, he made a strategic error by telling the French recipient of one of the two copies, Louis-Guillaume Le Veillard, of his intention to publish the memoirs along with several other of his grandfather's works.[27]

Before Temple could go to press, a French translation of the first part of his grandfather's autobiography appeared in Paris in 1791. Le Veillard denied that he had given his copy to anyone and the publisher never identified his source, who is still unknown. Intriguingly, the publisher acknowledged that his actions were somewhat dubious by titling his work the *Mémoires de la vie privée de Benjamin Franklin*. In 1791, a *vie privée* or private life was only beginning to lose its originally infamous purpose as the exposure of personal details that a famous person would not wish the public to know, or even the invention of anecdotes that he or she would nevertheless find it difficult to refute. The genre was the ancestor of the tabloid exposé of a celebrity. Before and during the French Revolution, many prominent individuals, including members of the royal family, had endured the publication of *vies privées* that were propaganda intended to trumpet the personal vice and systemic corruption of the old order. Some of these,

---

[26] Lemay and Zall, *The Autobiography of Benjamin Franklin*, xxi–xxiii.

[27] The tale of the multiple manuscripts is quite complicated; the full story is available in Lemay and Zall, *The Autobiography of Benjamin Franklin*, xxxiv–xlviii.

which appeared around the time that the first edition of Franklin's auto-biography did, were so defamatory that their printers did not put their names on the title pages, instead attributing them to the press of none other than Benjamin Franklin. It was just believable. Franklin was famous as a printer, and was known to have run a small press at his residence in Passy, France, where he published materials for the American republic that had removed itself from a monarchical system of government, as France was doing.[28]

The pirated *vie privée* of Benjamin Franklin was not quite the full and respectful edition of his grandfather's memoirs that Temple Franklin had hoped to publish. Worse, two English editions of the partial autobiography appeared in 1793, each one translated from the leaked French edition. (At this point, Franklin's original prose had become sadly garbled.) But, some-how believing that his own version of the manuscript might have more errors than either of the two copies, Temple offered it to Le Veillard in exchange for the Frenchman's copy, not realizing that his original included seven precious final pages that no other version contained. Temple pub-lished a six-volume edition of his grandfather's papers, including the Le Veillard version of the autobiography, in London, between 1817 and 1818. That edition of Franklin's memoirs had several flaws, notably, the absence of the final section. Also, Temple had polished some of his grandfather's plain, direct expressions because they would have seemed, to nineteenth-century readers, too characteristic of the leather-aproned worker Franklin had been for most of his life and unbefitting the statesman he had become. Yet this *Memoirs of the Life and Writings of Benjamin Franklin*, however compromised, however delayed, was the standard edition. It was regarded as Franklin's definitive 'memoirs' or 'life', first called an 'Autobiography' in the 1840s.[29]

Franklin's original and full manuscript resurfaced in 1867, and a printed version based on it was published in 1868, but not until 1981 did an accurate edition appear. That intellectual treasure was the handiwork of two scholars of literature, J. A. Leo Lemay and Paul Zall. They worked at the Huntington Library (which had acquired the long-misplaced full

[28] Robert Darnton, *The Devil in the Holy Water, or the Art of Slander from Louis XIV to Napoleon* (Philadelphia: University of Pennsylvania Press, 2010), 422–38.

[29] Lemay and Zall, *The Autobiography of Benjamin Franklin*, xlviii–lviii.

manuscript) to produce a genetic text of the manuscript that indicated, in printed form, the full nature of Franklin's composition, including emendations, corrections, and deletions. Following Lemay and Zall's lead, since 1981 the impetus has been to try to perfect, as much as possible, printed versions of the full manuscript. Indeed, the increased use of the term 'Autobiography' to describe the narrative proper had coincided with the increased tendency to publish it alone, rather than as part of a compendium, as Temple Franklin had chosen to do.[30]

Either option—solo narrative or weighty compendium—had precedent. Both the 'Poor Richard' of Franklin's almanacs and the 'Franklin of Philadelphia' who did electrical experiments had been predecessors. Both had been popular during the author's lifetime, meaning they each had successfully conveyed something central about who Franklin thought he was and why he wrote what he did.

Given Franklin's repeated efforts in expressing himself through curated letters, for example, it would not be surprising that he might have wished his memoirs to be published within an even more expanded *Oeuvres* or 'works'. Temple Franklin might have made his decision to use this format simply because he knew that his grandfather had valued his scientific compendia. Also, he had met Barbeu-Dubourg in France, and would thus have known the only other figure who had acted as his grandfather's biographer. It is even possible that he might have been following his grandfather's instructions, whether written in a now-lost document or else orally conveyed and therefore unrecorded.

Temple Franklin was also following the logic of the text itself. The narrative began, after all, as the patriarch's letter to William Franklin, and it included other works, such as other correspondence, along with Franklin's manuscript. Between the first and second sections of the narrative, Franklin had inserted letters from his friends Abel James and Benjamin Vaughan, each of whom urged him to complete the memoirs. He also reproduced the text of a broadside advertisement he had generated in 1755, soliciting wagons to carry provisions to troops in western Pennsylvania during the French and Indian War. At several points, as well, he noted where documents that he did not happen to have to hand should be

---

[30] Christopher Hunter, 'From Print to Print: The First Complete Edition of Benjamin Franklin's *Autobiography*', *Papers of the Bibliographical Society of America* 101 (2007), 481–505.

included; this was the case for his uncle's poem, an acrostic on the name, 'Benjamin Franklin', with the words 'here insert it' in the margin. Editors of the Autobiography have usually supplied the poem, since it was redis- covered in the mid-1800s. But it is typically reproduced in a footnote, not embedded within the narrative, even though it seems clear that Franklin had not wanted it to be hidden at the bottom of the page.

In most published editions of the Autobiography, editors have simply ignored Franklin's other references to parallel texts. When Franklin recounts his crossing of the Atlantic back to Philadelphia, in his twenties, for example, he refers to his 'journal' of his voyage and his 'plan of conduct' for the future. Temple Franklin dutifully included the whole journal in his edition of Franklin's memoirs and papers, because he had a copy of it— indeed, the only version of it that survives is in the printed *Memoirs* that Temple edited. But he did not include the moral itinerary that his grand- father mentioned. Franklin had allowed a friend in Philadelphia to copy that plan, and whatever original manuscript may have existed is lost. A fragment of the copy was published in 1815, and is included in the Yale edition of the *Papers of Benjamin Franklin*. But neither insert, either the journal or the plan, has appeared in recent editions of the 'Autobiography'. (Except for the present author's *Norton Critical Edition* (2013) which includes parts of the journal.) Nor does a dialogue Franklin wrote on the virtues of a Pennsylvania militia, nor does the resulting militia act, both of which appeared in the *Gentleman's Magazine* in 1756 and both of which he noted should be inserted into the text.[31]

Considering the stupendous fame and importance of Franklin's scientific writings during his lifetime, it is odd that no one has noticed that Temple Franklin might have been following the *Experiments and Observations* model when he published his grandfather's memoirs. This is the case because most subsequent editors of Franklin's 'Autobiography' have worked in literature, with little or no knowledge of the history of science. Despite the opening up of life-writing to a more inclusive sense of genres, scientific writing has yet to affect the larger field in very powerful ways. But in the case of Franklin's 'Autobiography', it probably should.

---

[31] Joyce E. Chaplin, ed., *Benjamin Franklin's Autobiography: A Norton Critical Edition* (New York: W. W. Norton, 2012), 225–8.

But maybe not. The second possible model for Franklin's memoirs, the pseudonymous relation of a fictional life, is of course different from that of the scientific writings. In life-writing, the use of an alias or even a constructed persona is not uncommon. And indeed Franklin's complex status as an author who used multiple aliases has solicited much attention, sometimes to praise his creativity as a writer. There have been comparisons between how he wrote while disguised under another name as opposed to how he wrote as 'Franklin', so comparisons between Franklin's 'Autobiography' and Father Abraham's 'Way to Wealth' (call it the 'Bonhomme Richard' model) are obvious ones to make. If anything, consideration of Franklin as a multiply constructed persona has augmented a warning that historians think twice about using any autobiography as an uncomplicated source, a simple narrative of facts rather than a complex literary creation. And the *vie privée*, as in the original title for the first and French edition of Franklin's memoirs, has also emphasized the capacity for that genre to be somewhat less than truthful, or even voluntary.[32]

A wealth of stand-alone, brief, and readable editions of the life of Benjamin Franklin have indeed followed the 'Bonhomme Richard' model. This has been driven, at least in part, by popular demand, but also by demand for college courses, for which a simple paperback of the 'Autobiography' is what's wanted; book publishers are pleased to accommodate both sources of demand. Personal experience at setting Franklin's 'Autobiography' for courses has made me conclude that, by and large, students tend to skim or just ignore the prompts within the narrative to pay attention to the other texts imbedded within it, all the better to appreciate the singular voice of Benjamin Franklin.

But the re-emergence of the compendium model of the memoirs is neither impossible nor unlikely. In 2007, the political scientist Alan Houston discovered at the British Library one of the missing inserts that Franklin had noted in his manuscript. This was a piece of correspondence from what Franklin called a 'Quire Book of Letters' that related to his duties in provisioning colonial troops during the French and Indian War. A quire is about twenty-four to twenty-five sheets. Franklin had evidently forgotten that his stash of war correspondence was even longer. The forty-seven

---

[32] On Franklin's self-invention, even in his memoirs, see David Levin, 'The Autobiography of Benjamin Franklin: The Puritan Experimenter in Life and Art', *Yale Review* 53 (1964), 258–75.

letters took up thirty-eight pages in the April 2009 volume of the *William and Mary Quarterly*. Franklin had indicated that he wanted at least two of the documents (much less than a full quire) placed at a point in the story where the reader would probably be challenged to remember the thread of the larger narrative after absorbing all the small details of what wagons carried which provisions where, and who had agreed or disagreed about their disposition. Nor did he consider that these documents would in their turn be sundered, possibly, from the other correspondence in the Quire Book that contextualized them.[33]

Which raises the question: did Franklin really mean to include these items, and if so, at the place he had said they should go? Had they been included, following his instructions, the narrative would look completely different. It would be composed not just in the author's voice, but in the multiple voices of his correspondents, even more than had been the case in his *Experiments and Observations*. It is revealing that Franklin complained several times of the inconvenience of being separated from documents, left in Pennsylvania, that would have helped him to write his memoirs, and especially to reconstruct long-past events in the right light. Had he ever been reunited with those papers, and had he completed his narrative and presided over its printing, would he have made the memoirs even more multi-vocal, breaking up his monologue in order to showcase key documents from the life being narrated? Editions of his *Experiments and Observations* had been getting longer and longer; a long set of his letters and papers would have been a logical next step for the retired and famous man of letters.

It would doubtless be hard for devotees of Franklin to accept that the work in question might have looked so radically different. The necessary back-and-forth between Franklin and a supporting cast of other writers would be a significant readjustment of the idea of a plain early American autobiography as authored by one self. I would maintain, however, that it would be intriguing evidence of Franklin's commitment to correspondence and to sociability in constructing his life—a characteristically and characterful eighteenth-century text. A compromise would be more like what Temple Franklin had attempted: to publish a long and even multi-volume

---

[33] Alan Houston, 'Benjamin Franklin and the "Wagon Affair" of 1755', *William and Mary Quarterly* (3rd ser.), 66 (2009), 235–86.

edition of the life and letters, with the narrative satisfyingly uninterrupted amid them, yet with all the parallel texts at hand to enact, if somewhat remotely, a dialogue between them and the prevailing monologue. An electronic edition, in which a reader could click various links that lead outward from a presumed central narrative, would make that even more possible. A recent trend has been to 'complete' Franklin's unfinished memoirs by trying to imagine how a full narrative would have looked, if run to the end of his life. That is an interesting project, but filling out the universe of relevant other writings must be part of it, not to diminish the voice of 'Benjamin Franklin', but to complete it with the other voices in which he established himself and his self.[34]

Nor should the science be forgotten. Perhaps because it was so obviously part of Franklin's life, so apparent at the time, his treatment of it within his memoirs is fleeting. This gives a false impression, a sense of the science being marginal to the other events of the life. Far from it. The experiments would have been absolutely obvious to Franklin's contemporaries—no need to mention them. And within the 'Autobiography', Franklin stated that the electrical experiments had fundamentally established his identity. In relating how a scientific critic in France had reacted to his experiments, Franklin said the man had doubted 'that there really existed such a Person as Franklin of Philadelphia'. The continued circulation, review, and acceptance of the *Experiments and Observations on Electricity* had settled the matter. There, within the canonical memoirs, is Franklin's claim that science had made him into a person who really existed. The wry claim mediated the non-existence of 'Poor Richard' and the embodied nature of 'Franklin of Philadelphia', both whom were, simultaneously, the historic Benjamin Franklin, man of many autobiographies, and therefore peerless representative of modern life-writing.[35]

---

[34] For a non-scholarly approach to this goal, see Mark Skousen, ed., *The Completed Autobiography* (Washington, DC: Regnery, 2006); for a scholarly one, see Douglas Anderson, *The Unfinished Life of Benjamin Franklin* (Baltimore, MD: Johns Hopkins University Press, 2012).

[35] *Franklin's Autobiography*, 145.

11

The Worst Thing I Ever Did: The Contemporary Confessional Memoir

Blake Morrison

Let me begin with a confession. In 1994, after spending four weeks the previous autumn attending the trial of Robert Thompson and Jon Venables, the ten-year-old boys charged with and found guilty of the murder of two-year-old James Bulger in Liverpool, and after deciding that the 10,000-word article I'd written about the case for the *New Yorker* didn't come close to saying all I needed to say,[1] I signed a contract with my publisher, Granta Books, to deliver an 80,000-word account of the case, provisionally entitled *The Worst Thing I Ever Did*. That previous year I'd published my memoir, *And When Did You Last See Your Father?*, and though the subject this time was a horrendous and very public death, not the quiet, private death at home of a seventy-five-year-old man, I intended the Bulger book to be narrated in the same first-person voice, and to be highly intimate in tone, not impersonal crime reportage. The book got written, and came out with Granta three years

---

[1] 'Children of Circumstance', *New Yorker*, 14 February 1994, pp. 48–60.

later, in 1997, and was indeed very personal, too much so for some reviewers. But I did change the title—from *The Worst Thing I Ever Did* to *As If*. Personal though the book was, and messianic though I felt in wanting to reclaim those two vilified children to a world where most of us (myself included) have done bad things of one kind or another, this wasn't a book about me. In fact I'm now rather ashamed I even considered that title—and relieved that, until now, only my editor and agent were aware of it. Still, I'm pleased to be able to expunge my shame by using the title in a context where it properly belongs: confessional literature, which has a great deal to say about the worst things that people do, or—no less important—have done to them.

The genre is a disreputable one. We live in the age of the selfie and there's a suspicion sometimes voiced in negative reviews that the confessional memoir is little more than a selfie, a look-at-me snapshot, a glorified ego trip. The very word memoir has narcissism inscribed in it: me–*moi*. To those who value reticence—and the English were once famed for their stiff upper lip—it's bad form to bang on about oneself, least of all about one's feelings. Isn't art supposed to be impersonal (T. S. Eliot's word) and the artist above the fray, paring his fingernails? There are gendered issues here, too: when a woman writes about herself, that's confessional literature, a columnist claimed in the *New Statesman* recently; when a man does it, it's just called literature.[2]

There's nothing new about confessionalism. It's usually dated back to St Augustine, in the fifth century, who owned up to impure sexual thoughts and to stealing pears, but I'd also want to include a number of Latin and Greek poets, not least Ovid, whose *Amores* possess or affect a candour that still seems fresh today and may well have been what led to him being sent into exile. The tradition has been with us ever since—from Rousseau and Thomas De Quincey to the confessional poets, mostly American (Robert Lowell, Sylvia Plath, Anne Sexton, W. D. Snodgrass, and others) who came to prominence in the 1950s and 60s. Still, it's fair to say there's been a resurgence of confessional literature in recent years. Looking over the life-writing shelves in my office at Goldsmiths the other day, I was struck by both the range and volume of non-fiction works that

---

[2] Laurie Penny, 'The Feminist Writer's Dilemma: How to Write about the Personal, without Becoming the Story', *New Statesman*, 2 July 2014.

could be called confessional—that's to say books that candidly narrate experiences that the authors themselves have difficulty owning up to and that some readers might feel would be better left unsaid. Kathryn Harrison in *The Kiss* (1997) recounting how she came to commit incest with her father. Rachel Cusk in *Aftermath* (2012) recalling the break-up of a marriage. Tim Lott in *The Scent of Dried Roses* (1996) trying to make sense of his mother's suicide. John Lanchester in *Family Romance* (2007) uncovering the lies that his mother told to conceal her real age and the years she spent as a nun. Julie Myerson in *The Lost Child* (2009), a book which caused such controversy that the television interviewer Jeremy Paxman felt obliged to lambast her on *Newsnight*, telling the story of her son's cannabis problems and the havoc they caused for the rest of the family. James Lasdun in *Give Me Everything You Have* (2013) documenting the ordeal of being stalked by a mentally unstable former student. Joan Didion, over two memoirs, *The Year of Magical Thinking* (2005) and *Blue Nights* (2011), describing the deaths of her husband and daughter. Mary Loudon in *Relative Stranger* (2007) piecing together the life of her sister, who in the years before her death, estranged from the family, had been living under a new identity, as a man. Julia Blackburn in *The Three of Us* (2008) telling how, as a teenager, she did exactly what her mother most feared and became the lover of her mother's lover, who was their lodger. Sathnam Sanghera in *The Boy with the Topknot* (2009) exposing the schizophrenia that afflicts his father and sister, a condition which, in his Sikh family and perhaps Sikh culture generally, is a taboo subject. A. M. Homes and Jackie Kay, both of them adopted children, recreating the belated adult meetings they had with their birth fathers. Karl Ove Knausgaard, the current doyen of life-writing, spreading himself over six volumes to tell of his childhood, marriage, impatient parenting, and literary agonies and enmities.[3] And so on...

Of course, these books aren't just confessional: they have purposes in mind other than lifting the lid, spilling the beans, revealing what has been swept under the carpet, rattling skeletons in the closet, and so on. Still, as those mostly pejorative metaphors imply, exposure of some kind is expected, perhaps of a messy or even sleazy kind—the equivalent of Tracey

---

[3] The six volumes were published in Norway between 2009 and 2011 under the composite title *My Struggle* (*Min kamp*). Those so far translated into English by Don Bartlett are *A Death in the Family* (2012), *A Man in Love* (2013), *Boyhood Island* (2014). and *Dancing in the Dark* (2015).

Emin's tent (with the names of her lovers written across it) or more likely her bed, the detritus of her private life spilled all over it. What confessional memoirs have in common is an intimacy we don't normally expect from literature—the reader is given privileged access to truths the author feels impelled to disclose, awkward or painful though those truths might be. Mortality is often at the heart of it: this kind of life-writing invariably turns out to mean death-writing—the loss of someone close to the author, or the author's own struggle to defeat a potentially terminal illness. Death and disease call the shots. But sexual transgression, madness, deceit, crime, and all manner of deadly sins are involved too.

Life-writing encompasses many genres other than the confessional memoir: biographies, autobiographies, letters, emails, diaries, blogs, atrocity narratives, prison writing, travel writing, obituaries, oral histories. Different institutions where it's studied and practised put their emphasis in different places: in Britain, at the University of East Anglia and the Life-Writing Centre at Wolfson College, Oxford, it's more likely to mean biography than memoir, because the leading figures associated with those places—Richard Holmes, Kathryn Hughes, Hermione Lee—are best known as biographers. At Goldsmiths University, London, where I'm based, the life-writing students who sign up for MAs and PhDs are usually people wanting to compose memoirs, mostly if not always confessional ones. In my seminar the other year I had two people whose adult sons had both died in tragic circumstances; a woman who'd been orphaned at the age of eight, and spent her childhood being farmed out to relatives, boarding school, and a housekeeper-cum-nanny; a man whose mother left home when he was 9 and, so he found out only years later, died shortly afterwards; another woman who was writing about both her own and her mother's alcoholism; and yet another young woman, in her twenties, who'd become a kind of parent to her schizophrenic Afro-Caribbean father. I suspect the final member of the group, a man in his eighties describing his upbringing in a Jewish family in the East End, felt like a jester on a stage full of tragedians.

The seminar wasn't uniformly bleak, though. None of them was writing a misery memoir. The orphan wrote briskly and amusingly about orphanhood; the woman whose son died after four years in a coma following a skiing accident wanted to celebrate the good times before it happened and to make serious points about the growing problem of patients kept alive in a vegetative state. There were a few tears in the group but plenty of laughter too. It was understood that the books they were writing needed light as well as shade. And many of the issues we discussed—to do with structure, tone of voice, characterization, narrative momentum, and so on—were issues that come up just as often in fiction classes. Still, why the writers were doing what they were doing was a question they frequently flagged, and they asked it not just of each other but of themselves. Why put themselves through this? Wasn't it self-indulgent—narcissistic? Was their story interesting enough? Were they? How to get readers involved or hooked without giving them cheap thrills or making them feel voyeuristic or depressing them to death? How to get publishers interested? Weren't memoirs—other than those written by or ghostwritten for the famous—on the wane? Why should anyone bother with them, with so much great fiction being written? Is there a right way to confess?

The word suggests a private transaction: a confessional box, a grille behind which an unseen priest sits, words of repentance directed at God through the agency of this priest, and absolution granted once the confessor's sins have been fully and honestly admitted—fessed up, as they say. In confessional literature, however, there's one huge difference: the transaction is a public one, between a writer and his or her readers, with neither God nor absolution officially part of the process. It's true these readers are unseen, except when they show up at readings and festivals. It's true, too, that a writer sitting at a desk may have an illusion of privacy. 'Many things that I would not care to tell any individual man I tell to the public', Montaigne said, and most of us have set down in writing at some point in our lives (in diaries or journals) stuff we wouldn't tell friends, for fear of upsetting or embarrassing them.[4] It's also the case that a writer may hope for some kind of absolution in recording, on the page, episodes which he or she regrets. Still, making confession to a priest—or as St Augustine intended in his *Confessions*, directly to God—is very different from publishing a confessional memoir.

So why the impulse? In his essay 'Why I Write' (1946) George Orwell gave four reasons for writing: aesthetic enthusiasm, historical impulse, political purpose, and, topping the list, 'sheer egoism', which he defined as the 'desire to seem clever, to be talked about, to be remembered after death, to

---

[4] Michel Montaigne, 'On Vanity', in *The Complete Essays*, ed. M. A. Screech (Harmondsworth: Penguin, 1993), 1109.

get your own back on grown-ups who snubbed you in childhood, etc etc'.[5] There's something in this. In *Why Be Happy When You Could Be Normal?* (2012) Jeanette Winterson gets her own back on her repressive mother and very entertaining it is too. But there are other motives in confessional literature beyond vanity and revenge, and I'd like to look at a few of those that are sometimes cited.

To begin with the least convincing...

(1) Spontaneous overflow of powerful feelings (Wordsworth) or free association (Freud). I couldn't help it, it just came out of me, unexpurgated, because the experiences I had were so immense there was no choice.

Unfortunately, this doesn't accord with the process of writing. Wordsworth qualified his definition of poetry as spontaneous overflow by adding that it began with 'emotion recollected in tranquility'. Emotion on the page is always manufactured emotion—retrospective, artful, a declaration of the author's heart but with calculated designs on the reader's. Samuel Johnson makes this point in his attack on Milton's 'Lycidas' in *Lives of the Poets*: 'It is not to be considered as the effusion of real passion', he says, 'for passion runs not after remote allusions and obscure opinions. Passion plucks no berries from the myrtle and ivy.'[6] On the Jerry Springer or Oprah Winfrey Shows, or one of their offshoots, people do come out with statements that are spontaneous rather than scripted. But everything we write is filtered, even diary entries, and words intended for publication are filtered several times—the first censor is oneself, revising the draft for publication, and then comes a further editor, or series of editors, before the confession ever reaches the printed page. So it *can* be helped. It's never involuntary. You make conscious and considered choices about what to reveal.

An opposite, slightly more plausible but overly cynical theory is as follows.

(2) Confession as an apologia or self-justification, a strategic bid for sympathy and admiration. Owning up to faults, vulnerabilities, and misdeeds is a way to win friends or keep them. Heroes are always fallible. Reveal

---

[5] Reprinted in *The Collected Essays, Journalism and Letters*, vol 1., ed. Sonia Orwell and Ian Angus (Harmondsworth: Penguin, 1970), 25.

[6] Samuel Johnson,; John Milton, *Lives of the English Poets*, 2 vols. (1779, 1781; London: OUP World's Classics, 1973), vol. 1, 112.

your Achilles heel, and rather than shoot a poisoned arrow at it, the reader will feel protective and on your side.

Well, certainly confessional literature always involves strategy—a judgement about what the impact on the reader will be, even if that judgement sometimes proves to be a *mis*judgement. When Julie Myerson wrote her book, or half of her book, about her son, she thought people would sympathize with her plight as a mother, and join her campaign to make the dangers of teenage cannabis addiction more visible—not that she would be vilified and Paxmaned as the worst mother in the world. It's always a matter of calculation, and brutally derogatory or mildly deprecating self-presentation is sometimes part of that calculation. Goody-goody narrators rarely win our sympathy: they're too perfect to be true, too perfect to be likeable anyway. Blank narrators aren't likeable either. Much better to say 'I'm bad' and hope the reader responds 'No, not bad, just human'. In my memoir about my father, I felt obliged to reveal embarrassing things about myself—things I wouldn't care to reveal to friends and acquaintances, in Montaigne's terms—out of a sense of justice, since I was doing the same with my father, subjecting his faults and foibles to public scrutiny. Fair's fair: I couldn't expose him and not expose myself. I hoped this would be a winning strategy, not a losing one. It was a choice, not the outcome of helpless humiliation.

(3) Confession as a desire to shock—the memoir as a screaming tabloid headline. Books have to make their way in the world, and to be noticed it helps if the story is sensational. Or, if it isn't sensational, to make it so, by spicing it up, exaggerating, even inventing.

When James Frey wrote his *A Million Little Pieces* (2003), he presumably judged that it would make for a more dramatic story to say he spent 87 days in a prison cell for causing a violent melee while high on crack, rather than stick to the truth, which is that he'd been held at a police station for five hours for a series of minor offences. As his case shows, though, the shocking facts had better not be shocking fictions, or you risk being rumbled by some intrepid investigative reporter.

Sometimes the facts *are* shocking, without any embroidery. Thomas Blackburn's memoir *A Clip of Steel* (1969) takes its title from the mechanical device which the author was sent as a boarding school pupil by his father, in order to discourage both involuntary ejaculation and masturbation: 'the instrument had an outer clip of thin firm steel whose inner edge was serrated with spiked teeth . . . if you had an erection then your expanding penis pressed into the sharp teeth of the firm outer clip. You were woken and an ejaculation was avoided.'[7] The reader winces even to think of it: how barbaric—no wonder the boy later ended up seeing a psychiatrist and turning to poetry. But torture of that kind makes for a powerful story: the author has our attention. I've heard it argued that the ante has been upped so much in confessional literature that only extremes of suffering like Blackburn's are now allowable, or at any rate publishable—misery piled on misery, rape and abuse multiplied and explicitness reaching new levels. But Blackburn's book came out nearly half a century ago. And perhaps whoever edited and published it felt more comfortable with the material involving erections and emissions than their equivalents would today. An equally striking example is J. R. Ackerley's *My Father and Myself* (1968), published the previous year, a book dedicated to the real love of his life, his dog Tulip. Ackerley was a respected literary editor and man of letters, so to publish a frank account of his homosexuality just two years after homosexuality had been decriminalized in the UK and twenty years before Alan Hollinghurst's novel *The Swimming Pool Library* (the novel often seen as a breakthrough in the portrayal of gay sex in this country) was courageous, surprising, and ahead of its time, though Ackerley died just before the book came out. Still, it's not his being gay but his expression of canine love in all its physicality that seems so shocking today. He saves it for his appendix: though he had already written about it at length in a previous memoir *My Dog Tulip* (1956), he was more cautious there about admitting to being sensually aroused by his Alsatian's body. He never had sex with her, he says, but he did sometimes press his hand against her swollen vulva when she was on heat, in order to ease or appease her. He also says that love for his dog cured him of sexual incontinence: once she came into his life, he spent less time pursuing boys. Whatever the case, his book and many before it (including Pepys' diaries) show that extreme candour isn't a modern invention.

(4) Confession as the desire to redefine what's shocking. To nail the hypocrisy and shallowness of polite society.

---

[7] Thomas Blackburn, *A Clip of Steel* (London: MacGibbon & Kee, 1969), 62–3.

Here's a more honourable motive and one not easily disentangled from the previous. Many a memoir composed by a writer in one generation sets out to expose the lies and secrets of a previous generation, on the grounds that those lies and secrets—about illegitimacy, say, or mental illness—seem unnecessary in a changed moral climate, no longer a source of shame, but 'normal', acceptable, and worth attending to rather than hiding away. When I showed the draft of my book about my father to my mother, one of the few things she asked me to remove was a reference to her being a Catholic. Why she should care so much about that became the subject of the book I later wrote about her. Disguising her Catholicism, losing her accent, giving herself a new name, and in effect renouncing her Irishness were choices she made in order to be quietly assimilated into English society in the 1940s and 50s. Religion, accent, name, and nationality were matters that she felt (or was made to feel) awkward about, whereas for me there was no shame attached to them—rather the opposite in fact. Did I betray her by revealing what she hid from all but a few close friends? I don't think so. I certainly hope not. It's true I'd not have revealed it in her lifetime. But I was confident that the prejudice she had feared and that she experienced in my father's family—a prejudice against Irish Catholicism—would no longer be shared by my readers; that if they read the story they would sympathize with the situation in which she found herself.

My book about my father had an agenda too: to look honestly and unflinchingly at the process of dying, just as he, a doctor, had always urged me. *As If*, the book I wrote about the James Bulger murder case, also had a polemical motive. Much shock had been professed in the media at the idea of children killing children, as though such an act was unprecedented. I wanted to show that such crimes have been committed throughout history, that the wonder is they don't happen more often, and that an equally shocking aspect of this case was to see 10-year-olds being put on trial in public in an adult court—shocking because they had limited understanding of the process, couldn't instruct their lawyers, and in almost every other country in the world would have been judged to be below the age of criminal responsibility. The confessional elements in the book—the emphasis on my *feelings*, not least as a parent—were there to highlight that polemical argument.

Confessional literature might be defined as literature that puts emphasis on feelings rather than ideas: a *cri de coeur*. 'I could inform the dullest author how he might write an interesting book', Coleridge wrote in 1797. 'Let him relate the events of his own life with honesty—not disguising the feelings that accompanied them.'[8] Well, yes, but the reader expects feelings not just to be declared, let alone paraded, but to serve a larger purpose, prompting recognition and extending our imaginative sympathies.

(5) Confession as performance and showmanship—even showoffery or boasting, its natural arena not a secret cloister but a soapbox or a stage.

Where those who bear witness say 'I saw this, I heard this, I was there', the confessional writer issues a challenge: 'Look at my often outrageous behaviour and judge me if you dare.' The desire isn't so much to shock the reader as in (3) above, but rather to stage a drama of the ego. Rousseau begins his *Confessions* by emphasizing his honesty and plain dealing: his intention is to paint 'a portrait in every way true to nature', 'simply myself', one that will 'bare my secret soul', he says. But the metaphor then shifts from realistic portraiture to theatre:

[L]et the numberless legion of my fellow men gather round me and hear my confessions. Let them groan at my depravities, and blush for my misdeeds. But let each one of them reveal his heart at the foot of Thy throne with equal sincerity, and may any man who dares say 'I was a better man than he'.[9]

He doesn't actually say 'Roll up, roll up', but the impression of a fairground barker or music-hall master of ceremonies is hard to miss. Honest or not, Rousseau is acutely aware of his audience and determined to put on a show. And what a show it is. He steals, he tells lies, he sends all five of his children to an orphanage, much to the despair of their mother Therese, and that's not even to mention his sexual transgressions—masturbation, flashing, sadomasochism, a long relationship with a woman 12 years his senior who takes his virginity, a visit to a brothel, deep frustration when he fails to perform for a beautiful courtesan because she has a malformed nipple, taking turns to have sex with a young girl kept by one of his friends . . . Rousseau relishes unburdening himself—and being watched: 'I must remain incessantly beneath [the reader's] gaze, so that he may follow me in all the extravagances of my heart and into every least corner of my life'

---

[8] Samuel Taylor Coleridge to Thomas Poole, 6 February 1797, in *The Oxford Authors: Samuel Taylor Coleridge*, ed. H. J. Jackson (Oxford: Oxford University Press, 1992), 494.

[9] Jean-Jacques Rousseau, *The Confessions* (1781), trans. J. M. Cohen (Harmondsworth: Penguin, 1953), 17 (henceforth cited within the text by page numbers).

(p. 65). Today's confessional memoirists follow where Rousseau led: self-dramatization is integral to the genre. And putting oneself on the page isn't a natural process; it means constructing a narrator, since narrators aren't born but made. It also means taking trouble to write inventively, so that the journey of the self becomes a docudrama, not just a circus act or ego trip.

Which isn't to deny the following.

(6) The confessional memoir as a piece of truth-telling—its primary impulse being to set the record straight, to bear witness or provide testimony.

And to be reliable: no matter how subjective the narrator, the reader wants to believe that he or she is honest. Good journalism works like this too. *I was there*, it says, reporting from the front line as an eye witness, or recounting first hand, from personal experience, what it's like to be in a war, say, or a prison, or, in the case of Primo Levi and other Holocaust survivors, a concentration camp. We don't tend to attach the word 'confessional' to this kind of memoir, when the subject is world history, rather than family history. But the intimacy of the witnessing often *is* confessional, and that's what sets it apart from mere reportage. There's a wonderful example of witness-bearing in George Orwell's essay 'A Hanging' (1931) about his experience of watching a man being hanged in Burma; there are details in it so odd but compelling they seem to guarantee its authenticity—a dog bounding around the compound where the hanging is about to take place and destroying the solemnity of the occasion; the condemned man carefully stepping aside to avoid a puddle even though he knows he's about to die; the relief and gallows humour among the assembled guards once he is dead. Few of us are witness to such dramatic events. But even with our smaller experiences, truth-telling is part of the contract—indeed the main clause. Confessional memoirists may not have the literary talent of poets or novelists, but their status as non-fiction writers is an invaluable asset. They're offering themselves as reliable narrators, and woe to those (like James Frey in *A Million Little Pieces* or Binjamin Wilkomirski in *Fragments: Memories of a Wartime Childhood*, 1995) who break that contract.

Finally, we come to what's perhaps the principal yet most contentious motive.

(7) Confession as catharsis, cleansing, or purgation. Something bad has happened, and putting it in writing, or putting it out there in the world, is a way of feeling better about it.

212 | **Blake Morrison**

'Give sorrow words', Shakespeare said, 'the grief that does not speak /
Whispers the o'er fraught heart and bids it break' (*Macbeth*, 4.3.209). Tennyson said something similar about the ease that comes from articulation,
though his imagery is less about expelling pain than numbing it.

> I sometimes hold it half a sin
> To put in words the grief I feel;
> For words, like nature, half reveal
> And half conceal the Soul within.
>
> But, for the unquiet heart and brain,
> A use in measured language lies;
> The sad mechanic exercise,
> Like dull narcotics, numbing pain. ('In Memoriam', verse V)

Get it on paper. Set it down in words. Writing as therapy.

Ah, therapy—a word generally held to be suspect when associated with
literature. The novelist Bernice Rubens said of one of her novels 'It was
good therapy for me, but a rotten novel. You should always write in
yesterday's blood.'[10] It's a quote which reinforces the idea that what's
therapeutic can't ever be literature, since literature needs to be shaped,
reflected on, set at a distance. Or to put it another way, that what's therapy
for the author won't ever achieve the necessary detachment or artistry
required to make it therapy for the reader.

Actually, I don't believe the therapeutic impulse need always be damaging. 'One sheds one's sicknesses in books', D. H. Lawrence said.[11] The
need to exorcise demons, and take control of the present by articulating the
past, is what drove Rousseau; writing eased his conscience: 'I can affirm that
the desire to some extent to rid myself of it has greatly contributed to my
resolution of writing these Confessions' (p. 88). Virginia Woolf took a
similar view. In an essay of 1939–40, notable for featuring the first known
use of the term life-writing, she talks of the 'horror' that comes when
buried memories are recovered, but adds that she realizes 'as one gets older
one has a greater power through reason to provide an explanation; and that

---

[10] Quoted in Janet Watts' obituary of Rubens in *The Guardian*, 14 October 2004.
[11] D. H. Lawrence to Arthur Macleod, 26 October 1913: *The Letters of D. H. Lawrence*, vol. 2: *June
1913–October 1916*, ed. George J. Zytaruk and James T. Boulton (Cambridge: Cambridge University
Press, 1981), 90.

this explanation blunts the sledge-hammer force of the blow'. More to the point:

[T]he shock-receiving capacity is what makes me a writer. I hazard the explanation that a shock is at once in my case followed by the desire to explain it. I feel that I have had a blow; but it is not, as I thought as a child, simply a blow from an enemy hidden behind the cotton wool of daily life; it is or will become a revelation of some order; it is a token of some real thing behind appearances; and I make it real by putting it into words. It is only by putting it into words that I make it whole; this wholeness means that it has lost its power to hurt me; it gives me, perhaps because by doing so I take away the pain, a great delight to put the severed parts together. Perhaps this is the strongest pleasure known to me. It is the rapture I get when in writing I seem to be discovering what belongs to what.[12]

To put the severed parts together, make them whole again, and move beyond pain and hurt—this sounds a little like psychoanalysis and, in literary terms, the process is one that a confessional memoir is ideally qualified to undertake. Its only rival in this respect is lyric poetry, like memoir an essentially first-person form. Ted Hughes spoke about the healing power of writing in terms not dissimilar to Woolf's. 'Poetry', he claimed, is 'nothing more than a facility for expressing that complicated process in which we locate, and attempt to heal, affliction—whether our own or that of others whose feeling we can share. The inmost spirit of poetry, in other words, is at bottom, in every recorded case, the voice of pain—and the physical body, so to speak, of poetry, is the treatment by which the poet tries to reconcile that pain with the world.'[13] Each of us, Hughes believed, has some story we need to articulate before we can realize our potential. In his case it was the story of his marriage to Sylvia Plath, which had become public property and which he wanted to reclaim. For years he couldn't do so. Look at his letters from the mid-1970s onwards and you'll find him describing himself variously as blocked, gagged, caged, kidnapped, hijacked, poisoned, 'populated by the deceased', caught in a logjam, immured in armour, and divided by steel doors or thick glass

---

[12] Virginia Woolf, 'A Sketch of the Past' (1939–40), reprinted in *Moments of Being*, ed. Jean Schulkind (Falmer: University of Sussex Press, 1976), 72.

[13] Ted Hughes to Bishop Ross Hook, 10 November 1982, in *Letters of Ted Hughes*, ed. Christopher Reid (London: Faber & Faber 2007), 458.

window from his real self, because unable to write about the trauma of Plath's suicide.

I once interviewed Hughes, who rarely gave interviews, about his children's book *The Iron Woman*, which he spoke of as a personal book and one intended to heal. 'Finally all works of art are just immense confessions of the central thing', he said. 'It's an illusion to think otherwise, to suppose it's good manners not to talk about yourself.'[14] I was surprised to hear him talking in this way. At the time I'd just published a memoir of my father—which I suspect Ted hadn't read, but which he knew about and the candour of which, again to my surprise, he approved. 'I often wish I'd done that at the time, with Sylvia', he said. 'It's like not mourning someone; if you don't it becomes damaging. It's better to try to get control of it . . . if you don't, it drifts away and takes a whole piece of yourself with it, like an amputation. To attack it and attack it and get it under control—it's like taking possession of your own life' (p. 171). He went on to criticize Auden's axiom that you 'should never write your autobiography, because it's your capital', and to praise Tolstoy—and Plath—for taking possession of the reality of their lives. 'Unless you do that, you're just tiptoeing round the edges of yourself', he said (p. 171).

Isn't this what life-writing amounts to—a way of taking possession of your own life, or, where biography rather than memoir is concerned, someone else's? Possession doesn't just mean immersion; detachment is required as well. J. R. Ackerley, in *My Father and Myself* (1968), talks of trying to see his life as if it were someone else's he was 'prowling about in'.[15] And there's a line on the first page of Susan Sontag's novel *Death Kit* (1967) which voices a similar sentiment: 'Some people are their lives', she says, others 'merely inhabit' them. A degree of watchfulness is implied here: a capacity to stand outside oneself, or float above, up on the ceiling, maybe, or be like a CCTV camera, constantly observing. You'll not take possession of your life unless you can see what it amounts to or where it's gone wrong, and that requires articulation as well as comprehension. Don't be coolly retrospective, I tell my students, plunge us into the heart of the action. Don't analyse, just say what happened—put us there. But putting us there also means

---

[14] See Blake Morrison, 'Man of Mettle', in *Too True* (London: Granta Books, 1998), 172.

[15] J. R. Ackerley, *My Father and Myself* (1968; London: Pimlico, 1992), 211.

putting the words in the right order: selecting, narrating, dramatizing, and establishing a consistent point of view—techniques associated with fiction that the non-fiction memoir depends on no less.

The idea that there's something rough-hewn or artless about confessional literature persists, though. There's a low-budget, improvised feel to it—the equivalent of the hand-held camera. Perhaps there's even a suspicion that if the confessional memoir is too well made it will lack authenticity. In Kathryn Harrison's memoir about incest, for instance, there's a passage where she describes feeling helpless and doomed in her relationship with her father, then gets up for a drink in the night, spots a cockroach in the kitchen, and rather than kill it traps it under a glass tumbler—and then watches it struggle.[16] This episode might have truly taken place, but the metaphorical aptness seems almost too convenient to be believable—the kind of thing a novelist might have invented.

Still, the idea that confessional narratives can't afford to be too well shaped is absurd; it's a form demanding artistry like any other. In Tobias Wolff's autobiographical novel *Old School* (2003), there's a wonderful passage describing a visit Robert Frost makes to a swanky private school, in order to present a prize and read his poems. During questions afterwards a clever, rather self-satisfied young teacher asks Frost whether poetry as well made as his fails to satisfy in a chaotic, war-torn modern age—isn't what's needed a kind of disorderliness that mimics the world out there? Frost is having none of it:

I lost my nearest friend in the one they called the Great War. So did Achilles lose his friend in war, and Homer did no injustice to his grief by writing about it in dactylic hexameters . . . Such grief can *only* be told in form. Maybe it only really exists in form. Form is everything. Without it you've got nothing but a stubbed-toe cry— sincere, maybe, for what that's worth, but with no depth or carry. No echo. You may have a grievance but you do not have grief, and grievances are for petitions, not poetry.[17]

Frost's distinction between grief and grievance might serve as the distinction between confessional memoirs of the best kind and misery memoirs of the worst. To put it another way, it's the difference between agency and

[16] Kathryn Harrison, *The Kiss* (London: Fourth Estate, 1997), 64–5 (henceforth cited within the text by page numbers).

[17] Tobias Woolf, *Old School* (London: Bloomsbury, 2004), 52–3.

victimhood, between taking responsibility (not least the responsibility to shape a story) and pointing the finger at a heartless world. I don't mean that victims of abuse or torture or a debilitating illness of some kind can't write powerful books—they can and do. But such books are never merely passive in their suffering: they look beyond the apportionment of blame to the darker recesses of the human heart. By contrast, when the author's message is a grievance against a world of motiveless malignity, with the innocent narrator passively enduring a succession of blows (shock and awe), then something counterproductive kicks in, the loss of that readerly sympathy which the narrator is angling for and craves.

Kathryn Harrison's memoir *The Kiss* is beautifully managed in that respect. As a young woman in an incestuous relationship with the father who has come back into her life after a long absence, she is, by definition, the victim. But she owns up to a certain complicity: 'Looking at him looking at me, I cannot help but fall painfully, precipitously in love', she says (p. 63), and feels jealous at finding him in bed with her mother, from whom he has separated. When she finally sleeps with him, the imagery is of a surrender, a giving in and letting go in the face of intense pressure. As for the act itself, it isn't described: 'The sight of him naked: at that point I fall completely asleep' (p. 136). The narcosis, or self-anaesthesia, is her way of coping—sleep in response to unbearable shame and desire: 'I sleep because I'm shocked and because I'm frightened. I want to avoid contemplating the enormity of what we're doing' (p. 138). Psychologically, this is convincing. And strategically, it's useful—as well as sparing herself, she is sparing us, as readers, who will only follow her so far, who aren't so prurient as to want a blow-by-blow account of the sex.

There's a similar boldness and astuteness and refusal of victimhood in Sharon Olds' poem 'First'. Olds finds the label 'confessional poet' uncomfortable. But awkward truth-telling is central to her art and this poem resembles Harrison's memoir not just in describing the sexual exploitation of a young woman by an older man, but in refusing victimhood. The episode takes place in a sulphur pool, and there's a reek of the devil about this man, but amid the fog and the steam comes an epiphany, and sense of triumph. 'I felt I knew / what his body wanted me to do', Old says. What he wants is a blow-job, and though it's a first-time experience for her it comes naturally, even innocently, 'like rubbing / my mother's back':

I gave over to flesh like church music
until he drew out and held himself and
something flew past me like a fresh ghost.
We sank into the water and lay there, napes
on the rim. *I've never done that before,*
I said. His eyes not visible
to me, his voice muffled, he said *You've been*
sucking cock since you were fourteen,
and fell asleep. I stayed beside him
so he wouldn't go under, he snored like my father, I
tried not to think about what he had said
but then I saw, in it, the unmeant
gift—that I was good at this
raw mystery I liked. I sat
and rocked, by myself, in the fog, in the smell
of kelp, night steam like animals' breath,
there where the harsh granite and quartz dropped down
into and under the start of the western sea.[18]

The young Olds gets one over the older man by turning his erroneous and
abusive taunt—'You've been sucking cock since you were fourteen'—into
a compliment, an 'unmeant gift'. Rather than feeling soiled by his insult,
she's cleansed and empowered by it.

If we feel resistant to this level of disclosure, that's also part of the charge.
TMI, people say, too much information, 'I don't wish to know that'. There
are revelations that make us feel uncomfortable, like voyeurs, or even
grubby, as if tarred with the same brush, and sometimes we take against
the author for that reason, for making us complicit. Confessional literature
rests on the premise of recognition and equivalence—'may any man who
dares say "I was a better man than he"', as Rousseau puts it (p. 17). But if
there is no recognition or equivalence, if we feel ugh, no way, the author's
on a different planet, I have never done, thought, or felt the things
described, then the mission fails. The author stretches out a hand but the
reader refuses to take it.

---

[18] Sharon Olds, 'First', from *The Wellspring* (1996), reprinted in *Selected Poems* (London: Jonathan
Cape, 2005), 72–3.

The confessional memoir has lost ground in recent years—as though the culture of emotion of which it was part of peaked at the end of the last century (in the UK in 1997, with the death of Princess Diana) and the genre has gone out of fashion. Back in the late 1980s and early 1990s, the memoir offered a return to veracity or believability, in reaction to magical realism and fabulism and metafiction; re-enter the reliable narrator. Now fiction is in the ascendancy again. The only memoirs that sell are celebrity memoirs. A few years ago, I supervised an MA student in her 70s, a vicar's wife, who had a fascinating story to tell about being brought up by two women, not knowing which of them, if either, was her mother. It was a beautifully written and ingeniously structured book about her quest to learn the truth, and the literary agent Peter Strauss took it on. But he couldn't find a commercial publisher. And in the end the author had to arrange for its publication herself.[19] In the new era of self- and e-publishing, perhaps it's unimportant that it failed to come out with a major press: it is at least out there, or on Amazon. But ten years earlier, before memoirs became the domain of TV chefs and soap stars, I think it would have found a publisher.

In the face of this downturn, the confessional memoir is itself changing and becoming bolder, tricksier, more playful in its relation to truth. Certainly Dave Eggers' memoir *A Heartbreaking Work of Staggering Genius* (2000) would suggest so. The book is, at heart, a heartfelt story: Eggers describes how both his parents died within a short space of time, and how he was left to bring up his 8-year-old brother. But around the central tale come a series of digressions, prefaces, rules, footnotes, clarifications, apologies, and suggestions for ways to enjoy the book that not only refuse the easy sentiment the story potentially offers but challenge common assumptions about life-writing. W. G. Sebald's books do this too, occupying an uncertain zone between fiction and non-fiction. What's truth, such memoirs ask? Isn't it relative? Does it matter whether the author is truthful or not?

Sebald and Eggers offer ways forward for life-writing, which is now branching out into new forms, including the lyric essay. Another path is that taken by Karl Ove Knausgaard, who shows how even the most humdrum of events can be made compelling: a fifty-page description of a

---

[19] Yvonne Craig Inskip, *Things My Mothers Never Told Me* (AuthorHouse, 2013).

children's party ought to be a recipe for disaster, but Knausgaard's account of such an occasion compels the reader's attention—it compelled this reader's anyway. His memoirs restore the centrality of family and childhood. The numerous genealogical websites that have sprung up in recent years have done so too, by making the writing of family history easier than it used to be—though against that we're also entering an era where certain kinds of written documents invaluable to biographers and memoirists will cease to exist. Without the letters my mother and father exchanged in the Second World War (and which he, a hoarder, made a point of keeping because he thought his children might be interested to read them), I'd not have been able to write my book about my mother. 'When a writer is born into a family, that family is dead', Philip Roth likes to say, quoting Czeslaw Milosz.[20] Well, yes, but that family will also have an afterlife—will exist in a new dimension, on the page.

In *The Journalist and the Murderer* (1990) Janet Malcolm famously said that every journalist betrays his or her sources—that a writer's only loyalty is to the story and getting it out there, not to the people it concerns. Betrayal is a troubling notion. 'What would your mother/father think?' I'm often asked. Well, they'd not like everything I've included in my accounts of them. But I'd still say I was honouring them, even while departing from their official versions of themselves. I doubt that those who knew my parents (a dwindling number) will think less of them after reading my books, and meanwhile others who never knew them now *will* know them, a little. That isn't resurrection. Perhaps it isn't quite redemption either. But it isn't an act of hostility. And though confession may play a part, it's only there to do right by the dead, which means being honest, not hagiographical. True, the dead don't give permission, but death itself is permission. And what it permits is elegy and homage.

Confessional literature, allegedly so inward-looking, is as much about other people as about the writer. And at best it's *for* other people: it opens up an intimate space for readers to inhabit. As the author of *The Empathy Exams* (2014), Leslie Jamieson says, 'confession is often the opposite of solipsism: it creates dialogue. It elicits responses. It coaxes chorus like a brushfire'.[21] There's even a case for saying that confessional literature is

---

[20] *New York Times* interview, 15 September 2011.
[21] 'Confessional Writing is Not Self-Indulgent', *Guardian*, 5 July 2014.

ultimately selfless: only authors lacking self-awareness could be so rashly candid, and only authors desperate to reach out to others are willing to lay themselves out for minute inspection. When private matters are made public, there'll always be protests: *Leave it out*, as the saying goes. But there'll also be those who feel consoled and affirmed, grateful for the risky stuff left in. Poetry and fiction may command more respect. But confessionalism shouldn't be dismissed as a dubious subgenre. If literature is the enemy of discretion and conformity, if its value lies in resisting obfuscation and euphemism by means of truth-telling, then confessional memoirs may be the truest literature of all.

12

The Rights to a Life

J. David Velleman

In *After Long Silence*, Helen Fremont tells the story of growing up in the
Midwest as the daughter of Polish Catholic parents.[1] She recounts some of
the stories they told of their courtship in eastern Poland, which was
occupied by the Germans, then occupied by the Soviets—who deported
her father to Siberia—and then occupied again by the Germans. She
recounts the stories they told of his escape back to Poland and, from
there, to Rome, where he was reunited with her mother, who had escaped
from Poland disguised as an Italian soldier. She recounts the stories they
told of their marriage in Rome and eventual emigration to the United
States. She tells her own story of growing up in the shadow of her parents'
wartime ordeal. She tells the story of coming out as a lesbian to her parents
and her Italian aunt.

Helen tells the story of discovering, in her thirties, that her parents were
actually Polish Jews—her mother, the daughter of an orthodox rabbi. She
tells the story of gradually uncovering the true history of her parents'
separation, escape, and reunification. She recounts that hair-raising history,
including all of the cover stories that her mother told in order to elude
arrest by the Germans, who had reoccupied eastern Poland; including her

---

[1] Helen Fremont, *After Long Silence: A Memoir* (New York: Dell Publishing, 1999) (henceforth
cited within the text by page numbers).

mother's new identity as a Polish Catholic girl named Maria, finally married in the Church to her revenant fiancé; including the cover stories that she told to her daughters as a way of fending off their questions about the past.

Helen tells the story of confronting her parents with what she had learned; she tells the story of their initial denials, their sleepless nights of returning memories, their grudging help in her project of reconstructing the past. She tells the story of discovering, and then explaining to her mother, how her mother's parents, Helen's grandparents, had died—not 'in a bomb', as her mother had always said, but in the gas chambers of Belzec. And, finally, she tells the story of telling all of these stories in a book of which her parents disapproved.

Helen tells these stories in telegraphic, Tralfamadorian style, jumping from wartime Poland, to post-war Italy, to Michigan in the 1950s, to Boston in the 1990s, and back again, unstuck in time.

Helen also enumerates the stories that she cannot tell, because they have been suppressed or repressed or simply forgotten by her parents: she doesn't even know her mother's given name. And in telling the history of her parents' wartime experiences, she deftly hints at the ways in which she is embroidering on shreds of evidence for the sake of telling a good story.

As a child, Helen heard many true stories from her parents and very few lies; they denied their heritage mainly by omission. Did her parents owe her the full story? Was it in any sense her story as well as theirs? What right did Helen have to undo her parents' repression and then to publish their story against their wishes? What right did she have to embellish the story with narrative details that were fictional, despite her insistence that they re-created some narrative truth?

More than most of us, Helen's parents lived through experiences that had the formal structure of a story: meeting and courtship, separation and trials, triumph and reunion: beginning, middle, and end. These events are 'their story' in a sense in which their later life in America is not, because the latter doesn't make for a story at all; the former make a story, and it is theirs.

The historiographer Hayden White says that the story form never inheres in events but can only be imposed on them.[2] My view is that the

---

[2] For Hayden White on the story form, see *Metahistory: The Historical Imagination in Nineteenth-Century Europe* (Baltimore: Johns Hopkins University Press, 1973); *Tropics of Discourse: Essays in Cultural Criticism*

story form is in essence an emotional cadence—an arc of emotions aroused, complicated, and resolved—and I would say that the wartime experiences of Helen's parents had an overall emotional arc of the right shape.[3] These emotions were the main engines of her parents' progress across Europe, and so the story form really was inherent in their journey.

Helen and her sister were told the outline of this story from their earliest childhood:

Their love story I had been fed early and often, until it seemed part of my bones. I knew that they had fallen in love before the war, and they had been separated for six years without knowing if the other was alive; my mother escaped Poland dressed as an Italian soldier, and my father walked across Europe after the war, found my mother in Rome, and married her ten years to the day after they had first met. That was the tale they liked to tell and retell, the story they used to summarize their lives. It was a good story, because it ran a thread across the war and connected the two lovers before and after. (p. 8)

Thus, Helen's parents exploited the arc of this story to distract attention from matters unspoken.[4] These matters included facts about the past, but they also included emotions that were very much in the present. Helen says:

I had been living my life with flawed vision, stumbling in the dark, bumping into things I hadn't realized were there. No one acknowledged anything. Yet each time I walked into my parents' house, I fell over something, or dropped into something, a cavernous silence, an unspoken, invisible danger. (p. 31)

The point of this and similar passages is not that Helen was continually stumbling into the six-year lacuna in her parents' story. There was indeed a narrative lacuna, because narrating those six years would have required her parents to reveal that they were Jewish; but that lacuna is not the 'invisible danger' of which Helen speaks here. The invisible danger is not even the danger that her parents faced as Jews in Nazi-occupied Poland. It is rather the danger of unleashing the emotions they retained from that experience.

(Baltimore: Johns Hopkins University Press, 1987); *The Content of Form* (Baltimore: Johns Hopkins University Press, 1987).

[3] I present this analysis of narrative in 'Narrative Explanation', *Philosophical Review* 112 (2003), 1–25. At one point, Helen says, 'Something happens, then something happens, then something happens. This is called a story' (p. 247). I disagree.

[4] 'The past was always like this, an empty space in our lives, a gap in our conversations, into which our mother tumbled from time to time, quietly, without warning' (p. 145).

When she says, 'No one acknowledged anything', she means that her parents didn't acknowledge the grief and fear they still carried with them. So whereas the often-repeated love story skipped but never falsified facts about the past, it did falsify emotions felt in the present, since their parents were not in fact living happily ever after.

When Helen discovers her Jewish background, she begins attending synagogue, and she eventually seeks instruction in Judaism from a rabbi. There are many reasons why Helen might have tried to enter Judaism, which after all remains foreign to many who identify themselves as Jews. What she suggests is that she was trying to fill out a newfound self-understanding: 'All our lives', she tells her mother, 'there's been something that just doesn't fit. This explains so much about who we are, our childhood, our family' (p. 45). Her sister Lara tells her, 'It's not just about *them*! . . . It's about *us*! About who *we* are!' (p. 159).[5] The prospect of explaining who she is leads Helen to embrace her Jewishness:

I had to admit, I wanted to be Jewish—if for no other reason than because it simply made *sense*. I began to recognize myself as a person with roots and a past, with a family history, with an identity. The stories of my childhood suddenly took on new meaning—everything seemed to be shifting, an underground movement of tectonic plates slowly clicking into place, finally *fitting*. (p. 32)

When it comes to explaining how things suddenly began to fit, however, Helen can offer little more than clichés about 'cultural' Jewishness. Voicing her first suspicions to her mother, she says, 'I don't know why . . . but I have the feeling that I'm Jewish':

'Like that time', I said, 'I went to visit Rachel after my first year of law school.' Rachel's mother was a Jewish Holocaust survivor. I'd spent a weekend at their house twelve years earlier. 'Remember what I told you when I came back. That it was just like being at home. With her father listening to a violin concerto in the other room, and the living room filled with books, and all her mother's plants in the window. And we sat at the kitchen counter, Rachel and her mother and I, and sipped coffee and talked and talked—and for a moment I thought I was with you and Dad—it was so much like *home*. I can't explain it—but I remember I told you about it—there was a deep resonance somehow.' (pp. 24–5)

---

[5] Helen tells her aunt, 'We needed to know about this, to understand our family, to know who we are' (p. 321).

After these suspicions are confirmed:

Lara and I laughed with recognition: the challah bread of our youth . . . the smoked fish that my father loved; potato pancakes. The matzos that we had always eaten at Easter. (pp. 34–5)

These passages fall flat. It's hard to believe that Helen gained much self-understanding from recognizing that her family's potato pancakes were *latkes*.

Similarly, Helen describes her parents' past at a level of detail that cannot be relevant to her self-understanding. Why does it matter to her that her grandfather was a rabbi? I can hardly believe that his membership in the clergy left any mark on Helen herself. Indeed, very little of her parents' life as Jews left any mark, precisely because they suppressed, repressed, and forgot it. Yet Helen herself regards it as worth reporting that her mother's family in Poland lit Sabbath candles, and that her grandmother shaved her head and wore a wig.

I doubt whether Helen's detailed reconstruction of her parents' past actually accounts for anything significant about herself or her childhood. When Helen says 'I began to recognize myself as a person with roots and a past, with a family history, with an identity', I suspect that she is describing, not a recognition of who or what she already was, but a fresh *cognition* of herself, as having some roots or other, some past or other, some history or other— and hence some identity or other—where previously she had nothing at all, because of the regime of repression in which she grew up. Embracing Judaism may not have been a way of recovering a pre-existing identity; it may rather have been an attempt to construct an identity for the first time.

What shaped Helen as a child may have been no more than the fact that her parents had lived through persecution and loss, ultimately emerging with an iron determination to leave it all behind. Helen was also shaped, I think, by inheriting characteristics of her parents that made them sur-vivors, starting with the sheer will to survive but also including, for example, a remarkable facility with languages, which enabled them to pass themselves off as Germans or Italians; an insight into others' motiv-ations, which enabled them to recognize who could and could not be trusted; a capacity for self-denial and self-control; and, finally, a talent for composing stories. In writing her book, I would say, Helen was employing a gift for self-narration that she had inherited from parents who self-narrated their way out of Nazi Europe.[6] And in fashioning her new identity as a Jew, she was employing the gift that enabled her parents to fashion their identities as Catholics, with the difference that Helen was aiming for consistency with an actual past. In achieving consistency with that past, however, Helen was not necessarily achieving consistency with a pre-existent self.

Helen embellishes the narrative of her parents' history with rich fictional details, as she herself reveals. In the midst of a fifteen-page narration of her mother's escape from Poland, she remarks:

I don't know if he said this. I don't know Polish, or Yiddish, or whatever language they spoke to each other. I wasn't there. My mother didn't tell me. The way she told the story was like this: 'And so I cut my hair short, dressed up as an Italian soldier, and marched out of Poland with the Italian army.' (pp. 233–4)[7]

Introducing the narration of her father's arrest, she says:

It's not clear exactly what happened. But nothing is ever exactly clear. History is a card table full of illusions, and we must sort through and pick the ones we wish to believe. And so I choose this one. (p. 130)

When Helen says 'I choose this one', she is speaking of one among many versions of a particular episode, but the same statement applies to her entire project. Her book is subtitled 'a memoir', but the story is not her own: she has appropriated it—chosen it—as the narrative on which to found a self-conception. And this appropriation raises the question of Helen's right to tell a story that had been buried by its actual protagonists.

Maybe by embellishing her parents' story, Helen gains the right to tell it, because it is now partly her creation. And maybe by revealing that the story is partly her creation, she blunts her parents' objections to its being told. For when she confesses to embellishing some parts of the story, she casts doubt over every part, any one of which could be fictional, for all the reader can tell. Once she has undermined her own credibility with the reader, she

---

[6] Helen says that her mother escaped from the Nazis by 'making up stories to save her life, spinning a tale of herself, shifting colors and sequences to suit her needs. She had invented herself a hundred times over by the time the war was over' (p. 47).

[7] Also: 'I can't explain it, and I won't stop trying. I will fill this vacuum with words until I recognize them as memory' (p. 186).

can no longer give the reader credible information about her parents. She thereby cloaks her parents in the reader's confusion about what to believe.

More pressing than the question of Helen's right to publish the story is the question of her right to confront her parents with repressed details of their past. Her mother implores her not to do the same to her Italian aunt, but she goes ahead anyway. These confrontations can seem like paternalistic 'interventions' of the sort that are partly benevolent and partly hostile. It's as if Helen is punishing her elders for keeping secrets from her, by forcing them to face the secrets that they have been keeping from themselves.

That repression is enacted in the book's crucial scene, as Helen and her sister Lara reveal the fate of their grandparents:

'I wrote away for information', Lara said, 'and I got back documentation about our family. We know what happened to your parents. We know what happened to Dad's mother.'

'What happened?' my mother suddenly cried. Her hands started trembling with a terrible urgency, while her face remained frozen—a wide-eyed mask of incomprehension. 'Then you know more than I do!' she exclaimed.

Lara nodded slowly, confused by my mother's sudden shift from anger to bewilderment.

'Tell me', my mother cried. 'What happened? I don't even know what happened to my parents!' She turned desperately from Lara to me and back again, her hands shaking. 'What happened?'

I hadn't been prepared for this. I had expected my mother to refuse to talk about it; I had been prepared for her to deny it, to get angry, to scoff at me and dismiss it, but I did not expect her to beg us to tell her how her parents were killed.

'Tell me!' my mother repeated. 'What happened to them?'

I screwed up my courage, looked directly in my mother's eyes, and spoke as calmly as I could: 'We found out', I said evenly, 'that your parents were gassed at Belzec.'

My sentence dropped like a bomb into a terrible silence. I bit my tongue. I hadn't meant to be so blunt, so harsh. Lara kicked me under the table, and with growing panic I waited for my mother's reaction. Seconds ticked by, and I was consumed by an excruciating sense of guilt that I had just shattered my mother's world.

But my mother did not react. She stared at me with the same puzzled look on her face, as if I hadn't spoken. 'Tell me what happened to them', she repeated, hands outstretched.

I kept quiet, shaken. I can't continue with this, I thought. I can't bear to do this . . .

'I don't even know what happened to my parents!' Mom cried. 'Tell me!' (pp. 42–3)

'My sentence dropped like a bomb into a terrible silence', Helen says. Her mother had always dismissed questions about the fate of her parents by saying, cryptically, that they had died 'in a bomb'. Helen is now, so to speak, killing her grandparents all over again, by dropping a verbal bomb. She drops it into 'a terrible silence', a brief fragment of the 'long silence' that had enabled her mother to unknow her parents' deaths. And Helen's mother bravely persists—perseverates—in not knowing.

At the end of the book, Helen is visiting her aunt Zosia in Rome, writing the book. So she is simultaneously writing the story and living what she writes. On the same visit, she reveals her discoveries about the family to her Roman cousin and faces the ire of her aunt for doing so.

The reader wonders to what extent the writing of this chapter influenced the living of it—to what extent it was lived so as to be written. Did Helen tell her cousin of his Jewish background for independent reasons, or she did tell him in order to write about it? And this question, raised by her contemporaneous narration of writing the book, echoes back through the preceding chapters. How much of her research was undertaken by the daughter and how much by the aspiring writer? In plotting with her sister to pry information out of their parents, was she also plotting her memoir?

Could it be that Helen came out as a lesbian in order to have the parallel storylines of uncovering her parents' secret and disclosing her own? Her mother refuses to believe that Helen is a lesbian, just as she refuses to take in the revelation of her parents' murder. As they say, you couldn't make that up—unless, of course, you made it up in order to make it happen in order to write it.

Or maybe it's the reverse. Maybe Helen wrote it in order to motivate herself to make it happen. In writing the book, she wrote herself into a corner, so to speak, since her friends and lovers would see the hypocrisy of her remaining closeted while outing her parents. How better to resolve her own indecision about whether to come out?

Or maybe Helen just researched her parents' past, came out as a lesbian, and wrote a book about it all.

After Long Silence is a book of stories about silence. Silence is the villain of the piece. The human villains, Nazis and Bolsheviks, make only the briefest appearance. Even Helen's description of the Petlura Days pogrom in Lvov, as witnessed by her mother and aunt, reaches its climax in Helen's own unwillingness to ask her mother whether she was raped. In a scene of horrors, silence takes centre stage.

The book has many heroes: Helen's father and mother, and those who helped them to escape. But the real hero of the book is the narrated truth, which triumphs over silence in the end. The book is one long testament to the healing power of The True Story.

Yet with some truths, there is nothing to do but forget. I believe in virtuous Holocaust deniers—namely, the survivors, many of whom, like Helen's parents, managed to achieve a merciful forgetfulness. 'Forget the past, live for the future', Helen's mother says. Hers was a past worth forgetting.

Once remembered, some of her mother's past can be domesticated by being told as a story, especially since it has an outwardly happy ending. But one part cannot be told as a story, because it has no narrative ending. It goes: 'And so they were herded into a windowless chamber and gassed to death.' One cannot imagine punctuating that sentence with 'The End'. It's a finish that isn't an ending, because it brings no closure. In the minds of the survivors, the final scene never ends.

Surely, this narratively intractable passage of history is the one that Helen's mother is struggling hardest to repress. Helen can't domesticate it for her, and so I continue to wonder whether she was entitled to tell it at all.

As for Helen's right to publish the story, she says that she is honouring her forgotten ancestors and expressing love for her parents:

My family is greater than just my parents and Zosia—my family extends backward in time and space. I want to put them on record, however imperfectly—I want them to be seen and heard.

And strangely enough, on the page I begin to recognize myself in my parents—a gesture here, a question there. My attachment to them grows stronger with each sentence that arranges itself before me. Perhaps this is the ultimate irony of my family: I express my love for them in ways that are invariably the opposite of what they would wish. (p. 344)

A complicated passage. The declaration of wanting her relatives to be seen and heard is an implicit rebuke to her parents, survivors who did not bear witness for the dead: they lived to tell the tale and then refused to tell it. Helen then disclaims responsibility for this rebuke: the sentences arrange themselves on the page, she says, as if the tale is telling itself. Finally, she expresses the mixed motives behind the whole complicated project, an expression of love that is also an expression of defiance.

I believe Helen when she says that writing her book is an expression of love; I believe the same of her family interventions. Still, I finished the book wishing to know more about how her parents received it. We are told only that they did not approve. As for the details, Helen is silent.

When I was a child, I was told that my father's sister Emma had perished in the Holocaust. That phrase made the Holocaust sound like a vortex into which people just disappeared, like sailors who are said to have perished at sea. The poetic vagueness of it expressed my father's perfect ignorance as to when, where, and how his sister had died.

When Germany invaded Western Europe in May of 1940, Emma was living with her husband and young daughter in the Dutch village of Borculo, which was close to the German border and immediately overrun. My father was living in Antwerp and was able to escape, together with his other sister, Molly, and their parents. They made their way through France and Spain to Portugal, and thence to the United States, where my father spent the war working for the Office of Strategic Services in Washington, DC. He travelled to Borculo immediately after the war, on one of the first post-war visas issued to civilians. When he knocked on the door of Emma's house, he found strangers sitting at her table, eating from her dishes—and claiming never to have heard of her.

In the early 1990s, an amateur genealogist in Holland wrote to my father in New York and to me in Ann Arbor, Michigan, seeking information about people with the last name of Velleman. He told us what he already knew about my father's family history, including many names and dates that my father could confirm. He also included information that my father had not previously known—in particular, the names of the camps where various aunts, uncles, and cousins had been killed, and the dates of their deaths. No such information was included for Emma, but we reasoned that information about Emma's death might have eluded his researches because it was recorded under her married name. My father wrote back, supplying Emma's particulars and asking the genealogist to apply his methods to the question of her fate.

One day my father called to say that a letter had arrived from our correspondent in Holland. He then began to read: Emma, her husband, and their daughter had been interned at the concentration camp Westerbork, in

Holland; had been placed on a transport bound for Auschwitz on 24 November 1942; and mother and daughter were presumed to have died on arrival, three days later. My father began to sob and dropped the phone. I had never before heard my father cry.

When my parents next visited Ann Arbor, my father silently handed me a manila folder full of yellowed correspondence. It had been given to him by his surviving sister, Molly, when he told her what he had learned about Emma and her family. In the years immediately following the war, Molly had corresponded with international relief agencies on behalf of the family in America, seeking information, in particular, about Emma's daughter, Rita, who might have survived without knowing how to contact her relatives. The folder now handed to me by my father contained carbon copies of Molly's enquiries, along with the original replies. The latter were all dead ends, with one exception. A letter from the International Red Cross, dated 1955, informed the family that Rita has been interned in the concentration camp Westerbork, in Holland; had been placed on a transport bound for Auschwitz on 24 November 1942; and was presumed to have died on arrival, three days later.

So my father had known Emma's fate all along. Why, I asked, had he recruited the genealogist to investigate what he already knew? Why had he reacted to the information as if hearing it for the first time?

He replied, 'I had repressed it.'

When I was a teenager, I quizzed my father about the war, and he told me the story of his escape: the chance encounter with a rich uncle who owned a car, which carried the family to safety; the time in Bordeaux when he helped stamp passports for the Portuguese Consul who was defying orders from Lisbon by issuing transit visas to thousands of refugees; the night they spent in a broken-down castle where the beds were full of lice; how he and his mother crossed the Spanish border on foot, mopping their brows with handkerchiefs holding diamonds from his father's workshop. (My grandfather was a diamond cleaver, and his occupation was noted in his passport, so that he would be searched.) My father also told me about his trip back to Europe after the war—a long story, mainly about coincidental meetings on-board ship.

After learning how he had repressed his knowledge of Emma's death, I realized that my father had turned his wartime experiences into a picaresque. Yes, his sister and her family had perished—he told that, too, though not of course the details that he had not yet recovered. But the central, significant event was lost in a series of adventures, all of which were bathed in the glow of a happy ending on the horizon.

Our brush with genealogy prompted me to start researching the family's history. This was just a few years before the Internet transformed genealogical research, and so I spent many hours in the basement of the local Mormon centre, reeling through microfilmed records of mysterious Mormon rites performed for my ancestors. Like Helen Fremont, I had found religion, though in my case, it wasn't Judaism.

Also like Helen Fremont, I was taking on the self-image of the so-called second generation, whose childhood was touched in some way by their parents' brush with the Holocaust. And I was adopting that self-image by hitching my life story to that of my father and, more importantly, to that of his sister Emma, whom I could never know. I even visited Borculo during a break from a conference in the Netherlands. But what is it to me, what is it about me, that I had an aunt who died in Auschwitz ten years before I was born?

I think that the death of my aunt is meaningful to me because she meant so much to my father, who meant so much to me. I would like to say that I grieve for her in solidarity with him, but the fact is that I doubt whether he ever really grieved for her. I once asked my father whether, after receiving confirmation of her death, the family had held a memorial of any kind. The idea had never occurred to him.

So I suspect that my father passed on to me an emotional task that he could not bear to do himself. And I suspect that Helen Fremont was given a much heavier emotional task, with the added burden of not knowing what it was. In this sense, discovering her parents' history really was a discovery of her own identity, after all. She was Jewish despite her Catholic upbringing because she was carrying the unresolved grief of Jewish parents for grandparents who were murdered for being Jews. Even if our parents don't pass on their stories, they still pass on emotions that only their stories can help us to resolve. To that extent, at least, their stories are ours.

13

Human 2.0? Life-Writing in the Digital Age

Patrick Hayes

In October 2000 Philippe Lejeune, who since the early 1980s has pioneered the scholarly research on diaries, reported back from a year spent sampling online diaries, or 'blogs'. *'Cher écran . . . ': Journal personnel, ordinateur, internet* took the unusual form of a journal, and what this form allowed Lejeune to do was tell the story of his gradual conversion from dismissal to approval. 'When you've been working on real personal diaries, everything in blogs feels like a caricature or prostitution', go the opening remarks: 'it all seems to ring hollow'.[1] At first he could not grasp how a diary, that most intimate of autobiographical forms, could be written for the gaze of strangers. The online environment is surely, he felt, 'the total opposite of the conditions that led to the development of the personal diary, which is based on a different notion of time (delay, maturation, and assimilation), and of communication (deferred or exclusive, that is, based on secrecy)' (p. 301). But gradually he started to be drawn to it as a venue for the diary. He began to find individual bloggers whose skills of narrative control and self-exploration compared favourably to book diarists. Then he found more

---

[1] Philippe Lejeune, *On Diary*, ed. Jeremy D. Popkin and Julie Rak, trans. Katherine Durnin (Manoa: University of Hawaii Press, 2009), 299 (henceforth cited in the text by page numbers).

positive ways of interpreting the impulse to make the intimate public. Blogging isn't like the vanity press market in the book world, 'with its naivety and pretentiousness', but more like 'self-publishing, which is active and responsible' (p. 314). Bloggers don't want artificial glory, only 'a response', much the same as when you show your diary to a trusted friend. Moreover, he concluded, writing for others might even create a new idiom that is 'looser', closer to 'a spoken style', and which contrasts favourably with the over-literary obsession with 'style' and 'depth' in book diaries. Online life-writing, he even-handedly concluded, has 'constraints and resources that are just beginning to be explored. It is a new frontier' (p. 316).

This was in 2000, and when Lejeune republished parts of '*Cher écran . . .* ' in English translation in 2009 he noted that the online environment had changed so fast that his research was now of purely 'archaeological value' (p. 299). The intervening period had witnessed not only exponential growth in the uptake of the Internet, but the emergence of a range of different channels for digital life-writing, such as social networking sites (Facebook, Google+), play and gaming sites (Second Life, World of Warcraft), and user-generated content (YouTube, Flickr), a development that has become cumulatively known as 'Web 2.0'.[2] As José van Dijck puts it, 'online services shifted from offering channels for networked communication', such as the blogs Lejeune researched, 'to becoming interactive, two-way vehicles for networked sociality'.[3]

Most obviously, Web 2.0 has made it very easy to write online. Whereas Lejeune's Web 1.0 bloggers needed at least some basic familiarity with internet programming to set up their sites and begin posting, Facebook enables anyone with a mouse and keyboard to set up their own slickly produced magazine-style webpage for free in a matter of minutes. And as this much more accessible interface took off, for many groups of people online life-writing ceased to be a wholly optional part of life, as it was for Lejeune's bloggers. Teenagers increasingly found they had to have a Facebook presence, and a well-maintained one at that, just to be socially included. Certain jobs, especially sales and public relations, increasingly

---

[2] According to Jaron Lanier, the phrase was coined by Tim O'Reilly, founder of O'Reilly Media, and a leading supporter of the open source movement. See Jaron Lanier, *You Are Not a Gadget* (London: Allen Lane, 2010), 65.

[3] José van Dijck, *The Culture of Connectivity* (Oxford: Oxford University Press, 2013), 11.

required employees to be on Facebook and Twitter, with the intimate and the corporate becoming increasingly blurred together.[4] Simultaneous with the rise of Web 2.0 was the development of the 'smartphone', a mobile internet device that further increased the uptake of social networking, and also the amount of time spent online. You could now write your life while you actually lived it. Parents started to text while pushing their children on the swings in the local playground; smartphones started to be placed on the table at dinner parties.

The benefits of these new developments have been rather self-servingly trumpeted by the corporations who own the social networking sites. In *The New Digital Age* (2013), Eric Schmidt, Executive Chairman of Google, and Jared Cohen, Director of 'Google Ideas', made great claims for the democratic value of Web 2.0 in its empowerment of ordinary people to find an online voice. But intellectuals have passed a mainly negative judgement on the quality of that online voice, and when Lejeune's optimistic account of blogging appeared in English in 2009 it was out of step with the dominant mood. In a 2010 article for the *New York Review of Books*, Zadie Smith revealed that she had sampled Facebook for two months (compare Lejeune's whole year on blogs) before quitting for good, and advising her readers to do likewise. Web 2.0, she claimed, creates 'People 2.0', a reduced and banalized kind of human being, obsessed with connection for connection's sake.[5] Jonathan Franzen has recently started to issue regular pronouncements on the power of the Internet to banalize and distract, which have earned him the rather amusing '#Franzenhates' Twitter stream in response.[6] More substantially, though, over the last couple of years a string of very notable books have been published in which prominent intellectuals, mainly from the social sciences, but also from within the technology industry, have publically revised their earlier enthusiasm for digital life-writing.[7]

The foremost of these intellectuals is Sherry Turkle, Professor of the Social Studies of Science and Technology at MIT, and a social psychologist

---

[4] Dave Eggers' dystopian novel, *The Circle* (London: Hamish Hamilton, 2013), explores the ramifications of the commercial appropriation of the intimate sphere: the novel is set on the so-called 'campus' of a company that bears many similarities to Google.

[5] Zadie Smith, 'Generation Why?', *New York Review of Books*, 25 November 2010.

[6] See especially Jonathan Franzen, 'What's Wrong with the Modern World', *Guardian*, 13 September 2013.

[7] These include Jaron Lanier, *You Are Not a Gadget*, and Nicholas Carr, *The Shallows* (London: Atlantic, 2010).

by training. In *Life on the Screen* (1995), a study of blogging and early virtual reality applications, Turkle claimed that she found herself in a 'liminal moment' in which it was an open question as to whether the virtual would enhance real life or ultimately degrade it. While she voiced concerns about the potential for 'social alienation' in people spending increasing amounts of time online, she tended to celebrate the potential for experiment and self-discovery in what were then known as multi-user domains (MUDs), in which fictional or real identities could be composed by participants for purposes of chat, storytelling, and gaming. But in *Alone Together: Why We Expect More from Technology and Less from Each Other* (2011), the title says it all. For Turkle, the liminal moment of the mid-1990s has turned into a contemporary dystopia in which the new forms of digital media are now actively deforming human relationships and depleting our most intimate experiences.

To intellectuals such as Turkle, Web 2.0 seems ever less like an exciting new frontier for life-writing. But this discourse of concern, powerful though it is, does not tell the whole story. A range of contemporary novelists who, unlike Smith and Franzen, work in more experimental literary traditions, have found much to admire in the new forms of self-presentation the Internet has made available. In *Super Sad True Love Story* (2010), Gary Shteyngart draws attention to the vitality of the more shallow and demotic diaristic voice promoted by social networking sites; in *Leaving the Atocha Station* (2011), Ben Lerner takes inspiration from the fractured self-expression of instant messaging; in *The Sluts* (2004), Denis Cooper explores the new kinds of pornographic writing created by the fantastical confessions left on anonymous message boards. In much of the leading scholarship on digital life-writing the view from literature, especially from more experimental literature, has not yet found a voice. My aim in this chapter is to place Turkle's concerns as a social psychologist, which I will explore in detail, in dialogue with the possibilities that imaginative writers have found in the newer kinds of online writing. Of course I cannot tell the whole story: a longer essay would go on to explore, among other things, the realm of virtual reality gaming, a rich field of life-writing which has attracted some interesting literary responses.[8] Instead I will offer three snapshots,

---

[8] See especially Jonathan Lethem, *Chronic City* (London: Faber & Faber, 2010), which draws upon Philip K. Dick's exploration of the virtual; also Ernest Cline, *Ready Player One* (London: Century, 2012).

each focusing on a different idiom, starting with social networking in general, then moving into some more specific reflections on instant messaging and the online confession.

One of the reasons Lejeune found himself able to warm to audience-oriented internet diaries was because his own ideas about the book diary actually tended to emphasize a chatty and dialogic trajectory for the genre. Against those who regard the modern book diary as a secular version of the spiritual diary, with its atmosphere of earnest self-exploration, Lejeune argued instead that it descends from, and is inflected by, the record-keeping practices of the family account book, and, above all, by the letter. The addressee in 'Dear Diary' evolves out of an imagined address to a real friend, a 'friend to whom you can tell everything, who will not judge you, who will understand you and say nothing'.[9] Even if the identity of the online confidant is unknown at the time of posting, the Web 1.0 blog can nonetheless, he claimed, take on the atmosphere congenial to intimate disclosure. In 'Growing Up Tethered', the most disturbing chapter of *Alone Together*, Sherry Turkle argues that this congenial atmosphere changes on social networking websites such as Facebook. Traditionally, she argues, adolescents have needed 'time to discover themselves, time to think', and above all time to reflect upon their feelings—all needs that were well served by the book diary. Social networking sites, combined with mobile technology, do nothing to encourage this kind of development, and instead promote a very different kind of self, which she refers to as 'hyper-other-directedness'.[10]

With 'other-directedness' Turkle has a specific sociological theory in mind. The concept was first developed by David Riesman, also a social psychologist, in his now-classic analysis of the impact of consumerism on American identity, *The Lonely Crowd: A Study of the Changing American Character* (1950). Riesman's argument was that as the post-war American economy began to reach a distinctively 'post-industrial' phase, there was taking place a correlative shift in the 'social character' of Americans, led in particular by the influence of mass media. He borrowed the concept of social character

---

[9] See especially the chapter titled 'Oh My Paper!', in Lejeune, *On Diary*, 93–102.

[10] Sherry Turkle, *Alone Together: Why We Expect More from Technology and Less from Each Other* (New York: Basic Books, 2011), 177 (henceforth cited within the text by page numbers).

from Erich Fromm: 'In order that any society may function well', Fromm had argued, 'its members must acquire the kind of character which makes them *want* to act in the way they *have* to act as members of the society... They have to *desire* what objectively is necessary for them to do.'[11] The rapidly expanding industrial economy of the nineteenth century had tended to create what Riesman called an 'inner-directed' character type, defined by strong inner values derived from powerful relationships with authority figures such as parents, and from the forms of self-reflection cultivated in solitude. But the consumer society, Riesman argued, is driven by new economic needs: to create an expanding domestic market of eager consumers, and for a workforce more attuned to working in concert with other people in large and complex bureaucratic corporations. Thus emerges the new, 'other-directed' self. 'What is common to all other-directeds', Riesman claimed, 'is that their contemporaries are the source of direction for the individual—either those known to him or those with whom he is indirectly acquainted, through friends and through the mass media. This source is of course "internalised" in the sense that dependence on it for guidance in life is implanted early.'[12] While Riesman tried not to pass judgement on the other-directed self, it is hard not to read his book as the diagnosis of a cultural catastrophe in the making. In their constant attunement to the signals of acceptability and desirability produced by the mass media and their peers, other-directed people become unusually prone to anxiety; as compulsive consumers they are more prone to fads and fashions; they are a 'lonely crowd', always together but alone together, with little independent capacity to reflect on themselves.

There are three main reasons why Turkle thinks that the kind of life-writing found on social networking sites takes 'other-directedness...to a higher power' (p. 176), as she puts it. She argues that it tends to promote a form of life-writing that is not contemplative but brief and attention-grabbing; not soul-searching, but conventional, seeking to 'fit in'; not reflective but written immediately, for immediate consumption by others.

---

[11] Fromm was a social psychologist affiliated to the Frankfurt School. The quotation is from *Man for Himself: An Inquiry into the Psychopathology of Ethics* (1947), italics in original; quoted in David Riesman, Nathan Glazer, and Reuel Denney, *The Lonely Crowd: A Study in the Changing American Character* (New Haven, CT, and London: Princeton University Press, 1950), 5.

[12] Riesman, Glazer, and Denney, *The Lonely Crowd*, 22.

By way of illustration she discusses the case study of 'Brad', one of a number of teenagers and young adults she interviewed for *Alone Together*.

Brad is a particularly articulate informant, with a highly developed aversion to Facebook. On the one hand, he complains about the 'preferences' section of the site, which fills the left-hand side of the screen with images of favourite music and books: 'You get reduced to a list of favourite things. "List your favourite music"—that gives you no liberty at all about how to say it.' These choices, he claims, tend to breed anxiety: 'What does it matter to anyone that I prefer the band Spoon over State Radio? Or State Radio over Cake? But things like Facebook . . . make you think that it really does matter' (p. 185). He also complains about having to write in a shallow, attention-grabbing way, and a glance at the Facebook interface suggests why this is so. Blogs in Web 1.0, in contrast, would typically fill long stretches of the screen with continuous prose.[13] The most sustained form of writing Facebook allows is on the 'wall', where you post an update about yourself for all to see within an extendable box in the middle of the screen. On either side of this box (which can also be posted on by others, displacing the centrality of your own text) there are numerous other attractions, such as your photos, your other contacts, and a 'bar' featuring adverts. These are all rather tempting to click on, so—mindful of your readers—the tendency is for relatively short and attention-grabbing entries, often combined with photos, just as a teen magazine, full of colour and loud headlines, tends to feature only short articles about hot topics. As Brad points out, this format delimits 'permissible' topics, and further reduces the self into conventional shapes: 'in a conversation, it might be interesting that on a trip to Europe with my parents, I got interested in the political mural art in Belfast. But on a Facebook page, this is too much information. It would be the kiss of death. Too much, too soon, too weird' (p. 185). Above all, the other-directed qualities of the site create in Brad what Turkle calls 'presentation anxiety' (p. 182). Instead of Lejeune's model of freewheeling intimate disclosure, Brad is preoccupied by an other-directed concern that his writing doesn't sound right, or isn't having the right effect—in short, that he is falling short of the right standards of adolescent 'cool'. 'I write for effect', he admits. 'I sit down and ask, 'If I say this, will it make me sound like I'm too

---

[13] Lejeune disliked blogs with too much extra presentation, which he described as 'the sort of window-dressing you might see at a fancy pastry-shop' (p. 304).

uptight? But if I say this, will it make me sound like I don't care about anything?' (p. 273). He feels that Facebook 'perverts' efforts at truthful disclosure because such revelations should be to 'another person who cares', rather than to the lonely crowd.

As well as posting on your Facebook wall, you can also interact with a particular individual via the instant messaging box, through which you can communicate in real time. Here, Turkle argues, there is an even stronger tendency to brevity because the exchanges take place in real time, which encourages a phone-style idiom of chat. Messaging (or its precursor, text-ing) encourages a particular quality of high-speed unreflectiveness, in which writing can emerge from within the very middle of an emotional response, even during a quarrel or a breakup. Turkle illustrates the effects of this through a study of 'Julia', who 'turns texting into a kind of polling':

> If I'm upset, right as I feel upset, I text a couple of my friends . . . just because I know that they'll be there and they can comfort me. If something exciting happens, I know that they'll be there to be excited with me, and stuff like that. So I definitely feel emotions when I'm texting, as I'm texting . . . Even before I get upset and I know that I have that feeling that I'm gonna start crying, yeah, I'll pull up my friend . . . uh, my phone . . . and say like . . . I'll tell them what I'm feeling. (p.175)

Julia's smartphone closes the gap between feeling and writing: 'What is not being cultivated here', Turkle points out, 'is the ability to be alone and reflect upon one's emotions in private. On the contrary, teenagers report discomfort when they are without their cell phones. They need to be connected in order to feel like themselves.' Julia's messaging is 'close to being a generational style' (p. 176), Turkle claims, and the consequence of this anxious other-directedness is to bring the kind of conventionality and shallowness Brad described into the innermost realm of the emotions. 'Technology does not cause but encourages a sensibility in which the validation of a feeling becomes part of establishing it', Turkle argues, 'even part of the feeling itself' (p. 177).

One can feel compassion for Julia's anxiety, and for Brad's resentment, while also observing that there is a conspicuous absence, in *Alone Together*, of any respondents who actually enjoy writing in this mode. Focusing on resenters like Brad (he returns in no fewer than three chapters) leads Turkle to ignore the aesthetic dimension of this idiom, by which I mean simply the extent to which the particular qualities it enables, however humanly limited these might be, can nonetheless be well or badly performed.

This point is made by the anthropologist Daniel Miller in *Tales from Facebook* (2011), a study of digital behaviour in Trinidad. Rejecting Turkle's attempt to establish a general framework for evaluating social networking, he argues that Facebook can only be understood as 'the aggregate of its regional and particular usage'.[14] Much of the book is taken up with case studies emphasizing the cultural specificity of the Trinidadian appropriation of Facebook, and it echoes Michel de Certeau's emphasis on the way in which powerful technologies and institutions are always apt to be appropriated, and in all kinds of ways subverted, by ordinary users.[15] But what Miller also sees is that a form that requires an ability to compose at speed in the middle of one's feelings, using high levels of conventionality and mindfulness of one or more interlocutors, is an adolescent ritual that can by all means be done badly (as with Brad), or mawkishly (as with Julia), but can also be done very well indeed, creating a sense of power and accomplishment rather than anxiety. He presents the case study of 'Aaron', a Trinidadian teenager who spends six hours a day (when he can) posting, messaging, and responding. In contrast to Brad's resentment at a form he has struggled to master, Aaron is gleefully learning to be 'articulate and savvy' within what Miller calls 'the aesthetic of Trini posting'. He manages his interactions with his friends adroitly, expertly timing 'the incredibly complex weave between being sufficiently funny, sufficiently interesting, sufficiently concerned with other people, quick in banter, and learning how to hint just the right amount so that he doesn't lose face when the other fails to respond' (p. 86). As Miller emphasizes, there is a very determinate utility to all this, as Aaron is acquiring, in an other-directed culture, 'key social skills that could make the difference between a happy life and an unhappy one'. But he is also delighting in his growing power.

Aaron's fun takes place in the baffling jargon of Trinidad youth-speak, which Miller, perhaps out of politeness, leaves untranslated. Consider, instead, a wholly impolite example taken from Gary Shteyngart's *Super Sad*

---

[14] Daniel Miller, *Tales from Facebook* (Cambridge: Polity, 2011), 163 (henceforth cited within the text by page numbers).

[15] See Michel de Certeau, *The Practice of Everyday Life*, trans. Steven Rendall (Berkeley and London: University of California Press, 1984).

True Love Story, a dystopian novel set in an America of the near future, which, in a zany elaboration upon Riesman's *Lonely Crowd*, is on the verge of being taken over by media corporations. The Internet has migrated onto a ubiquitous hand-held device with the rather sinister name of 'äppärät', a next-generation smartphone which holds credit data and continually updates your ratings, on such criteria as 'Personality' and 'Fuckability':

> She actually came up to me PHYSICALLY and VERBALLED me like 'Oh, I thought you were a lez cause you went to Elderbird, I didn't know you were a feminazi too' and I was like 'Yeah, but even if I was the biggest lez in America I wouldn't thresh you with a fucking combine' and then guess where she ended up by the end of the party? In the bathtub getting ass-reamed and face-pissed by Pat Alvarez and three of his friends who taped everything and then put it on GlobalTeens the next day. GUESS how high her ratings went up? Personality 764 and Fuckability 800+. What is WRONG with people?[16]

The quoted text is sent over the äppärät by a young woman with the webname of 'Grillbitch' to 'Euni-Tard' (aka Eunice, the heroine of the novel) via 'GlobalTeens', which has taken over from Facebook as the standard platform for social networking. Here Grillbitch is explaining what happened when she texted a warning to the girl who appeared to be making a move on 'Gopher', her erstwhile boyfriend.

It is evident that Grillbitch's writing makes little attempt to reflect on the scene, other than to call for approval at the end of the passage. The emotions themselves are simple (rage, grim satisfaction), and are vented, rather than explored, in a barely punctuated flow. The language is highly conventional ('I was like . . . ', 'biggest lez'); it is brief, and gives the impression of having been written at high speed—indeed, Grillbitch and Euni-Tard often refer to the various other activities they are doing while writing (usually shopping). In short, it is highly other-directed, picking up every bit of slang possible, oriented wholly to the interlocutor, trying to be 'cool'. But 'trying' is the wrong word: Grillbitch is not anxiously trying to be cool; like Aaron she pulls it off. To read her is to behold her power, a power that derives from the dexterity with which she can handle conventional language at speed. She redoubles the other girl's insult, crisply closing it with

---

[16] Gary Shteyngart, *Super Sad True Love Story* (London: Granta, 2010), 27 (henceforth cited within the text by page numbers).

that hard 'c' on 'combine', accenting the GUESS and WRONG to capture the irate passion of a speaking voice. She is adroit with the technical language of slang: 'ass-reamed' and 'face-pissed' nail the humiliation of her rival with all the visceral energy of the gutter. Shteyngart has acknowledged Philip Roth as an influence on his work, and passages like this resonate with Roth's interest, in *Portnoy's Complaint* (1969) and elsewhere, in gaining access to the vitality to be found in forms of speech and writing perceived to be crude and shallow, such as (for him) Jewish street-corner comedy and sports banter.[17] As with the gamut of vulgar voices in *Portnoy's Complaint*, Grillbitch puts on a bravura display: unlike Brad she isn't just learning how to fit in, she is learning how to shine, taking pleasure in the capacity of this form for verbal hijinks.

My suggestion, then, is that by ignoring the qualitative differences between different performances of social networking Turkle is led towards an over-normative assessment of its risks, even if attention is confined to the vulnerable group of teenagers and young adults that concern her. But she is more right than Daniel Miller suggests in her wider claim that there is a shaping power within the form itself. When he argues that the adolescent socialization rituals it embodies are 'an intrinsic condition of social life, irrespective of the technologies so employed' (p. 217), Miller simply dismisses Turkle's fears about the psychological consequences of networked life-writing. But in doing so he pushes his argument too far. No small part of the cleverness of Shteyngart's novel lies in the way he avoids Miller's rather blandly uncritical stance, and the way he does so takes another kind of inspiration from Philip Roth.

There are many similarities between *Super Sad True Love Story* and *Portnoy's Complaint*. Alexander Portnoy is the highly literate, very dutiful only son of Jewish immigrants from Poland; Lenny Abramov, the hero of Shteyngart's novel, is the highly literate, very dutiful only son of Jewish immigrants from Russia. These good Jewish sons are both fascinated and appalled by Shiksa women from mainstream consumerist America who seem to promise release from the oppressive earnestness of their upbringing. More important than this homage, though, is the critical stance that Shteyngart takes from Roth's novel. Roth had himself been strongly influenced by

---

[17] Shteyngart has discussed Roth in 'Hello, Columbus', *New York Times Book Review*, 4 December 2005.

David Riesman's analysis of the other-directed self, and while he came to distrust Riesman's over-homogenizing assumptions, in no sense did he seek merely to exchange the concerns of *The Lonely Crowd* for a role as cheerleader of the consumer culture. Instead, through the figure of Portnoy, Roth set up a series of ironies around a man whose strenuous efforts to acquire a lower and more shallow life are repeatedly undone by his seemingly unshakable high-mindedness. The way Shteyngart adapts this doubly ironic mode is by structuring his narrative around a running contrast between the GlobalTeens exchanges on social media, and a written journal kept in a book by Lenny.

Lenny's diary entries are long, narrative in form, and rich in self-irony. They are written at a reflective distance from the action and emotions described, and for himself only—not for publication. He makes great claim to be a lover of books, alluding throughout to figures such as Tolstoy, Chekhov, Nabokov, and Musil. His writing is 'a tribute to literature as it once was' (p. 325), and he looks nostalgically back to 'Lionel Trilling and those guys', an earlier generation of Jewish intellectuals who 'came from poor, hardy families' and who 'were realistic about dying' (p. 214). This is from the end of his first entry, where he is describing falling in love with Eunice:

> I touched my expertly brushed teeth and petted the flurry of grey hairs sticking out from beneath my shirt collar, which she had thoroughly examined in the morning's weak early light. 'Cute', she had said. And then, with a child's sense of wonder: 'You're old, Len.'
>
> Oh, dear diary. My youth has passed, but the wisdom of age hardly beckons. Why is it so hard to be a grown-up man in this world? (p. 24)

The slow pace of Lenny's book diary, together with its distance from the immediacy of events, allows for a complex reflection on the beauty and folly of his love for young Eunice. It does indeed resonate with 'Trilling and those guys', pulling back from the moment to make a studied reflection on death, its pathos, and the need for wisdom before it. Quite unlike the absorption in emotional immediacy found in Grillbitch, a light irony plays over his self-exploration: like Nabokov's Humbert, one of his models as a diarist, there is a nice *frisson* of self-parody in his self-regard.

The complex literariness of Lenny's book diary shows up the shallowness of Grillbitch's online diary—the conventionality of her feelings, her immersion in her own crude immediacy. But by bringing the inner and other-directed diaries together, Shteyngart's larger irony also cuts against the conventionality of Lenny's bookish writing. His prose has a rather dead quality to it when placed against Grillbitch's speedy prose: 'hardly beckons' isn't quite an archaism, but it exudes stuffiness; his closing complaint, 'Why is it so hard...', strains at the sonorous, but sounds a duff note against Grillbitch's 'What is WRONG with people?' Moreover, while Turkle defined the other-directed self as afflicted by the need to perform rather than explore the self, there is surely more than a little of the performance in the stagey melancholy of Lenny's prose. Was it really with a 'child's sense of wonder' that Eunice told him he looks old? Hard to imagine so from the next page, where Eunice messages Grillbitch: 'Respect yourself, hoo-kah!' While it may be reassuring for someone educated in the culture of the book to read Lenny's diary, the troublingly ironic structure of *Super Sad True Love Story* suggests that there is every bit as much potential for inauthenticity, imitativeness, and self-deception in the supposedly inner-directed book diary as in its more overtly other-directed online counterpart.

To reflect upon the performed qualities of online life-writing is therefore to complicate, not to reject, Turkle's claims about this new idiom. The same is true of a more specific argument she makes about mobile instant messaging technology. The mobile Internet, she argues, has a tendency to distract from the felt immediacy of experience itself: people who are 'always on', messaging and texting, cannot simultaneously be giving full attention to their children, or to their friends. One of Turkle's core claims, as a social psychologist, is that children who struggle to get attention from parents who are 'tantalisingly [close], but mentally elsewhere' (p. 267), preoccupied with their smartphones, tend to become insecure and resort to increased use of social networking for reassurance. Heightening the other-directed cycle, 'these same children', she argues, 'are insecure about having each other's attention' (p. 268).

It is hard to disagree with Turkle on this level, and she goes on to make telling claims about the way in which instant messaging is used, particularly by anxious 'lonely crowd' teenagers, to insulate the self from those more complex and unpredictable emotional exchanges that can take place over the phone or face to face. As her informant 'Audrey' puts it, 'texting offers protection': 'When you instant-message you can cross things out, edit what you say, block a person, or sign off. A phone conversation is a lot of pressure. You're always expected to uphold it, to keep it going, and that's too much pressure.' Audrey prefers texting to calling because in texting 'there is a lot less *boundness* to a person', by which she means that in a call she could learn too much or say too much, and things could get emotionally 'out of control' (p. 190).

But while Turkle gives a disturbing account of the power of mobile messaging technology to distract and to deplete human relationships, she also has a more questionable tendency to define genuine immediacy in physical terms, bound up with voice and facial expression. In fact it is Brad (again) who makes this point for her: 'Brad sums up his discontents with an old-fashioned word: online life inhibits "authenticity". He wants to experience people directly' (p. 273). This tendency to connect authenticity with physical presence or voice, rather than with text, comes through most strongly in the case study of 'Meredith', who tells of how she learned about the death of a friend on her instant messaging service. According to Turkle, Meredith was glad the news came to her this way, rather than through a phone call, because it protected her from losing control of her emotions in front of someone else. For a day after the news, Meredith only communicated with friends via instant messaging: 'Just about the fact of it. Conversations like, "Oh, have you heard?" "Yeah, I heard." And that's it' (p. 205). Turkle reads Meredith in the same way she read Audrey—as an other-directed individual using instant messaging to stage-manage real human contact. The distance from immediacy allowed for by this technology enables her to avoid the reality of the experience, and thereby avoid genuine emotions. 'I see a vulnerability in this generation', she warns. 'Under stress, they seek composure above all. But they do not find equanimity. When they meet and lose composure, they find a new way to flee: often they take their phones out to text each other and friends not in the room . . . They keep themselves at a distance from their feelings' (p. 206).[18]

This idea that the immediacy of an experience can only really be disclosed by voice, or (preferably) face to face, is challenged in an interesting way by Ben Lerner in *Leaving the Atocha Station*. This novel turns on two quite

---

[18] Turkle's phonocentrism compares to Zadie Smith's in *NW* (London: Hamish Hamilton, 2011). This novel, which is also influenced by ideas about the other-directed self, ends with a scene in which a character who has become disastrously addicted to social networking sites decides, in a redemptive moment, to pick up the phone rather than send an email.

different experiences of death: the Madrid train bombings of 2004, which the protagonist Adam Gordon witnesses while in Spain on a research fellowship; and his friend's account, delivered over instant messaging, of witnessing a young woman drown while on holiday in Mexico. As a rebuff to over-facile ideas about voice and immediacy, when Adam later tries to convey the terror of this death face to face to a Spanish friend, he finds his own description bedevilled by the empty conventionality of spoken language, and is met by an equally empty conventional response. 'My God', his interlocutor dutifully replies, and takes his hand, before starting to talk about something else.[19]

Not least among the many reasons why Lerner distrusts the idea that embodied experience necessarily has greater immediacy than textual experience, is because he follows through on the implications of David Riesman's claims about the power of culture and economics to shape the self in a more rigorous way than Turkle does herself. 'That *I* was a fraud had never been in question—who wasn't?' asks Adam. 'Who wasn't squatting in one of the handful of prefabricated subject positions offered by capital or whatever one wanted to call it, lying every time she said "I"; who wasn't a bit player in the looped infomercial for the damaged life?' (p. 101). If the self is always already a 'fraud', immersed in stock responses and stock perceptions, felt immediacy is as mediated as anything else. Instead of distrusting instant messaging, Lerner explores a special way of valuing its expressive powers, and in doing so he takes inspiration from the poetry of John Ashbery.

Prior to writing *Leaving the Atocha Station*, Lerner had published a long review essay of the new Library of America edition of Ashbery's poetry. Here he drew attention to the way in which Ashbery's poems flaunt their own process of fabrication rather than hide it, not only announcing their 'mediacy', but taking mediation as their theme, and revelling in the experience of mediation itself. 'Instead of making a bid for lyric immediacy', Lerner claimed, 'the poems always refer to its displacement, as if the poem we have describes a poem for which we've always arrived too late.'[20] In doing so, however, Ashbery paradoxically takes us—Lerner argues—closer to experience itself than a more naive rhetoric of presence would be able to

---

[19] Ben Lerner, *Leaving the Atocha Station* (London: Granta, 2012), 96 (henceforth cited within the text by page numbers).
[20] Ben Lerner, 'The Future Continuous: Ashbery's Lyric Mediacy', *boundary* 2:37.1 (2010), 207.

describe. By focusing attention on the means by which experience is mediated, 'Ashbery's poems allow you to attend to your attention, to "experience your experience", thereby enabling a strange kind of presence.'[21]

What Lerner values in instant messaging is precisely this capacity to break with the self's immersion in the seemingly authentic immediacy of everyday expressions and emotions, and thereby generate 'a strange kind of presence' from the experience of mediacy itself. In particular, he is intrigued by the potential for time-delay effects that both accentuate the experience of mediacy, and create unpredictable imaginative consequences. As you are composing and reading in an instant-message chain, your response can be inadvertently directed to a remark that your interlocutor has already moved beyond, if you happen to be slower at texting or typing. So within a form that gives a strong sensation of presence, there is simultaneously a high potential for misidentification and accidental meanings as the message chain unfolds. Consider the following passage from *Leaving the Atocha Station*, where Cyrus is explaining to Adam how the young woman who ends up drowning was first tempted into the fast-moving river:

Cyrus: So there I was opposite the girlfriend on the bank, both of us being pressured
   by the swimmers to join them. The girlfriend and I kept looking at each
   other with nervous smiles.
Me: if one of you got in the other would have to
Cyrus: I felt that
Me: a game of chicken. you two should have left the others and gone off and had
Cyrus: Or at least if she got in I would have to. But she probably could have
   remained on the bank
Me: a wonderful life together!
Me: right. she would not be emasculated. (pp. 70–1)

In their desire to keep up the typed exchange Adam and Cyrus keep breaking into each other's sentences, accentuating the felt mediacy of the experience. But in attending to the act of attention, as Lerner puts it, a peculiarly intense experience of the event itself emerges from this otherwise

---

[21] This quotation is taken from *Leaving the Atocha Station* (p. 91), though it echoes, with a significant modification, a passage from Lerner's essay: 'Ashbery's poems allow us to attend to our attention, to "experience our experience"; they offer what we might call *lyric mediacy*.' 'The Future Continuous' 209.

rather flat prose. Consider the break on 'had' in Adam's second remark. It is accidental, but it opens up a space for the sombre tone of Cyrus' narrative to be disrupted in a way that is desecrating: 'gone off and had...' what? Is he making a very silly joke—does 'had' lead to 'had sex'? It does not—it becomes 'a wonderful life together', a phrase that now stands on its own line. A desecration of the serious tone breaks out into a strangely resonant moment, in which the phrase made famous by the Frank Capra film, *It's a Wonderful Life*, a film that is almost the definition of kitsch, suddenly becomes haunting. The accidental juxtaposition of Cyrus' image of the girl's last moment of life on the bank breaks the cliché into a genuinely mournful exclamation.

The resonances within the passage just quoted could easily be skimmed over within a fast-moving exchange of messages. But compare the narration of the death itself:

Cyrus: she moved downriver where the current became pretty strong, and she was getting upset
Me: so someone went and helped her?
Cyrus: Things
Cyrus: things got very bad very fast. she went underwater for a second, and when she resurfaced, she was a little farther down and totally panicked
Me: jesus
Cyrus: She was screaming and water was
Me: jesus
Cyrus: getting in her mouth and she was struggling (pp. 71–2)

In this most desperate moment the consciousness of mediation is at its most acute, but the experience of textuality does not place emotions at a distance, it intensifies them by allowing us to 'experience our experience' on highly unconventional terms. The reduction of the young woman to a thing floating downriver finds a horrific echo in the fragmentation of the language, which invites us—accidentally—to reflect upon materiality itself: 'Things', as Cyrus' second line puts it, in their awful inhuman thingness. This happens again with 'water was', which dangles at the end of Cyrus' penultimate line, the disjointed phrase itself casting attention onto the non-meaning of sheer matter, which is exactly what the woman is confronting in her own death. The seemingly dehumanizing effects of this highly mediated exchange do indeed fracture the relationship between writing and experience. But what emerges is not detachment, instead a 'strange intensification of presence' that takes us into the depths, not the shallows.

In placing Turkle's concerns against Lerner's Ashbery-inspired insights into the poetics of instant messaging, I am again not seeking simply to discount her claims about the power of this technology to distract and deplete, nor do I suggest that informants such as Audrey and Meredith are somehow deliberately misrepresenting their experience. What I am suggesting is that, as with the other-directed diary, Turkle's tendency to overprivilege the fears and complaints of teenagers and young adults leads her to judge digital life-writing in an over-normative way.

These limitations are most evident in her response to online confessional writing. Focussing on the website PostSecret, where anonymous postcards featuring a confession of some kind are sent in and scanned, Turkle admits to being puzzled by the genre—of which there are many more examples, including MySecret, and message boards serving various kinds of interest groups. Online confessions often seem peculiarly exaggerated and lurid; they invite responses that often mock rather than give counsel and support, or themselves start to indulge in counterfantasies. When she examines the genre in *Alone Together* Turkle confronts the possibility that 'these confessions are fiction' (p. 230), written for an audience. In what sense could they then have value?

Her suggestion is that the value of these probably fictitious online confessional performances lies in their therapeutic possibilities, an argument she had previously made about the psychological function of fictional identities in virtual reality gaming in her earlier book *Life on the Screen*. 'Perhaps online confessions are a new genre altogether', she speculates. 'When people create avatars [in virtual reality], they are not themselves but express important truths about themselves. Online confession, another internet performance zone, also occupies an intermediate space. Here, statements may not be true, but true enough for writers to feel unburdened and for readers to feel part of a community' (p. 230). Yet Turkle now has little enthusiasm for this argument, and tends instead to regard the practice of anonymous unburdening as a simple decline from the real confession. In her study of 'Sheryl', who confesses online to illicit affairs, and to spending her parents' retirement money on holidays, Turkle points out that confessing leads to no change of behaviour: 'Sheryl's online confessions do not lead her to talk to those she has wronged or to try to make amends. She goes online to feel better, not to make things right. She thinks that most people use confessional sites this way' (p. 233). Online spaces, she concludes, 'offer themselves as "cheap" alternatives to confronting other people', both because they avoid an unruly confrontation with another voice (as with Audrey's use of instant messaging) and because they avoid the challenge of making an apology. The online confession is thus more symptom than cure, 'a shot of feeling good that can divert attention from what a person really needs' (p. 234).

In one sense, Turkle is surely right. When measured by the moralistic assumptions of confessional discourse, in which the aim is to discover the truth of the self through dialogue, and which, as Peter Brooks has argued, descends in its modern form from the disciplinary procedures of Church and State, the anonymous online confession falls woefully short.[22] But the limits of this way of responding to online confession are evident even if we confine ourselves to Turkle's informants. There is an interesting moment in which she presents a case study to clinch the argument that confessional sites are bad therapy:

One high school senior tells me that she visits online confessional sites at least twice a week. Most recently, she has been writing descriptions of sleeping with her best friend's boyfriend. When I ask her what she does after she writes her confessions, she says that she stays alone in her room, smoking. She thinks that she has unburdened herself and now wants to be alone. Or perhaps the confession has left her depleted. (p. 237)

Turkle's reading may be correct, but it may also be a touch naive. This 'high-school senior' might be a rather different character to the emotionally defensive Audrey, or the overcautious Meredith, let alone the resentful Brad. Hard to know, but perhaps her confession is itself a form of sexual arousal, possibly fantasized (note the 'writing descriptions of'), in which case the cigarette, which Turkle seems to read only as a sign of depletion, might be a virtual-post-coital pleasure, to be consumed once the self is thus 'unburdened'. Or perhaps it is even her way of accessing a fantasy of being discovered in the act of betrayal: she sits there after writing, smoking

---

[22] Peter Brooks, *Troubling Confessions: Speaking Guilt in Law and Literature* (Chicago and London: University of Chicago Press, 2000), 35–64.

and looking at a text that could take her best friendship into emotional terrain that will certainly be more complex, but may also be more interesting. In short, it may be the case that what online confession creates is a space in which the intimate idiom of confession is being appropriated by users for aesthetic aims, bound up with the imaginative transformation of experience, rather than for therapy or self-knowledge.

This aspect of the online confession is explored by Denis Cooper in *The Sluts*, a novel that reproduces, among other things, a fictional gay sadomasochistic message board, where men post descriptions of sex with an escort named 'Brad', complete with their ratings of his 'fuckability'. The message board rapidly turns into a full-blown confessional site, in which Brad's clients start to confess to an ever-escalating series of crimes, including rape, arson, and murder. As with the confessional sites Turkle reviewed, it is wholly anonymous, and one of the chief pleasures of the novel lies in its play with the fictional potential of internet anonymity. All Cooper gives us are the postings, without any narrative commentary: we follow X's confession, which is then contradicted by Y's, only for Z to confess, pages later, that he was posting for both X and Y; followed by A's confession that really he was Z, and so on. As the novel progresses, it becomes ever more difficult to establish whether anyone is telling the truth, or if Brad even exists.

Cooper's inspiration for the novel was twofold. The figure of Brad, he claimed in an interview, is a 'fantasy figure' designed to explore the way in which internet message boards create a space in which sexual fantasy can flourish, and *The Sluts* resonates with the online cult of Peter Azur, a gay Czech porn star from the 1990s who spawned an extraordinary variety of admiring message boards and chatrooms.[23] What interests Cooper in these virtual spaces is the way they create a mode of pornographic writing in which, protected by anonymity, men can collaboratively, or competitively, fantasize through the idiom of an erotic confessional. As with Grillbitch's messages to Euni-Tard, this is not fine writing. It is what Cooper calls 'horny everyman rhetoric', an altogether 'blabbier writing' than you would normally find in a novel.[24] Here is an example:

---

[23] See <http://denniscooper.blogspot.co.uk/2006/01/floppy-haired-czech-porn-star-peter.html>.

[24] 'It's blabbier writing', Cooper remarks, 'but the blab is as tight as I could get it.' <http://www.dennis-cooper.net/sluts_interview.htm>.

The hatred I feel when I rape and humiliate and torture and beat and dismember their beautiful young faces and bodies is as close as I can get to the fury of love I felt for Brad. The thing about Brad is that he was right—killing a boy who wants to die is an experience beyond any other in the world.[25]

This is from a message left by 'Brian', whose conventional name belies his self-presentation as a Byronic overreacher. While his actions go beyond the human norms in a frenzied way, reaching for 'the fury of love', he is ultimately just an 'everyman' with a gift for fantasy and a rather flat prose. While 'the fury of love' could be Byron, the tumbling bathos in 'the fury of love I felt for Brad' most certainly could not.

Cooper stands in a line of pornographic writing that descends from de Sade through Georges Bataille, and the particular value he discovers in the 'horny everyman rhetoric' generated by online erotic confessionals can best be appreciated if *The Sluts* is compared to *The Story of the Eye* (1928), Bataille's first pornographic novel, and Cooper's other main source of inspiration. What Cooper shares with Bataille is an interest in using the idiom of pornography to violate the normal ways in which the self is immersed in cultural values. As the young male narrator of *The Story of the Eye* puts it, 'decent people have gelded eyes': their perceptions are 'gelded' by moral taboos that have become so ingrained they barely notice their own confinement.[26] Bataille's attempt to 'ungeld' the eye depended upon a highly wrought style that drew inspiration from Surrealism. He created a disorienting form of writing that, as Roland Barthes put it in his essay on the novel, 'transforms all experience into language that is *askew* (*devoyé*) ... demolishing the usual contiguities between objects and substituting fresh encounters'.[27] Bataille rendered language 'askew' by setting up complex chains of metaphor connected with the eyes, and with liquidity, and by pushing these metaphors into ever more disorienting combinations as the erotic story progressed. In one scene, the eye becomes 'sucked like a breast'; in another the narrator finds his lover Simone 'drinking my left eye between her lips'; in further scenes the eye metamorphoses into an egg crushed into a woman's anus, into bull's testicles, and so on. Through these

---

[25] Denis Cooper, *The Sluts* (New York: Carroll & Graf, 2004), 140.

[26] Georges Bataille, *The Story of the Eye*, trans. Joachim Neugroschal (London: Penguin, 1979), 42.

[27] Roland Barthes, 'The Metaphor of the Eye', trans. J.A. Underwood, in Bataille, *The Story of the Eye*, 127 (henceforth cited within the text by page numbers).

surreal combinations Bataille's writing creates a special transgressive charge: 'The world becomes *blurred*', Barthes argues, 'properties are no longer separate' (p. 125). What Cooper finds in 'horny everyman rhetoric' is a surrealism of the everyday that circumvents Bataille's rather stagey play with metaphor.

As just one example, consider the following passage from *The Sluts*, which was posted by Brad himself. Brad is (allegedly) sixteen years old and mentally ill. Here he describes the aftermath of an erotic encounter with a man known only by his webname, 'builtlikeatruck', an encounter that culminated in his attempt to burn down his client's business:

I'm sorry about what I did to him but he kind of played with my head if you know what I mean. He told me he really liked me and it wasn't about sex and I believed him like the stupid fucker I am, but then he turns around and rapes me when I needed a friend. He should be so fucking grateful that I didn't say anything about that to my lawyer. I'm a nice person. (p. 121)

This is not only leaden prose, it is brilliantly askew, from the 'I'm a nice person' at the end to the flatfooted threat in the penultimate sentence, and the self-exposing 'stupid fucker I am'. In particular, though, note the awful comedy of 'rapes me when I needed a friend', the audacity of which lies in the way it jostles against something like the everyday 'avoided me when I needed a friend'. Cooper has spoken of the 'weird' mix of the comic and horrific in his prose: in this passage, as the very serious slips into bathos, our conventional emotional responses are thrown out of joint.[28] For an instant, within what might be called the emotional surrealism of Brad's prose, rape becomes normalized within the range of perfectly ordinary human actions, and we find ourselves in a space where, as Barthes put it, 'the world becomes *blurred*'. Through the bathos of the writing the concept of rape blurs into the everyday, suddenly losing its moral and emotional charge.

This desecration of the morally prudent register for discussing rape is of course due to the fact that Brad is mentally ill, and drugged to numb his hysteria. But a few pages later a man with the webname 'likeemyoung' confesses that it was in fact he who posted the above message, not 'Brad'. Why? The answer is complex, but it was at least in part for the sheer

[28] 'It's weird: some people who've read it think it's a comedy, but others don't see the comedy at all. But then that's always happened with my books. For some people, the intensity of the content erases the tone.' <http://www.dennis-cooper.net/sluts_interview.htm>.

exhilaration of imagining rape and arson not in a well-judged and responsible way, but for seeing how it feels when projected through the dis-
oriented idiom of a mentally ill teenage rent boy. The fiction of Brad gives
likeemyoung (and participants in such message boards in general) a space
for ungelding their eyes. As we move through the manifold erotic confessions and counter-confessions of the novel, descending ever further into a
space where the boundary between the fictional and the real is undecidable,
we enter into a weirdly ecstatic realm, where the ordinary controls on what
can be felt cease to hold.

Back in 2000, Philippe Lejeune described online life-writing as a 'new
frontier' that has 'constraints and resources that are just beginning to be
explored' (*On Diary* p.316). He was of course speaking as an early frontiers-
man who had reached, say, the plains of Ohio, but was as yet unaware of the
heights of Colorado, let alone the bewildering California that was to come.

Following this admittedly very partial review of the territory as it now
stands, my own inclination is to intensify both sides of Lejeune's even-
handed remark. On the one hand, with the rise of a pervasive and invasive
'always on' mobile social networking technology, 'constraints' now seems
too mild. It doesn't capture the genuine concerns raised by social psychologists such as Sherry Turkle, and 'dangers' might be a better word for
today's digital environment. Imagine, for example, your teenage son or
daughter getting lost in one of Cooper's pornographic message boards; or
(worse?) imagine them *only* acquiring Grillbitch's capacity for self-reflection
after all that time at secondary school. But on the other hand, 'possibilities'
is also too restrained. In the hands of writers such as Shteyngart, Lerner and
Cooper, the Internet emerges as the new Wild West of life-writing, rich in
imaginative energies, a sublime space in which experience can be pushed to
its outer limits. These writers speak to the enthusiasm that Kevin Kelly,
former editor of *Wired* magazine, feels for life on the screen:

At times I've entered the web just to get lost. In that lovely surrender, the web
swallows my certitude and delivers the unknown. Despite the purposeful design of
its human creators, the web is a wilderness. Its boundaries are unknown, unknowable, its mysteries uncountable. The bramble of intertwined ideas, links, documents,
and images create an otherness as thick as a jungle. The web smells like life.[29]

---

[29] Kevin Kelly, 'Technophilia', *The Technium*, 9 June 2009 <http://kk.org/thetechnium/archives/
2009/06/technophilia.php>.

Kelly's metaphor of the jungle is perhaps even more apt than Lejeune's 'frontier'. Social psychologists such as Turkle, focused on developmental norms, are surely right to see it as an uncivilized space full of hazards and risks that have the potential to make you very small indeed. But seen through the lens provided by some of the more experimental directions in contemporary fiction, it also emerges as a place for exploring, regressing, fantasizing, and pleasurably losing yourself.

14

Autobiography and Psychoanalysis

Laura Marcus

How should we understand the relationships between psychoanalysis (as theory and practice) and life-writing (as a set of genres and practices)? This question has absorbed analysts, critics, and theorists from the early decades of the twentieth century onwards. Life-writing has been of central importance to psychoanalysis: Sigmund Freud wrote on autobiography, including that of Goethe, and produced psychobiographical accounts of, amongst others, Leonardo da Vinci (1910) and, in collaboration with William C. Bullitt in the 1930s, Woodrow Wilson (published 1966). 'We must lay hold of biography', Freud wrote in a letter to Carl Jung in 1909.[1] The Minutes of the Vienna Psycho-Analytical Society (which begin in 1906) contain reports of a number of presentations and discussions of 'pathography' and of psychoanalytic biography between 1907 and 1912, at a time when Freud and his followers were particularly concerned to extend psychoanalytic thought into broader cultural spheres.[2] Writing the biographies of great artists and writers seemed a direct way of reaching a wider,

---

[1] *The Freud/Jung Letters* (abridged), ed. William McGuire (Harmondsworth: Penguin, 1991), 161.

[2] See Herman Numberg and Ernst Federn, eds., *Minutes of the Vienna Psychoanalytic Society*, 4 vols. (New York: International Universities Press, 1962–76), vol. 1, 1974.

non-medical readership. In a related way, twentieth-century biographical writing, including the 'new biography' of the 1920s and 30s, became profoundly shaped by psychoanalytic theories of human development and sexuality.[3]

The specific focus of this chapter is autobiography and psychoanalysis. In this context, critical and theoretical approaches to the topic reached their height with the ego-psychology of the mid-twentieth century (as in the work inspired by the analyst Erik Erikson, whose biography *Young Man Luther: A Study in Psychoanalysis and History* was published in 1958) and in the structuralist 'moment' of the 1970s and 1980s. In this later work, a Lacan-influenced theory was highly critical of an Eriksonian model, in which the ego would be strengthened and secured through analysis, positing instead a radically fragmented understanding of identity. The focus here was, in Jeffrey Mehlman's words, on 'the search for repetitions, aberrant details, seeming contradictions, surprising omissions',[4] and the exemplary autobiographer was the ethnographer and writer Michel Leiris, whose autobiographies, including *L'Âge d'homme* (1939) and *La Règle du jeu* (1948–76), circle around key images and obsessions.

In the last few decades, there have been competing views about the centrality of psychoanalysis to the writing, and reading, of autobiography. For the theorist Michel Neyraut, though 'both provide one or more versions of a life ... their paths diverge for many reasons, one of which is fundamental and relates to the presence of the psychoanalyst in the first case and the omnipresence of the reader in the second. I mean that whereas in analysis transference is constitutive and discoverable, in autobiography it

---

[3] 'The new biography' was a term used in the 1920s and 1930s to define the work of a cluster of biographers, from Britain, France, Germany, and the United States, amongst them Lytton Strachey, André Maurois, Emil Ludwig, and Gamaliel Bradford. Key tenets and characteristics of their work included 'brevity, selection, and an attention to form and unity traditionally associated with fiction rather than history; the discovery of central motifs in a life and of a "key" to personality; and a focus on character rather than events' (Laura Marcus, 'The Newness of the "New Biography"', in *Mapping Lives: The Uses of Biography*, ed. Peter France and William St Clair (London: British Academy/Oxford University Press, 2002), 193–218; 196). Strachey's biographies, in particular his *Elizabeth and Essex* (1928), engaged extensively with psychoanalytically inflected debates about androgyny and sexual identity, and it could be argued that Strachey and Freud were the two primary influences on the writing of biography in the 1920s.

[4] Jeffrey Mehlman, *A Structuralist Study of Autobiography: Proust, Leiris, Sartre and Lévi-Strauss* (Ithaca, NY: Cornell University Press, 1974), 16.

is problematic and indiscernible.'[5] John E. Jackson, author of *Passions du sujet* (1990), makes the point more fully: 'Where the autobiographer is alone with himself to narrate and to understand his past or his identity, the analysand has from the beginning to hang his relation to himself on his relation to the analyst, whose interventions serve not only to short-circuit the self-seduction which often marks writing about oneself, but also to modify this relation of the self to itself.'[6]

Discussions by two practising psychoanalysts and essayists, Charles Rycroft and Adam Phillips, extend the topic in helpful ways. Rycroft's 1983 essay 'On Autobiography' starts from the premise that, while we might speak of the autobiographer and the subject 'as by definition the same person', in fact 'neither the autobiographer nor the autobiographee are single selves but are rather multiple sets of selves ... The appropriate visual analogy ceases to be that of a painter painting a self-portrait and becomes that of someone occupying a temporal corridor of mirrors and communing in turn with images of past and present selves.'[7] As a psychotherapist, Rycroft writes, 'I am compelled to question both the conception of himself and the history of his life that each person brings to me initially', and thus 'it has become natural to me to think of myself as an assistant autobiographer', helping his patient 'to discriminate between his own true voice and his learned imitations of other, typically ancestral voices'. It is not surprising, he adds, 'that my own ideal conception of an autobiography should be one in which the autobiographer remains in pursuit of himself while recounting himself, and that I should betray impatience with autobiographers who are merely advertising the continued existence of a long-standing ego'.[8]

Rycroft, however, expressed doubt that such an ideal autobiography could ever be realized. No record of a life could ever achieve completeness, 'since it would take a lifetime to record a lifetime'; autobiographies are unavoidably selective, not least because they 'underestimate the part played

---

[5] Michel Neyraut, 'De l'autobiographie', in *L'Autobiographie: VIes Recontres psychanalytiques d'Aix-en-Provence 1987* (Paris: Société d'édition, 1988), 7–45; 9 (my translation).

[6] John E. Jackson, 'Mythes du sujet: A propos de l'autobiographie et de la cure analytique', in *L'Autobiographie*, 135–69; 136 (my translation).

[7] Charles Rycroft, 'On Autobiography', in *Psychoanalysis and Beyond* (London: Chatto & Windus, 1985), 191–7; 192.

[8] *Ibid.*, 193.

by bodily processes in the story of one's life'; 'falsification' is an inevitability, because 'the process of detaching that thread, which is one's own life, from the fabric which has been simultaneously woven by those around one introduces an inherent bias towards egocentricity at the expense of object-ivity, and towards exaggeration of one's difference and alienation from others'.[9] Ultimately, he concluded, autobiographies are not free from the moral charges that can be levelled against 'our individualistic society'.

Adam Phillips' essay 'The Telling of Selves: Notes on Psychoanalysis and Autobiography' (1994) makes a similar argument about the analyst as, in Rycroft's phrase, 'assistant autobiographer', in his suggestion that 'in psychoanalytic treatment it takes two to make a life-story'.[10] His concern in the opening section of his essay is with Freud's concept of 'screen memory', first explored in an 1899 essay, in which what appear to be memories of childhood are in fact understood to be constructions, concealing repressed experiences, and with the question of, in Freud's words, 'whether we have any memories at all *from* our childhood; memories relating *to* our childhood may be all that we possess'.[11] With concepts like deferred action (*Nachträglichkeit*) and screen memories, Phillips suggests, 'Freud multiplied our way of remembering', with significant consequences for the connections between psychoanalysis and autobiography' (p. 67).

Psychoanalytic interpretation is made possible by free association, 'memory in its most incoherent and therefore fluent form'. This is memory, and thought, in fragments, and pursuing it entails, for the analysand, a giving-up on the 'conventional satisfactions of narrative' (p. 68). Such anti-narrative, Phillips argues, would make a written autobiography unreadable. He finds important points of contact between psychoanalysis and autobiography: 'psychoanalysis is clearly akin to autobiography in the sense that it involves a self-telling, and the belief that there is nowhere else to go for the story of our lives' (p. 69). He nonetheless argues that they should not be seen as identical practices. The aim of analysis, he suggests, 'is not to recover the past, but to make recovery of the past possible, the past that is frozen in

---

[9] *Ibid.*, 195.

[10] Adam Phillips, 'The Telling of Selves: Notes on Psychoanalysis and Autobiography', in *On Flirtation* (London: Faber, 1994), 68 (henceforth cited within the text by page numbers).

[11] 'Screen Memories', in *The Standard Edition of the Complete Psychological Works of Sigmund Freud*, trans. James Strachey, vol. 111 (London: Hogarth Press and the Institute of Psycho-Analysis, 1893–99), 303–22; 322.

repetition; and in this sense psychoanalysis might be more of a prelude to autobiography'.

Adumbrating the differences between the projects of psychoanalysis and autobiography, Phillips argues that psychoanalysis is 'a deliberate attempt at a cure' and that psychoanalysts work with 'normative development stories... sponsoring very specific ways of describing and redescribing a life-story' (p. 71). They turn to autobiographies, biographies, and novels 'to find other ways of plotting lives'. Secondly, 'psychoanalysis is self-telling to, and in the presence of, a particular other person, the analyst. The analyst's reticence invites the patient to recreate him or her from the significant figures in the patient's past' (p. 71). This is the psychoanalytic process known as 'transference'. The autobiographer, by contrast, 'spreads out his audience, most of whom are anonymous' (p. 72). Psychoanalysis is a conversation, an immediate and continuing dialogue: the writing of auto-biography (and autobiography is above all a written form) entails a rela-tionship to the genre and its traditions. Considered as an autobiographical performance, psychoanalysis is highly selective: 'childhood memories, dreams, mistakes, the vagaries of erotic life; where there is conflict, wher-ever continuity is disturbed or composure undermined, our other lives are in the making' (p. 75). A life is made up of too many autobiographies, though the problem of 'multiple plots' concerns autobiographers as much as it does psychoanalysts and their patients.

Rycroft's and Phillips' suggestive discussions affirm the widely shared view that the practices and projects of psychoanalysis and autobiography, while having some important connections, miss each other at a number of crucial junctures. As the philosopher Stanley Cavell, who has engaged extensively with psychoanalytic thought, puts it: 'For philosophy, speaking for oneself is, let us say, too personal; for psychoanalysis, what we are likely to call autobiography is, in a sense, wrongly personal, about the wrong person, serving to avoid hearing (roughly paraphrasing Lacan) who it is who is dictating your history.'[12] Following Cavell's argument, it is not only that, as Rycroft and Phillips argue, autobiographies tend falsely to unify the multiplicities of lives that make up a life, in their attempt to create narrative coherence: they are also false records of the self, or selves.

---

[12] Stanley Cavell, *A Pitch of Philosophy: Autobiographical Exercises* (Cambridge, MA: Harvard University Press, 1994), 5.

Adam Phillips suggests that 'there are surprisingly few case-histories or fully fledged autobiographies by patients or analysts' (p. 75). We can take on board his argument that, because 'psychoanalysis is autobiography by other means', a 'psychoanalytic autobiography' is 'a contradiction in terms', or perhaps a tautology. There are, nonetheless, many significant examples of psychoanalytically informed autobiographies and of autobiographies which are structured in relation to the psychoanalytic project and process, as well as records of analysis, by patients and analysts. A number of psychoanalysts, including Freud's biographer Ernest Jones, produced autobiographical works.[13] I discuss a number of such texts in this chapter, focusing on some of the ways in which psychoanalysis—as a theory of the self and its formation, an exploration of the workings of the unconscious mind, an approach to family relations, and a therapeutic practice—has informed, and been represented in, works of autobiography. I am also concerned with the ways in which autobiographies of this kind have negotiated, if not overcome, the problems that have been identified by Rycroft, Phillips, Cavell, and many others: the monologic nature of autobiography as against the dialogic formation of psychoanalysis; the question of the unity as against the multiplicity of identity; the narration by autobiographers of constructed and partial selves, as distinct from of the more difficult and demanding self-projections which psychoanalysis brings forward. Thus, to take one example, the psychoanalyst Wilfred Bion prefaces his autobiographical text *The Long Week-End 1897–1919: Part of a Life* with these words:

In this book my intention has been to be truthful. It is an exalted ambition; after many years of experience I know that the most I can claim is to be 'relatively' truthful. Without attempting any definition of terms I leave it to be understood that by 'truth' I mean 'aesthetic' truth and 'psycho-analytic' truth; this last term I consider to be a 'grade' of scientific truth. In other terms, I hope to achieve, in part and as a whole, the formulation of phenomena as close as possible to noumena.[14]

I am further concerned with the ways in which accounts of psychoanalysis, as a relationship and dialogue between analyst and analysand, enter into autobiographical texts, and with the connections made between the analyst

---

[13] See Ernest Jones, *Free Associations: Memories of a Psycho-Analyst* (London: Hogarth Press, 1959).

[14] Wilfred R. Bion, *The Long Week-End 1897–1919: Part of a Life* (London: Free Association Books, 1986), 8.

and the reader, through their shared placing as both the receivers and the interpreters of the life history. Psychoanalysis was early defined (by one of Freud's and Breuer's 'hysterical' patients) as the 'talking-cure', and the centrality of speech and hearing, represented as a talking-out and talking-through of life stories within the analytic encounter, is frequently reproduced in autobiographies in which psychoanalysis centrally figures. My discussion moves from accounts of analysis with Freud in the 1930s to more recent texts, including autobiographical works written by the historians Ronald Fraser and Barbara Taylor. I close with a more detailed discussion of the philosopher Richard Wollheim's memoir *Germs*, published in 2004, soon after his death.

Psychoanalysis, as a science and theory of the mind, began with Sigmund Freud's self-analysis, undertaken as a conscious task in the summer of 1897, and worked through in his correspondence with his, at this time, intimate friend Dr Wilhelm Fliess. Amongst the formative 'discoveries' to which Freud's introspection led him was 'the definite realization that there is no "indication of reality" in the unconscious, so that it is impossible to distinguish between truth and emotionally-charged fiction'.[15] Freud's concept of the inseparability of truth and fiction in memory and history has had profound implications for understandings of autobiographical writing and the complex nature of autobiographical recall. So too have his emphasis on the role of dreams as 'the royal road to the unconscious' and his theorisations of 'screen memories'.

The Interpretation of Dreams, first published in 1900, has often been defined as Freud's true autobiography, by contrast with his *An Autobiographical Study* (1925, English translation 1927) which is an account of a professional life, relatively free from introspection and silent on the topic of the self-analysis. Ernest Jones endorsed Freud's universalizing tendencies (his unconscious coming to stand for everyone's unconscious) in describing the self-analysis as Freud's 'most heroic feat—a psycho-analysis of his own unconscious . . . Once done it is done forever. For no one again can be the first to explore those depths.'[16] A work by another disciple of Freud's, the analyst Theodor

---

[15] Sigmund Freud, *The Origins of Psycho-Analysis: Letters to Wilhelm Fliess, Drafts and Notes: 1887–1902* (New York: Basic Books, 1954), 216.

[16] Ernest Jones, *The Life and Work of Sigmund Freud*, vol. 1: *1856–1900* (New York: Basic Books, 1953), 319.

Reik, was titled *The Inner Experience of a Psychoanalyst* (1949), and, picking up on Freud's anthropological metaphors for psychoanalysis's discoveries, as well as his image of femininity as 'the dark continent', promised 'the story of the strange adventure that is the most important work of a psychoanalyst: the story of an expedition into the last dark continent on earth'.[17] For Reik, 'It was self-observation and self-analysis which led to the fundamental convictions which Freud presented to an unbelieving world' (p. ix) and, like Jones, he represented Freud's self-analysis as an act of unparalleled heroism, writing of 'the process by which Freud arrived at his results by a heroic mental deed, by a victory over his own inner reluctances and resistances. Nothing said to us, nothing we can learn from others, reaches so deep as that which we find in ourselves' (p. 19).

The broader context for Reik's discussion is his conviction that the 'training analysis' which, for the profession, is an essential part of qualifying as a psychoanalyst, cannot substitute for the self-analysis which, he argues, is the route to the most profound self-knowledge. For Reik and for Jones, Freud's self-analysis is represented as a journey into the interior undertaken by the isolated individual. Yet, Reik notes, self-knowledge can only come about through acts of self-observation in which, in the words of William James, 'The *I* observes the *Me*' (quoted in Reik, p. 5). Self-knowledge comes about when the self becomes an other to itself, and Reik recommends to the reader an experiment in writing, along the lines of free association:

The reader is invited to take paper and pencil and to write down whatever occurs to him during the next half-hour. He should eliminate all censorship of his thoughts while he writes . . . just as if they had been dictated to him by another person . . . He should then put the written sheets into a drawer and leave the room. When he takes them out the next day, he will meet a person there who reminds him of himself in many ways but is in other ways an unknown man. Was it he who thought all that? Here is a new *I* to whom he gets introduced. (p. 26)

The concept of dictation (from the self to the self or, rather, from one part of the self to another) is pursued, in more literal terms, through Reik's recommendations of the use of a Dictaphone to record one's words, thus allowing for 'the possibility of listening in comfort to one's thoughts the

---

[17] Theodor Reik, *The Inner Experience of a Psychoanalyst: Listening with the Third Ear* (London: George Allen & Unwin, 1949), ix (henceforth cited within the text by page numbers).

next day, as one might listen to a third person. The advantages compared with writing are clear. The road from thought to speech is shorter than from thinking to writing. It is really a return to the original, because what we think is only what we say within ourselves without pronouncing the words' (p. 27). Reik connects the distinction between thought and spoken words to the Catholic confession, which cannot be merely thought or written down, but must be '*vocalis*, spoken; it must be articulated, vocalized . . . The advantage of the dictaphone is that one can "hear oneself think"' (p. 27).

Autobiographies in which the experience of psychoanalysis features prominently tend, as I have suggested, to foreground the role of speech and dialogue, and the focus is frequently on the speech acts and dialogic engagements—as well as the play of silence and of interruption—entailed in the psychoanalytic session. Returning to Freud's self-analysis, we might note that, *contra* Ernest Jones' account of the process as a lonely heroic act, Freud's discoveries about himself, which became the founding tenets of psychoanalytic models of identity, were frequently produced in dialogue with another individual and that, in the first decades of his career in particular, he engaged intensely with a series of interlocutors: Josef Breuer, Wilhelm Fliess, Carl Jung. The relationship between self-analysis (in which the 'I' observes the 'me') and the intimate communications (with Fliess in particular) which shaped Freud's conceptual 'discoveries' also have a crucial part to play in psychoanalytically informed autobiography and in the representation, in life-writings, of the psychoanalytic encounter.

In 1954, the American doctor and psychologist Joseph Wortis published his *Fragments of an Analysis with Freud*, the title an echo of one of Freud's best-known case histories, that of 'Dora', or 'Fragments of an Analysis of a Case of Hysteria' (1905 [1901]). Wortis' book is 'a first-hand account' of his analysis in Vienna in the early 1930s: it is not, he insists, 'about me' but 'about Sigmund Freud and his theories'.[18] The autobiographical and self-revelatory dimensions of his account are more or less absent, while Wortis emphasizes the documentary nature of his record of the analysis:

Our conversations were all in German, but I kept my notes in English, with frequent inclusion of the German words and phrases that Freud used. All the quotations are

---

[18] Joseph Wortis, *Fragments of an Analysis with Freud* (1954; New York: McGraw Hill, 1975), vii (henceforth cited within the text by page numbers).

exactly as they stand in my notes, usually written down immediately after each session, in a nearby coffeehouse, on the 4x6-inch cards I always carried with me. The impulse to keep a record of our talks arose quite naturally out of the realization that my period of contact with Freud would be limited, and I wanted to reconsider the experience at leisure. (p. x)

The main part of the book is organized as a diary of the times, each entry being given over to an account of that day's analytic session. Wortis' dreams were central to these sessions, but he gives little indication of the past experiences to which their interpretations might have led. He also records Freud's own resistance to self-revelation, articulated in his response to Wortis' suggestion that there would be significant interest in the 'personal factors' underlying Freud's scientific work. Wortis quotes Freud thus:

'My personal experiences?... I certainly don't intend to tell them. No man could tell the truth about himself.'

'But you could come nearest to being the exception', I suggested. 'The world would be most anxious to hear, and would profit from the knowledge.'

'It won't hear anything from me; I have told enough about myself in my *Traumdeutung* [*The Interpretation of Dreams*]', said Freud. 'If it discovers things in some other way, that is not my concern. People should interest themselves in psycho-analysis, and not in my person.' (p. 121)

'No man could tell the truth about himself': Freud's scepticism towards biographical and autobiographical 'truth' ran deep, despite his extensive engagements with various forms of life-writing. The opacity of the self is a corollary of the concept which founds and grounds psychoanalysis: the existence of an unconscious which reveals itself only in disguised and distorted forms. Freud's assertion, as Wortis reports it, however, suggests that there are also more strongly willed forms of self-concealment. Thus it may be, on the one hand, that we can never know the truth about ourselves, however intently we seek for it and, on the other, that we possess knowledge of the self that we find too shameful to reveal, and that a protective narcissism defends against the humiliations attendant on con-fession and disclosure.

In the year following the analysis, Wortis sent the notes he had taken on his sessions to the psychologist Havelock Ellis, who commented on the interest and value of the 'Freud notes': 'They do not, however, reveal anything about you. Their value is that they constitute *an analysis of Freud*, and a precise revelation of his technique...I am almost afraid that the notes might in a future age be regarded as a *reductio ad absurdum* of psycho-analysis: But, *anyhow*, they will be valuable' (pp. 173–4). In his 'Retrospect' to the published volume, and indeed throughout the notes themselves, Wortis makes clear his sense of the limitations of Freudian psychoanalysis:

The series of inept and inappropriate interpretations early in the analysis (that a house represents the womb, that a stage show represents coitus, etc.) and the general foraging in a false direction indicated to me as the analysis went on that I was not likely to get any deep or valid insights from it. Actually I think a dividing of the ways came at about the middle period of the analysis when I began to realize that people by and large must work their problems out in the arena of real life and action and not by endless probing into the reaches of an obscure unconscious repository of instincts and childhood repressions. (pp. 186–7)

In 1934, the year in which Joseph Wortis undertook his analysis, the American poet H.D. was also in Vienna for analysis with Freud. Like Wortis, H.D. was close to Havelock Ellis, and she also saw herself as a 'student' rather than as a 'patient' of Freud's. She too based her account of the analysis in part on her notes and diaries of the time. The tenor of her accounts of her analysis is, however, very different to that of Wortis: any resistances she expressed relate not to psychoanalysis's failures in 'real life' engagement but to what she perceived as Freud's 'materialism', including his interpretation of experiences which she held to be 'inspiration' (vision-ary, mystical) as 'symptom'. She produces, her arguments with some of Freud's ideas notwithstanding, a homage to him and his methods. *Tribute to Freud* (1956) (which contains 'Writing on the Wall' (1945–46) and its com-panion text 'Advent' (assembled from the 1933 notebooks in 1948)) is a text composed of fragments, and H.D. uses archaeological imagery to represent the relationship between the 'objects' in Freud's consulting rooms (includ-ing classical and Egyptian pottery and figures) and the contents of mind and memory: 'there are priceless broken fragments that are meaningless until we find the other broken bits to match them'.[19] Associations between present and past are made through spatial rather than temporal connec-tions: the architecture of Freud's rooms becomes the passageway into other remembered spaces (in particular her father's study and the hotel room in Greece in which she had her 'visionary' experience of 'the writing on the

---

[19] H.D., *Tribute to Freud* (Manchester: Carcanet, 1970), 35.

wall').[20] The text is at once intended to suggest the processes of free association and is clearly crafted to represent the ways in which patterns are both found and made.

While H.D.'s *Tribute to Freud* is certainly closer in form to 'memoir' than to 'autobiography' in any conventional understanding of the latter genre—there is no attempt to structure the fragments into a linear, chronological account nor to produce a 'coherent' life story—it could be argued that its search for different kinds of pattern, meaning, and significance are part of the changes that psychoanalysis has wrought upon modern autobiography. We should also note, however, that earlier developments—such as literary impressionism—had opened up the space for the autobiography of fragments and the representation of discrete experiences and perceptions: John Ruskin's *Praeterita* (first published in twenty-eight parts between 1885 and 1889) is a central example here. 'Aesthetic autobiography', such as that of Ruskin, has tended to emphasize not only the visual dimensions of experience and memory but also an acute awareness of spatiality, and this is heightened in the works of many of the twentieth-century writers, artists, and art theorists for whom psychoanalysis and autobiographical writing, and the connections between the two, have become central ways of exploring the relationship between the inner and the outer or object world.

I will return to these representations in my brief discussion of autobiographical works by the art theorist Adrian Stokes, who was for many years in analysis with Melanie Klein, and give a fuller account of *Germs: A Memoir of Childhood* (2004), the posthumously published autobiography of the philosopher and aesthetician Richard Wollheim, who also wrote extensively on Stokes' theories of art and psychoanalysis. For the moment, I wish to pursue a different version of the relationship between the inner and the outer world, psyche and polis, using two texts of recent decades in which the representation of psychoanalysis as a therapy is made central.

---

[20] In *Tribute to Freud*, H.D. describes the experience she called 'the writing-on-the-wall', where she saw a 'series of shadow- or of light-pictures . . . projected on the wall of a hotel bedroom in the Ionian island of Corfu, at the end of April 1920 . . . For myself I consider this sort of dream or projected picture or vision as a sort of halfway state between ordinary dream and the vision of those who, for lack of a more definite term, we must call psychics or clairvoyants' (p. 41). Freud, H.D. writes, 'picked on the writing-on-the-wall as the most dangerous or the only actually dangerous "symptom"' (p. 41).

On its publication in 1984, historian Ronald Fraser's *In Search of a Past: The Manor House, Amnersfield, 1933–1945* appeared as a new kind of autobiography. Fraser brought together oral history, through the interviews with the former servants on his parents' country-house estate, and accounts of his psychoanalytic sessions. The intention was to explore the past through two different lenses: those of social history, in which he would look at his childhood and family through the perspectives of others, as objective 'evidence', with the servants testifying not only to an historical past (the world before the Second World War) but to his personal past; and his past as he lived and experienced it, with the processes of analysis unlocking buried memories. *In Search of a Past* opens with a record of a psychoanalytic session: 'There's a long silence, and then I say: "I remember . . . "'.[21] Throughout the memoir, Fraser draws attention to such silences, initially threatening, and hence to the fact that speech in psychoanalysis differs from other kinds of conversation. It is represented as a way of speaking into a new kind of silence. 'Anticipating a dialogue', Fraser writes of this first encounter with the analyst, P., 'I looked at him, but his eyes had vanished again' (p. 5).

To a large extent, Fraser's project acts as confirmation of Adam Phillips' suggestion that psychoanalysis might be a prelude to autobiography. *In Search of a Past* explicitly follows the autobiographical example of the French writer and political theorist André Gorz, whose 'existentialist' autobiography *Le Traître* (1958, translated as *The Traitor* (1959)), moves from the pronoun 'We' to 'They' to 'You' to the authenticity of the 'I'. Gorz's narrative strategy is to present the writing of *The Traitor* as the necessary condition for the construction of the 'I', while Fraser depicts the construction of the 'I' as the condition for the writing of the autobiography. In a central passage, which raises a number of issues about the relationships between psychoanalysis, autobiography, and history, Fraser records telling his analyst about the book he is planning—the book we are now reading:

I outline the newly discovered aim of combining two different modes of enquiry— oral history and psychoanalysis—to uncover the past in as many of its layers as possible. 'At first, I thought I wanted your help to overcome the difficulty of writing about the past'; now I see that the difficulty is part and parcel of the past. This

---

[21] Ronald Fraser, *In Search of a Past: The Manor House, Amnersfield, 1933–1945* (London: Verso, 1984), 3 (henceforth cited within the text by page numbers).

"voyage of inner discovery", as I think you once called it, has to be combined with the account of the other voyage into the social past.

'Uh-huh...' After a time, he adds: 'Yes, through them you set out to discover the external objects; now, through analysis, you're seeking the internal objects.'

'And the two don't always coincide', I reply. 'That's my split vision. Formed by the past, a person is also deformed by it.'

He doesn't reply at first. 'Well, it's not the past but what we make of the past that shapes our future and present', he says firmly at last. 'But I can see that the two voyages share common elements of language and memory. Perhaps you could contrast them in the book.'

'Well... Yes, they're similar in reconstructing a remembered past, not the past as it actually was. In that respect, analysis is more limiting because it recreates the past only in the forms in which it was internalized or repressed. The infantile aspects...' (pp. 118–19)

At the text's close, 'silence' ceases to be threatening and becomes the productive element of the analysis—'I rest in the silence'—as figures from the past enter, in imagination, 'until they fill the emptiness around me' (p. 186). In the final lines, the dialogue between analyst and analysand expresses both understanding and agreement over the relationship between the inner world which psychoanalysis explores and the evidential basis of history, 'subject', and 'object':

'It's the synthesis of the two, isn't it?'
'The author of your childhood then, the historian of your past.'
'That's what I intend—to write about it from inside and out.' (p. 187)

Another historian, Barbara Taylor, in *The Last Asylum: A Memoir of Madness in Our Times*, intertwines an account of her childhood and family history, her mental illness, her psychoanalysis, her stay as a patient, in the 1980s and the early 1990s, in one of the last of the Victorian asylums, and the history of the asylum movement in Britain. She writes of the memoir that it 'is a work of history—my own and many other people's':

It is also a book about the work of turning the personal past into history. The sources of self run deep. In my case, exploring them required me to become a historian of my own life, through the peculiar and demanding labour of a long-term psychoanalysis, of which *The Last Asylum* is also an account.[22]

---

[22] Barbara Taylor, *The Last Asylum: A Memoir of Madness in Our Times* (London: Hamish Hamilton, 2014), xii–xiii (henceforth cited within the text by page numbers).

In her 'Prologue', Taylor defines the difference between standard psychiatric procedures, which manage and suppress thoughts and symptoms, and the psychoanalytic project, 'which instead of suppressing the lunatic psyche engages with it, unleashing its dynamism inside the therapeutic relationship. Solo madness becomes shared madness, with one side of the relationship hopefully remaining sane enough to feel the craziness without getting lost in it' (p. xiv). Throughout the memoir, she recounts the conversations (in the italicized portions of the text) between herself and the analyst she calls Dr V, which she describes as 'true to my recollections of them—in substance if not in detail—but it is I alone who am responsible for recalling them in this way' (p. xvii).

'Before I went into analysis, I knew nothing of me', Taylor writes in the first chapter of the book, 'Beginning':

After several years of analysis, when I finally began to meet myself, the person that I encountered was so angry she could destroy the world. To take her seriously meant entertaining a tumult of grief and despair so intense that my body folded up with it, so bloody with rage and hate that no one could survive it.

We can't go there
We are already there.
Will I survive?
I believe that you and I and the analysis will all survive. (p. 8)

After Taylor had spent a couple of months in analysis, 'talking about it incessantly', a friend gave her a notebook: ' "I thought you might like to write some of this down" ... By the time I left analysis, in 2003, I had thirteen notebooks, plus various unbound scribblings.' 'I wrote mostly about V [the analyst] and me', Taylor records, but 'also about my friends, my family, childhood memories. I recorded many dreams' (p. 11). She describes the writing as a form of talking to herself: talking about it in the memoir becomes a way into her family history, 'about my early life as I rediscovered it during the first decade of my psychoanalysis' (p. 19). Writing and talking come to represent both compulsion and cure.

Fraser's 'inside' and 'outside' map onto the psychoanalysis/inner world and the project of 'recording' the past, by means of a different kind of communication, the oral history interview. Taylor's memoir, too, has its 'inside' and 'outside': the experience of madness and the work of the historian, researching and charting a history of attitudes, treatments, and institutions. Both writers bring to their works awareness of the criticism that could be levelled not only against autobiography—we recall Rycroft's critique of its 'individualism'—but against psychoanalysis. Their orientations are theoretical as well as experiential, and Fraser's memoir might seem to move, in too assuredly recuperative a way, towards narrative and psychological resolution. Yet both texts are important attempts to represent the immediacy of the articulations, and disarticulations, of the psychoanalytic dialogue, as well as to bridge what is, for Adam Phillips, a 'significant gap' between 'the written and the spoken in the telling of lives' (p. 74).

I return now, in the final part of this chapter, to the connections between psychoanalysis, aesthetics, and philosophy, especially as they relate to issues of the unity and 'pattern' of a life. These were central concerns for the art theorists and philosophers Adrian Stokes and Richard Wollheim, who became close friends in the early 1960s, and who both produced important experiments in autobiography. Stokes wrote extensively on numerous dimensions of art and culture, including painting, sculpture, architecture, and ballet. His two-decades-long, though intermittent, analysis with Klein, which began in 1929, and his increasing absorption in the question of art's role in externalizing our 'inner objects', was a shaping force on two autobiographical works, *Inside Out* (1947) and *Smooth and Rough* (1951). These works bear, in interesting ways, on Adam Phillips' suggestion that every psychoanalytic theorist tells us:

implicitly or explicitly, his or her own version of what a good life-story is; so, for example a Kleinian good life-story would not be one inspired and gratified by revenge; a Winnicottian good life-story would not be defined by its states of conviction but by the quality of its transitions; and so on. In choosing a psychoanalyst of one persuasion or another, one is choosing the kind of life one wants to end up speaking. (pp. 70–1)

The Preface to *Inside Out* opens with these words: 'In the nursery, that is where to find the themes of human nature: the rest is "working-out", though it also be the real music.'[23] The opening section of the text describes

---

[23] Adrian Stokes, *Inside Out*, in *The Critical Writings of Adrian Stokes, Vol. II*, ed. Lawrence Gowing (London: Thames & Hudson, 1978), 139–82; 141 (henceforth cited within the text by page numbers).

the London parks, in which Stokes spent much time as a child, in terms which resonate with Melanie Klein's models of the destructive, depressive, and reparative or restitutive stages of identity formation:

My governess and I used to read outside the park police station the notices recounting...all the crimes that had recently occurred, chiefly suicides in the Serpentine. A police description of a dead body exactly expressed my predominant impression of the park as a whole. Yet I did not altogether give up hope of infusing these remnants with life. I would return again and again to the fountains and hope against hope that the engine-house activity would spell out something good. (p. 143)

The walk home from the park, Stokes writes, 'was marked by the passage underneath the Serpentine bridge', a 'dirty echoing tunnel' and an 'obscene hole' to which 'I attributed the home of the animus that tore the body of the park to shreds' (pp. 152–3). Beyond childhood, it was a different tunnel, 'a long railway tunnel, the Mont Cenis' (through which he passed in journeying from France to Italy) which 'was the approach to the counter-landscape, to the rested mother, to love and life' (p. 153). 'Forms arranged in space' are the connective link between inner and outer worlds, and the 'two landscapes' of *Inside Out* describe, he writes, 'basic human relationships': 'Hyde Park is especially a destroyed and contaminated mother, Italy the rapid attempt to restore. In their terms, and it would seem to me in their terms alone, could I re-create succinctly the division, the incorporation of opposites' (p. 158).

Stokes' autobiographical writings were, Richard Wollheim argues, the first texts in which he fully used psychoanalysis, as if Stokes, like Freud, felt that he could only incorporate these discoveries once he had, Wollheim writes, 'confronted them with his own experience and seen their necessity'.[24] To this extent, Stokes' autobiographies (or semi-autobiographies, in Wollheim's phrase), laid the ground for his most complete workings-out of the relationships between art and psychoanalysis, in the five volumes of art theory written in the 1950s and published by the psychoanalytic Tavistock Press. When Wollheim came to write his own autobiography, *Germs: A Memoir of Childhood*, Stokes' autobiographical example would appear to

---

[24] Richard Wollheim, 'La pensée d'Adrian Stokes', *Les Cahiers du Musée National d'Art Moderne*, 25 (Automne 1988), 39–51; 46. ['...après les avoir confrontés avec sa propre expérience et avoir reconnu qu'ils s'imposaient'.]

have been an important influence, not least its focus on the 'geography' of childhood experience and the spatial and bodily dimensions of our memories of childhood.

Wollheim's self-explorations are also significantly connected to his theoretical writings. *Germs* can certainly be characterised as a 'philosophical autobiography'.[25] There are also important uses of autobiography in Wollheim's philosophical texts, and an imbrication, throughout his work, of philosophy, autobiography, and psychoanalysis. In his philosophical study *The Thread of Life* (1984), Wollheim conjoins the philosophy of mind and psychoanalytic theory in a study of personhood. Freud's case histories—including that of the patient known as the 'Rat Man'—are central, and Wollheim discusses at some length the obsessive-compulsive behaviours of the 'Rat Man' as expressions of ambivalent feelings, in particular towards the figure of his father, and the 'conflict of desire' that governed his life. In one of the early chapters of the text (which was based on a series of lectures) Wollheim writes, as if the examples were themselves randomly or 'idly' chosen, of 'desires that are idle or have no role—my desire to have seen the *Oresteia* in the twilight of ancient Athens, my desire to have had another mother'.[26]

The general point Wollheim draws out of this discussion is that, psychologically, no clear line can be drawn between 'idle' and 'working' desires, but he does not return to the terms of 'my desire to have had another mother' until later in the text, in an example chosen 'from my own experience of psychoanalysis', which rests on his recurrent identification of certain men with the figure of his father, and an accompanying distance from, and 'embarrassment about', the women to whom these men are married, though 'the personality of the woman is a matter of indifference'. The interpretation rests on the calculation: 'Your mother is just the woman to whom your father is married: that is all she is' (p. 193). The 'revelation' is at one level misleading, in that the pursuit of self-examination leads only to the compounding of self-error: 'My desire to

---

[25] See Julia Straub's illuminating essay on *Germs*, in *Haunted Narratives: Life Writing in an Age of Trauma*, ed. Gabriele Rippl, Philipp Schweighauser, Tiina Kirss, Margit Sutrop, and Therese Steffen (Toronto: University of Toronto Press), 85–100.

[26] Richard Wollheim, *The Thread of Life: The William James Lectures, 1982* (New Haven, CT: Yale University Press, 1984), 89–90 (henceforth cited within the text by page numbers).

have another mother remains unexamined so long as the thought "My mother is just the wife of my father, she has no direct connection with me" remains inviolate.' Yet, Wollheim suggests, there is a 'supplementary piece of projection' (p. 195): could it be that the 'curious void in the picture' (indicated by the 'indifference' towards the women married to the men with whom he has strong emotional identifications) is also a projection into them of 'the blankness, the nothingness, the sense of absence that I felt in relation to my mother?' (p. 195).

Versions of this material emerge, in recast forms, in the memoir, in which Wollheim expresses, through the laconic nature of his prose, something of this affective 'blankness': 'my mother ... continued to put her trust in phrases like, "I do what I do", "That's what I'm like", "You can't change what a person's like." I do not know that I wanted to change what my mother was like, or at any rate not until many years later, by which time what I really wanted was to change her for someone else, but I wanted to know, because I needed to know, why it was that what my mother spent so much of her life doing was so important to her.'[27] The detailed accounts Wollheim gives of his antecedents—his father's German-Jewish family, members of the intelligentsia[28]—and his mother's, 'altogether different', West Country ancestry—not only serve as genealogy: they also point up the nature of the difference (in a text in which the question of 'sexual difference' is represented as the great conundrum of childhood) that was, confoundingly, the background to his ill-matched parents' meeting and marriage and, subsequently, to Wollheim's being.

Wollheim's lack of feeling for his mother is not fully analysed in the text, though it emerges frequently through anecdotes and in passing comments, many of which relate to the impossibility of exchange and understanding:

[27] Richard Wollheim, *Germs: A Memoir of Childhood* (London: Waywiser Press, 2004), 146 (henceforth cited within the text by page numbers).

[28] Julia Straub takes up the threads of the text relating to questions of Jewish identity and anti-Semitism, suggesting that, though these are significant, they are understated in *Germs*, particularly in the context of the Second World War, in which Wollheim served. Wollheim does note the fate of some family members, victims of the Nazis, though his father was able to bring others out of Germany. He also records an episode in 1933, when his father, whose professional life was imperilled by the situation in Europe, was staying in a Berlin hotel: 'as he got into the old-fashioned lift, he found himself alone with Hitler, and very slowly they travelled up several floors together. From that moment onwards he was a terrified man' (p. 170).

'she never answered any question that I put to her. She did not like it if one person talked to another' (p. 19); 'my mother . . . liked rules without reason' (p. 41); 'She never opened a book, a newspaper, a woman's magazine, or anything that I ever wrote' (p. 134). By contrast, *Germs* indicates Wollheim's strong affective relationship to his father. He expresses regret for what he thinks of as 'the buried life': 'My father had turned his back on a life he had buried, and, by turning his back on it, he buried it deeper, he buried it from me' (p. 55). The image seems linked to his father's 'reticence' in dressing in front of him: 'as to the body itself, what I learnt was strictly limited by the fact that, at a certain moment, my father invariably turned his back to me [so that] by the time he turned round to face me, the lower part of his body was completely swaddled in linen shirt and silk underwear'. Wollheim's fascination with his father's collection of erotic literature suggests that it offered a glimpse of 'the buried life': 'Bound in exotic covers . . . Their meaning only partially buried in a foreign language, these books offered me . . . all the stolen pleasures of instruction, and delight, and adventitiously the lure of danger' (p. 70). In his semi-autobiographical novel, *A Family Romance* (1967), Wollheim devotes a full chapter to his narrator's account of his father's library, including 'the various pornographic works' (p. 44): 'What I took away from these books is, I most often feel, some kind of poison, which I have ever since carried round with me, somewhere on the person, perhaps in a little bottle or phial' (p. 45).

In *A Family Romance*, the 'poison' connects the book, the body and its fluids, and sexual knowledge, a set of associations which take various forms in *Germs*, one of them being Wollheim's account/confession of his aversion to newspaper, and in particular the smell of newspaper, which is 'the most persistent thread in my life . . . It was like a ghost in a house that could be expelled only by demolishing the house' (p. 248). The newspaper phobia is, at the close of *Germs*, linked to an early memory, 'which I have recently, after much effort, called out of decades of dormancy, and which internal evidence dates to November 1925, when I was two and a half'. The memory is of his older brother flicking newspaper pellets, moistened with saliva, at the sheet of newspaper, reporting the death of Queen Alexandra, the Queen Mother, being read by their Nanny in the teatime nursery: 'As the pellets hit the paper with a slight thud, they clung to the page like the scabs in some children's disease' (p. 249). The newspaper was of the type that reported murder trials and sexual scandals: its desecration 'by spit, and smell, and the signs of disease' made it 'hard any longer to believe that, as the Nation had been told, death had come to the Queen peacefully' (p. 250). The ('screen'?) memory is connected to later episodes of his newspaper aversion but there is no other aspect of the memoir which would make us confident of so neat a relationship between cause and effect. We might further question whether buried memories could ever be retrievable, in the perfection of the detail provided by Wollheim, out of 'decades of dormancy', though (and this is at no point explicitly stated), the 'effort' (and the connection) could be interpreted as the labour of psychoanalysis.

Wollheim compared the writing in *Inside Out* and *Smooth and Rough* to the intricate work of a goldsmith,[29] and the question of pattern and design recurs throughout *Germs*. It was also a central philosophical issue for Wollheim. In his essay 'On Persons and their Lives', he wrote of his concern with 'the varying degrees to which people, persons, manage to give their lives a pattern, an overallness, or the different measures of success that they have in making their lives of a piece', and of the relationship between this 'ideal unity' (the ideal of 'the life of wholeness' that has been present in many cultures through the ages) and 'the formal unity that a life possesses in virtue of being one and the same life, a person's one (and only) life'.[30]

Wollheim's memoir opens with a scene from early childhood, the first memory, and deploys the forms of linguistic and phenomenological immediacy that Wollheim elsewhere finds characteristic of 'experiential memory' and of 'centrally imagining' (pp. 306–7), in which 'I centrally imagine whatever it is from the inside'. In the first, long paragraph of *Germs*, the 'I' as a child finds the front door of the house open and walks out into the garden, entering a world in which everything moves: 'The flowers move, and the lavender moves, and the tree above me is moving.' Then comes the trip and the fall, and the large rose-thorn, 'which had been lying in wait on the gravel path . . . slid itself under my thumb-nail, and then, like a cold chisel, worked its way up into me, making its own channel as it went, until it came to rest on the pad of pink, quivering flesh that forms a cushion

---

[29] Wollheim, 'La pensée d'Adrian Stokes', 46. ['Nous voyons ce processus à l'oeuvre dans la complexité du travail d'orfèvre de *Inside Out* (1947) et *Smooth and Rough* (1951)'.]

[30] Richard Wollheim, 'On Persons and their Lives', in *On Emotions*, ed. Amélie Oksenberg Rorty (Berkeley and Los Angeles: University of California Press, 1980), 299–322; 299 (henceforth cited within the text by page numbers).

underneath the nail'. Cries of pain and outrage bring an adult, clad in a starched apron, and the narrator as child is safely returned to the house, 'set down in the darkness, and the dank smell of the hallway rose up and blended with the sharp, chastising smell of the apron ... And then it was the turn of oblivion'. 'Oblivion came down', Wollheim writes, 'with a swish, with the great, heavy swish of velvet curtains suddenly released from the high gilded arch of an opera house, or an old music hall, stirring up as they fell the smell of sawdust aerated with the cold dusty draught that blew in from the wings and dried the nostrils.' The curtains are at once the mechanism of forgetting and the literal fabric of the backstage world of Wollheim's father, the ballet and theatre impresario Eric Wollheim: the passage moves from the curtains as image of oblivion to the stage and the troupe of female dancers who swerve round the young Richard Wollheim on his visits backstage:

Whenever I recall such moments, I noticed how a look of apprehension passed over my father's face as he turned from them to me, and then a look of relief as he turned back from me to them.

It was, as my readers will have guessed, a long, a very long, time before I succeeded in brushing against a woman's body. (p. 13)

This opening sequence is overdetermined, to borrow the Freudian term for the plurality of determining factors to which formations of the unconscious (such as symptoms and dreams) can be attributed. Wollheim offers us a version of the Creation (the first morning) and then the Fall, introducing the terms of innocence and experience central to the memoir as a whole. He weaves in something of the syntax and sensations of Joyce's *Portrait of the Artist as a Young Man* (1914–15), with its recreations of the language of childhood and of bodily feeling—'When you wet the bed first it is warm then it gets cold. His mother put on the oilsheet. That had the queer smell'—merging these with echoes of Stokes' anthropomorphising and animistic/mechanistic lexicon: 'The keepers carried whistles. Emergence from a telephone booth is always associated by me with the fingering of something tucked away on one side of the chest, a cold, punishing little organ that it was a positive duty to handle.'[31] The invocation of 'the sharp, chastising smell of the apron', also sets in train the masochism, and its

---

[31] Stokes, *Inside Out*, 144.

sadistic obverse, which is a central theme, or drive, throughout Wollheim's memoir, in which we glimpse the structures of fantasy and the complex identifications explored in Freud's 1919 essay 'A Child is Being Beaten' (a text explored in some detail in Wollheim's *The Thread of Life*).[32] Sexuality emerges from behind the curtains, with the 'strong, horse-like bodies' of the dancers, who look down through their artificial eyelashes 'to take stock of my little boy's body': the emotions that the young Wollheim attributed to them, and which he now records, run (as if vertically) from a surface surprise, to the desire to protect him, to shame 'at whatever it was about them from which I needed protection', and, 'deepest of all', withering contempt 'for whatever weakness there was in me that made me need, or made them feel I needed, protection from them' (p. 13). There is a break on the page, and then this paragraph:

For many years, and all of them long before I set out, with Dr S as my pilot, to sail back up the stream of my life—an image I clung to for those strained, pipe-filled sessions, in which the unity that I longed to find in my life seemed to slip further and further away into incoherent anxieties—I loved to trace back to this isolated event, of which I know no more than I have set down, a number of the emotions that have patterned themselves over the subsequent years of my life. (p. 13)

---

[32] ' "A Child is Being Beaten": A Contribution to the Study of the Origin of Sexual Perversions' (1919), was described by Freud, as he was working on the paper, as a study of masochism. In the essay Freud explored the ways in which pleasure and pain become connected, through an analysis of what he found to be a widely shared childhood beating fantasy, which 'had its issue in an act of pleasurable auto-erotic satisfaction' (Standard Edition vol. 17 (1955), 180). The essay looks at the passive linguistic form of the fantasy—'A child is being beaten'—in relation to the impossibility of deciding whether 'the pleasure attaching to the beating-phantasy was to be described as sadistic or masochistic' (p. 181), and goes on to explore the transformations in the structure of the fantasy and its protagonists. In his discussion of the essay in *The Thread of Life*, Wollheim writes: 'mode, viewpoint, repertoire, oscillate, and . . . as a result of these oscillations the same phantasy—same, that is, judged by the identity of the events it represents—can become the expression of different desires or acquire different significance' (p. 96). Throughout *Germs*, Wollheim records his childhood fantasies and memories of imagined and real scenes in which punitive fathers, or father figures, beat male and female children, though he at no point represents himself as the child being beaten.

'A Child is Being Beaten', and the structures of fantasy it explores, is also central to the psychoanalytic autobiography, *A Dialogue on Love* (Boston: Beacon Press, 1999), of the literary and gender theorist Eve Kosofsky Sedgwick. I have not had space to discuss Sedgwick's memoir in this chapter but, in its representation of the process and 'dialogue' of psychotherapy, it is highly relevant to my topic.

This is the first mention of the psychoanalyst, Dr S, who is invoked on only a few occasions in the text, and never through direct quotation, by contrast with the extensive presence of the analyst and his recorded (or ventriloquized) discourse in the autobiographical works by Ronald Fraser and Barbara Taylor discussed earlier in this chapter. The 'naming' of Dr S, however, makes a subtle alteration in the nature of the memoir, suggesting to the reader that the memories and episodes recounted in the text have already passed through the articulations and the interpretative processes entailed in psychoanalysis. To 'sail back up through the stream of my life' is not only the province of autobiographers, but also of analysands, and the memoir suggests an oblique but none the less significant relationship between the two identities.

Dr S is invoked again a little later in the text, in the context of a memory of a different pair of velvet curtains, those at the foot of the stairs in Wollheim's parents' house, from behind which he, at the age of eight or nine, 'planning upon making a surprise return to the company' rather than going up to bed, overheard the mezzo-soprano from Vienna, Lea S, commenting unfavourably on his prominent ears: 'Believe me, I know a surgeon in Vienna, he could do it, he would do it for me. No more than a small cut, snip, snip, and they'll lie down. Close to the head, very neat' (p. 26). We might make the link to the cigar cutter which, we have been told a few pages earlier, was (allegedly) used to perform Wollheim's circumcision, but the narrative moves us, through memory, to another pair of curtains, 'seen just a few weeks before on a visit to Madame Tussaud's', concealing, though inadequately, a replica of an instrument of torture used 'in Algiers under foreign domination' (p. 27): a large wheel whose rim had been removed to be replaced by long, curving blades:

The different ways in which the bodies were lacerated, and the time it took for death to arrive, depended directly upon the postures in which the prisoners had been set . . . Sometimes the prisoner had been forced to his knees, and then tied into this position, so that, more mercifully, the knife decapitated him on the first turn.—I have to recount that, of all the discreditable things I felt obliged to reveal to Dr S, nothing caused me more shame than recalling the words of the Viennese singer, for which I, of course, bore not the slightest responsibility. She spoke, I merely overheard. (p. 28)

The narrative thus circles back to the 'shame' of what was overheard (Wollheim comes back repeatedly to episodes of overhearing, on one occasion in relation to a college friend's description of him as a 'total masochist', and to the ear as receptacle), having passed through the curtains obscuring the replica of the instrument of torture, which has been described in relation to the sadism of its (imagined) operators and the grotesque 'postures' into which they placed their prisoners. The text does not necessarily lead us to read the 'shame' of the singer's overheard words as a 'displacement' from the feelings evoked by the wheel of torture (which is apprehended only through the shadows it casts on the ground under the inadequately concealing curtains), though it is there as an interpretative possibility. This becomes a reminder of the roles, at once shared and very different, of reader and analyst. How should the reader take the (implied) invitation to follow the connections between the different kinds of cutting (the piercing of the 'pink, quivering flesh' by the rose-thorn, the circumcision with the cigar cutter, the 'snip snip' of the Viennese surgeon's knife, applied to the ear, as summoned up in Lea S's 'melodious voice', the lacerating knives operated by the prison guards) and from there trace the associative paths between sexuality and wounding, fantasized or real?

In 'On Persons and their Lives', Wollheim wrote of autobiography as 'a literary genre singularly dedicated to the notion of pattern in life or the idea of wholeness . . . it is poised between the writing and the rewriting of a life; and a life may be rewritten so as to impart to that life a unity that it never had—that is, malignly; or it may be rewritten benignly—that is, so as to achieve, even at a late hour, some reconciliation with the past' (p. 315). In *Germs*, Wollheim alludes to the presence of both modes of rewriting in his own autobiographical venture. The associations traced back to the first memory (of the garden and the fall) were, Wollheim writes at one point, 'mere associations after the fact, telling me nothing about the past, or why it has the power to repeat itself in the present' (p. 18). In Part 2 of the memoir, in a fully recursive and reflexive narrative move, Wollheim describes his adult self, of two decades previously, having 'the distinct feeling that I was about to start work on this memoir in earnest':

The truth is that, with a kind of refined cruelty towards myself, I had, in the writing of the first paragraph in which the early fall is recounted, set myself a task that lacked all rationale, except that it blocked all progress. For I had decided, though without full consultation with the side of myself that would have to do the work, that each sentence, beginning with the first sentence, which was three words long, would be one word longer than its predecessor, up to the moment when I trip, and then the words would stream out, one tumbling over another, like a body in free fall. I soon saw that this device was pointless, in that the ear, which is sensitive to the greater structural complexity of the sentence, has no way of taking in mere changes in word-length, but I could think of no way of accommodating to this criticism . . . As a result, I was set back some twelve or fifteen years. (p. 104)

The reader, turning back to the book's opening, finds that Wollheim did indeed carry out his plan—'It is early. The hall is dark. Light rims the front door'—gradually accumulating words in sentences until the 'free fall' of words inaugurated by the body's fall, as if to attempt an erasure between the word and bodily sensation, in a 'writing of the body' to which many auto-biographers have aspired. The 'pointless' patterning of the opening sentences' number sequence—which almost certainly goes unnoticed on a first reading—could be understood as a compensatory strategy. It might be an attempt to give pattern (of a formal kind) to a 'memory' whose 'causal influence' and 'affective tendency'[33] (the capacity to be rethought and refelt, with the power to shape present and future identity) are held to be insufficient.

From a different perspective, the 'device' not only draws attention to the artifice of the representation of the 'first memory', but also points up both the arbitrariness and the excessiveness of the many other patterns which Wollheim describes in close detail throughout the memoir—patterns of association, habit, behaviour, compulsion—of his own and of those who looked after him as child. He recounts, in an exquisitely structured set piece, his mother's house-cleaning, undertaken in a residence with a number of servants: it was, for his mother, an inflexible 'daily routine' and a system of her own devising for the eradication of 'germs'. It was challenged only by the arrival of a governess 'who very much had her own idea of things' (p. 143), and whose 'special procedures' (p. 144) Wollheim depicts in terms which recall the more extreme obsessive behaviours of Freud's clinical subjects. Wollheim, who was a sickly child, also describes, over and again, the ways in which he was, quite literally, wrapped up: the covering and protecting of the body in layers of clothing emerge as attempts, like the 'special procedures', on his parents' and carers' behalf, to ward off the arbitrary, the dangerous, and the uncontrollable, in their own lives as in his.

[33] Wollheim, 'On Persons and their Lives', 309.

It may be, however, returning to the patterning of the opening paragraph, that it is not to be understood as entirely 'pointless' or as merely compensatory. In the closing lines of the memoir, in the context of a meditation on the end of childhood, from which Wollheim moves to occasions 'when I was ready to whisper into the delicate shell of a woman's ear, needs that I never had, desires that I knew only from my father's books, in the hope that one thing I could say, but only just, would, once said, lead to the saying of another thing, once impossible, but now just conceivable' (p. 255), he reflects upon the indirection (or metonymic 'displacement') that has structured his memoir:

[W]e try obliquely to conquer the inability to say one thing through the hard-won ability to say another thing that neighbours on it . . . However little there was in the way of truth to the first thing said, there might be more to the second thing said, and eventually, or such was the hope, I would, in saying one thing after another after another after another, each with a grain more of truth to it than its predecessor, come to spill the beans: I might, if only the ear stayed steady, and that was another hope, find myself, with one broad archaic gesture, scattering the germs. (p. 255)

We travel, then, from the memoir's opening, where each sentence is 'one word longer than its predecessor', to its ending, with its hope for a discourse in which each element would possess 'a grain more of truth to it than its predecessor'. Spilling the beans, scattering the germs: the word 'germs', in this context, acquires additional associations to those of the threat and contagion which it has accumulated throughout the memoir, and becomes allied to 'germination' (the link reinforced by the image of the 'grain' of truth). Further, through the unwritten but surely implied substitution of 'seeds' for 'germs', we close with a model of 'dissemination' ('scattering seeds'): speaking/writing as both 'poison' (poured into the 'delicate shell' or, pace *Hamlet*, into the 'porches' of the ear) and 'remedy', words/germs/seeds sent out to fall on who knows what manner of ground.

15

The Unstoried Life

Galen Strawson

> I want Death to find me planting my cabbages, neither worrying about it nor the unfinished gardening.
>
> Michel de Montaigne

'Each of us constructs and lives a "narrative"... this narrative *is* us, our identities.' 'Self is a perpetually rewritten story.' 'In the end, we *become* the autobiographical narratives by which we "tell about" our lives.' 'We are all storytellers, and we are the stories we tell.' 'We invent ourselves, but we really are the characters we invent.' A person 'creates his identity by forming an autobiographical narrative—a story of his life'. We're 'virtuoso novelists, who find ourselves engaged in all sorts of behaviour, and we always try to put the best "faces" on it we can. We try to make all of our material cohere into a single good story. And that story is our autobiography. The chief fictional character at the centre of that autobiography is one's self.' 'The story of a life continues to be refigured by all the truthful or fictive stories a subject tells about himself or herself. This refiguration makes this life itself a cloth woven of stories told.'[1]

---

[1] Montaigne, *The Complete Essays*, 1563–92, trans. M. A. Screech (London: Penguin, 1991), 99; Oliver Sacks, *The Man Who Mistook His Wife For a Hat* (London: Duckworth, 1985), 110; Jerome Bruner, 'The "Remembered" Self', in *The Remembering Self*, ed. U. Neisser and R. Fivush

According to these theorists, the *narrativists*, life is life-writing, a narrative—autobiographical—activity. We story ourselves and we are our stories. There's a remarkably robust consensus about this claim, not only in the humanities but also in psychotherapy. It's standardly conjoined with the claim that such self-narration is a good thing, necessary for a full human life.[2] I think it's false that everyone stories themselves, and I think it's false that it's always a good thing. These are not universal human truths, even when we confine our attention to human beings who count as psychologically normal, as I will do in this chapter. They're not universal human truths even if they're true of some, or even many or most. Their proponents, the narrativists, are—at best—generalizing from their own case, in an all-too-human way.[3]

What exactly do the narrativists have in mind, when they say things of the sort just quoted? I have not yet been able to find out, but it does seem that there are deeply *Narrative* types among us, where to be Narrative with a capital 'N' is (here I offer a definition) to be:

naturally disposed to experience or conceive of one's life, one's existence in time, oneself, in a narrative way, as having the form of a story, or perhaps a collection of stories, and—in some manner—to live in and through this conception.[4]

The popularity of the narrativist view is *prima facie* evidence that there are such people. But many of us aren't Narrative in this sense. 'Time travels in divers paces with divers persons',[5] and it also travels in divers guises. This

(Cambridge: Cambridge University Press, 1994), 53; Bruner, 'Life as Narrative', *Social Research* 54 (1987), 15; D. McAdams, R. Josselson, and A. Lieblich, 'Introduction', in *Identity and Story: Creating Self in Narrative* (Washington, DC: American Psychological Association, 2006), 1–11, 3; David Velleman, 'The Self as Narrator', in D. Velleman, *Self to Self* (Cambridge: Cambridge University Press, 2006), 206; Marya Schechtman, *The Constitution of Selves* (Ithaca, NY: Cornell University Press, 1996), 93; Dan Dennett, 'Why Everyone is a Novelist', *Times Literary Supplement*, 16–22 September 1988, 1029; Paul Ricoeur, *Time and Narrative* (1985; Chicago: Chicago University Press, 1988), vol. 3, 246.

[2] Sartre, at least, disagrees on the second point, arguing in *La Nausée* (Paris: Gallimard, 1943) that self-storying, although inevitable, condemns us to inauthenticity—in effect, to absence from our own lives. Proust agrees—see p. 290 below.

[3] I doubt that what they say is an accurate description even of themselves.

[4] I use the upper-case 'N' to mark this out as an adjective denoting a psychological trait. Thus the (lower-case) *narrativists* think we're all ($\pm$ should be) *Narrative*.

[5] *As You Like It* 3.2. Rosalind considers variations in the experienced pace of time that arise from temporary circumstances, but individual differences in temporal phenomenology run much deeper. Zimbardo and Boyd sort human beings into 'Pasts', 'Presents', and 'Futures' on the basis of

chapter offers dissenting testimony from many sources. Some of us are not just not naturally Narrative. We're naturally—deeply—non-Narrative. We're anti-Narrative by fundamental constitution. It's not just that the deliverances of memory are, for us, hopelessly piecemeal and disordered, even when we're trying to remember a temporally extended sequence of events. The point is much more general. It concerns all parts of life, the 'great shambles of life', in Henry James' expression.[6] This seems a much better characterization of the large-scale structure ($\approx$ structurelessness) of human existence as we find it.

Non-Narratives are fully aware of life's biological temporal order (birth, infancy, childhood, adolescence, adulthood, prime of life, maturity, decline, old age, and death),[7] and its associated cultural temporal order and rites of passage (including, in these parts, acquisition of the right to drive, marry, drink, vote, adopt, retire, get a free bus pass). Even with all this knowledge of life structure they find themselves 'weltering through eternity', even on the most ordinary mornings or under clear temporal duress (late for work), and not just (as in Shelley's lines) when thickly dreaming.[8]

It makes no difference to non-Narratives whether something has 'burst the spirit's sleep', that is, caused them to wake up to life in a way that makes their past seem like sleepwalking.[9] This Shelleyan experience is orthogonal (as philosophers say) to any experience of narrative coherence or narrative self-determination or 'self-authorship'. The two forms of experience appear to be 'doubly dissociable', in the terminology of experimental psychology: one can experience either in the absence of the other (or both together, or neither).

their different temporal proclivities (*The Time Paradox* (New York: Random House, 2008)), and classify us further as 'past-negative' or 'past-positive', 'present-hedonistic' or 'present-fatalistic'. It's a familiar point that different cultures experience time very differently (see e.g. Robert Levine, *A Geography of Time: The Temporal Misadventures of a Social Psychologist* (New York: Basic Books, 1998)).

[6] James, *The Awkward Age* (New York: Harpers, 1899), 198.

[7] A recent medical classification distinguishes between 'young–old' (65–74), 'old' (74–84), 'old–old' (85+).

[8] Shelley, 'Lines Written among the Euganean Hills', 1818, in *'Percy Bysshe Shelley: The Major Works*, ed. Z. Leader and M. O'Neill (Oxford: Oxford University Press, 2003), 198.

[9] Henderson in Bellow's *Henderson the Rain King* (1959; London: Penguin, 1996), 312, echoing Shelley, *Revolt of Islam*, 'Dedication: To Mary —', in *'Percy Bysshe Shelley: The Major Works*, ed. Z. Leader and M. O'Neill (Oxford: Oxford University Press, 2003), 138.

The experience of 'self-authorship'—the sense that one is engaging in self-determination in and through some process of 'life-writing' or narrative self-constitution—is one thing, mysterious to my kind. The existence of such a thing is another. Perhaps some people have the experience, or aspire to it; some seem to believe in the possibility of self-creation. 'The tendency to attribute control to self is a personality trait', as the psychologist Dan Wegner says, possessed by some and not others.[10] There's an experimentally well-attested distinction between human beings who have what he calls the 'emotion of authorship' with respect to their thoughts, and those who, like myself, have no such emotion, and feel that their thoughts are things that just happen.[11] This may track the distinction between those who experience themselves as self-constituting and those who don't, but whether it does or not, the experience of self-constituting self-authorship seems real enough. When it comes to the actual existence of self-authorship, however—the reality of some process of self-determination in or through life as life-writing—I'm sceptical.

Mary McCarthy appears to speak for many when she says:

I suppose everyone continues to be interested in the quest for the self, but what you feel when you're older, I think, is that you really must make the self. It is absolutely useless to look for it, you won't find it, but it's possible in some sense to make it. I don't mean in the sense of making a mask, a Yeatsian mask. But you finally begin in some sense to make and choose the self you want.[12]

And this, I take it, is how she experiences things, and how—with an attractive degree of caution—she believes them to be. Germaine Greer is less nuanced. She thinks 'human beings have an inalienable right to invent themselves', and she presumably has experiences to match.[13] I go with Emerson: 'we are carried by destiny along our life's course looking as grave & knowing as little as the infant who is carried in his wicker coach thro' the street'.[14] We may be busy all day, intensely engaged in our work, but 'sleep

---

[10] Dan Wegner, *The Illusion of Conscious Will* (Cambridge, MA: The MIT Press, 2002) , 202, citing J. B. Rotter, 'Generalized Expectancies for Internal Versus External Control of Reinforcement', *Psychological Monographs* 80/1, whole number 609 (1966).

[11] Wegner, *The Illusion of Conscious Will*, 318, 325–6.

[12] Interview, in *Writers at Work*, second series (London: Secker & Warburg, 1963), 313.

[13] *The Times*, 1 February 1986.

[14] Emerson, notebook entry, October 1837, in *Journals and Miscellaneous Notebooks of Ralph Waldo Emerson, Volume V: 1835-1838* (Cambridge, MA: Harvard University Press), 392.

lingers all our lifetime about our eyes, as night hovers all day in the boughs of the fir-tree. All things swim and glimmer. Our life is not so much threatened as our perception. Ghostlike we glide through nature, and should not know our place again.'[15] This is the price we pay for our mental complexity, a great difficulty in our condition, unknown to animals, but a price that may be worth paying.

Emerson can be overpowering and for that reason unhelpful, even when he's right. And he uses the ever-tempting general 'we'—just like the narrativists. Deep down, he says, we're all equally unknowing; he proposes a universal human truth. So it's not clear that one can use his words to try to distinguish one group of people from another—non-Narratives from Narratives, or (a different distinction) people who believe in life as life-writing from people who don't. And some Narrative types probably experience the pull of Emerson's remarks, even if others feel their lives to be glimmer-free. So I'll put Emerson aside. The issue remains, the claim that all human life is life-writing, and that life-writing is not only a necessary task for any self-respecting human being, but also, at least in the best case, an exercise of autonomy—self-determination.

This view seems extraordinarily unappreciative of fate, but above all comic, like Einstein's moon—

If the moon, in the act of completing its eternal way around the earth, were gifted with self-consciousness, it would feel thoroughly convinced that it was traveling its way of its own accord on the strength of a resolution taken once and for all.... So would a Being, endowed with higher insight and more perfect intelligence, watching man and his doings, smile about man's illusion that he was acting according to his own free will[16]

—or the all-too-human monkey in *Journey to the West*, in which the Buddha challenges Monkey, aka The Great Sage, to get out of his (the Buddha's) right hand with a single somersault. Monkey, who knows he can cover thirty-six thousand miles in one somersault, accepts the challenge, jumps onto the Buddha's palm, performs a maximal somersault, and marks the distant place of his arrival by writing 'The Great Sage Equaling Heaven

---

[15] Emerson, 'Experience', 1844, in *Essays and Lectures* (New York: Library of America, 1983), 47. The last phrase echoes Psalm 103.

[16] Einstein, 'About Free Will', in *The Golden Book of Tagore: A Homage to Rabindranath Tagore from India and the World in Celebration of His Seventieth Birthday*, ed. Ramananda Chatterjee (Calcutta, 1931).

Was Here' and urinating—before returning to the Buddha's palm to claim his prize.

'I've got you, you piss-spirit of a monkey', roared the Buddha at him. 'You never left the palm of my hand.' 'You're wrong there', the Great Sage replied. 'I went to the farthest point of Heaven, where I saw five flesh-pink pillars topped by dark vapours. I left my mark there: do you dare come and see it with me?' 'There's no need to go. Just look down.' The Great Sage looked down with his fire eyes with golden pupils to see the words 'The Great Sage Equaling Heaven Was Here' written on the middle finger of the Buddha's right hand. The stink of monkey-piss rose from the fold at the bottom of the finger.[17]

If there is any defensible sense in which life is life-writing, I think it is—at best—'automatic writing'. One's life isn't 'a cloth woven of stories told', in Ricoeur's words, threaded with varying degrees of fiction. Never mind the fact that claims of this kind seem to insult those who have suffered greatly. Never mind the adamantine fact that one's life is simply one's life, something whose actual course is part of the history of the universe and 100 per cent non-fictional. For now it's enough to hold on to the point that Alasdair MacIntyre made right at the start of the current narrativist movement: 'we are never more (and sometimes much less) than the co-authors of our own narratives. Only in fantasy do we live what story we please.'[18]

It's worth adding that every life comes with a thrilling stack of counterfactuals. You might so very easily never have met the person you love, or believe you love. And what are the chances of your coming into existence? There's a sense in which they're vanishingly small. Your parents might so very easily never have met, and their parents in turn, and their parents in turn. And if you hadn't gone to X because Y fell ill, you'd never have discovered Z. The irony is that these counterfactuals are great material for good stories, and easily give rise to a sense of wonder or providence. But the wonder has no justification, if only because spectacular counterfactuals hold true of one's life whatever happens. Consider X, amazed at his astonishing good fortune in meeting Y: it might so easily never have

---

[17] *Xiyouji (Journey to the West)*, attributed to Wu Cheng-en, trans. W. J. F. Jenner (1592; Beijing, 1993), vol. 1, ch 7.

[18] *After Virtue* (London: Duckworth, 1981), 199.

happened. But if he hadn't met Y he might now be weeping with happiness at his good fortune in meeting Z.

So I'm with Bill Blattner in his criticism of Alexander Nehamas' influential book *Life as Literature*: 'We are not texts. Our histories are not narratives. Life is not literature.'[19] Somebody had to say it. You might think that Proust disagrees, and not only shows himself to be of a Narrative disposition, but also sides theoretically with the narrativists, when he states that

real life, life at last uncovered and illuminated, the only life really lived, therefore, is literature—that life which, in a sense, lives at each moment in every person as much as in an artist.[20]

But this would be a mistake, a perfect mistake, given the way in which Proust is using the word 'literature'. Proust's conception of how we can enter into our real life is complex, but one thing that is clear is that Narrativity—a tendency to self-narration—constitutes one of the greatest obstacles to doing so. Literature as *la vraie vie*, literature in Proust's special sense of the word, is a matter of a certain rare state of self-awareness which is not generally much in one's control, and has absolutely nothing to do with Narrativity. Roughly speaking, it's a state of absorbed, illuminated consciousness of what one most deeply loves. It's an awareness of an aspect of one's essence (a term one shouldn't hesitate to use) which is itself a participation in one's essence—something from which one is generally alienated. And this awareness is emphatically not a matter of narrative. It is, on the contrary, out of time. The unhappy truth of the human condition, according to Proust, is that we run a great risk of dying without ever knowing our real or true life in his sense ('cette réalité que nous risquerions fort de mourir sans avoir connue'). Our Narrative tendencies are one of the principal reasons why this is so.

Keats says that 'A man's life of any worth is a continual allegory.'[21] Suppose we allow this. Does it follow that he or she should know this, or try

---

[19] 'Life is Not Literature', in *The Many Faces of Time*, ed. L. Embree and J. Brough (Dordrecht: Kluwer, 2000), 187.

[20] 'La vraie vie, la vie enfin découverte et éclaircie, la seule vie par conséquent réellement vécue, c'est la littérature. Cette vie qui, en un sens, habite à chaque instant chez tous les hommes aussi bien que chez l'artiste': *A la recherche du temps perdu* (1922 ; Paris: Gallimard, 1989), vol. 4, 474.

[21] Letter of 14 February–3 May 1819 to George and Georgiana Keats, in H. Rollins, ed., *The Letters of John Keats, 1814–1821*, 2 vols. (Cambridge, MA: Harvard University Press, 1958), vol. 2, 102.

to work out what it is? I don't think so. The search might occlude—distort, destroy—its object. Suppose we further allow that allegories are narratives, so that (if Keats is right) lives of worth are always narratives. It certainly doesn't follow that anyone should be a Narrative type, or that all worthy people are Narrative types. 'Very few eyes can see the Mystery of his life', Keats continues, and I think he knows that this includes the worthy person in question.

If Proust is right about life, 'real life' in his special normative sense of the term,[22] then it may be that non-Narratives have a certain advantage—however small, and however easily nullified by other encumbrances (it's a merely negative advantage—absence of a hindrance—not in itself a positive one). The narrativists, however, may refuse to admit the reality of non-Narratives: 'Look', they may say, 'we're sure that you're sincere when you claim to be non-Narrative, but really you're as Narrative as the rest of us.'[23] In the last twenty years the philosopher Marya Schechtman has given increasingly sophisticated accounts of what it is to be Narrative and to 'constitute one's identity' through self-narration. She now stresses the point that one's self-narration may be very largely implicit and unconscious, and that's an important concession, relative to the strong version of her original 'Narrative Self-Constitution View', according to which 'one must be in possession of a full and explicit narrative [of one's life] to develop fully as a person'.[24] It's certainly an improvement on her original view, and it puts her in a position to say that people like myself may be Narrative and just not know it or admit it.

In her most recent book, *Staying Alive* (2014), Schechtman modifies her original thesis still further, but she still thinks that 'persons experience their lives as unified wholes'[25] in some way that goes far beyond their basic awareness of themselves as single finite biological individuals with a certain *curriculum vitae*. She still thinks that 'we constitute ourselves as persons . . . by developing and operating with a (mostly implicit) *autobiographical narrative* which acts as the lens through which we experience the world',[26] and

---

[22] One's real life in Proust's normative sense is not one's actual life as this is ordinarily understood. It's a matter of one's essence.

[23] 'That's precisely why Proust is so pessimistic', they may add.

[24] Schechtman, *The Constitution of Selves*, 93, 119.

[25] Schechtman, *Staying Alive* (Oxford: Oxford University Press, 2014), 100.

[26] *Ibid.*, 100; my emphasis.

I still doubt that this is true. I doubt that it's a universal human condition—universal among people who count as normal. I doubt this even after she writes that ' "having an autobiographical narrative" doesn't amount to consciously retelling one's life story always (or ever) to oneself or to anyone else'.[27] I don't think an 'autobiographical narrative' plays any significant role in how I experience the world, although I know that my present overall outlook and behaviour is deeply conditioned by my genetic inheritance and sociocultural place and time, including, in particular, my early upbringing, and also know, on a smaller scale, that my experience of this bus journey is affected both by the talk I've been having with A in Notting Hill and the fact that I'm on my way to meet B in Kentish Town.

I am, like Schechtman, a creature who can 'consider itself as itself, the same thinking thing, in different times and places', in Locke's famous definition of a person; I know what it's like when 'anticipated trouble already tempers present joy'.[28] In spite of my poor memory, I have a perfectly respectable degree of knowledge of many of the events of my life; I don't live ecstatically in the present moment in any pathological or enlightened manner. But I do, with Updike and many others, 'have the persistent sensation, in my life..., that I am just beginning'.[29] Pessoa's 'heteronym' Alberto Caeiro is a strange man, but he captures an experience common to many (in some perhaps milder form) when he writes that 'I always feel as if I've just been born / Into an endlessly new world'.[30] Some will immediately understand this, others will be puzzled—and perhaps sceptical. The general lesson is the lesson of human difference.

In a rare interview Alice Munro speaks about her writing:

there is this kind of exhaustion and bewilderment when you look at your work... it's all in a way quite foreign—I mean, it's quite gone from you....And all you really have left is the thing you're working on now. And so you're much more thinly clothed. You're like somebody out in a little shirt or something, which is just the

---

[27] *Ibid.*, 101.

[28] *Ibid.*, 101; for the Locke quotation see Locke, *Essay*, 2nd edn (London 1694), §2.27.9.

[29] John Updike, *Self-Consciousness* (London: Penguin, 1989), 239. Updike's testimony shows that this experience of life has nothing essentially to do with poor memory.

[30] Fernando Pessoa, 'The Keeper of Sheep', 1914, in *Fernando Pessoa & Co., Selected Poems*, ed and trans. R. Zenith (New York: Grove Press, 1998), 48. Pessoa's heteronyms are not *noms de plume*; see e.g. R. Zenith, 'Introduction', in Fernando Pessoa, *The Book of Disquiet* (London: Penguin Classics, 2002), vii–xxvi.

work you're doing now and the strange identification with everything you've done before. And this probably is why I don't take any public role as a writer. Because I can't see myself doing that except as a gigantic fraud.[31]

Here Munro is speaking specifically of writing, and (as I understand her) of her bewilderment at being identified with her previous work, but one's general relation to one's past can have a similar form. It can in any case be radically non-narrative and find its ideal representation in list form, as in Joe Brainard's *I Remember*, which contains over 1,000 'I remembers':

> I remember when my father would say 'Keep your hands out from under the covers' as he said goodnight. But he said it in a nice way.
> I remember when I thought that if you did anything bad, policemen would put you in jail.
> I remember one very cold and black night on the beach with Frank O'Hara. He ran into the ocean naked and it scared me to death.
> I remember lightning.
> I remember wild red poppies in Italy.
> I remember selling blood every three months on Second Avenue.[32]

There's an echo of Munro's experience in Updike's complaint about biography:

The trouble with literary biographies, perhaps, is that they mainly testify to the long worldly corruption of a life, as documented deeds and days and disappointments pile up, and cannot convey the unearthly innocence that attends, in the perpetual present tense of living, the self that seems the real one.[33]

One may be suspicious of Updike, but one shouldn't think that those who feel that their pasts fall away are motivated by a desire to escape responsibility.[34]

According to Schechtman, 'the sense in which we have autobiographical narratives . . . is cashed out mostly in terms of the way in which an implicit understanding of the ongoing course of our lives influences our experience

[31] Munro, 'Go Ask Alice', *New Yorker*, 19 February 2001.

[32] Brainard, *I Remember* (1970–73; New York: Granary Books, 2001), 20. Georges Perec wrote a memorable work in the same form (*Je me souviens* (Paris: Hachette, 1978)).

[33] Updike, 'The Man Within', *New Yorker*, 26 June 1995.

[34] See G. Strawson, 'Episodic Ethics', in *Real Materialism and Other Essays* (Oxford: Oxford University Press, 2008), 209–31.

and deliberation'.[35] And there's one natural reading of this claim given which it's obviously true. One is, say, in the second year of one's apprenticeship, and one knows this; one is coming up for promotion, or two years from retirement, or engaged to X, or about to move to Y, or four months pregnant or terminally ill, and one's knowledge of these facts is of course influencing one's experience and practical deliberation. But the obviousness of this claim understood in this basic way doesn't support the idea that it's also true in some further sense. I don't think that it can be asserted in any stronger sense without flipping from true to false—false of many people, even if still true of some.

Schechtman concludes her discussion of narrativity in *Staying Alive* with a further concession:

> it seems more accurate and less liable to generate misunderstanding to give up the locution of 'narrative' in this context and to describe the type of unity that defines a person's identity not as a *narrative* unity but simply as the structural unity of a person's life.[36]

It's the idea of a life as 'a diachronically structured unit' that 'is doing the real work' for her view, and many things which form diachronically structured units are not narratives at all.[37] I think she's right to drop the word 'narrative', but what now comes to mind, given this reformulation, is the degree to which any sense of specifically diachronic structural unity seems to be lacking, for at least some human beings, in their experience of existence from moment to moment, day to day, month to month, year to year.

The lack may seem remarkable—hard to credit—given the profound diachronic/structural unity that does actually exist in any human life. A human being is a single-bodied creature whose constancies and continuities of character through adult life tend to be as powerful as his or her bodily constancies and continuities.[38] Many things conspire to underwrite a person's experience of the diachronic unity of their life; for we are, again, creatures who can and do explicitly 'consider [themselves] as [themselves], in different times and places', in Locke's phrase. We're capable of 'mental

---

[35] Schechtman, *Staying Alive*, 101. [36] *Ibid.*, 108. [37] *Ibid.*, 108.

[38] Putting aside genuine trauma. Being 'born again' is a superficial change, relative to one's deep structure.

time-travel', in Tulving's abbreviation of Locke, and some of us do a lot of it (some biased to the future, others to the past).[39] As far as the future is concerned, we all know that we will die. This is not a small matter. But none of these things support the narrativist thesis as usually expounded, the thesis that all human life is, in some sense, life-writing, and also ought to be. We can reduce the thesis to the thin claim that we have some sense of the unity of our life, and ought to. But I don't think it looks any better. The unity is there, no doubt, but it's not something one needs to be aware of. To think about it, to try to nurture it, is to risk fantasy and self-deception.

'No', you say. 'It's a necessary part of self-possession.' But what is it to be self-possessed? Does it involve 'self-authorship'? Self-editing? The claim that someone is very self-possessed can carry the suggestion that they're self-alienated, out of touch with their reality. Self-possession as self-alienation; it's a paradox of a familiar sort, but it captures a truth. 'It is all very well', as the great Lewis Thomas said, 'to be aware of your awareness, even proud of it, but do not try to operate it. You are not up to the job.'[40] It's a familiar point in sports that self-control can depend on a kind of thoughtlessness.

According to Dan McAdams, a leading narrativist among social psychologists:

Beginning in late adolescence and young adulthood, we construct integrative narratives of the self that selectively recall the past and wishfully anticipate the future to provide our lives with some semblance of unity, purpose, and identity. Personal identity is the internalized and evolving life story that each of us is working on as we move through our adult lives . . . I . . . do not really know who I am until I have a good understanding of my narrative identity.[41]

If this is true, we must worry not only about the non-Narratives—unless they are happy to lack personal identity—but also about the people described by Mary Midgley and Erik Erikson:

[39] E. Tulving, 'Memory and Consciousness', *Canadian Psychology/Psychologie Canadienne* 26 (1985), 1–12, 5. 'Chronesthesia' is another recent and unnecessary term for the capacity described by Locke.

[40] 'The Attic of the Brain', in *Late Night Thoughts on Listening to Mahler's Ninth Symphony* (New York, NY: Bantam Books, 1983), 141.

[41] Dan McAdams, *The Redemptive Self: Stories Americans Live By* (New York: Oxford University Press, 2005), 287–8.

various selves ... make up our composite Self. There are constant and often shock-like transitions between these selves.... It takes, indeed, a healthy personality for the 'I' to be able to speak out of all these conditions in such a way that at any moment it can testify to a reasonably coherent Self.

[Doctor Jekyll] was partly right: we are each not only one but also many.... Some of us have to hold a meeting every time we want to do something only slightly difficult, in order to find the self who is capable of undertaking it.... We spend a lot of time and ingenuity on developing ways of organizing the inner crowd, securing consent among it, and arranging for it to act as a whole. Literature shows that the condition is not rare.[42]

Erikson and Midgley suggest, astonishingly, that we're all like this, and many agree—presumably those who fit the pattern. This makes me grateful to Midgley when she adds that 'others, of course, obviously do not feel like this at all, hear such descriptions with amazement, and are inclined to regard those who give them as dotty'. At the same time, we shouldn't adopt a theory that puts these people's claim to be genuine persons in question. We don't want to shut out Paul Klee:

My self ... is a dramatic ensemble. Here a prophetic ancestor makes his appearance. Here a brutal hero shouts. Here an alcoholic *bon vivant* argues with a learned professor. Here a lyric muse, chronically love-struck, raises her eyes to heaven. Her papa steps forward, uttering pedantic protests. Here the indulgent uncle intercedes. Here the aunt babbles gossip. Here the maid giggles lasciviously. And I look upon it all with amazement, the sharpened pen in my hand. A pregnant mother wants to join the fun. 'Pshtt!' I cry, 'You don't belong here. You are divisible.' And she fades out.

Or W. Somerset Maugham:

I recognize that I am made up of several persons and that the person that at the moment has the upper hand will inevitably give place to another. But which is the real one? All of them or none?

Or Philip Roth's Nathan Zuckerman, who is more or less intimately related to his author:

All I can tell you with certainty is that I, for one, have no self, and that I am unwilling or unable to perpetrate upon myself the joke of a self.... What I have

---

[42] Erikson, *Identity: Youth and Crisis* (New York: Norton, 1968), 217; Midgley, *Wickedness: A Philosophical Essay* (London: Ark, 1984), 123.

instead is a variety of impersonations I can do, and not only of myself—a troupe of players that I have internalised, a permanent company of actors that I can call upon when a self is required. . . . I am a theater and nothing more than a theater.[43]

What are these people to do if the advocates of narrative unity are right? I think they should continue as they are.[44] Their inner crowds can perhaps share some kind of rollicking self-narrative. But there seems to be no clear provision for them in the leading philosophies of personal unity of our time as propounded by (among others) Marya Schechtman, Harry Frankfurt, and Christine Korsgaard.

There is, furthermore, a vast difference between people who regularly and actively remember their past, and people who almost never do. In his autobiography *What Little I Remember*, Otto Frisch writes 'I have always lived very much in the present, remembering only what seemed to be worth retelling' . . . 'I have always, as I already said, lived in the here and now, and seen little of the wider views'.[45] I'm in the Frisch camp, on the whole, although I don't remember things in order to retell them. More generally, and putting aside pathological memory loss, I'm in the Montaigne camp, when it comes to specifically autobiographical memory: 'I can find hardly a trace of [memory] in myself; I doubt if there is any other memory in the world as grotesquely faulty as mine is!' Montaigne knows this can lead to misunderstanding. He is, for example, 'better at friendship than at anything else, yet the very words used to acknowledge that I have this affliction [poor memory] are taken to signify ingratitude; they judge my affection by my memory'—quite wrongly. 'However, I derive comfort from my infirmity.' Poor memory protects him from a disagreeable form of ambition, stops him babbling, and forces him to think through things for himself because he can't remember what others have said. Another advantage, he says in his *Essays*, 'is that . . . I remember less any insults received'.[46]

---

[43] *The Diaries of Paul Klee, 1898–1918* (London: Peter Owen, 1965), 177; Somerset Maugham, *A Writer's Notebook* (London: Heinemann, 1949), p. 21; Roth, *The Counterlife* (1986; New York: Vintage, 2005), 324.

[44] 'There never was a good biography of a good novelist. There couldn't be. He is too many people, if he's any good': F. Scott Fitzgerald, *The Notebooks of F. Scott Fitzgerald* (New York: Harcourt Brace Jovanovich, 1978), 159. He's wrong, but one can see what he has in mind.

[45] Frisch, *What Little I Remember* (Cambridge: Cambridge University Press, 1979), ix, xi.

[46] *The Complete Essays* (1563–92; London: Penguin, 1991), 32–3. 'My memory is not only in itself very short', he wrote to his father in 1563 after the death of Étienne de La Boétie, 'but in this case

To this we can add the point that poor memory and a non-Narrative disposition aren't hindrances when it comes to autobiography in the literal sense—actually writing things down about one's own life. Montaigne is the proof of this, for he is perhaps the greatest autobiographer, the greatest human self-recorder, in spite of the fact that:

> nothing is so foreign to my mode of writing than extended narration [*narration estendue*]. I have to break off so often from shortness of wind that neither the structure of my works nor their development is worth anything at all.[47]

Montaigne writes the unstoried life—the only life that matters, I'm inclined to think. He has no 'side', in the colloquial English sense of this term. His honesty, although extreme, is devoid of exhibitionism or sentimentality (St Augustine and Rousseau compare unfavourably). He seeks self-knowledge in radically unpremeditated life-writing: 'I speak to my writing-paper exactly as I do the first person I meet.'[48] He knows his memory is hopelessly untrustworthy, and he concludes that the fundamental lesson of self-knowledge is knowledge of self-ignorance.[49]

Once one is on the lookout for comments on memory, one finds them everywhere. There is a constant discord of opinion. I think James Meek is accurate when he comments on Salter's novel *Light Years* (1975):

> Salter strips out the narrative transitions and explanations and contextualisations, the novelistic linkages that don't exist in our actual memories, to leave us with a set of remembered fragments, some bright, some ugly, some bafflingly trivial, that don't easily connect and can't be put together as a whole, except in the sense of chronology, and in the sense that they are all that remains.[50]

Meek takes it that this is true of everyone, and it is perhaps the most common case. Salter finds a matching disconnection in life itself: 'There is no complete life. There are only fragments. We are born to have nothing, to have it pour through our hands';[51] and this, again, is a common experience:

affected by the trouble which I have undergone, through so heavy and important a loss, that I have forgotten a number of things which I should wish to have had known': *Essays of Montaigne*, trans. C. Cotton and ed. W. C. Hazlitt (London: Reeves and Turner), xxxii.

[47] 'On the Power of Imagination', in *The Complete Essays*, 120.
[48] 'On the Useful and Honourable', in *The Complete Essays*, 891.
[49] See in particular 'On Experience', *The Complete Essays*, 1220–1.
[50] 'Memories We Get to Keep', *London Review of Books*, 20 June 2013, 3–6.
[51] James Salter, *Light Years* (1975; New York: Vintage International, 1995), 35.

Examine for a moment an ordinary mind on an ordinary day. The mind receives a myriad impressions—trivial, fantastic, evanescent, or engraved with the sharpness of steel. From all sides they come, an incessant shower of innumerable atoms; as they fall, as they shape themselves into the life of Monday or Tuesday, the accent falls differently from of old; the moment of importance came not here but there; so that, if a writer were a free man and not a slave, if he could write what he chose, not what he must, if he could base his work upon his own feeling and not upon convention, there would be no plot, no comedy, no tragedy, no love interest or catastrophe in the accepted style, and perhaps not a single button sewn on as the Bond Street tailors would have it. Life is not a series of gig lamps symmetrically arranged; life is a luminous halo, a semi-transparent envelope surrounding us from the beginning of consciousness to the end.[52]

It's hard to work out the full consequences of this passage. What is certain is that there are rehearsers and composers among us, people who not only naturally story their recollections, but also their lives as they are happening. But when Sir Henry Taylor observes that 'an imaginative man is apt to see, in his life, the story of his life; and is thereby led to conduct himself in such a manner as to make a good story of it rather than a good life',[53] he's identifying a fault, a moral danger, a recipe for inauthenticity.[54] We should therefore worry if the narrativists are right, and such self-storying impulses are in fact universal.

Fortunately, they're not right. There are people who are wonderfully and movingly plodding and factual in their grasp of their pasts. It's an ancient view that people always remember their own pasts in a way that puts them in a good light, but there is solid evidence that it's far from universally true.[55]

In his poem 'Continuing to Live', Philip Larkin claims that 'in time,/We half-identify the blind impress / All our behavings bear'. The narrativists think that this is an essentially narrative matter, an essentially narrative

---

[52] V. Woolf, 'Modern Fiction', in *The Essays of Virginia Woolf*, vol. 4: *1925 to 1928*, ed. Andrew McNeillie (London: Hogarth Press, 1925), 160.

[53] *The Statesman* (London: Longman, Rees, Orme, Brown, Green, & Longman, 1836), 35.

[54] Cases in which the storying is done with perfect self-consciousness—'I was telling myself the story of our visit to the Hardys, & I began to compose it' (see Lee, this volume, p. 135) —are not at issue.

[55] See e.g. W. Waggenaar, 'Is Memory Self-Serving?', in *The Remembering Self: Construction and Accuracy in the Self-Narrative*, ed. U. Neisser and R. Fivush (Cambridge: Cambridge University Press, 1994), 191–204. See also the final pages of Tolstoy's story 'The Death of Ivan Illich'.

construal of the form of our lives. But many of us don't get even as far as Larkinian half-identification, and we have at best bits and pieces, rather than a story. We're startled by Larkin's further claim that 'once you have walked the length of your mind, what / You command is clear as a lading-list', for we find, even in advanced age, that we still have no clear idea of what we command.[56] I for one have no clear sense of who or what I am. This is not because I want to be like Montaigne, or because I've read Socrates on ignorance, or Nietzsche on skins:

How can man know himself? He is a dark and veiled thing; and whereas the hare has seven skins, the human being can shed seven times seventy skins and still not be able to say: 'This is really you, this is no longer outer shell.'[57]

I think of Simon Gray in his *Coda*, written when he knew himself to be dying of cancer:

the truth is that I don't really know even quite elementary things about myself, my wants and needs, until I've written them down or spoken them.[58]

Gray is perhaps wise, given the continuation of the above passage from Nietzsche:

Besides, it is an agonizing, dangerous undertaking to dig down into yourself in this way, to force your way by the shortest route down the shaft of your own being. How easy it is to do damage to yourself that no doctor can heal. And moreover, why should it be necessary, since everything—our friendships and hatreds, the way we look, our handshakes, the things we remember and forget, our books, our handwriting—bears witness to our being?

I can't, however, cut off this quotation here, because it continues in a way that raises a doubt about my position:

But there is a way in which this absolutely crucial enquiry can be carried out. Let the young soul look back upon its life and ask itself: what until now have you truly loved, what has raised up your soul, what ruled it and at the same time made it happy? Line up these objects of reverence before you, and perhaps by what they are and by their sequence, they will yield you a law, the fundamental law of your true self.

---

[56] Philip Larkin, 'Continuing to Live', in *Collected Poems* (London: Faber & Faber, 2003), p. 94.

[57] Nietzsche, 'Schopenhauer as Educator', trans. R. Gray (1874; Stanford, CA: Stanford, 1997), 174 (translation modified).

[58] Gray, *Coda* (London: Faber & Faber, 2008), 114.

'Perhaps by what they are...they will yield the fundamental law of your true self.' This claim is easy to endorse. It's Proust's greatest insight. But Nietzsche is more specific: 'perhaps by what they are *and by their sequence*, they will yield...the fundamental law of your true self'. Here it seems I must either disagree with Nietzsche or concede something to the narrativists: the possible importance of grasping the sequence in progressing towards self-understanding.

I concede it. Consideration of the sequence—the 'narrative', if you like—may be important for some people in some cases. For most of us, however, I think self-knowledge comes best in bits and pieces. Nor does this concession yield anything to the sweeping view with which I began, the view—in Oliver Sacks' words—that all human life is life-writing, that 'each of us constructs and lives a "narrative"', and that 'this narrative *is* us, our identities'.

NOTES ON CONTRIBUTORS

Alison Booth, Professor of English at the University of Virginia, has published widely in Victorian studies, feminist criticism, and narrative theory, with a focus on reception of authors. Her studies of prosopography began with *How to Make It as a Woman: Collective Biographical History from Victoria to the Present* (2004), and continue in a forthcoming book, 'Homes and Haunts: Touring Writers' Shrines and Countries' (Oxford, forthcoming). The Collective Biographies of Women project is supported by ACLS and NEH grants.

Joyce E. Chaplin is a historian of science and an environmental historian. She is the James Duncan Phillips Professor of Early American History at Harvard University, author of *The First Scientific American: Benjamin Franklin and the Pursuit of Genius* (2006) and editor of *Benjamin Franklin's Autobiography: A Norton Critical Edition* (2012).

Michael Dobson is Director of the Shakespeare Institute, Stratford-upon-Avon, and Professor of Shakespeare Studies, University of Birmingham. His publications include *The Making of the National Poet* (1992), *The Oxford Companion to Shakespeare* (with Stanley Wells, 2001 Stanley Wells, Will Sharpe, and Erin Sullivan, 2015), *England's Elizabeth* (with Nicola Watson, 2002), *Performing Shakespeare's Tragedies Today* (2006), and *Shakespeare and Amateur Performance* (2011).

Adam Foulds is a poet and novelist who lives in London. In 2013 he was named as one of Granta's Best of Young British Novelists. In 2014 he was named as one of the Poetry Book Society's New Generation Poets. His 2009 Man Booker-shortlisted novel, *The Quickening Maze*, concerns the poets John Clare and Alfred Tennyson in and around a private mental asylum in Epping Forest in 1840.

Janis Freedman Bellow teaches in the English Department at Tufts University, and lives half the year in Boston and half in Vermont.

Patrick Hayes is Associate Professor of English Literature at Oxford University and a Fellow of St John's College. He is the author of *J.M. Coetzee and* *the Novel: Writing and Politics after Beckett* (2010) and *Philip Roth: Fiction and Power* (2014). He is currently at work on the *Oxford History of Life-Writing: 1940 to the Present Day.*

Zachary Leader is Professor of English Literature at the University of Roehampton. He is the author of *Reading Blake's Songs* (1981), *Writer's Block* (1991), *Revision and Romantic Authorship* (1996), *The Life of Kingsley Amis* (2007), a finalist for the 2008 Pulitzer Prize in Biography, and *The Life of Saul Bellow: To Fame and Fortune 1915-1964* (2015), volume one of a two-volume biography. Among the books he has edited are *The Letters of Kingsley Amis* (2001), *On Modern British Fiction* (2003), and *Percy Bysshe Shelley: The Major Works* (with Michael O'Neill, 2003). He is General Editor of the forthcoming 'Oxford History of Life-Writing', a seven-volume series from Oxford University Press.

Hermione Lee is a literary biographer, Professor of English at Oxford University, and President of Wolfson College, Oxford. Her books include biographies of Virginia Woolf, Edith Wharton, and Penelope Fitzgerald, and she is the author of *Biography: A Very Short Introduction* (2009), and of a collection of essays on life-writing, *Body Parts* (2004).

Laura Marcus is Goldsmiths' Professor of English at the University of Oxford. She has published widely on nineteenth- and twentieth-century literature and culture, including life-writing. Her publications include *Auto/biographical Discourses: Theory, Criticism, Practice* (1994) and *Dreams of Modernity: Psychoanalysis, Literature, Cinema* (2014). She will be writing the early twentieth-century volume for the forthcoming 'Oxford History of Life-Writing'.

Blake Morrison is Professor of Creative and Life writing at Goldsmiths, University of London. He has written poetry, fiction, libretti, and literary criticism, and is a regular reviewer for the *Guardian*. His two memoirs are *And When Did You Last See Your Father?* (1993) and *Things My Mother Never Told Me* (2002).

James Shapiro teaches at Columbia University. His books include: *Shakespeare and the Jews, 1599: A Year in the Life of William Shakespeare, Contested Will: Who Wrote Shakespeare?,* and *1606: William Shakespeare and the Year of Lear.*

William St Clair FBA is the author of *The Reading Nation in the Romantic Period* (2004), *Lord Elgin and the Marbles* (1998), *The Godwins and the Shelleys, The Biography of a Family* (1989), and other works, including co-editing and contributing to *Mapping Lives, The Uses of Biography* (2002). He is Senior Research Fellow at the

Institute of English Studies, School of Advanced Study, University of London.

Alan Stewart is Professor of English and Comparative Literature at Columbia University, and International Director of the Centre for Editing Lives and Letters. He is the author, most recently, of *Shakespeare's Letters* (2008) and editor of volume 1 of the *Oxford Francis Bacon* (2012). He is currently working on the second (early modern) volume of Zachary Leader's series on *Life-Writing* for Oxford University Press.

Galen Strawson holds the President's Chair of Philosophy at the University of Texas at Austin. His books include *Freedom and Belief* (1986), *The Secret Connexion* (1989), *Mental Reality* (1994), *Selves* (2009), and *Locke on Personal Identity* (2011).

J. David Velleman is a Professor of Philosophy and Bioethics at New York University. His latest book is *Konrad Morgen: The Conscience of a Nazi Judge* (2015), co-authored with Herlinde Pauer-Studer. His book *How We Get Along* (Cambridge 2009) explores the role that self-enactment and self-narration play in the foundations of ethics.

Karen A. Winstead is a Professor of English at the Ohio State University. She has written *Virgin Martyrs: Legends of Sainthood in Late Medieval England* and *John Capgrave's Fifteenth Century*. She has also edited and translated Capgrave's *Life of Saint Katherine* and translated a volume of Middle English virgin martyr legends. She is currently working on the medieval volume of the 'Oxford History of Life-Writing'.

INDEX

NOTE: Page numbers in *italic* refer to captions to illustrations and figures